The 'Hood Comes First

MUSIC / CULTURE

A series from Wesleyan University Press

Edited by George Lipsitz, Susan McClary, and Robert Walser

My Music
by Susan D. Crafts, Daniel Cavicchi, Charles Keil,
and the Music in Daily Life Project

Running with the Devil:
Power, Gender, and Madness in Heavy Metal Music
by Robert Walser

Subcultural Sounds: Micromusics of the West
by Mark Slobin

Upside Your Head!
Rhythm and Blues on Central Avenue
by Johnny Otis

Dissonant Identities:
The Rock 'n' Roll Scene in Austin, Texas
by Barry Shank

Black Noise:
Rap Music and Black Culture in Contemporary America
by Tricia Rose

Club Cultures:
Music, Media and Subcultural Capital
by Sarah Thornton

Music, Society, Education
by Christopher Small

Listening to Salsa:
Gender, Latin Popular Music, and Puerto Rican Cultures
by Frances Aparicio

Any Sound You Can Imagine:
Making Music/Consuming Technology
by Paul Théberge

Voices in Bali:
Energies and Perceptions in Vocal Music and Dance Theater
by Edward Herbst

Popular Music in Theory
by Keith Negus

MURRAY FORMAN

✳

The 'Hood Comes First

RACE, SPACE, AND PLACE

IN RAP AND HIP-HOP

✳

WESLEYAN UNIVERSITY PRESS
Middletown, Connecticut

Published by Wesleyan University Press, Middletown, CT 06459
© 2002 by Murray Forman

Printed in the United States of America
Designed by Kathy Kimball
Set in Carter & Cone Galliard type by B. Williams & Associates

ISBN 0-8195-6396-x cloth
ISBN 0-8195-6397-8 paper

5   4   3   2

CIP data appear at the end of the book

To my parents, Jo and Joyce Forman
To my daughter, Bayla Silver Metzger
Para mi corazón y alma, Zamawa Arenas
and to all citizens of the hip-hop nation

Contents

❋

Acknowledgments

❋

Writing this book has been a fascinating experience encompassing much work and much play. Along with the research and writing—the heavy labor of the process—I attended dozens of hip-hop shows, spent hours perusing rap magazines, viewed countless videos, and listened to hip-hop records, compact discs, and tapes at every opportunity (despite the setback of losing virtually my entire hip-hop CD collection in an ugly b&e). Many people aided and abetted me in my efforts, some in concrete, tangible ways and others through the strong voice of encouragement. All deserve thanks, though not all are mentioned here.

I want first to recognize the fine work of several campus and community radio stations that have, over the years, deeply influenced my music listening and consumption habits while providing a central site through which local hip-hop cultures circulate. They are unquestionably the best sources in their localities for reggae, R & B, and hip-hop: in Ottawa, CKCU-FM (*Reggae in the Fields*); in Montreal, CKUT-FM (*Weekend Groove* and *Masters at Work*); and in Boston, WERS-FM (*Rockers* and *WERS @ Night*). In New York, the commercial station Hot 97 is essential listening, rocking the old-school and "now"-school jams.

For those who know me best, the marathon metaphor can be aptly applied to this project. Mile by mile, day by day, I have been surrounded by some of the brightest minds and most loving hearts imaginable. George Szanto and Will Straw of the Graduate Program in Communications at McGill University were able and helpful advisors throughout the initial research and writing stages. George has since retired from academia, but he remains a valued confidant and a dear friend. Will alerted me early in my academic career to the viability of popular music as an area of study. It was he who introduced me to the International Association for the Study of Popular Music (IASPM), where many of the ideas in this book were first given a public voice, and I continue to benefit from his insights and assistance. Other members of my "Mont Real"/Montreal posse who offered their ongoing encouragement include Melanie "Queen Bee" Aube and Johanna "Jo" Visser (whose ear is well tuned to my occasional rage against the machine).

Murray Pomerance of Ryerson Polytechnical University, Toronto, has been a dear friend and a keen editor over the past several years, and my writing and conceptual thought (especially in chapter 8) have benefited from his counsel. Keir "K-Mack" Keightley, at the University of Western Ontario in London, Ontario, deserves special mention for sharing a veritable warehouse of knowledge about popular music and the industry. The value of his initial input and sustained camaraderie weighs a ton. Simon Jones, of Birmingham, England, was with me during the earliest phase of the writing process, and his knowledge and love of music from reggae through salsa continue to impress me. You're missed over here, mate! I have also enjoyed the collegiality and friendship of Jeff Melnick and Rachel Rubin, who with Reebee Garofalo, Deb Pacini Hernandez, and myself coedit the *Journal of Popular Music Studies*. Muchas, muchas gracias a la familia Arenas—Omar, Zunilde, Kathar, Claudia, Zayi, y Samuelito—en Caracas, Venezuela, por toda su amibilidad y apoyo. Nothing I do should go without a huge expression of gratitude to "my real deal homies" of "the Soo crew" who have always backed me: Paul "PAK" Kaihla, Gaston "Gus" Lelievre, Lyle "L-Love" Robinson, and Steve "Big Poppa" Stinson.

My students at Northeastern University, Boston, shared their knowledge and experiences with hip-hop freely, often supplying tapes or CDs of new or obscure material. My former students at Queens College, City University of New York, also provided much useful information about the New York and Queens hip-hop scenes, and they, too, were a constant source of insight and discussion. Many thanks to the ranks for helping me to "keep it real." Also, genuine appreciation and thanks are warranted for the support of my colleagues in the Media Studies department at Queens College.

On the Boston front, I continue to enjoy the company of what I call my "Five Mic Friends," in reference to *The Source* magazine's famous record ranking system. Thanks to my colleagues at Northeastern University's Department of Communication Studies for their friendship and encouragement, especially Kevin Howley and Joanne Morreale. La familia at Argus Communications—Zamawa Arenas, Lucas and Damaris Guerra, and Luis Soto—are amazing and maintain an unwavering dedication to "doing well by doing good." Special thanks to Lucas for the amazing cover to this book. I am incredibly fortunate to call Deb Pacini Hernandez and Reebee Garofalo friends. Their intellectual electricity and political commitment to fighting the good fight remain a constant inspiration. Over the past several years they, more than anyone else, have presented the most important intellectual challenges and academic insights that inform my own work. The easy hang time has sure enough been fine too! Judith Brown has seen this book progress from the start and has perhaps heard more about it than anyone else; thanks, JB—"I got nuttin' but love for ya."

The undiluted family support of Jan and Shawn and my parents, Jo and Joyce Forman, has sustained me throughout the years I have been working on this project and before. Their patience (after all, they had to hear each moment of my musical evolution at often bone-crushing volumes), material sustenance, and unconditional love smoothed the work immeasurably. Thank you from the heart. Much love to my daughter Bayla, whose musical tastes continue to evolve and fascinate me. Our spirited discussions over the past five years about popular music, high school culture, and the teen scene have been invaluable to my own understanding of youth today.

Finally I offer unconditional gratitude to Zamawa Arenas. Not only has my range of cultural and musical experiences widened by her influence, but so, too, have my critical and analytical perceptions been sharpened. Words in any language cannot say thank you/gracias fully, so I'll leave it to a smile, a bolero by Cheo Feliciano, and a slow dance. . . .

Introduction

❄

On a trip traversing almost a dozen states along America's eastern seaboard, I relished the opportunity to surf the local and regional radio stations, sampling broadcast formats and musical styles from one area to the next. The uniformity of "classic" stations (i.e., "timeless" classics from the 1940s and 1950s, "classic rock" from the 1960s and 1970s, pop hits from the 1980s, etc.) and the relative homogeneity of Top 40 "hit" radio and of mainstream country music programming, however, was at odds with my actual movement through space, reinforcing a sense of placelessness that was matched by the standardized rest areas and gas, food, and lodging complexes along the interstate highways.

The radiophonic journey did not correspond to the physical journey through space, over distance; rather, it was constituted as a recurring array of formats, with the distance being measured in spaces on the dial along the broadcast spectrum. Though I moved through disparate and distinct areas and regions, a prevailing sense of cultural stasis overdetermined the experience. As Jody Berland points out, "The accelerating conquest of space through media is inseparable from the increasing disunity of our place in it, our relationship to it" (1988, 343). She suggests that this contributes to the formation of a "soundscape" that is commercially derived and conceived according to a rational corporate logic based on a concept of demographically coherent listening audiences.

The point of this example lies in the exceptions that I encountered, particularly as I converged on the larger urban centers such as New York, Philadelphia, and Washington, D.C. In these cities, the crucial identifying distinction was the presence of at least one urban-format station and, often, lively and upbeat campus stations that featured playlists with an abundance of vintage funk or reggae and contemporary R & B and rap music. These stations stood out for several reasons: first, the music spoke almost exclusively to black American cultural sensibilities, differentiating them in distinct ways from stations featuring the pop, heartland rock, and country music that dominated the radio throughout the journey. Second, in several instances the urban format had been isolated and identified as the musical and cultural "other" among mainstream commercial stations. Classic and contemporary rock stations in particular frequently announced their musical affiliations and program content in contrast to those of urban formats, broadcasting their station identification with the antagonistic slogans "no rap, no crap," "no funk, no junk," "classics . . . without the rap," or my personal favorite, "music you can understand." These explicit distinctions expose the underlying, interwoven contexts of racial difference, cultural taste, and audience demographics that have been part of American popular music throughout the twentieth century. They simultaneously inscribe a racial and spatial economy of meanings and values onto the broadcast spectrum in what can be regarded as the segregation of the airwaves. This "othering" of funk and rap generally parallels the cultural and geographical ghettoization of black communities in American cities and thus can be reimagined in terms of a cultural geography of the radio bandwidth and, by extension, of the entire contemporary music industry.

Throughout the journey another factor also emerged: stations whose formats either accommodate or prominently feature rap and hip-hop in their multiple forms also tended to convey a much more clearly enunciated sense of locality and place. The abstractions of classic or hit radio formats (which, as Berland indicates, tend to elide spatial specificities in favor of more generalized broadcasting styles and appeals to an audience "out there," especially among syndicated programs) were not nearly so evident on urban hip-hop stations. Both DJs and audience callers made repeated "shout outs," citing urban neighborhoods and various other sites of significance by name, including housing projects, schools, workplaces, and streets. In this context, urban radio (encompassing both commercial and community broadcasters) functions as a cultural mediator, influencing localized cultural tastes and facilitating a musical and spoken dialogue within the various cities. As Mark Anthony Neal observes, "Hip-hop recordings began to resemble digitized town meetings"(1999, 161), and though he is skeptical of the relationships between rap music and commercial radio's profit imperatives, the community engagements and interaction facilitated through the medium often function in valuable ways that reinforce community ties. Furthermore, this highly interactive broadcast style corresponds with other secular and religious practices that shape the historical past and the present of black popular culture, contributing to an elaborated sense of the black public sphere.

While it is true that other radio formats have in the past—and may still —function in a similar manner, they tend not to do so today to the same extent or degree. Stations with urban formats and rap or R & B programs (particularly those on weekend nights), actively acknowledge civic locality in ways that are generally unmatched by classic rock, country, or Top 40 hit radio. Urban stations communicate through a range of expressive and vernacular forms that reflect and reinforce a youth culture and a black public sphere in which it coheres. As this suggests, the music industry and accompanying commercial media structures are influential in the organization of popular music in America and affect the production, dissemination, and reception of culture. It is therefore necessary to engage with both the social and the institutional realms of rap music in the process of explaining its various elements as a force and presence in American society over the past twenty-five years.

Rap's lyrical constructions commonly display a pronounced emphasis on place and locality. Whereas blues, rock, and R & B have traditionally cited regions or cities (i.e., "Dancing in the Street," initially popularized in 1964 by the Motown artists Martha and the Vandellas and covered by the rock acts Van Halen in 1982 and David Bowie and Mick Jagger in 1985), contemporary rap is even more specific, with explicit references to particular streets, boulevards and neighborhoods, telephone area codes, postal service zip codes, or other sociospatial information. Rap artists draw inspiration from their regional affiliations as well as from a keen sense of what I call the *extreme local*, upon which they base their constructions of spatial imagery.

I raise these issues anecdotally as a means of introducing a series of factors contributing to hip-hop culture and rap music's unique character. Foremost among these are the intensely articulated emphases on space, place, and identity, which are rooted in wider circulating discourses of contemporary urban cultures and the complex geographies of the postmodern or global city. Since its inception in the mid-1970s and its subsequent commercial eruption with the release of the Sugarhill Gang's 1979 hit, "Rapper's Delight" (Sugar Hill Records), rap has evolved as the dominant cultural voice of urban black youth. Rap's urban origins and continued urban orientations (in terms of performance, production, and highest concentration of consumption) provide the primary environment for the music's evolution. Just as important, the music's ubiquity and tactile qualities have also reciprocally altered the sound of the city. The transformation of the urban soundscape since the early 1980s has been partially accomplished via the rolling bass beats of hip-hop music booming from convertibles, Jeeps, customized low riders and tall SUVs, luxury cars and sedate family sedans. The convergence of new car-stereo technologies and the fetishization of bass and volume in tandem affect the sonic character of the city. As rap constitutes the music of choice for large segments of mobile youth, their means and contexts of consumption and enjoyment redefine the aural contours of the city. Rap's presence as a central facet of all contemporary North American urban centers (and those on a much wider, global scale) is unavoidable, and owing in part to this intensified audibility, it has come under scrutiny from various institutional sites, having been exposed to numerous forms of surveillance, critique, and analysis.

Rap music takes the city and its multiple spaces as the foundation of its cultural production. In the rhythm and lyrics, the city is an audible presence, explicitly cited and sonically sampled in the reproduction of the aural textures of the urban environment. Throughout the 1980s and 1990s, however, the specificity of references to urban locale has become increasingly evident as rappers illustrate their awareness that the city is not an evenly structured space but one that is prone to a tangible unevenness, with different places constituting distinct zones of activity. The rap genre has provided an important site for the examination and critique of the distribution of power and authority in the urban context. *The 'Hood Comes First,* therefore, takes as one of its primary interests the rising *urgency* with which minority youth use rap in the deployment of discourses of urban space and more proximate scales of urban locality, or place. It examines in detail the ways through which members of the hip-hop culture articulate notions of subjective and collective identities, urban experience, racial consciousness, and spatially structured patterns of power.

"The real" has also emerged through the years as a uniquely resonant concept within hip-hop culture and has accordingly been granted close attention here. In most cases it stands as an ill-defined expression referring to combined aspects of racial essentialism, spatial location, and a basic adherence to the principles and practices of the hip-hop culture. It emerged with the most clarity following rap's transitional phase from an underground or alternative musical form to a multi-platinum-selling facet of the popular music industry. Yet the boundaries between real or authentic cultural identities and those deemed inauthentic are carefully policed from within the hip-hop culture, and the delineations that define "the real" are taken with deadly seriousness by those who ascribe to hip-hop's cultural influences. In the context of this study, the emphasis on "the real" can also be linked to a range of emergent spatial concerns, especially those that are sedimented within the geocultural construct of "the 'hood." *The 'Hood Comes First* illustrates many of the complex manifestations of a place-based concept of "the real" and provides a culturally relevant analysis of its resonance within hip-hop.

At the core of this book is the belief that by examining and exploring the multiple articulations of the terms "the ghetto," "inner city," and "the 'hood," as well as other key spatial configurations that emerge from rap's discourses and hip-hop media generally, the cultural production of urban sites of significance can be illuminated. It is too frequently accepted without evaluation that rap is implicitly conjoined with spaces of urban poverty, existing as a both a product and a legitimate voice of a minority teen constituency that is also demographically defined as part of the social "underclass." Although urban housing projects and areas of chronic economic depression do comprise major sites of hip-hop's production and consumption, the culture has, in its diverse modes of expression, evolved and the range of its influence has expanded, rendering its lingering status as "ghetto" music increasingly problematic. Today many top rap acts, like their audiences, hail from middle-class or more affluent suburban enclaves, complicating the commonly held impressions about the music, the artists who produce it, and its origins. In these pages, then, I will trace the ways in which several of the central elements of race, class, and cultural identification are recast and revised within a coherent if not entirely consistent spatial discourse, one that relies on the spatial construct of "the 'hood."

Because of its pervasiveness, the term "the 'hood" warrants special attention. It is literally an abbreviated version of the word "neighborhood" and, as such, defines a territory that is geographically and socially particular to the speaking subject's social location. Quite simply stated, the 'hood exists as a "home" environment. It is enunciated in terms that elevate it as a primary site of significance. The correlative terms "homeboy," "homegirl," and "homies," which have been regular components of the hip-hop lexicon, are similarly meaningful in spatial terms, as they identify a highly particular social circle encompassing friends, neighbors, or local cohorts who occupy the common site of the 'hood.[1] The term's usage is especially notable for its prevalence and ubiquity in rap's lyrical structures and in various other textual forms produced concurrently with the music, such as the ancillary music press and black cinema that have emerged in the wake of rap's popularity as signposts in the mapping of hip-hop culture.[2] In *The 'Hood Comes First,* these cultural texts constitute the objects of analysis and will be assessed for their role in the diffusion of new urban sensibilities.

The existing historiography of rap is another matter, however, since it has been narrowly concerned with several primary interests. These include descriptions of the genre's emergence from the ghetto neighborhoods of

New York, with a focus on the cultural conditions within which its artistic elements acquired shape and definition; the development of a critique of rap and hip-hop practices as they manifest contributing elements of a contemporary black aesthetic; and discussions of rap's technological production and the prowess of its young black innovators. These are undoubtedly important issues and are accordingly taken up and assessed in this book. Music journalists, cultural critics, and academics alike have been following rap and hip-hop through their evolutionary phases since their inception, tracking their paths and commenting on their various transformations over the years. What has subsequently evolved is a sizable body of work addressing hip-hop culture and its numerous facets, producing what can be reasonably defined as a rap and hip-hop canon.

There remain, however, several shortcomings in hip-hop studies. The links between ghetto or inner-city spaces and rap are frequently drawn without significant interrogation of the discursively produced value systems that always influence our social perceptions of these spaces. In many earlier instances, the ostensibly "raw" reality of hip-hop's formative spaces is valorized and romanticized, creating misperceptions that position its cultural expressions as the apparently organic product of a particular sociospatial milieu. Even more conspicuous is the limited analytical rigor applied to describing and explaining the influential role of the music industry throughout rap's history. Considering the abundance of research on rap, there has been a relative paucity of critical study on the facilitating or constraining factors within the popular music industry that have, in various ways and at various times, aided or restricted its development. This absence is addressed here in an attempt to reconnect rap with the forms of industrial and cultural analysis that have been so important to country, pop, rock, blues, and jazz scholarship. In this book, I seek to intervene in the canonical body of work surrounding rap and hip-hop; I want to challenge many of the uncritical assumptions and unanswered generalities that, through the years, have had the effect of reifying the history of rap and hip-hop. By my intervention, I hope to introduce a complementary analysis that contributes greater specificity to the study of hip-hop across the mediascape and from geocultural and spatial perspectives.

There are three distinct but related aspects of rap and hip-hop under scrutiny in the following pages, constituting three spatial modalities. The first involves the detailed examination of hip-hop's geocultural origins and the spatial factors of its developmental trajectory. The second involves the rise and evolution of a unique spatial discourse within rap and hip-hop culture that defines resonant social and cultural issues with increasing specificity and emphasis on physical terrains or imagined spaces and places. The third involves the analysis of the spaces of commerce and industrial activity that have influenced hip-hop's development as it expanded beyond its local enclaves outward onto the national and international stage. This is an achievement that is best understood within the institutional contexts of the wider music and culture industries.

Each of these analytical perspectives can be applied, for instance, to the Will Smith video "Freakin' It," which was also the lead single from his full-length release *Willennium* (2000, Columbia). The images and the track's lyrics amplify Smith's celebrity status while reconnecting the megastar of music, television, and film fame with his hometown roots in Philadelphia. The video is a virtual travelogue featuring detailed images of Philly locales and neighborhoods familiar to the artist, including other architectural landmarks such as the city's African American Cultural Museum. The Philadelphia theme is further reinforced by employing distinct icons of the city's cultural landscape, especially the city's professional basketball team, the 76ers. Intentionally shot on a shoestring budget, the video focuses viewer attention on the scenery and urban terrains that constitute Smith's "home."

In another example, in midsummer of 2000, St. Louis native Nelly's hit single "(Hot Shit) Country Grammar" (2000, Fo' Reel) was perched at number one on the *Billboard* Hot Rap Singles chart and was in heavy rotation on BET and MTV's rap programs. The video is replete with place references to St. Louis, Missouri, that are coded sartorially through sportswear displaying the professional team logos of the city's baseball squad, the Cardinals, and the hockey team, the Blues. Additional shots of the city's distinctive span over the Mississippi River and lyrical references to the midwestern corridor between Texas and Illinois proliferate, delineating the cultural and geographic environment that informs Nelly's frame of experience and identity. The collective posse shots and crowd scenes that are standard in today's hip-hop videos round out the images of the artist's home turf, with members of Nelly's "St. Lunatics" crew, neighbors, and various characters from "the 'hood" literally dancing in the streets. By January 2001 the CD *Country Grammar* had sold five million units (and was positioned at number fifteen on the Billboard 200 chart), and through interviews and an array of media articles, a much larger portion of the hip-hop audience was cognizant of the artist's roots and cultural ties to his home place in St. Louis. By midsummer of 2001, the CD had posted sales of over seven million copies, and it shared the charts with a posse recording featuring the St. Lunatics (*Free City*, 2001, Fo' Reel) that continued to extol the virtues of St. Louis.

The project in *The 'Hood Comes First* is to draw the artifacts and practices of hip-hop together in order to engage with questions relating to the formation of a politics of place and of race, culture, and identity. By critically engaging with theoretical and practical problems upon which similarities and differences between discourses of race, nation, and the 'hood are based, the spatial component of rap music and hip-hop culture will be revealed as a crucial characteristic of one of the most influential areas of contemporary black popular culture.

The 'Hood Comes First

CHAPTER ONE

Space Matters
Hip-Hop and the
Spatial Perspective

❉

In his preface to *Race Matters,* Cornel West describes in detail an incident he experienced in New York City:

> I dropped my wife off for an appointment on 60th Street between Lexington and Park avenues. I left my car—a rather elegant one—in a safe parking lot and stood on the corner of 60th Street and Park Avenue to catch a taxi. I felt relaxed since I had an hour until my next engagement. At 5:00 P.M. I had to meet a photographer who would take the picture for the cover of this book on the roof of an apartment building in East Harlem on 115th Street and 1st Avenue. I waited and I waited and I waited. After the ninth taxi refused me, my blood began to boil. The tenth taxi refused me and stopped for a kind, well-dressed, smiling female fellow citizen of European descent. As she stepped in the cab, she said, "This is really ridiculous, is it not?"
>
> (West 1993, x)

In this description West communicates the irony that even a well-dressed, professional, and prominent intellectual of African-American heritage must confront the all-too-common systemic racism of American society. The words spoken to him by the "female fellow citizen" offer both truth and understatement as her utterance implies an arguably embarrassed shrug of regret and acceptance: after all, she still took the cab ahead of him. But West's own words are of interest also in terms of what is stated explicitly and what is rendered implicit.

While exposing one or two things about race and class in the United States, his brief narrative exposes a geography of difference that underlies his experience as a black man standing on the street in New York. He has left his "rather elegant" car in a secure parking lot in a relatively safe area of the city. The assumption is that taxis will not stop for him *because* he is black, even though his dress and demeanor are completely normal for the upscale contexts of midtown Manhattan. The attention to such details as street names, however, is an important facet of his story. They are centrally significant in their communicative capacity to provide information about the cultural locations through which West circulates. His emphasis on local geographies is absolutely essential to the inherent meaning of his anecdote, for by relating street names and neighborhoods he effectively maps the cultural terrains of the city and their distinct and differential qualities along a spatial axis encompassing race and class. Race matters, but it is clear that space does too.

Space is an influential factor in contemporary culture. It can be at once unifying or differentiating and is structured in and through numerous institutional agendas and public discourses. It is today obvious that the spaces we inhabit are generally susceptible to bids, in various forms, for increased influence, authority, and power. Spatialized power is expressed within a range of contexts, whether these be official housing policy and localized politics of urban development, the struggles between combative street gangs, or conflicts between members of minority populations and urban police forces. Spatial conflict involves engagements of fluctuating intensities and, importantly, fluctuating scales as various transformative strategies are deployed in the attempt to extend control and domination over the social landscape. Power and authority are unevenly distributed throughout society, with space emerging as one important vector among many for the expression of dominant-subordinate relations within the hegemonic order.

Over roughly the past twenty-five years, space and place have acquired prominence in cultural research. Concern with spatial issues has intensified, developing as a mainstay of critical cultural analyses and a response to what some theorists (Jameson 1984; Harvey 1989; Soja 1989) attribute to the evolution of new social sensibilities, in which theoretical preoccupations with time (and concerns related to an earlier period of modernity) shift to space (and conditions of postmodernity). While the earliest emphasis on space or spatiality was most frequently generated within the fields of abstract geometry and physics, the spatial turn to which I refer suggests a transition toward a new paradigm that seeks to explain social and cultural phenomena in relation to various human, institutional, and natural geographies. The convergence of scholarly interest around questions of space, culture, and geography is based on a belief that human interrelations are simultaneously constituted by and constitutive of the spaces in which they occur. Social subjects ground their actions and their identities in the spaces and places in which they work and play, inhabiting these geographies at various levels of scale and personal intensity. From this perspective, it might be said that today space is everywhere.

Space is not an overdetermining factor, but it is influential in ways that often remained unexplained. Interest in the social elements of spatial habitation and use illustrates an emphasis on what Henri Lefebvre refers to as "spatial practices," which project space onto "all aspects, elements and moments of social practice" (1991, 8). The evidence of new vernaculars featuring spatially oriented metaphors, expressions, and narratives, such as those that emerge from a range of social sectors, may be considered a crucial component inflecting the articulation of experiences, identities, practices, and so forth within various cultural milieux or "social spaces." Indeed, there is very little about contemporary society that is not, at some point, imbued with a spatial character, and this is no less true for the emergence and production of spatial categories and identities in rap music and the hip-hop culture of which it is a central component.[1]

Hip-hop has evolved into one of North America's most influential youth-oriented forces. It provides a sustained articulation of the social partitioning of race and the diverse experiences of being young and black or Latino in North America. As the cultural influences of hip-hop's varied forms and expressions have gradually spread through global systems of diffusion, these themes can be heard in other languages around the world, expressed with a shared emphasis on spatial location and identity formation but informed by radically varied contexts and environments. Space and place figure prominently as organizing concepts delineating a vast range of imaginary or actual social practices that are represented in narrative or lyric form and that display identifiable local, regional, and national aesthetic inflections. Youths who adhere to the styles, images, and values of hip-hop culture (in which a distinct social sector displays relatively coherent and identifiable characteristics) have demonstrated unique capacities to construct different spaces and, simultaneously, to construct spaces differently. The prioritization of spatial practices and spatial discourses underlying hip-hop culture offers a means through which to view both the ways that spaces and places are constructed and the unique kinds of space or place that are constructed.

A highly detailed and consciously defined spatial awareness is one of the key factors distinguishing rap music and hip-hop from the many other cultural and subcultural youth formations currently vying for popular attention. In hip-hop, space is a dominant concern, occupying a central role in the definition of value, meaning, and practice. How the dynamics of space, place, race, and cultural differences are articulated among youths of the "hip-hop generation"—including artists, producers, and executives working in hip-hop's diverse media forms—and how they are located within a range of social discourses emerge as phenomena worthy of concentrated analysis.

It is first necessary, however, to clarify what space and place mean in relation to each other. Spatial analyses and place studies do not share precisely the same history or trajectory, for although place clearly displays spatial characteristics and thus conforms to some elements of spatial analysis, its study has been shaped through its own unique developments. The relationships between space and place are organized around differences in focus and object as well as differences of scale and value. Therefore, in order to account for these distinctions, space and place warrant separate attention.

Space and Spatiality

As Lefebvre has explained, space is "produced," or, more precisely, "(social) space is a (social) product" (1991, 26). He qualifies this by noting that it is not a produced object or commodity; rather, "social space is produced and reproduced in connection with the forces of production (and with the relations of production)" (77). His main criticism of early forays into spatial analysis is that space has traditionally been regarded as "innocent" or apolitical, unimplicated in the patterning of power, authority, and domination across the social spectrum. He writes that produced space also "serves as a tool of thought and action; that in addition to being a means of production it is also a means of control" (26); and that it can and must be critically scrutinized to determine in whose interests it is produced and manipulated and by what social factions it is policed and dominated. Seen as a social product, space is also more easily understood as political and ideological, and the interrelationships forged within space are, accordingly, politically or ideologically laden.

For Lefebvre, spatial practices, which are invested with political or ideological values, are effected in the social realm through myriad formal or institutional systems, such as the production of property laws and the contracts, licenses, and other legal means of regulation through which they are officially maintained; public curfews; trespassing laws; and so on. In his efforts to identify the distribution of spatial practices and the accompanying dissemination of spatial knowledges, which are continually in flux, he further challenges the common, uncritical acceptance of space as a rigidly defined construct. Lefebvre states that "every society—and hence every mode of production with its subvariants . . . produces a space, its own space" (1991, 31). Within a critical approach that conceives of contemporary culture as a lived process and a site of ongoing struggle and negotiation, space (and place) can be regarded as constructions that are neither organic nor fixed for all time. Space is foremost a cultural construct. It is the "product of a sequence and set of operations" (73), and as such it is bound up in cultural tensions and conflicts that, in their inherent fluctuations, invariably display spatial attributes.

As Lefebvre and others (Relph 1976; Meyrowitz 1985; Entrikin 1991) argue, there is no pure, authentic, or "true" space to which social subjects are bound. No overarching concept of space provides the grounds for a generalized meaning and application of the concept, and it is impossible to discuss space in homogeneous terms, since no single space nor any single conception of space has authority over another. This emerges as a point of contention in the study of race and the spatial arrangement of urban social landscapes in hip-hop, especially when considered in the contexts of an enunciation of spatial authority and the anchoring primacy of the terms "the ghetto" or "the 'hood"(the latter of which is etymologically derived from "neighborhood" but has developed its own unique meanings). For instance, the ghetto, 'hood, street, and corner all surface as representations of a particular image inscribing an ideal of authenticity or "hardcore" urban reality. Space is the subject of a broad system of classification whereby different spaces and different conceptualizations of space coexist in a multiply imbricated arrangement. Even in theory, the question of space is a highly contestable construct produced according to various and often competing intellectual interests or disciplinary agendas.

It should also be emphasized that space does not possess an inherent capacity to dominate, although spaces may be invested with power and thus become part of an apparatus of domination, as Foucault (1980) and Harvey (1989) have concluded. Simon Duncan and Mike Savage observe that "space does not actually exist in the sense of being an object that can have effects on other objects," including social subjects and collectivities (1989, 179). For instance, to use a blunt example, a social "center" cannot impose its will on a social "margin," although this particular description of relational power and its spatial character is not uncommon. There is a certain allure to the simplistic idea of autonomous, active spaces such as "the center" or "the margin," but this misrepresents the relational dynamics and the actual human motivations and agencies that are in play, not to mention ignoring the influences of historically established institutions and systems of authority that are imbued with spatial characteristics and biases.

The social practices and relationships among human agents that produce power or authority are organized along continually shifting and contingent territorial lines. Space therefore appears to be mobilized as various social boundaries are renegotiated and transformed. Upon examination, however, it is clear that active social processes and relationships in space have themselves been improperly endowed with spatial features through a kind of metonymic conferral. This means that space is not, in and of itself, a causal force; it is influential but does not determine outcomes. It is not a self-motivated entity capable of action. Rather, returning to Lefebvre's terminology, it is a "product" that is shaped by human agency and the subsequent social practices that occur within a given frame of action or within a range of human relationships. Duncan and Savage explain that fallacious notions of spatial determinism actually conceal the institutional composition of "spatial patterns" in society that shape material practices and processes, which in turn reproduce social life. Inculcated through systemic institutional processes that include acculturation and socialization, the spatial constructs around which we organize our lives become more and more patterned until they acquire a naturalized character.

Space is, in this sense, an important facet of the hegemonic order, for spatial relationships are also organized along the lines of subordination and domination—relationships of power—that are consensually and, when deemed necessary by those in positions of authority, coercively maintained. Harvey identifies the dynamics of difference thus: "'Difference and 'otherness' is [sic] *produced* in space through the simple logic of uneven capital investment and a proliferating geographical division of labor" (1993, 6). As citizens and members of various diverse agglomerations, we inhabit the spaces around us with relative autonomy while simultaneously enacting boundaries through our regular social practices and constructing the underlying differences that separate various cultural "milieux," "territories," "realms," or "domains." Critical research into social spatialization challenges prevalent tendencies toward the normalization of space and spatial differences and their "commonsense" status. It refutes the acceptance of benign space, interrogating the potential meanings and values that are ensconced in the language and logic of capitalist societies (encompassing patriarchal and racist tendencies, among other biases) and their particular mechanisms for the maintenance and extension of power and authority.

Spatial Frames and Hip-Hop Culture

In his insightful collection of essays *Black Studies, Rap, and the Academy*, Houston Baker, Jr., points to the presence of cultural conflict along particular sociospatial lines when he writes: "The black urban beat goes on and on and on in the nineties. The beat continues to provide sometimes stunning territorial confrontations between black expressivity and white law-and-order" (1993, 33). The "black urban beat" to which he refers encompasses a history of African-American urban musical forms, but in its contemporary manifestation the musical genre to which it refers most directly is rap. The primary territory under inspection is that of the urban public sphere, which is the space where, in an idealized liberal bourgeois sense, public cultures in their diversity and multiplicity define their identities, exert their proprietary rights to open self-representation, and enter debates germane to the structure and order of society. But the site of confrontation is more complex. Where is this site and how is the territory demarcated? What are the social and cultural institutions that have been erected along the boundaries of conflict, and how are they maintained and reinforced? To what degree are the different territories either autonomous or mutually reliant, and are the divisions between them insurmountable or are they relatively permeable?

Baker explores several of these questions by isolating numerous cultural phenomena in hip-hop that display spatial components, in the process revealing subtle details of their socially produced character. As he notes, the spatial dimensions of experience and practice are thoroughly embedded in our understandings of the city. We explicitly and implicitly account for the differences that space makes when we consider urban phenomena; it is one of the key factors that modern citizens draw on to make sense of the urban worlds they inhabit daily. This is evident in the urban themes and narratives of the hip-hop culture as well.

In a related context, John Jeffries writes: "In black popular culture, the city is hip. It's the locale of cool. In order to be 'with it,' you must be in the city. . . . The city is where black cultural styles are born" (1992, 159). In fact, urban spaces and places have figured prominently in various studies of African-American culture, including W. E. B. Du Bois's monumental study *The Philadelphia Negro,* first published in 1899, with its sociological research on the community structures of black life in the civic wards or neighborhoods of Philadelphia at the end of the nineteenth century. With a highly specific spatial focus, Du Bois isolates a community within a community, or, as Charles Scruggs (1993) has suggested, an "invisible city . . . a city within a city," mapping the concentrations, lifestyles, and occupations of Philadelphia's black population:

The new immigrants usually settle in pretty well-defined localities in or near the slums, and thus get the worst possible introduction to city life. . . . Today they are to be found partly in the slums and partly in those small streets with old houses, where there is a dangerous intermingling of good and bad elements fatal to growing children and unwholesome for adults. Such streets may be found in the Seventh Ward, between Tenth and Juniper streets, in parts of the Third and Fourth Wards and in the Fourteenth and Fifteenth Wards. (Du Bois 1967, 81)

The localized references and the depiction of a concentrated black citizenry reach new and fearsome proportions by the mid-1980s, as revealed in Mike Davis's *City of Quartz* (1992), with its descriptions of a "carceral city" and the enforced military-style zoning of public and residential spaces according to criteria of race, class, and age. In Davis's historical study of urban development in Los Angeles, the containment of what the dominant classes often consider to be "undesirables" or "aliens" (which include an inordinate proportion of blacks and Chicanos) is explicit. This illustrates that the contemporary city, like that at the turn of the century, remains the primary space of racial division and racial tension and that, despite progress in some quarters, apparatuses of urban racial segregation have taken new, sophisticated, and highly technologized forms.

Within hip-hop culture, artists and cultural workers have emerged as sophisticated chroniclers of the disparate skirmishes in contemporary American cities, observing and narrating the spatially oriented conditions of existence that influence and shape this decidedly urban music. It is important to stress the word "existence" here, for as hip-hop's varied artists and aficionados themselves frequently suggest, their narrative descriptions of urban conditions involve active attempts to express how individuals or communities in these locales live, how the microworlds they constitute are experienced, or how specifically located social relationships are negotiated. It is the modes of existence, or what Massey (1992) refers to as the "social content," that give rap its vitality. Baker, for instance, focuses on the "simmering energies" of young black men and women, "diffused over black cityscapes" (H. Baker 1993, 87), as an indicator of the character and content of black urban life and of the apparent contradiction between the images and statistics of embattled urban existence and the vibrant responses of the youths who inhabit such locales.

In the face of dismal social-research reports, the fact remains that the urban spaces most reviled by the mainstream and elite social segments are lived spaces where acts of atrocity and conditions of desolation and desperation are often matched by more promising conditions steeped in optimism, charity, and creativity. The latter, of course, frequently go unnoticed and thus remain underreported in the social mainstream. These conditions of optimism and nihilism occur in a common spatial context, contributing to particular ways of experiencing the world, and out of the prevailing contradictory tensions comes incredible activity as youths engage in hip-hop's spatial practices in their attempts to produce spaces of their own making.[2] This includes their enunciation of patterns of circulation and mobility, the renaming of neighborhoods and thoroughfares; the specific reference to city sites, including nightclubs, subway stops, and so on; and the "claiming" of space that makes existence, no matter how bleak or brutal, something with stakes, something worth fighting for.

Tricia Rose also defines rap and its recuperative function in spatial terms, noting that "Hip Hop gives voice to the tensions and contradictions in the public urban landscape during a period of substantial transformation . . .

and attempts to seize the shifting urban terrain, to make it work on behalf of the dispossessed" (1994b, 72). As the music and surrounding practices within the frames of hip-hop's cultural activity continue to display the creativity and dexterity of young urban artists and producers, it is increasingly evident that the careful explanation of space and its relevance is of crucial significance. The issue of space and place remain central to hip-hop, whether it emerges from Los Angeles, Long Beach, Houston, Atlanta, New Orleans, or the boroughs of New York. The questions remain, however: which spatial modes are of most significance to the cultural processes and social practices that underlie the hip-hop culture, and through what spatial apparatuses is their relative significance expressed and articulated?

Rap's Spatial Dimensions: Discourse, Text, Industry, and "the Real"

There are several primary spatial terrains that can be identified within rap music and hip-hop culture. The first encompasses the discursive spaces (or discursive fields, regimes, etc.) within which the culture's communicative structures cohere, as well as the varied discursive sites, such as the mainstream and alternative media or published academic tracts such as this that comprise the expressivity of the wider hip-hop culture or the articulations of its casual observers or detractors. Stuart Hall describes discourse as "sets of ready-made and preconstituted 'experiencings' displayed and arranged through language which fill out the ideological sphere" (1977, 322). Discourse, which encompasses language and other symbolic forms enabling communication and the production of meaning, enacts the processes through which the conditions of human existence are thought and explained, how they are made sensible and bestowed with values and meanings in social terms. In rap and hip-hop, the denotative and connotative representations, through both language and images of the urban terrain, are discursively rendered, describing and narrating a perceived social reality that is further invested with values of authenticity.

Hip-hop's discourses have an impressive influence among North American teens of all races and ethnicities, providing a distinctive understanding of the social terrains and conditions under which "real" black cultural identities are formed and experienced. The connective logic that links space, place, and race to this ostensible reality has been a point of much debate among critics (i.e., Boyd 1997; Kelley 1997), and it remains central to any engaged discussion on the topic of hip-hop. Discourse must, therefore, be an essential element of the study of hip-hop's relationships to the social production of race and space, for it is in and through discourse that the imaginings of cultural authenticity and the lived practices that express it are merged. Harvey's observation that "representations of places have material consequences insofar as fantasies, desires, fears, and longings are expressed in actual behavior" (1993, 22) offers an instructive view on the discursive articulation of spatialized and racialized identities.

The emphasis on "experiencings" is important to Hall's definition of discourse from two perspectives. First, it reinforces the interrelationships between language and life and between the systems of symbolic representation and the social world, conceived as an arrangement of institutional and organizational patterns within which individual subjects and collective populations circulate. Second, it foregrounds the active element of language; that is to say, discourse consists primarily of sets of linguistic and symbolic practices that are enacted or mobilized by social subjects who continually strive to make sense of the world around them. It is in and through discourse that the world of experience acquires meaning, and it is likewise in and through patterned discourses that social subjects are located or positioned, suggesting important implications for aspects of human agency (i.e., the range of what can be conceived or done) and identity formation that are fundamentally rooted in spatial relations. Discourse sets the stage for practice, producing the conditions in which the world is actively perceived and apprehended by social subjects; practice or the active expression of agency and experience is "talked into life" (Wagner-Pacifici 1994). From this we might conclude that it is through the complex dynamics of discourse and practice that race is spatialized and space is racialized; these are two sides of the same coin.

Any approach to discursive space must remain sufficiently flexible to account for ruptures and breaks in the capacity of discourse to shape experience and perspective. In fact, discursive space is a stratified space where competing discourses collide and jostle with each other, providing the basis for a system of relationships across disparate fields. Pertaining to the heterogeneous and stratified character of discourse, Robin Wagner-Pacifici argues against the notion of inherent coherence, or the "internal fixity and insularity of given discourses":

No one discourse can stand on its own; it will always be partial in the eyes of the differentiated audiences of the modern world. Thus an analyst will inevitably find alien images, stylistic flourishes, unanticipated lexical features, and so forth embedded within a given discourse that promises an intact, wholecloth worldview.
(Wagner-Pacifici 1994, 8)

He notes that "the practical acknowledgment of the incompleteness, the partiality of a given discursive formation," forms the grounds for a progressive hybridity that is capable of producing "discursive flexibility to move back and forth across several discursive formations, to self-consciously cobble together speech acts through borrowings and reframings" (1994, 146). The rap genre, musically and discursively, is constructed in ways that thwart absolute coherence and closure, instead remaining highly ambiguous, multivalent, and open ended.

Extending the scope of its meaning as it is implemented by Tricia Rose (1994a), rap music's "flow" is relevant to the discussion of discursive space, for rap artists are actively and intentionally involved in what might be termed discursive bricolage, enacted through the accumulation of fragments and shards from an array of social discourses and stylistic elements of popular culture. The flow across and through multiple fields of discourse may be, on the one hand, a strategy of refusal, a conscious rejection of discursive lockdown. On the other hand—sidestepping the rush to identify "resistance" everywhere—it may simply be a case of highly conscious play within the free-ranging signifiers of contemporary popular culture. In practice, rap displays elements of each to varying effect. The lyrical speech acts of rap artists, although they meet the prerequisites of the entertainment industry (i.e., supplying the content and commodity for sale and eventual consumption), also articulate disparate and apparently unrelated social phenomena (i.e., age, race, class, gender, location, and each artist's own stock of cultural capital), in the process establishing a unique and complex means of mounting what can at times be insightful commentary and a withering critique of prevailing social relationships. It can be said from this perspective that the discursive spaces of rap are distinct, providing a unique arena for particular kinds of expression and articulation that in various instances reinforce, challenge, and play with the dominant social codes.

Since rap music's popular and commercial debut, it has undergone numerous transformations and developed several notable subgenres reflecting and announcing various social practices that have remained submerged within dominant discourse. In the same general time frame, there have been both radical and more subtly nuanced changes in "the black public sphere," that sphere within a sphere that has always existed as a facet of American society but has been systematically and systemically rendered invisible, secondary, or problematic within dominant discourse and inquiry.[3]

It is not an empty claim to suggest that rap music and the spectacularity of the extended hip-hop culture have been central factors in the circulation of cultural counterdiscourses among many black and Latino teens and in the contemporary transformations of African-American cultural identities and politics that are formed within the public sphere. This is especially true in view of the fact that rap and its associated hip-hop practices have provided a lightning rod for heated debates about musical "quality" and aesthetics, as well as social values, moral and ethical parameters, gender inequality, sexism or misogyny, class conflict, intergenerational dissonance, and the ongoing antagonisms of racial disharmony in America today. Beyond this, rap and the accompanying facets of hip-hop have also been integral to the production of new stylistic sensibilities that have had an unavoidable impact on a vast expanse of popular culture and have extended far beyond their source in the cultural domains of urban minority youth.

Nancy Fraser's (1992) theoretical model defining the conditions in which socially disenfranchised collectives might formulate alternative discursive arenas provides a compelling approach to the study of hip-hop cultural production and the capacity to construct what she calls "subaltern counterpublics," which are founded upon oppositional counterdiscourses. Fraser explores a spatial conceptualization of an arena where publics and counterpublics converge through dialogue and discourse. Her theoretical formulation conveys an expansive ideal as she argues for a multiplicity of discursive formations that, despite the prevalence of contradictory agendas, are in dialogue across disparate social settings and cultural contexts—across space. She stresses the importance of articulated alternatives that are culturally and politically oriented and that conjoin different discourses and connect divergent positions. This is to say that she envisions an alternative discursive arena that encompasses and encourages forms of social action that can, under historically specific conditions, lead to coalition-based political aggregates. Although Fraser's theory does not address geography and social dispersion explicitly, it is obvious that the cultural and subcultural formations comprising the objects of her analysis occupy separate—if overlapping —social spaces and can be located upon a cultural map of difference.

Fraser also acknowledges the multiple forms of existing social oppression and disenfranchisement and the ways that marginalized social factions maintain an active presence within the dominant public arenas and within the dominant social discourses where systemic oppression tends to be reproduced most consistently. Marginality is always only partial, and its geocultural conceptualization as a site at the edges of social power is often wrongly expressed as a tangible element, something that can actually be pointed to. The theoretical notion of margin/center dynamics must also acknowledge the particular ways that each is codependent and mutually influential as a set of social forces. This perspective refutes the simple and commonly misapplied oppositional bipolarity of margin/center relations, instead opting for a more connective and interrelated model that accepts these power differentials as relationships in tension and struggle. In this view, then, the arena of public discourse is seen to be hierarchically structured: centrality and marginality (or domination and subordination) coexist within a structure of relational difference where, in fact, each relies on the presence and definition of an "other."

Fraser's approach is consistent with that of Angela Davis (1981, 1989), who points out that effective struggle against hegemonic hierarchies of domination must be founded on an integrative logic that emphasizes the various interlocking forms of oppression experienced by individuals and social groups across a broad spectrum of social experience. In a slightly different sense, throughout her work focusing on themes of resistance and cultural transformation, bell hooks (1988) advocates a cultural project that subscribes to the radical processes of "talking back" and "coming to voice" that initiate the articulation of personal or collective politics—whether these be politics of resistance or of identity formation. None of these theoretical formulations are intended as precise programs for change, however, for society is an unruly amalgamation of competing and contradictory forces, and the terrains of culture are characteristically prone to variation and unevenness. There are no guarantees that progressive change can be achieved or that the kinds of desired changes will result (Grossberg 1992). Yet, in each of these theoretical and practical propositions is a theme that conforms to the ways in which rap has been taken up, implemented, or deployed by members of the hip-hop culture.

The articulation of experience and the influences of contemporary conditions that inform cultural identities frequently emerge within the arena of the hip-hop culture as a series of counterdiscourses, representing an attempt to circumvent constraining and outdated programs for social empowerment. While there are many examples of conservative and even regressive positions that are articulated within hip-hop (i.e., the reinforcement of restrictive patriarchal values, the expression of traditional notions of heterosexual masculinity, a preponderance of racist or bigoted sentiments, and a pronounced commitment to narrowly conceived capitalist ideals of wealth and power), they tend to generate the most controversy at the exclusion of other alternative positions. The disjuncture produced by rap's alternative or progressive counterdiscourses also illustrates the problems with identifying the black "voice" as homogeneous or the black public sphere as a unified concept when, in fact, they display several overlapping points of antagonism.

With rap, predominantly black and Latino teenagers have established an identifiable discursive arena, a forum where the ideas and concerns as well as the expression of powerful strains of both nihilism and optimism of a generation can be heard in multiple articulative modes. Rap's young creators have located a cultural voice that is both an adaptation to and a departure from earlier voices of nationalism and black unity politics. It is an adaptation in the postmodern dialogic sense that the past is often revisited as an archival repository of ideas, discourses, symbols, or styles that continually resurface (albeit radically reworked) in contemporary contexts. Examples of this can be seen in the adapted personae of rappers who express their identification with the images and political stances of the Black Panther party and other political facets of the earlier black power movement.[4] It is a departure inasmuch as the dialogue between generations and between different classes of African-Americans is often strained, reflecting the extent to which evolving social and cultural conditions of existence often result in divergent rather than convergent cultural strategies.

TEXTUAL SPACE AND RAP EXPRESSIVITY

The second spatial component of hip-hop is identifiable in the textual spaces of its recorded form and other related media and ancillary texts that either focus on rap and hip-hop explicitly (such as the music press and teen-oriented fan magazines or television and radio broadcasts) or embrace it for its thematic content or background (i.e., film and television). This aspect of hip-hop's spatial composition also encompasses the dynamics in popular culture of production and consumption as they involve textual commodities. The textual sites of recordings, magazines, and music videos or films comprise the material product that is disseminated regionally, nationally, and globally and that is encountered and consumed by audience members within the practices of capital exchange in the commercial market.

Like discourses, these texts should not be approached as unified, closed objects for analysis, for, as Graeme Turner cautions,

> the point of textual analysis is not to set up a canon of rich and rewarding texts we can return to as privileged objects. . . . Analysis should not limit itself to the structures of individual texts, but should use such texts as the site for examining the wider structures that produced them—those of culture itself.   (Turner 1990, 23)

Textual space, rather than texts themselves, attains prominence from a theoretical point of view here, for the concept of space offers a means of isolating the point where a range of influential factors converge and interact, as well as accommodating intertextual and extratextual cultural elements that are crucial to our understanding of texts and their production, distribution, and actual or potential uses.

Popular texts are polysemic in form, serving as a crossroads for a wealth of words, images, ideas, and ideologies that are linked together to construct representations of social reality. Reality, conceived as the physical and material plane where actual social practices occur, exists at a crucial remove from the textual representations that circulate in its name, for while the representational forms are based in a foundation that can be identified as "reality," it is essential to recognize that this always can be only partial. It is with this in mind that the limits to textual analyses must be recognized. The text exists as "a site where cultural meanings are accessible to us" (Turner 1990, 23), although the meanings are neither accessible solely in the text itself, nor are they guaranteed in some preordained and thus over-determined manner.

From a critical perspective, hip-hop's various texts "cannot be the whole story" (Grossberg 1992) of youth, minority existence, racial identities, or spatial affinities. Rather, the encoded text, be it in the form of recorded music, printed articles, film, or radio and television programming, becomes part of each individual's own economy of meaning upon its decoding. Texts are consequently made meaningful according to each individual's cultural frames of reference and cultural capital, since the textual content is reintroduced to the social realm through interpretive practices (the act of making meaning) and social actions based upon interpretation. Texts can be studied as representations of reality, but the textual rendering can never guarantee the produced outcome or the "reality effects" that result when they are swept up and into people's lives.

Lawrence Grossberg suggests that textual and other elements of popular culture acquire their meanings when they are charted along individuals' "mattering maps" and are situated within social practices that are charged with affective intensities. As an influential facet of popular culture in which individuals invest (both monetarily and affectively), rap is highly implicated in this cartography of everyday life. For Grossberg, "affective investment" is the dominant factor in the process of making popular culture meaningful:

The image of mattering maps points to the constant attempt to organize moments of stable identity, sites at which people can, at least temporarily, find themselves "at home" with what they care about. . . . But mattering maps also involve the lines that connect the different sites of investment; they define the possibilities for moving from one investment to another, of linking the various fragments of identity together. They define not only what sites (practices, effects, structures) matter but how they matter. And they construct a lived coherence for those enclosed within their spaces.   (Grossberg 1992, 84)

In a society prone to both excess and alienation, individuals chart their course and navigate their lives around sites of reproducible intensity that, like ports in the storm, provide a position or location at which to anchor oneself, a mooring of relative security. Following Grossberg's instructive lead, it is important to circumvent the risk of improperly locating meanings in the texts themselves and to consciously undermine the authority of the text. Hip-hop's textual forms are more aptly thought of as intrinsic elements involving processes of social mapping that provide the coordinates for charting issues and practices within the broad terrains of popular culture. Hip-hop does not comprise the essences of authentic urban black identity, but it can, from this perspective, offer social texts that make sense to young minority youth who dwell in urban environments and who accordingly identify themselves within their codes and meanings.

According to Michel de Certeau,

narrative structures have the status of spatial syntaxes. By means of a whole panoply of codes, ordered ways of proceeding and constraints, they regulate change in spaces (or moves from one place to another) made by stories in the form of places put in linear or interlaced series. . . . Every story is a travel story—a spatial practice. (1984, 115)

De Certeau's emphasis on narrative as a crucial cultural element in the inscription and delimitation of boundaries offers insights as to how narrative space (stories and texts) and spatial narratives rendered in textual form operate in tandem. The narrative descriptions of tours and journeys, for instance, circulates into the social space of meanings, where they might, in turn, inform people's common practices. Over time, through our encounters with spatial narratives, we adopt a set of spatial dispositions, developing a repertoire of potential ways of being in relation to particular geographies or social settings. These stories or narratives present more than an imaginary locus that is visited in the mind—they introduce spatial sensibilities and cues that are continually enacted throughout our social lives. In similar fashion, rap's textual forms provide spaces where stories cohere and where descriptive mobilities within its narratives can also be encountered, emerging as influential components in the ways that youths imagine their worlds and chart their paths through urban and nonurban terrains.

In rap, the vocalist or MC constructs elaborate rhymes that interact with the digitally produced electronic rhythms, telling stories that vividly depict contemporary life and are laden with references to popular-culture icons, people, situations, and sites. The rap narrative is, in effect, a highly mobile form that ranges widely across our cultural spaces, touching on many walks of life in multiple ways. For instance, in a thoughtful article addressing the interweaving of voices and electronic technologies in rap, Rose (1989) repeatedly alludes to the various spaces that either influence the music as a genre or that inform its narrative structures, providing the basis for its "stories."

Rose frames these sites and spatial practices within a history of hip-hop that foregrounds the impoverished locales of New York City's South Bronx and the generalized spaces of the ghetto. Yet she also cites the recording studio, for instance, as a transformative space of technological innovation and production, where digital samplers and rhythm machines are merged with the lyrical narratives and in tandem circulate in commodity form into the spaces of audience "communities." There is no single dominant space in these descriptions, yet there can be no denying the relatively narrow racialized character of the spatial sites that are central to the music's production. Rap is not necessarily unique in these aspects, for any recorded music generally displays similar spatial elements. But rap texts are the product of particular kinds of spatial relations and spatial histories, and they therefore feature a distinct spatial repertoire that characterizes the music, identifying it as a unique genre without essentializing its cultural meanings.

Additionally, as the central expressive voice of hip-hop culture, rap is, in its textual forms, extended through people's daily circulation (through the mobile listening practices enabled by car stereo systems and portable cassette and CD players) or through its own retextualization and recontextualization (grafted onto other media or infused into various common social settings). The sonic qualities of rap texts transform the spaces into which they flood in ways that are quite distinct from those seen in other musical genres. It is not at all uncommon to hear ambient music of any style in one's daily circulation in the city and to process it quickly and almost absentmindedly for cues about its relevance or appeal to one's own life, tracing it onto our own subjective mattering maps. Throughout the day we hear music from numerous sources over which we have literally no control, and yet we continue to locate and position it according to our cultural knowledges or assumptions about how the music might be linked to particular audience formations, fan groups, or what Grossberg terms "affective alliances." For instance, the slow, rumbling bass of rap, hip-hop, or reggae dancehall music alters and redefines space differently than the high-pitched and frenetic guitar solos of heavy metal music. Each suggests unique textual distinctions that we "read" from and that position us differently in relation to it.

In this sense, every musical genre provides a wide variety of relevant characteristic elements that can be organized (albeit in an initially perfunctory manner) cartographically according to individual and collective cultural maps and values. The textual spaces of rap can therefore be conceived as points or positions among various audience members and fans, as well as having spatial and relational relevance to corporate and other institutional entities. They provide sites in which disparate formations converge and are mobilized. In corresponding terms, Iain Chambers explains:

we all become nomads, migrating across a system that is too vast to be our own but in which we are fully involved, translating and transforming bits and elements into local instances of sense. It is this remaking, this transmutation, that makes such texts and languages—the city, cinema, music, culture and the contemporary world

—habitable: as though they were a space borrowed for a moment by a transient, an immigrant, a nomad. (Chambers 1993, 193)

Rap's content is the result of a process of inscription whereby social relationships are reiterated within textual spaces that are themselves then returned to the public sphere. The recorded and performative texts are opened up and revealed as sites where social practices and their informing histories can subsequently be read.

INDUSTRIAL OR ORGANIZATIONAL SPACE
AND HIP-HOP'S COMMODIFICATION

Hip-hop's ascendance into the popular social consciousness is not the result of an accident. Although it initially emerged with apparent spontaneity from a series of distinct cultural conditions and social contexts, its popularization has involved a complex process of institutionalization that is not remotely spontaneous. It has since been intentionally and strategically connected to commercial procedures, linking the forms, images, and statements of hip-hop with commercial interests, with production, distribution, and promotional apparatuses, and with national and international commodity markets. In this context, the space under review is that of organized global corporate enterprise, or what Arjun Appadurai (1996) calls "financescapes."

The spatial or geocultural components of the modern culture industries are recognizable in the work of many academic theorists. Focusing on music, Theodor Adorno, the grandfather of critical mass-culture theory, denounced the commercial character of popular music as early as the 1930s, expressly citing the dilution of musical aesthetics and the prevalence of vulgar public taste, both of which are informed by the commercial imperatives of the market. As Adorno notes, the production and distribution of songs in the popular idioms of the twentieth century adhere to the dominant modes of commodity production and the rational logic of corporate efficiency evident in most other industrial sectors as well: "in the advanced industrial countries pop music is defined by standardization: its prototype is the song hit" (1989, 25). Discussing the globalization of the contemporary music and entertainment industries in the late twentieth century, Roger Wallis and Krister Malm write:

Through a process of integration and concentration different sectors of the music, electronic, and communications industries have been amalgamated into giant conglomerates, so complex in their organizational structure that even individual employees do not know who owns what. (Wallis and Malm 1990, 161)

Roy Shuker states that "the music industry is big business, an international multi-billion dollar enterprise" (1994, 31), and in Keith Negus's view, "the industry needs to be understood as both a commercial business driven by the pursuit of profit and as a site of human activity from which some very great popular music has come and continues to emerge" (1996, 36). In each of these views, the spatial components of the industry are foregrounded, whether the emphasis is on the corporate sites of executive management and musical production or on the international and postnational character of today's market, characteristically fragmented into large-scale geographic regions or more nuanced demographic niches.

The global corporate entertainment industry is commonly portrayed as a dominating space, a zone that represents authority and influence, with the indicators involving either economic might or international reach. These are the geographies of power, and the financial titans overseeing their landscapes, mapping the flow of manufactured, mass-produced goods, and charting the entries into new, unexploited markets have honed and extended their capacities to dissolve not only the boundaries of nations, but also the boundaries of places on a reduced scale, infiltrating both broad and minute social domains with awesome force. The "executive suite" (Negus 1999) comes into focus in its portrayals in mainstream business news and industry media as a particular site or locus inhabited by a majority of exorbitantly well paid men (and a few women). Their labor involves organizing and allocating corporate resources in the production of cultural content—nonmaterial goods—and the objects and images of massified public and private leisure.

Decisions made by executives, producers, promoters, and others who together comprise the various divisions of the entertainment industry are defined primarily in business terms, but their efforts also affect the structures of contemporary pleasures and desires that are organized through images, music, and other popular media texts. This is not to say, however, that they maintain an irrefutable hold on the manifestations of pleasure and desire or that theirs is a determining authority in the mass production of common, homogeneous sets of pleasure and desire that are circulated throughout the world via media and cultural commodities. Despite fears of global cultural homogenization, considerable evidence exists that the meanings and uses of leisure and entertainment commodities are far from singular. It is more accurately stated that the gatekeeping and agenda-setting powers of mass media and entertainment conglomerates have an inordinate influence over the character and parameters of the systems of pleasure and desire, and their affective composition, on an increasingly global scale.

As evidence against global homogenization theory, it might be casually observed that Bob Marley and Michael Jackson have, at different historical moments over the past thirty years, attained relatively widespread global recognition through the systems of mainstream media diffusion. Yet in their circulation as contemporary signs of celebrity, their music and associated representational images are adopted into peoples' lives and reimagined according to radically different regional and localized contexts. The Maori adaptations of Bob Marley and the Wailers' "Get Up Stand Up," for example, celebrates the cultural contribution of the Jamaican Rastafarian artists while redefining the content of that contribution within the politics of race, resistance, and social struggle in New Zealand. The pattern is true also of contemporary hip-hop, for, as Mark Schwartz states, "across the globe, hip hop has been customized, souped up, or retrofitted into local relevance" (1999, 362). Michael Jackson's celebrity status as the "King of Pop" is much more secure on the global stage than in the United States, in part because his sexual ambiguities and complex racial stance with regard to his own physical blackness are of less importance in foreign cultural contexts where the intense and divisive debates about sexuality, race, and cultural identity that rage in the United States do not apply. For the same reason, Public Enemy never had the impact on the international stage that it did in the United States: the mediating politics of race and culture in other international contexts defused the potency of their symbolic (connotative) or literal (denotative) meanings. Thus, while transnational media enterprises and the global culture industries have a powerful influence over what gets circulated into world markets, there are no guarantees as to how cultural commodities will be incorporated into localized practices and the lived experiences of subjective pleasure and desire.

Since the 1970s the trend in the media entertainment industries (and most other major industrial sectors) has been toward consolidation and corporate concentration. Competition among the largest corporate conglomerates is steadily being cleared, and the umbrellas of major organizational entities grow larger and larger, throwing a greater portion of the cultural markets into their shadow. Market competition still exists across social sectors and within media structures, but for some time now it has exceeded local, regional, and national geographies, entering and altering diverse cultural landscapes throughout the world. Thus, the dynamics between the head office, or the particular sites of executive decision-making within systems of global corporate domination, and the dispersed sites of cultural innovation on the one hand and distant markets on the other emerge as a further example of spatial othering characterized by radical disjunctures and uneven distributions of spatial power, and the different capacities to deploy space in the ongoing production and reproduction of this power.

Robert McChesney, writing in the *Nation* (one of the most consistent sources of critical discussion on the globalization of commercial culture and consciousness), explains that "when audiences appear to prefer locally made fare, the global media corporations, rather than flee in despair, globalize their production. This is perhaps most visible in the music industry" (McChesney 1999, 14). McChesney's skeptical and derisive argumentative thrust is standard among political-economy theorists and commentators who are critical of trends of Western cultural imperialism (among them Armand and Michele Mattelart, Marc Crispin Miller, and Herbert Schiller). Yet it should also be acknowledged that under certain conditions the broad sweep and transnational circulation of contemporary culture industries have the potential to introduce new cultural forms and artists to a much wider audience base, to contribute to the panoply of cultural voices in dialogue on a global stage, and to provide the basis for unforeseen, hybrid interactions. In hip-hop, an example of this might be France's MC Solaar, whose rise on the international stage has been facilitated through the extended francophone diaspora, including the hip-hop scene in Montreal, as well as connections he has forged with the anglophone New York rapper Guru (of the prominent rap group Gang Starr), who has publicly supported Solaar's work. For all the positives that might emerge, however, the question of access to the production, distribution, and broadcast mechanisms on the global stage remains a nagging and pernicious issue.

Furthermore, McChesney's view does not account for the ways that, as Negus phrases it, "culture produces an industry":

production does not take place simply "within" a corporate environment created according to the requirements of capitalist production or organizational formulae but in relation to broader cultural formations and practices that may not be directly within the control or comprehension of the company.   (Negus 1999, 490)

Industry mechanics and the human practices at each level of organizational structure are continually and inextricably entwined with the cultures surrounding them, although the transnational scale of larger corporate entities means that they are wrapped into a much broader cultural system than are smaller or independent companies. The idea of one-way flows of influence is patently false; executives, managers, and basic laborers who comprise the culture industry's workforce do not live in vacuums but are themselves active consumers of cultural commodities, and they too adopt and adapt cultural products into their daily lives. Thus, there is always a fluid interaction between the society and culture in which a corporation is based and the corporation itself, though the balance of influence may not be equally distributed in every instance.

From its inception, hip-hop has been exposed to the logics and practices of the cultural industry system, "comprised of all organizations engaged in the processes of filtering new products and ideas as they flow from 'creative' personnel in the technical subsystem to the managerial, institutional, and societal levels of organization" (Hirsch 1990, 129). The emphasis is on the systemic character of the culture industries and the various constitutive divisions that operate in the service of larger entities but also function according to their own internal logics. The segmented industrial terrain, including artists, producers, managers, agents, publicists, distributors, retailers, and consumers, also presents a series of spatial points or nodes in the filtering process that can, under specific historical, cultural, or social conditions, either facilitate or constrain the flow of new cultural products or creative innovations. The spatial orientations of these industry segmentations in relation to hip-hop and rap music are also a major factor in the organizational and economic dynamics between independent cultural producers, which generally operate at a more localized micro-scale, and major transnational corporate enterprises in the music, film, publishing, and promotions sectors.

RAP, HIP-HOP, AND THE MATERIAL SPACES OF "THE REAL"

The final space of central relevance to this study encompasses what is referred to variously as actual space, physical space, natural space, or, to use Lefebvre's term, "the space of experience." It is the space of the world around us, where social practices and relationships are enacted. This is also the space of the senses and of sensual practices—the space of activities that have tactile quality. It is the visceral space through which physical bodies roam, interact, and collide. Physical space is commonly taken for granted and infused with assumptions about its "natural" or organic characteristics, leading to a descriptive terminology that Lefebvre suggests is passive and relatively unreflective. Yet for all of its obviousness (because it surrounds us and demarcates each of our individual "worlds"), it can also be the most elusive kind of space.

In regular social contact, the physical spaces in which we live and work are frequently regarded unproblematically as containers for our experiences of the world. This perspective regards physical space as a kind of preceding emptiness that is filled by our human subjective presence. Produced and reproduced by statesmen, corporate leaders, architects, planners, and, crucially, each of us in our own daily peregrinations according to variances of scope, scale, ability, and autonomy, physical space is more or less unconsciously transformed into social space by the human interactions that demarcate parameters of existence. Its "real" meanings are thought to reside in our actions and practices or their outcomes, which, of course, have to happen somewhere. Such an approach casts space as a setting or a back-drop to the important activities of everyday life without adequately taking up the question of the spatial composition of life's events—a question that, as I mentioned previously, has gradually become a central concern in the fields of cultural geography and cultural studies. In fact, physical space *is* a container of sorts, but caution must be taken not to designate it as *simply* a container of social performance and practice.

Humans co-opt physical space in many ways. All involve the establish-ment of coordinates that have relational meaning and have been rendered in readable forms, as in the creation of terrestrial and oceanic maps or even the descriptive tensions between "here" and "there." In Lefebvre's terms, this is a process of production; through human action we attribute sym-bols and signs to physical spaces, providing both visual (i.e., maps and car-tography) and lexical (i.e., descriptive terminology) means for defining multiple spaces upon which society is structured. It also involves the intro-duction of built structure to physical landscapes: constructing buildings or highways and streets as routes of passage and flow, or erecting signs as markers that help orient residents. The process of rendering space mean-ingful in cultural terms involves more than just isolating distinct spaces or objects in space. It also encompasses the reproduction of society by defin-ing spaces according to the ways they are inhabited and used as lived, expe-riential space.

In hip-hop's physical and localized expressions and in rap's narratives, the authority of individual experience is generally built upon what is con-ceived as the self-evident truth of natural or material spaces, where events occur and experience is registered. To reduce the myriad of experiential tes-timonies (which will be taken up in greater detail later) to a basic formula-tion, the statement "this happened to me" is often and increasingly re-inforced by the spatial qualifier "here." The "where" of experience has a powerful influence over the social meanings derived from the experiences themselves, for just as our actions and mobilities bring space into cultural relief, so, too, does socially produced space bring meaning to our actions. The category of space comprises the social arena in which individuals re-produce or challenge their experiential boundaries of action and inter-action.

Spatial scale thus emerges as a crucial factor for the apprehension and un-derstanding of spatial difference, since, like many other elements of the prevailing capitalist system, it is subject to uneven development and distri-bution among people of different social classes and groups. For example, the spatial patterns that define territorial boundaries and that frame circula-tion and mobility are structured unevenly between individuals and institutions, the scale of the latter being much larger than that of the former. Similarly, age, class, gender, and race variables can be regarded as social factors that frequently affect scale and the range of physical space accessible to individuals as well as collective formations (i.e., adults versus youth, the wealthy versus the impoverished, men versus women, and whites versus minorities). In each of these contexts, the issue is one of scale, including the scale or extent of social interrelationships through which individuals and group agglomerations express their autonomy and define their identities.

Encapsulating the influence of discursive, textual, and physical spaces in rap and hip-hop, Rose's sketch of rap's formation and growth is illuminating as she identifies their multiple, stratified influences, tracing a spatial arc through urban America's cultural landscapes:

Out of a broader discursive climate in which the perspectives of younger Hispanic, Afro-Caribbeans and African-Americans had been provided little social space, hip hop developed as part of a cross-cultural communication network. Trains carried graffiti tags through the five boroughs; flyers posted in black and Hispanic neighborhoods brought teenagers from all over New York to parks and clubs in the Bronx and eventually to events throughout the metropolitan area. And, characteristic in the age of high-tech telecommunications, stories with cultural and narrative resonance continued to spread at rapid pace.   (Rose 1994a, 60)

Context and conjunctural forces can be discerned in the first segment of this description, in which Rose isolates the relationships between discourse and cultural spaces of enunciation simultaneously at hip-hop and rap's source. Hip-hop culture was carried outward along both physical and technological pathways, disseminated more widely as its practices evolved away from the central spaces of their origin. Finally, through the circulation of textual materials and human mobilities, the culture took root in other spaces, such as the corporate spaces of the music, film, television, and publishing industries as well as dispersed and disparate audience environments existing at a substantial distance from the sites of hip-hop's origins. At each historical moment and in each spatial juncture, hip-hop underwent processes of transformation that reflect the influences of sociospatial difference and produce the contexts for adaptation.

As hip-hop culture gradually merged with formal institutional structures of the mass media and expanded its range of cultural influence, it displayed a dual directionality operating at different levels of scale: hip-hop developed and expanded outward as its impact and influence were circulated onto the regional and national scales, yet as young people throughout the nation (and the world) encountered hip-hop in all of its forms, they quickly adapted it to their own localized patterns and practices, reinventing hip-hop according to entirely contingent and locally relevant logics. This dynamic, which involves dimensions of scale, resides at the core of much of the spatial orientation of the hip-hop culture and can be heard in the themes of rap music as well as in other popular texts relating to the culture. The spatial complexities of hip-hop, far from being incidental or insignificant, are central to all that emerges from it.

From Space to Place: The Production of Scale and Value

Like space, place has been the object of much thought and scholarly interrogation, emerging in numerous contexts as either an adjunct to the study of spatiality or as the central focus in the analyses of society and spatial processes. For example, Yi-Fu Tuan notes that "'space' is more abstract than 'place'" (1977, 6), whereas Lawrence Grossberg expresses the distinction between space and place in terms of a "structured mobility," stating that "places are the sites of stability where people can stop and act, the markers of their affective investments," and "spaces are the parameters of the mobility of people and practices" (1992, 295). As each of these statements on space and place illustrates, the two concepts are mutually entwined. Yet there is no easy agreement as to how they should be separated to explain their distinctions and what these distinctions might mean culturally. Two dominant themes emerge, however, that can be seen as primary points distinguishing place from space: scale and value.

According to John Agnew, scale "refers to the spatial *level*, local, national, global, at which the presumed effect of location is operative" (1993, 251). In a relational sense, place as a dimensional arena exists in contrast to the larger and more general scales of space (Tuan's position). Place defines the immediate locale of human interaction in the particular, whereas space is the expanse of mobile trajectories through which subjects pass in their circulation between or among distinct and varied places (Grossberg's position). The produced character of place remains central; like space, it is a social construct, but one that is shaped according to different logics and meanings.

Place is structured along more narrowly circumscribed parameters than is space; it is defined by its closeness and proximity to individuals and groups and by its localized character, distinguished by its contrast with the distant and external character of abstracted space or of other distinct places. Its reduced scale allows individuals to inhabit it more fully, permitting greater intimacy, awareness, and involvement with the particularities of its geographic and social composition. Recognition and affiliation grounded in place facilitate certain kinds of investments in those places of greatest familiarity or significance. This closeness introduces the further ability to organize places in concrete and material ways as part of individuals' daily lives, leading David Ley (1989) to suggest that place is a more highly ordered concept than space. At reduced scales, however, it is clear that individuals are more capable of imagining lines of mobility and circulation routes from a perspective of close proximity. This subsequently influences one's awareness of the range of possible options and, in a literal sense, paths of action, giving material consequences to the often-hazy affective and subjective sense of place that individuals carry within themselves.

Just as space and place are produced according to differing logics of scale, so, too, is place subject to its own varied classifications. For some individuals and in some social contexts, a sense of place as a site of significance may be grounded in the immediate environments of personal experience, such as the home or the near neighborhood. In other contexts place may be conceived more broadly, encompassing the entire city where one lives and works (an aspect that is often tied to civic pride and booster campaigns) or even the wider region, depending upon levels of affiliation and identification with a given social or natural terrain. In hip-hop and rap, the naming of streets and neighborhood locales, cities, and regions of production activity reflects this spatial pattern with impressive consistency. This approach to place and scale returns us to the crucial notion that social relations produce and reproduce our comprehension of spatiality; there is no sense of place that can be derived in the absence of social processes, for it is these lived processes themselves that ultimately inform our affective affiliations to sites of significance.

The vast majority of spatial articulations within hip-hop emerge from within the contextual boundaries of the urban sphere, a factor that has remained consistent since the culture's inception and remains true even as hip-hop's forms and expressions have circulated globally. As John Jeffries observes, it is the city that provides the frame for "the repertoires of black popular culture," including style, music, and "black popular culture's deliberate use of the body as canvas" (1992, 158) but he notes that the concept of the urban environment itself remains an abstraction composed of generalities, for no city reveals itself in all of its complexities, nor is any city open and accessible to all.

The abstraction of "the city" can be productively reduced through additional clarification and qualification by references to specific cities, for example, as well as to specific micro-spaces and places within any given urban environment. Thus, without disputing Jeffries's point that cities constitute a crucial element in the formation and expression of black popular culture in its multifaceted idioms, it is necessary to further acknowledge and illuminate the diverse practices that produce distinct kinds of urban spaces in America's cities. The cultural histories as well as the cultural present of, for instance, New York, Miami, Detroit, Houston, New Orleans, and Los Angeles differ vastly, and despite similarities that might be shared at the scale of "the city" or "the American urban environment," the distinctions are pronounced, as are the nuanced forms and expressions of popular culture that emerge from each urban locale. This is no less true of the distinctions and disparities that occur at the micro-levels of individual boroughs and neighborhoods, whether this be in the Roxbury section of Boston, the Bronx in New York, or Houston's Fifth Ward, where hip-hop culture exerts a pronounced influence.

A refinement can be seen developing in the areas of music, film, and various performance arts among young urban cultural workers, who make up the group most noticeably influenced by hip-hop. Their work frequently reduces the spatial scale, shifting focus from the broad, generalized spaces of the city to more localized environments of the borough and, in a further reduction, to the scale of the neighborhood. This refinement should not be regarded as a simple reduction that, in its focus on particularity and local levels of experience, is capable of producing more authentically knowable spaces (although this claim is often made among hip-hop's cultural producers and consumers, a point to which I will return in later chapters). Even as an example of a highly localized and particular scale, the narrowed parameters of the neighborhood refuse totalization, offering instead a highly complex range of experiences that are shaped by the overlapping effects of internal and external influences (i.e., local and nonlocal forces). From an analytical perspective, however, it is appropriate to shift the emphasis from larger scales of the urban environment to reduced scales, since these micro-levels of experience are today receiving intensified attention through the many forms of black cultural expression now current.

According to Jeffries, black popular culture is undergoing a transition that is largely motivated by concurrent transformations of the late-capitalist, postmodern urban sphere:

> The cultural signifiers that black popular culture employs [to continue its reaffirmation of black humanity in the upcoming century] may already be overdetermined—overdetermined in the sense that the significance of place, and the presumed authenticity associated with the signifier "black," are both being displaced.
>
> (1992, 162)

It seems accurate to say that these elements of significance—place and "blackness"—rather than undergoing a once-and-for-all displacement, are being redefined at multiple levels of experience and meaning. As the global-local nexus described by Kevin Robins (1991) evolves into *the* primary frame of social interaction in late-twentieth-century America, there is a renewed investment in the significance of place, and new attempts are being made to revalorize and reinvigorate the places of social meaning.

Similarly, it can be seen among examples emanating from the hip-hop culture that new signifiers of blackness are also closely aligned with the revitalized significance of place, for they are often, though by no means always, grafted onto one another. In the extreme and more publicly visible cases, this tendency is evident in the formation of and explicit identification with neighborhood "crews," "cliques," and "posses"—defined as relatively cohesive and locally identified peer groups—associated with the cultural forms and collective affiliations within hip-hop culture. In less optimistic but no less significant ways, they can be discerned in the highly locational and place-bound practices of "gangsta-ism" that resounded audibly in the discourses emerging from hip-hop in the late 1980s and early 1990s.

The active process of making spatial sites significant—or the active transformation of space into place—involves the investment of subjective value and the attribution of meanings to components of the socially constructed environment. Tuan describes place as "a special kind of object . . . a concretion of values" (1977, 12). For him, place is rendered meaningful (and hence significant) precisely through the lived practices of circulation and habitation. It emerges as a meaningful domain through experience, perception, and the visceral contact that occurs as one interacts with the physical and social environment. One's sense of place is the product of a particular proximity and familiarity with the environment of one's routine circulation and is encompassing of those elements that are frequently described as the "practices of everyday life," accounting for the minutiae and subordinated details that may be overlooked due to their apparent insignificance.

In other words, place is produced according to rhythms of movement and patterns of use. The dynamic apprehension of space through personal and subjective processes of meaning conferral consequently encompasses the overlapping duality of both habitation and habituation. Habitation and habituation are themselves part of what I call a reiterative process that includes locally repeated practices as well as recurrent narratives and discourses that are part of the explanatory and communicative apparatus of everyday life. Reiterative processes simultaneously influence the real and the symbolic foundations of experience. They also involve the saying and the saying again (literally, rendering experience meaningful by introducing it into language) and the accompanying repetition of actions, as well as the ensuing talk about them and about their real or potential implications. The significance of place consequently acquires definition through discursive articulations and narrative descriptions that are formed within a myriad of contradictory and competing cultural forms, a variety of genres, and a wide array of expressive apparatuses. Both our subjective and our collectively held senses of place begin to take shape and cohere once they are rendered into language, acquiring what Ryden (1993) refers to as a "discursive depth."

The "sense of place" that individuals acquire, however, is not based solely on a positive relation to a known environment, for, as Tuan suggests, topophilia or "love of place" (1974) exists alongside and often in tandem with one's experience of "landscapes of fear" (1979), which are capable of producing what might be termed topophobia. For the hip-hop culture, place may be significant for its familiarity, its nurturing factors, and its supportive infrastructures, but it may also harbor other, more menacing elements that are also centrally implicated in establishing criteria of significance. From this perspective, place is not always a close and positive spatial frame. It may be threatening, alienating, and dangerous to its inhabitants.

It is important to stress here that neither the individual and subjective affiliation to place nor the collective inhabitation of proximate spaces can be reduced to a simple notion of community, although communities do cohere within bounded parameters of localized places. As Deyan Sudjic (1992) argues, the overarching notion of community is frequently a myth in the context of today's sprawling global cities, which are characteristically diverse and prone to rapid transformation. The sustainable communities of the past, based traditionally in strong family connections to locality, wide ethnic or immigrant support systems, and a shared sense of collective purpose, have been altered by, among other factors, the influences of modern communications technologies, which both eliminate the need for face-to-face contact and provide leisure and news options that mitigate the need for direct community engagement. The contemporary appeal to community values employed by many politicians as well as urban planners often harks back to an earlier, idealized notion of urban cooperation and place-based affiliations, where the community is "presented as desirable in itself, a reflection of a natural order of life that is tampered with at society's peril," or understood as "the anchor of social stability" (Sudjic 1992, 283).

Community is organized around a much more complicated and long-standing structure of interrelationships, a relatively strong sense of common cause (whether it is ever enacted or visible in concrete practices), and at least a modicum of localized cooperation that exceeds geosocial, place-bound affiliations. Yet the sense of community that coheres around localized issues and interests is still primarily grounded in a shared sense of place that accompanies either explicit or implicit mapping of community boundaries and in a descriptive lexicon recognizable by the majority of those who ostensibly comprise the community in question. Herein lies an important element of place identification: in order for a place to emerge as a social product, there must be a point where the description of its attributes is rendered explicit or where the value invested in one's relationships to place are communicated with others who may either express a shared identification with it or, conversely, have little or no relationship to it. This points to the necessary stage at which language enters into the definition of place, for it is in and through language that the values of places are produced. For example, localities under duress (from, for instance, a major local fire, an outbreak of crime and violence, intense devastation, or conditions of extreme hardship) commonly gravitate toward the themes and discursive articulations of "the community" with little effort or forethought. Prior to the catalytic incident, "community" existed in the collective mind of the local citizenry, an imagined construct to which they might turn should the need arise. The language and meanings of community exist as resources to which people turn when community, with all of its attendant comforts, is most needed.

As a contemporary medium of cultural and aesthetic expression, rap music provides a unique medium for defining a series of enunciative positions, accommodating the locational coordinates (both physical and cultural) of experience that enable young artists to articulate their emergent sense of place and, as need arises, community. The kind of place values to which I refer here constitute more than ephemeral positionings along a spectrum of possibilities. The investment of self in place and the concurrent identification of self within an economy of place-based factors ultimately shape and influence the ways in which subjective perspectives evolve in relation to others who occupy the same places or, further removed, spaces of similar character.

The close relationships of person and place that are structured around scale and value have important implications for the construction of subject identities among the inhabitants of a given place. Evolved social norms have produced strong relational influences between place and identity, which is evident, for instance, in the common casual inquiry about where one is from or where one currently resides. This is an efficient way of filling in information about a person's character and identity and assumes a latent relationship between spatiality and identity. Indeed, it is a core defining factor of hip-hop culture and its communicative logics.

Individual and collective identities are connected to place, although rarely to a single place and, owing to contemporary influences such as increased travel and global communication technologies, never in a pure or unmediated way. Individuals are more likely today to feel strong, value-laden affinities to several places at once rather than to a single homogeneous locale, although identification with a dominant home environment remains strong. This pattern of multiple, even hybrid spatial identifications is largely a result of highly mobile social patterns that produce corresponding forms nomadic identities, leading Iain Chambers to write that "our sense of being, of identity and language, is experienced and extrapolated from movement. . . . Identity is formed on the move" (1994, 24–25). This movement may be across an ambiguous and ill-defined mediascape in the realm of the popular, but it is also crucially encompassing of patterns of circulation and motion that comprise our daily lives and lead us across and through sociospatial boundaries in a process of endless encounters with different places and their accompanying localized discourses.

Consequently, whether looking to the practices of subway train graffiti in the late 1970s and early 1980s or to the more recent proliferation of territorial affiliations within a corporate institutional structure as hip-hop has attained commercial stability and international popularity, it is evident that identity formation in hip-hop culture is strongly linked to spatiality, mobility, and fluctuating differences between the near and the far, or between "here" and "there."

Perspectives on the Global-Local Nexus

In a world increasingly prone to transnationalism, or what Arjun Appadurai (1996) calls "deterritorialization," it is common to encounter the idea of human and corporate interaction defined in terms of new global "flows." The concept of "flow" encompasses global economies and the exchange and transfer of huge volumes of manufactured goods, financial information, news and media images, and human bodies around the world according to a prevailing logic of maximized efficiency and rational order. This is the cultural effect that can be discerned in such disparate examples as the rise of continental free-trade agreements and economic unification strategies; the internationalizing efforts of the 1985 Live Aid concerts for famine relief and USA for Africa's theme, "We Are the World"; and the technological achievement of the digitally linked 1999 NetAid concerts.

It is said that these and other examples of a "global culture" reduce the difference of space (Meyrowitz 1985; Harvey 1989), drawing the world and its dispersed peoples closer—through, for instance, style, fashion, and global taste—into ever more intimate contact via telecommunications technologies, mass media, and popular culture. These link individuals and social groups across what were once, in earlier iterations, perceived as incommensurable cultural and spatial divisions, even as the trend reproduces hierarchically stratified inequalities of information access and storage. It can be seen that a diverse array of capitalist forces is in motion, forces that introduce a transitional global sensibility. These examples point to the extension of economic power and the conquest—or, to use David Harvey's term, "compression"—of time and space. As we are beginning to realize, the impact is one not solely of spatial proportions but "also [of] the stretching out over space of relations of power, and relations imbued with meaning and symbolism" (Massey 1992, 4).

By the year 2000, we witnessed a dual pull in apparently opposite directions, toward the micro-spaces of particularized geographies and the vast macro-spaces of a global scale. What, we might ask, is the relationship between these two directionalities, and what are the consequences of their divergences? How can this be understood "on the ground," where meanings are made within the systems and structures of social interaction? Where does power enter and exert itself within these social interactions, and, pursuant to this, what stakes are involved? Who stands to win (and profit), and who loses? In either oblique, vague references or, by contrast, explicit and articulate critique, contemporary cultural workers, including hip-hop's break-dancers, graffiti artists, and rap musicians, have encountered similar questions. They have initiated their own intense debates on the topic within the expressive cultural spaces they build and inhabit.

These "competing centrifugal and centripetal forces that characterize the new geographical arena" (Robins 1991, 24) have reorganized the sense of the world as well as the sense of self. The cultural apparatuses that organize our individual and collective senses of social belongingness are being altered by the newly emergent global-local nexus. This is defined by Kevin Robins as being "associated with new relations between space and place, fixity and mobility, center and periphery, 'real' and 'virtual' space, 'inside' and 'outside', frontier and territory" (1991, 41). Among some factions in the fields of critical sociology and cultural studies, this may be celebrated as an indication of the declining constraint of boundaries and rigidly structured terrains (as well as the accompanying erosion of faith in the metanarratives or *grands récits* of fixed histories, unified centers, and coherent, unmediated subjectivities). Advocates see the positive possibilities as leading toward the potential for a radical new hybridity formed in the limitless options of contingency (Bhabha 1990; Chambers 1994), contributing not to new ordered forms and aesthetics but to wildly disruptive, incoherent, or chaotic forms that thwart the rigidified tendencies of institutionalized dominant culture.

The oppositional images of place that often spring forth on behalf of marginalized social formations in attempts to recast them within the global-local nexus are not, however, always progressive. Akhil Gupta and James Ferguson explain that

the irony of these times, however, is that as actual places and localities become ever more blurred and indeterminate, *ideas* of culturally and ethnically distinct places become perhaps even more salient. It is here that it becomes most visible how imagined communities come to be attached to imagined places, as displaced peoples cluster around remembered or imagined homelands, places, or communities in a world that seems increasingly to deny such firm territorialized anchors in their actuality. . . . Territoriality is thus reinscribed at just the point it threatens to be erased. (1992, 10–11)

They caution that "often enough, as in the contemporary United States, the association of place with memory, loss, and nostalgia plays directly into the hands of reactionary popular movements" (13). What they describe is a fundamentally reactionary posture that frequently arises from either a sense of encroaching loss or, from a conservative impulse, an attempt to preserve existing conditions and to thwart the onslaught of rapid change on a national or global scale. Similarly, Kevin Robins writes that

globalization is profoundly transforming our apprehension of the world: it is provoking a new experience of orientation and disorientation, new senses of placed and placeless identity. . . . The driving imperative is to salvage centered, bounded, and coherent identities—placed identities for placeless times.

(Robins 1991, 40–41)

For Robins, there is a danger that, in the midst of a global trend that threatens to erase territorial divisions and the boundaries upon which national identities have been historically based, individuals and groups will desperately seek to supplant this sense of loss and "disorientation." They urgently attempt to introduce either a rejuvenated nationalism or, conversely, a hyper-localism framed within powerful notions of nostalgic pride, tradition, and racial or ethnic purity that might reaffirm or reify unified and unambiguous identities.[5]

These concerns also correspond with David Harvey's and Doreen Massey's views. Harvey writes: "Indeed, there are abundant signs that localism and nationalism have become stronger precisely because of the quest for the security that place offers in the midst of all the shifting that flexible accumulation implies" (1989, 306). His Marxist analyses of the condition of postmodernity accommodate various geographical perspectives as he fluctuates between a critique of illusory ideals of large-scale nationalisms (citing the charismatic leadership of Ronald Reagan and the patriotism of the British Falklands War effort as two examples of how the image of nationalism has been advanced) and corporate relocation strategies, to which the rise of an urgent localism can be read as a reaction against corporate indifference to labor and communities. Massey warns of the inward-turning and reductive responses that can result from panicked reaction to globalization's effects:

There is today all too much evidence of the emergence of disquieting forms of place-bound loyalties. There are the new nationalisms springing up in the east of

Europe. . . . There are also burgeoning exclusive localisms, the constructions of tightly bounded place-identities [that are] static, self-enclosing and defensive.

(Massey 1992, 7)

Relating specifically to rap music and the hip-hop culture, the "place-bound loyalties" and "localisms" described by Massey and others can at times be discerned in the discourses and textual images of space and place that are associated with the pervasive articulations of "the ghetto" and "the 'hood."

A new, spatially oriented terminology that reflects the contours of the current historical moment and the conditions of existence within which the world is experienced and explained by mainly urban black and Latino youths has emerged through hip-hop's diverse cultural practices. It is within hip-hop's referential frames that subjective and group identities among urban minority youth and, to a growing extent, nonurban youth are increasingly located and defined. Space, place, and race, cast within the discursive articulation of identities has since the early 1980s ascended as a cultural dominant (Williams 1977) in the cultural lexicon and expressive repertoires of North American youth; today, they are rendered visible and audible with the greatest urgency in the various forums of hip-hop culture.

CHAPTER TWO

"Welcome to the City"
Defining and Delineating the Urban Terrain

❋

The "city" (or, more appropriately, cities) is central to the discussion of race, space, place, and hip-hop. It encompasses the physical city and its material features, including architectural edifices, the above- and below-ground crossroads, and the public and private spaces within a delineated geographic boundary, as well as the symbolic city, which is to say the representational city, encompassing images, verbal articulations, or other artistic expressions of urban cultures, experiences, and identities. The evidence of urban emphasis is abundant: each of several top-selling CDs from the late 1990s has a track that explicitly cites the city as a geographic locus and resource. Jay-Z's "The City Is Mine" (1997, Roc-a-Fella/Def Jam) appropriates the chorus from Glenn Frey's 1985 hit "You Belong to the City" (MCA) to frame his boastful descriptions of the urban lifestyles of hip-hop's rich and famous. On "Welcome to the City" (1998, No Limit), Master P structures tales of social struggle, criminal behavior, and underground economies around the chorus of Stevie Wonder's "Living for the City" (1973, Tamla). Lauryn Hill's "Every Ghetto, Every City" (1998, Ruffhouse/Columbia) gives a slight nod to the rhythmic pulse of Stevie Wonder in his *Innervisions* (1973, Tamla) phase, offering a retrospective meditation on the urban terrains and hip-hop culture that inflected Hill's own identity in her formative teenage years. Her track is in fact representative of how far hip-hop has come in its expressive attention to urban detail, citing specific locational place names and the activities and cultural practices associated with them.

Cities are, of course, complex in both their physical and symbolic character, and like most complex systems, they are subject to imbalances, hierarchically structured divisions, competition, and contradictions that can in turn produce the uneven conditions in which chronic social tension and civic unrest might unfold. As David Theo Goldberg observes,

The built environment is made in, and reifies, the image and architecture of "pyramidal power." . . . Citizen and strangers are controlled through the spatial confines of divided place. This urban geometry—the spatial categories through, and in which, the lived world is largely thought, experienced, disciplined—imposes a set of interiorities and exteriorities. (Goldberg 1993, 45)

Moreover, the city is a historical construct, and the evolution of urban spaces has been marked by deep contestatory battles over space and its uses. Spatial power is always open to negotiation or renegotiation. Political maneuvers and strategies of outright resistance—the power plays of contemporary society—are liable to change according to shifting needs over time, which has resulted in radically different experiences of cities among victors and the vanquished in these sociospatial struggles and among older and younger social groups.

Over the roughly twenty-five years since hip-hop's earliest identifiable characteristics emerged, much has been written on the topic that traces the links between this profoundly urban form and the influences of the city on its cultural and spatial formations. A quick check of books on rap and hip-hop in general at Amazon.com's online store, for example, reveals over seventy titles on the subject. The plethora of writing and analyses on hip-hop has resulted in what can be confidently described as a hip-hop canon, with the citation of several key books and authors being de rigeur. It is therefore important and necessary to reexamine these texts and to assess the propositions set forth within their pages, for as canonical texts they have the power to sediment certain histories or historical accounts that may, in retrospect, require critical revisitation. This is not to suggest that the history of hip-hop has been falsely inscribed, but that the evolutionary construction of a hip-hop canon is itself now part of hip-hop's lore. These texts and their content do not exist outside of the culture—they do not provide externalized objective views. Rather, they, too, are internally significant facets of what is today recognized as hip-hop culture. The authors generally are urban dwellers themselves who include hip-hop in their lives as participants and members of an active audience. Analyzing the contributions of literary or academic workers who, in the popular and alternative press or academic and popular publishing industries, have influenced the understanding of the urban character of the hip-hop culture is as essential as analyzing the contributions of early musicians, break-dancers, and graffiti artists who forged and have maintained hip-hop over time.

Hip-Hop Historiography: Sourcing Urban Culture

The story of rap's rise from the black ghettoes of America has by now become a familiar tale, diffused through a range of sources that include academic publishing and both mainstream and minor media. Historically it has been framed as part of a surge of artistic creativity formed at street level, and it is frequently described as an example of radical innovation under duress (i.e., Hager 1984; Toop 1984; Rose 1994a), which further points to the cultural vitality and inventiveness of various black youth subcultures. As rap has expanded in terms of its popularity and scope of cultural influence, this narrative has had a powerful effect on how the music, the artists who produce it, and its audiences are perceived within a general system of social tastes and values. Much of rap's earliest journalistic coverage in the mainstream media was inaccurate, dismissive, or heavily biased against the form and its informing cultural practices, a continuing example of which can be seen in a *Newsweek* feature story ("The Rap Attitude") that, at the time it was published (March 19, 1990), raised the collective ire of artists and producers in the rap music industry and throughout the hip-hop culture. The mainstream media's diffusion of images of the hip-hop scene into the American popular consciousness continues to be uneven at best. The spatial specificities of rap's origins, which include the twin factors of where the music emanates from and how those social spaces are constructed within critical discourse by various social commentators (including academics), can thus be regarded as an enduring facet in the definition and comprehension of hip-hop's contemporary character. Whether represented in a positive or a negative light, these competing perspectives have influenced public perceptions of the genre in relation to other forces within popular culture.

Much academic coverage of hip-hop's historical development features a detailed description—not necessarily analysis—of its spatial particulars. While hip-hop's capacity to circumvent the constraints and limiting social conditions of young African-American and Latino youths has been examined and celebrated by cultural critics and scholars, attention to hip-hop's spatial logics has been notably inconsistent. These histories often rely on a brief geographical explanation, establishing hip-hop's earliest locales in a manner that highlights the first stages of the emergent movement and the flow of people and cultures through a defined environment: the Bronx borough of New York. It is not, however, solely the geography of the city that makes the historical narratives of rap's emergence unique. The histories of the blues and jazz and their related cultural practices in the 1920s and 1930s, for example, are also often structured around the importance of regional and local geographies.[1] With virtually all the mainstream and critical academic work on hip-hop and rap, no matter how the culture and the music are explained, the emphasis is almost exclusively placed on their urban composition in a manner that accepts the city as a transparent, self-evident entity.

This is evident, for instance, in David Toop's *Rap Attack: African Jive to New York Hip Hop*, which has for years (and through three editions) provided one of the more concise historical overviews of rap, hip-hop, and their cultural origins. Toop begins his narrative with references to New York streets and night spots, localizing the base of the music's roots in the Bronx:

Hip hop's home, the Bronx, is an area with a fearsome reputation caricatured by films such as *Bronx Warriors* and *Fort Apache: The Bronx*. Its grim project housing and burnt-out buildings have little of the political and cultural resonance of neighboring Harlem, let alone the material assets further downtown; it was within the Bronx and, to a lesser extent, Harlem that black youths developed their own alternative to gang warfare that had risen from the dead in the late 1960s to dominate and divide neighborhoods north of Central Park.   (Toop 1984, 12)

Using a terminology that bespeaks "the ghetto," Toop describes architecture and geography, social structure and territory. The mapped spaces of the Bronx, Harlem, and Central Park are identified by name precisely because those names speak of particular places in particular ways (although the veiled reference to a territory "further downtown" is easily decipherable as Manhattan). They already have semiotic value and, thus, significance that has often been constructed through the entertainment and news media.

It is interesting to note, however, that the cultural resonance of "the Bronx" and the deeper symbolic values attached to its geographies within the public imagination are not so closely or uncritically held among residents of the borough itself. Reporting in the *Bronx Beat* (March 13, 1995), a community newspaper serving the area, Edward Lewine interviewed local residents, asking them to define the spatial parameters of the South Bronx, presumed to be ground zero in hip-hop's history. Under the headline "The South Bronx? It's a State of Mind," Lewine observes that there are no official cartographic designations for the South Bronx section of the borough on civic records or maps: "No one could agree on exactly where the South Bronx is. But they all said that wherever it is, it has a bad reputation." Despite its apparent absence as a mapped and territorially inscribed space, one respondent noted that "the people that come from the South Bronx hold it as a badge of honor. It means they're tough." As interviewees debated the possible zones comprising the South Bronx, the place-image of urban ruin and danger emerged quite clearly, with several borough citizens suggesting that "the term 'South Bronx' came into common use in the 1970s after the release of the movie *Fort Apache, the Bronx* and Jimmy Carter's much-publicized visit to Charlotte Street." Toop and many others, however, paint a particularly bleak image of the entire borough, overlooking the uneven distribution of urban desolation in the Bronx (and other urban loci) that led one man, standing in a central location in his Bronx neighborhood, to state, "It don't look dilapidated. That's what I associate with the South Bronx."

The urban spaces from which hip-hop emerged are made meaningful in a further sense according to a general mapping of New York's interborough organization. This is conveyed in Toop's descriptions of the greater New York metropolitan area, which provide basic geographic information, but also assume some level of prior knowledge pertaining to the geo-cultural arrangement and spatial dimensions of the city. New York's iconic presence, its identity as a global city, allows Toop and others to implement a descriptive shorthand that facilitates the efficient communication of spatial and cultural coordinates. He relies on the assumption that most people know in advance that Harlem and the Bronx are predominantly inhabited by blacks, Latinos, or immigrants, distinguishing it from Manhattan and other boroughs. This assumed knowledge makes it easier to graft onto these places further images (as well as stereotypes) pertaining to the cultures that cohere there.

Dick Hebdige's (1987) description of rap's invention introduces a further extension of the cultural constituencies that inhabit local urban neighborhoods as he acknowledges the crucial influences that were experienced over the years with the influx of various immigrant and ethnic groups. He demarcates the Bronx in more historically precise terms than does Toop, referring explicitly to the black and Latino cultural melange that has contributed to the borough's character for over seventy years:

Both reggae and rap also grew out of city slum environments. Rap started in the South Bronx of New York, which had been a mainly black and Hispanic ghetto for decades. By 1930 nearly a quarter of the people who lived there were West Indian immigrants. And most of the Spanish speakers living in the Bronx nowadays either came originally from Caribbean islands like Puerto Rico and Cuba or are the children of Caribbean immigrants. . . . There are now three million Puerto Ricans living in New York—as many as live in Puerto Rico itself. The Bronx had never been prosperous. But in the 1960s it went into a sudden decline and by the end of the decade it had become the poorest, toughest neighborhood in the whole of New York. (Hebdige 1987, 137)

This narrative delineates the Bronx and the local neighborhoods therein as a dynamic, if depressed, environment that is the product of historical fluctuations of people and cultural flavors. It is represented here as a territory of cultural hybridity, formed along the cultural axes described by Trinh Minh-ha when she points to "a Third World in every First World" (1987, 138–39). By foregrounding the historical and cultural elements of the borough, Hebdige mitigates the constraints that a narrative of urban devastation or economic decline might imply. He works against the sense of closure and containment that often accompanies popular images of the Bronx in film, television, and musical lyrics. The dominant image of the Bronx, reinforced by photographs or television and movie footage, is one of poverty, disease, violence, and danger, all coded as black. Yet a preliminary understanding of the vitality of the borough and its various communities and an attempt to locate the urban spaces of the South Bronx in a historical light challenges the linear narrative equation *Bronx + black = doomed wasteland*.

Among the most in-depth historical examinations of hip-hop's geographical origins is that undertaken by Rose (1994a). Noting that "rap's primary context for development is hip hop culture, the Afrodiasporic traditions it extends and revises, *and* the New York urban terrain in the 1970s" (26), Rose carefully analyzes and assesses the postmodern and postindustrial city, first in the abstract (i.e., "the city") and then in the particular, focusing on the urban conditions of New York City and the South Bronx. She details the clever artistry of hip-hop's producers and their wily creativity, which are reflective of an endless capacity for altering the implied or preferred uses of technologies and space. Rose explains that the city is much more than a backdrop to hip-hop practices; rather, it is the very factor that "provided the context for creative development among hip hop's earliest innovators, shaped their cultural terrain, access to space, materials, and education" (34). Without avoiding the darker influences of economic and infrastructural decline and a prevailing sense of "loss and futility" among many impoverished or marginally prospering urban dwellers of the late twentieth century, Rose identifies a positive and progressive agency in hip-hop that refutes conceptualizations of the city as an architectural and human disaster.

Like Hebdige, Rose introduces a historical perspective that accounts for the flow and dynamic interrelations of diverse ethnic and racial groups. In fact, this point is developed with varying degrees of detail by virtually all chroniclers of rap history when acknowledging the profound impact of the Jamaican cultural presence in the Bronx and Harlem neighborhoods, and of the influences of the Jamaican sound systems, such as the hip-hop pioneer Kool DJ Herc's, and reggae's lyrical "toasters" whose vocal styles gradually evolved into those of the rap MC and who played a crucial role in community-oriented leisure practices (i.e., Holman 1984; Hager 1984; Gilroy 1987, 1993b; Fernando 1994; Stolzoff 2000). Accompanying this, academics and members of the hip-hop culture themselves have begun to explicitly recuperate the previously overlooked or ignored Latino presence that has been evident and vital to the growth of hip-hop throughout its history, pointedly correcting erasures that have contributed to a generalized popular perception that rap and hip-hop are the invention solely of urban black youth.[2] Juan Flores correctly isolates the spatiality of this historical dynamic:

> Of course it is possible to identify specifically Puerto Rican ingredients that went into the original brew of hip hop, that formative contribution being even more apparent in breakdance and graffiti than in rap. But this line of analysis usually leads to the notion of the "tinge" or touches of salsa thrown in to add zest to the recipe. The beginnings of rap are connective not so much because they link black traditions and Puerto Rican traditions, but because they mark off one more step in a long and intricate black-and-Puerto Rican tradition of popular culture, based primarily in the long-standing black-and-Puerto Rican neighborhoods of New York City.
> (Flores 1994, 91)

The relationships between localized urban conditions and the rise of rap as a response, dialogue, or statement by black and Latino teenagers is indeed central to an understanding of hip-hop's cultural origins.

Hip-hop did not spring forth from the Bronx magically; it emerged from within an economically limiting context as a new means of negotiating the immediate environment and of motivating individual and collective cultural practices of opportunity on a day-to-day basis. As Robin Kelley (1997) is careful to explain, the economics of the Bronx and other similarly designated "ghetto" communities are not based on chronic impoverishment alone; they are also brimming with hard workers whose labor, reinvestment, and community commitments are beyond reproach. This was the case in the mid-1970s, when hip-hop's expressive forms of graffiti, break-dancing, DJing, and MCing began to develop, and it remains so today. Hip-hop was not founded simply in the organic creativity of a homogeneous American urban youth population. It emerged from within particular geographies of oppression and opportunity combined, where the interlocking forms of race and class (and, as Rose [1990, 1994a] explains, gender) often tend to reproduce the most intense conditions of lack, but which also portend positive and optimistic perspectives among the inhabitants. It thus becomes necessary to approach hip-hop's evolution from within a matrix of influences that are most prevalent in high-density urban localities inhabited predominantly by black, Latino, and multiethnic immigrant working and nonworking populations.

Hip-hop and rap have, in tandem, been crucial in the redefinition of the

American urban environment and, more pointedly, the redefinition of the relationships between minority youth and the American metropolis. The culture of hip-hop embodies a range of activities that not only display but consciously foreground spatial characteristics, whether through the sonic appropriation of aural space, the appropriation of street corners (where, at an earlier stage in hip-hop's development, rap improvisation and break-dancing were common), or appropriation of the city's architecture through the ubiquitous display of spray-painted graffiti tags, burners, and pieces.[3] Hip-hop comprises a deliberate, concentrated, and often spontaneous array of spatial practices and spatial discourses that are both constituted by and constitutive of the spaces and places in which its primary cultural producers live and work. Its expressive forms have therefore been exceedingly influential in both the representation and the transformation of the urban environment throughout the 1980s and 1990s.

The Symbolic Meaning of "Inner City"

Pointing to a defining aspect of the modern city and the trends of suburban development in the post–World War II period that were implicated in the shaping of contemporary urban environments, Stephen Haymes writes, "The consequence of capitalism's spatial reordering of the city is the creation of conditions that gave rise to inner-city black ghettoes" (1995, 81). It is worth exploring the term "inner city," for in the media and elsewhere its usage has attained a status of acceptability that tends to elide deeper, underlying assumptions. "Inner city" is, literally, a term that points to sites or spaces at the core of urban America. It occupies the opposite pole of the outer city, the suburbs and strip malls, or what Joel Garreau (1988) refers to as "edge cities," that surround the perimeters of all major cities.[4] In this sense, the inner city is purely geographic, delineating a specific spatial locus. Beyond its spatial coordinates, however, in its symbolic representational forms, the term has a resonance that reaches through the urban cores and the suburban and nonurban sectors of society, cutting to the very heart of the contemporary body politic.

Timothy Maliqalim Simone seizes on the spatial biases of language, criticizing the often subtle practices of signification that can influence social dialogue and the production of meaning:

In the aftermath of the civil rights movement of the sixties and seventies, American culture has discovered that racial effects are more efficiently achieved in a language cleansed of overt racial reference. Although conceptual precision in discussions about American social life demands that racial discourse employ racial categories, such categories may or may not make the explicit reference to perceivable and acknowledgeable racial characteristics such as skin color. (Simone 1989, 16–17)

The commonsense meanings of the term "inner city," especially in language constructions such as "inner-city youth" or "inner-city violence," constitute a buzzword that comes fully loaded with extenuating implications, assumptions, and stereotypical ideas of who occupies these spaces and in what ways. For instance, when a term such as "inner-city youth" is applied offhandedly by policy makers, educators, and the media, it refers not simply to teens from the geographic city center but exclusively to minority teenagers. Yet in its very status as common language, it masks the fact that race, space, and class have been historically and systemically ordered in the collective consciousness, especially among the white middle-class population. This underlying principle is evident, for example, in a policy report released by the Heritage Foundation, a conservative American think tank, that predicts a correlation between a growing urban black youth population and increases in urban crime by the year 2010 (Whitmire 1995).[5]

When mobilized in particular contexts, then, the term "inner city" implicitly refers to racialized images or racially inflected conditions of danger, violence, and depravity that can be contrasted with the ideals of calm, safety, and security attributed to nonurban or suburban spaces:

The boundaries of race provide particularly conducive conditions for the construction of distorted cultural representations. In the United States, for example, a pernicious white mythology about black culture was historically consolidated by the media, legitimated by the social sciences, and institutionalized by the state. Its consequences, grounded in the cultural fiction of "the black ghetto," included the creation of unequal life-chances for households confined within the stigmatized collectivity of the inner-city. (J. Duncan and Ley 1993, 6)

The term is also used in some contexts to signify an earlier, mythical period when the modern city was ostensibly freer of threat or danger, particularly from minorities and immigrants. Discussions that attempt to identify inner-city constituents and the means through which urban core environments are constituted as communities of concentrated poverty often summon a range of images, including the specter of chronic family welfare, nonworking single mothers, substance abusers, gang members, and so on. Less frequently accounted for are the impact and produced outcomes of inadequately funded and unresponsive educational systems, health services, and recreational services and a concurrent intensification of urban policing and surveillance. Thus, the decontextualized and ahistorical uses of the term "inner city" have a potentially negative, reductive, and neutralizing effect on those who actively inhabit urban core communities.

The spatial distinctions implied by the term "inner city" are important, as they are figured into the common logic of a center-versus-margin paradigm. As Iain Chambers explains:

There is the emergence at the center of the previously peripheral and marginal. For the modern metropolitan figure is the migrant: she and he are the active formulators of metropolitan aesthetics and life styles, reinventing the languages and appropriating the streets of the master. This presence disturbs a previous order. Such an interruption enlarges the potential as the urban script is rewritten and an earlier social order and cultural authority is now turned inside out and dispersed.

(Chambers 1994, 23)

In spatial terms, the inner sanctums of elite and institutional dominance—the central power bloc—do indeed exist in what might be geographically identified as the city core, if not precisely the inner city as I have discussed it above. Rob Shields emphasizes that "marginal places that are of interest are not necessarily on geographical peripheries but, first and foremost, they have been placed on the periphery of cultural systems of space in which places are ranked relative to each other" (1991, 3). The buildings that house the contemporary cultural power bloc are shells at the end of the workday and on weekends, empty edifices that continue to articulate the authority of the "power elite." They symbolize the elite's presence in an ongoing way even, or perhaps especially, when they are vacant. By night, individuals converge on the buildings as a virtually invisible ethnic labor force, cleaning and maintaining them and then departing before the "official" workforce returns. Manuel Castells provides further insights on the phenomenon:

The issue arises that in such a structure organized around flows, people, activities, and cultures that are not valued (or priced) could easily be switched off the network. And in a city where only the meaningful places are the ones associated with the highest functions, the space with meaning for only a few tends to be the space of exclusion for the most.

(Castells 1985, 19)

Urban minorities, immigrants, refugees, undocumented workers in the underground economy, welfare recipients, and the homeless all conform to Castells's notion of "switched-off" communities. Yet hip-hop arises in a manner that presents a powerful switched-on art form, literally connecting young cultural laborers with electronic technologies and digital knowhow, figuratively linking them to new social conduits that can lead out of the constraining spaces of the inner city, the ghetto, or the 'hood.

However, the people who comprise the dominant hegemonic classes and who motivate the institutional discourses of authority in business, commerce, and politics do not, en masse, inhabit the core. The suburbs ostensibly offer a safer haven from both the intensities of the urban professional work world (constituted in the dominant capitalist mindset as a site of civilized threat and legitimate combat) as well as the dangers that emerge, in the popular imagination more than reality, on the streets after dark (constituted as zones of primitive, uncivilized, and illegitimate or unlawful combat). Tom Wolfe impressively captures these tensions and the spirit of late-1980s urban class antagonism in his best-selling novel *The Bonfire of the Vanities*, placing the conflictual elements of race, space, and class at the core of the book's narrative.

Displaying a considerably less optimistic view than Chambers, Ronald Formisano describes "white flight"—the gradual evacuation of America's urban cores in the postwar years and into the 1960s—as "the greatest exodus in America's history. It drained the white population out of the city limits and engorged the near and far suburbs. . . . The suburbs were almost entirely white, while blacks, Hispanics, and later Asians were ringed into the central city by the suburban noose" (1991, 11–12). Examining neighborhood selection processes and the distribution of white and black metropolitan populations, Joe Darden more precisely reveals the extent of racial separation and the formation of segregated environments: "Almost one-half of the white population lived in neighborhoods in the suburbs compared to less than one-quarter of the black population. On the other hand, more than half of the black population (57.8%) lived in neighborhoods in central cities, compared to exactly one-quarter of the white population" (Darden 1987, 27). As new industries and a service sector requiring education and skills emerged, the tendency through much of the late twentieth century was for companies to locate at the edges of the cities, nearer to the majority-white populations that benefited most from the transition to a new electronic and information-based economy.

The depression of America's cities in the period throughout hip-hop's gestational period of the 1970s and much of the 1980s resulted in spatial variations of urban geographic composition. Complicated by misguided urban renewal projects (sometimes referred to as "black removal" projects), unscrupulous development plans, and racially and ethnically motivated political struggles, these trends contributed to the decline of opportunity and quality of life for many people living in the central urban sectors. *Pace* Chambers, those in the urban core and inner cities actually appropriated very few of the "master's" streets in a real or tangible sense, despite the eruption of spontaneous hip-hop practices enacted in public spaces, or of low-level displays of kitsch culture of an often religious nature, as identified by Celeste Olalquiaga (1992). The streets were surrendered and abandoned by departing white and middle-class families, for, "rather than repair the damage to our cities, it seemed simpler, and certainly less dangerous and more profitable, to rebuild the American city somewhere else" (Sam Smith 1994, 61).

A strong economy and the rise of an electronic information sector throughout much of the 1990s, however, began to reverse the trend, stimulating urban real estate markets and producing intensified gentrification.

Thousands of young single professionals, including a general increase of well-skilled minority workers, have been lured back into the city by new opportunities and are reclaiming urban zones that had previously been abandoned to urban dwellers with the onslaught of white flight. Many electronic information (or "dot-com") companies also swept into urban core areas (such as New York's Silicon Alley), establishing offices in warehouses and long-empty or undeveloped loft spaces, and substantially altered the urban character in the neighborhoods where they settled. This has produced an interesting boomerang effect, as it repositions those returning to occupy chic apartments or high-security urban condominiums as new pioneers, active revanchists whose newfound economic prosperity positions them in a unique relationship to exploitable space.[6] Such trends have redefined the inner city as the next frontier of American capitalist conquest, as the nation turns inward on itself after several centuries of imagining the frontier as an external beyond.[7] It should also be noted that the rapid rise in the number of Latinos in cities such as Boston, New York, Miami, Houston, and Los Angeles are today changing the character and spatial images of the inner city in these urban settings, necessitating the reimagining of the dominant, long-standing, and inaccurate image of a primarily black inner-city culture.

Chambers is somewhat more accurate, however, when he suggests that the streets of America's major cities were transformed, in terms of aesthetics and lifestyles, at the level of popular culture. With the rise of hip-hop, and subsequently through rap music and various hip-hop-influenced films and videos, young black artists have demonstrated an unprecedented capacity to influence language, style, and image among the wider youth population. Throughout the 1980s and 1990s, the linguistic, sartorial, and musical expressions of urban minority America have been virtually unavoidable. The influences of hip-hop culture, while adapted and refined in various contexts, occur with regularity across the social spectrum, emerging forcefully (though in lesser concentration) within rural and suburban spaces as well.

This has been further facilitated by the expansion and ubiquity of such media as cable music-television networks (especially MTV and BET in the United States and MuchMusic and MusiquePlus in Canada) that daily feature images of North American cities in rap videos. While at one level this extended range of influence can be credited to the power and scope of the mass media in all of its forms, it also reflects the complex cultural dynamics that identify hipness with black popular culture and that associate the urban core with authenticity and the city's streets as a legitimating space of cultural value among youths.

Youth, Race, and Space

The cultural tensions that are produced through the convergence of issues of race and space are intensified when the variable "youth" is introduced as an active element (or complication, depending on one's perspective) in the organization and ordering of society. The image of youth that has pervaded the popular imagination through film, television, and musical promotion since at least the 1950s, when American youth culture (as it is generally conceived today) came into full bloom, is often one of either optimism and unbounded promise or, conversely, threat, danger, and crisis. In Grossberg's assessment, youth was perceived as the designated demographic group that would, in effect, embody the ideals of the American dream for an unbounded future. Youth was invested with the nation's hope: "The baby boomers became the living promise of the possibility of actually achieving the American dream. They were to be the best-fed, best-dressed, best-educated generation in the history of the world. They were to be the living proof of the success of the American experiment" (Grossberg 1994, 35–36).

When one surveys texts—both popular and academic—that address generational social formations, one finds that youth, in its idealistic postwar baby-boom configuration, is commonly coded as white and, more often than not, middle class and suburban in the popular imagination as well as in the nostalgic recollections of many contemporary social commentators. Thus, despite the ethnic working-class characterization and themes permeating such texts as the 1955 film *The Blackboard Jungle* (starring a young Sidney Poitier and directed by Richard Brooks), the clichéd images of young love, a car, and expendable teen income accompanied by a nonstop sound track of period hits continue to resonate in the dominant perception of youth. This is evident, for example, in the images of early 1960s youth represented in George Lucas's cinematic landmark *American Graffiti* (1973).

Youth continues to be framed against the American middle-class ideals of a liberated consumer culture. In his book *Populuxe* (1986), Thomas Hine sets out to examine "the look and life of America in the '50s and '60s," yet he reproduces many standard inaccuracies of what he refers to as America's "golden age" by erasing racial and class disparities from the historical account:

The decade from 1954 to 1964 was one of history's greatest shopping sprees, as Americans went on a baroque bender and adorned their mass-produced houses, furniture and machines with accoutrements of the space age and of the American frontier. . . . There was so much wealth it did not need to be shared. Each householder was able to have his own little Versailles along a cul-de-sac.   (Hine 1986, 3)

In this particular permutation—and this is a standard image-ideal rather than an anomaly—there is no acknowledgment of the fact that millions of black Americans and poor whites faced the entrenchment of racial and spatial segregation in the form of massive urban housing projects (such as Chicago's infamous Cabrini-Green housing development or Toronto's Regent Park complex). Even the conflicting images of more radical and less idealistic white youth practices (at least from a traditional or conservative standpoint) are all too frequently ignored in this kind of selective recollection. The political struggles of civil rights activism linking white and black political causes, such as the 1964 "Freedom Summer" voter registration drive, are either romantically reimagined in the white liberal mind or "disappeared" beneath the steamroller effects of mainstream revisionism. They are often reduced to a series of gestures, styles, or political positions without history or substance.

It should be recognized that these historical moments produced some of the first and arguably most influential political and cultural engagements of a youth culture that embraced new visions of hope and attempted to connect the values of both black and white Americans outside of formal institutional spaces. The category "youth" should not be cast in general terms that fail to account for "interlocking forms of oppression" having a pronounced spatial dimension. Referring to urban black youths, Venise Berry remarks on the distinct difference of cultural experience that informs not only racial or ethnic identities but also identities of youths in ghetto environments: "The term 'youth,' which came to mean a specific attitude including pleasure, excitement, hope, power, and invincibility, was not experienced by these kids. Their future was mangled by racism, prejudice, discrimination, and economic and educational stagnation" (1994, 170).

As many of the baby boom generation now confront their own middle age with an uneasy combination of embarrassment and nostalgia, anxiously reshading their youthful hues through revisionism, they are also forced to confront a new generation—their own offspring—that they find largely incomprehensible.[8] The predominant mass-mediated image of youth in the 1980s and early 1990s was of a generation composed of scared, scarred, mistrustful, angry, and apathetic "slackers" and "dead-end kids" who have given up on today, let alone tomorrow.[9] This was true across the color line and in the suburbs as well as in the city core, as Donna Gaines (1991) has pointed out. Conversely, the "Gen-Next" demographic of preadolescents to twenty-five-year-olds is now targeted almost rabidly by aggressive marketers who seek to open new commercial opportunities in the age of extreme sports, relatively widespread Internet access, and affordable digital electronic commodities (Lopiano-Misdom and De Luca 1997). The scope and intensity of economic duress and systemic racism, however, continue to set minority youth apart from their white counterparts.

How have the conditions of minority existence been described in previous academic critique? Young black males have been discursively rendered as one of the primary threats to "law and order" (Hall et al. 1978) in the city, a primary focal point of social anxiety in a rising "moral panic" (S. Cohen 1972) fueled by strong talk of deviance, delinquency, and danger. Black youths are repeatedly cast as contemporary society's "folk devils" (S. Cohen 1972) to whom an array of negative consequences is attributed and who provide visible targets of "official" retribution: "Unwanted as workers, underfunded as students, and undermined as citizens, minority youth seems wanted only by the criminal justice system" (Lipsitz 1994b, 19). Lawrence Grossberg writes that "youth is the last and almost always ignored category in the traditional list of subordinated populations (servants—i.e., racial and colonized minorities, women and children) who, in the name of protection, are silenced" (1992, 176). This has not been lost on members of the hip-hop culture: Public Enemy—perhaps the best-known rap act from the late 1980s—fashioned its band logo in the image of a defiant black youth lined up in the crosshairs of a sniper's rifle scope. Public Enemy articulated a cynical belief that society's number-one threat was the young black male. The group's song titles—for instance, "Countdown to Armageddon," "Party for Your Right to Fight," "Don't Believe the Hype," and "Bring the Noise" (all from the 1988 LP release *It Takes a Nation of Millions to Hold Us Back* [Def Jam])—emerged as rallying cries enunciated and disseminated through the discourses and cultural forms of hip-hop.

When W. E. B. Du Bois wrote of a "double consciousness, this sense of always looking at one's self through the eyes of others, of measuring one's soul by the tape of a world that looks on in amused contempt and pity," he was describing the "two-ness" of being "an American and a Negro" (1994, 2). He was right, of course, that "the problem of the Twentieth Century is the problem of the color-line."[10] Despite major transformations in society and general improvements in social well-being and the overall quality of life since Du Bois first wrote those words, the color line remains a crucial and costly obstacle. Blacks and many other racial and ethnic minorities tend to benefit least and last from social improvements, and they are often the first to feel the negative effects of cutbacks and decreases in social-services spending. Attitudes of bigotry and racist intolerance are still widely evident. Yet the "problem of the color-line" and the "double-consciousness" of which Du Bois wrote are exacerbated in contemporary contexts by the convergent "problem" of youth.

In his detailed study on youth in crisis, Charles Acland examines the distinct discourses of "youth" and "crisis" that form a crucial conjunction encompassing numerous social issues relating to moral decline or "trouble." As he explains, whereas "youth . . . is increasingly symbolically central as that internal Other defined as a threat to the stability of the social order but central in the composition of that order" (1995, 41) the situation is magnified for black youth. Building on several of the themes found in the important British study *Policing the Crisis* (Hall et al. 1978), Acland describes what he sees as "a crisis-in-process" or the continuance of "hegemony through crisis," involving the maintenance of the prevailing hegemonic order in the midst of a concurrent and overlapping series of crises. Like the authors of *Policing the Crisis,* Acland acknowledges Gramsci's perspectives on "the crisis of authority." Writing of a generational divide, Gramsci notes that "the crisis consists precisely in the fact that the old is dying and the new cannot be born; in this interregnum a great variety of morbid symptoms appear" (1971, 276). The emphasis on multiple and simultaneous crises that saturate society provides the proper context for the analysis of youth, race, and space and their influential relationships to hip-hop, for by accessing the means through which each category is discursively constructed and socially organized, it becomes possible to more fully illuminate the extensive apparatuses of contemporary hegemonic power in the urban terrain.

In the case of minority youth, the crisis can be seen as being discursively oriented toward the localized practices of certain social groups who cohere in specific social environments, that is, the ghetto or the public housing projects. For the dominant hegemonic classes, the crisis lies not in the simple existence of minority youth, but in their potential to extend their influence and grow in importance beyond the confines of the ghetto, which constitutes a socially sanctioned area designated primarily to the uses of minority populations. Fundamentally, it is a problem of containment: containment in a spatial and physical sense pertaining to the institution of "vertical ghettoes" or public housing high-rise structures, or, in broader cultural terms, containment as a crisis founded in the inability to sustain the traditional authority of European-based value systems. The dual recognition of hip-hop's cultural reach beyond the ghetto and its ability to galvanize members of both the white and the black bourgeoisie to a sense of imminent crisis has, in some cases, been exploited by rap artists themselves as they deliberately taunt mainstream sensibilities, stoking prevailing racially inscribed social anxieties. The title of Ice Cube's "The Nigga You Love to Hate" (1990, Priority Records) articulates an understanding of the fear and disdain involved. In another example, the cover of Ice-T's album *Home Invasion* (1993, Priority Records) graphically represents the means through which the black urban threat will enter the white suburban home: rap music and the ears of white children.

In this regard, hip-hop and its varied cultural and spatial practices are easily implicated by social authorities as catalytic elements in the crisis threatening mainstream society and the dominant white majority, for it is today among the most widely disseminated forms of contemporary black popular culture. Its impact is felt throughout society, including those enclaves that are traditionally defined as white and middle-class. As Acland writes:

Crisis operates as a *mobile signifier* that migrates from debate to debate and carries with it a field of connotations and referential indices. It implies a common set of standards, values, and ethical questions that set the debate in motion and guide the institutional responses. The discourse of crisis is a potential point of conjuncture of a series of such points; it is the logic of a form of hegemony.   (Acland 1995, 41)

The confluence of youth, race, and class that occurs within inner city or urban environments has been discursively constructed, from the outside, as a visible and troubling blight on American society. It has accordingly been nominated across numerous discursive fields as a profound threat to American core values. Of course, these values are not unqualified foundations of an American ideal; they do not exist in the form of inscribed tablets. Rather, they are highly contestable and, as the so-called culture wars of the past twenty years indicate, subject to diverse interpretations.

In many cases the discursive patterning of race and youth in this country essentializes the general character image of the threatening force (black, poor, uneducated, undisciplined, from single-parent homes, etc.) by simultaneously homogenizing and essentializing the dominant system of "standards, values, and ethical questions," writing them into the national body as the ideals upheld by the mainstream majority. This is racism in action, conducted within the patterns of social discourse. Discursively constructed as foundational components of the variegated social structure in what Acland refers to as a "common" frame of knowledge, these ideals also establish the grounds of society's stratified relations of domination and subordination; they are ideals that the internal other has not and, in fact, cannot uphold once "it" is discursively constructed as "other," as Paul Gilroy (1987) has convincingly argued in relation to blacks in England.

As the color line continues to assert itself in contemporary America along with the accompanying crisis of youth, more recent attempts to redefine American society (including California's controversial Proposition 187 immigration law and the Republican Congress's 1995 "Contract with America," through which welfare programs, single-parent assistance, and affirmative-action initiatives, among other things, all fell under attack) reflect a continuing racial split, contributing to new forms of exclusion and separatism that are deeply felt among the nation's minority and majority populations alike.

Constructed as the doubly threatening other, young blacks and Latinos are exposed to thorough and intense regimes of discipline and surveillance by the parent culture of mainstream society. They are positioned defensively on a daily basis, knowing that they are the objects of socially inscribed fear, mistrust, and blame for many of the problems that comprise a widely perceived sense of social disorder. For instance, in his analysis of the coverage of African-Americans in television news broadcasts in the Chicago area, Robert Entman notes a prevalent pattern of stereotyped representations of black youth and a high frequency of cases in which black leaders as well are portrayed negatively compared to their white counterparts. He notes further that

because television news offers only implicit information about the relationship between poverty, race and crime, viewers are left with no coherent explanation of poverty issues. Only indirectly does TV news suggest, for example, that racial discrimination might have something to do with poverty, which in turn may help explain all that crime. (Entman 1994, 35)

Entman also explains that the tendency to show images of young black defendants in police mug shots with no identifying captions has an additional negative influence on white perceptions of black youths, who can, as a result, be more easily lumped together in the mainstream white imagination as a homogeneous criminal set, undifferentiated from one another in their racial and criminal composition.

Contemporary North American analyses of youth and race reveal similarities to British conditions examined by Hall et al. (1978) and Gilroy (1987), who isolate the dominant discourse on black youth and crime as a patterned response to a perceived "threat from within." Despite the different social histories of race relations in the United Kingdom and the United States, there are many pertinent lessons to be gleaned from research on Britain. As Hall and Gilroy have both illustrated, the discursive project linking minority youth to wider social and moral collapse provides a knowable (visible, familiar, and institutionally coded) culprit. Having labeled the causal force of social ills, it is then easier to generate support among the white majority (especially those of the working class, who often maintain a stronger sense of tradition and nostalgia for the "better days" of an idealized past) for increased policing, more prison facilities, capital punishment, and other options.

By identifying the "enemy" and then mobilizing the forces of the state in a highly publicized series of domestic counterattacks, such as the U.S. government's "War on Drugs" or the heavy-handed (and frequently illegal, even murderous) initiatives of the street-crime units of the Los Angeles, New Orleans, and New York police, the growing uneasiness of the majority population is temporarily allayed by the impression that *something* is being done. Increasingly, the white perception of black youth—isolated, redefined, and amplified as a threat via conduits of authority, including the mainstream media—is based on fear and anxiety. This is not the same fear and anxiety that white and middle-class America experienced in the wake of the black power movement of the late 1960s and 1970s, but a terror that is rooted in the apparent irrationality of black youth today. In the absence of any recognizable program or politic that informs actions, the image of black youth out of control is gradually emblazoned on the collective American mind. Members of America's minority populations have become major casualties in the discursive, symbolic, and physical violence perpetrated by political and cultural authorities and their police arms throughout the 1980s and 1990s.

In the face of intense scrutiny and surveillance, how are the manifestations of black youth identity perceived within the social mainstream, and where on the map of urban cultural differences is this social subset located? We might look at a series of mid-1990s U.S. studies in which the predicted growth of America's teenage population over the next decade is tied to estimated increases in armed violence and crime, leading James Fox, former dean of the College of Criminal Justice at Northeastern University to state: "I truly believe we will have a bloodbath when all these kids grow up" (Strauss 1995). With predictions of a more rapid population growth among black and Latino teen groups being associated with the greater likelihood of crime and violence, the study subsequently raises concerns about this particular youth population. The report further identifies "inner-city areas" as the primary site of the worst violence because of the crack cocaine trade and refers to "black and Hispanic ghettos" as landscapes of exceptional danger and desolation, virtual "black" holes in society.

George Lipsitz observes that "since the 1970s, a series of moral panics about gangs, drug use, teenage pregnancy and 'wilding' assaults have demonized inner-city minority youths, making them the scapegoats for the chaos created in national life by deindustrialization and economic restructuring" (1994b, 19). This demonization is discursively reproduced within issues and incidents that arise across numerous institutional and social domains of power and authority (education, unemployment, teen pregnancy, black-on-black violence, drugs, gang activity, etc.). Each locates minority youth uniquely within its discursive repertoires, bringing to bear its own distinct forms of evaluation, judgment, surveillance, and containment.

Accompanying this construction of minority youth as scapegoat, demon, and folk devil is the sense that today's youth are somehow less caring and more vicious than earlier generations of their same age group. Despite generally declining national urban crime rates in the latter half of the 1990s, violent youth crimes have been widely invoked to illustrate that violent crime remains more prevalent among black, Latino, and increasingly, Asian immigrant or refugee teenagers. As a process of social labeling, this facilitates the patterned framing of minority youth in the racist terminologies of savagery and provides public justification for the institution and installment of new forces of power such as the "three strikes and you're out" legislation for young criminal offenders in several states or the stunning show of police might throughout the 1980s and 1990s, culminating in the horrific 1999 shooting of Amadou Diallo in the Bronx by four members of the New York City Police Department. In fact, white-collar corporate crime is much more costly to Americans than street crime, and there are estimated to be up to "six times the number of work-related deaths as homicides" (Donziger 1996, 66). It seems, then, that in America divisions along the color line are exacerbated by other factors, including class and corporate privilege and various phenomena that are only indirectly related to race and ethnic differences.

The cultural geographies of difference and the "embedded contexts" that help form identities become extremely important to the ways that youth exists as a stratified construct. Youth is influenced by the local conditions of daily life, for, as Milbrey McLaughlin writes, "even within the same community, differences in neighborhood, history, families, and structural and spatial arrangements of parks, schools, and public transit create substantially distinct conditions for the evolving self" (1993, 38). As a social category, then, "youth" is highly susceptible to the differences within multiple systems of power and influence that frame issues of race, class, and gender and that reveal an ineluctable spatial dimension in the cities of America.

Ghetto Space, Ghetto Identities

The discourse of ghetto authenticity and the evolution of a "real nigga" mentality in the late 1980s and 1990s emerge as prominent and complicated features of hip-hop culture. These expressions are actually continuations of prior discourses of difference within black cultural spaces and in relation to white society, as can be found in the words and writings of Malcolm X (1966) and others who have noted contestatory attitudes relating to the inherently different social-class positions occupied by the "house nigger" and the "field nigger" in the antebellum South. First and foremost spatial distinctions, they are highly value laden and carry the weight of a deeply ingrained caste system within the repressive structures of plantation slavery. Their spatial demarcations are implicated in the distribution of power as it was negotiated among slave owners and the domestic servants and field laborers under the owner's authority, as indentured human property. For Malcolm, the "house nigger" was the embodiment of passive black subservience, while the "field nigger" embodied a core militancy as the activist figure among disgruntled and resistant masses of black Americans. Turning his point toward the social and political conditions of his time, Malcolm X contrasted what he described as the "Uncle Tom" institutional structures of 1960s Negro leadership (most notably the Congress of Racial Equality (CORE), the National Association for the Advancement of Colored People (NAACP), and the Southern Christian Leadership Conference (SCLC) with what he perceived as the more authentic and radically politicized positions of blacks in the streets and ghettoes of the nation, who most resembled the resistant "field nigger" in a symbolic sense.

Space and spatial variations across the black social spectrum continue to be central to a comprehension of black identities (and this is no less true of other races and ethnicities). Even the historical distinctions between "field nigger" and "house nigger" acquire contemporary resonance in the Boogie Down Productions (BDP) track "House Niggas" (1991, Zomba), which explicitly summons the terms but then rechannels their meanings toward more contemporary contexts in a rhetorical strategy reminiscent of that of Malcolm X. As BDP illustrates, the spatial discourses of contemporary hip-hop culture are capable of mobilizing a historical awareness of socially distributed power that continually frames and influences the identities and experiences of black teenagers in contemporary America. While the group's lyricist and producer, KRS-One, stands out for his consistent attention to historical politics, African-American cultural traditions, and the spatial distribution of power, he also shares similarities with his contemporary peers, who make frequent references to the primacy of the urban ghetto in the cultural experiences of the hip-hop generation.

In a study commissioned by the U.S. Department of Housing and Urban Development in 1985, members of the Committee on National Urban Policy, in their analyses of urban conditions, use the terms "ghetto" and "poverty neighborhoods." For the purposes of their research, the ghetto was defined as "an area in which the overall census tract poverty rate is greater than 40 percent. We define the ghetto poor as those poor, of any race or ethnic group, who live in such high-poverty census tracts" (Jargowsky and Bane 1990, 19–20). It is also important to note that the report disproves the notion that in the 1980s the majority of America's poor lived in urban ghettos. Jargowsky and Bane found that "in 1980, there were 2.4 million poor people living in ghettos—8.9 percent of all U.S. poor people. Thus it is clearly not true that the typical poor person was a resident of an urban ghetto." The passage goes on to state, however, that the burden of ghetto poverty falls most heavily on blacks and Hispanics: of the total number of America's poor whites, 2.0 percent are ghetto dwellers; of poor blacks, 21.1 percent; and of poor Hispanics, 15.9 percent. The researchers' findings conclude that "nearly two-thirds of the ghetto poor are black and most of the rest are Hispanic" (Jargowsky and Bane 1990, 10).

Despite their reliance on census findings and statistical evidence, however, the authors admit that the 40 percent poverty rate is "inherently arbitrary" and that they turned to various city and census bureau officials to aid their judgment of which areas could accurately be defined as ghettos (Jargowsky and Bane 1990, 20). This reflects the extent to which the image and idea of what a ghetto is and where a ghetto lies inform and validate statistical data. The illusion of a carefully maintained scientific objectivity (which is primarily intended to conform to the requirements of government policy makers at the civic, state, and federal levels) is negated by this appeal for a legitimating affirmation. The biased input from civic or census officials who confirm for them that the research data affirm the social images tends to ignore the lived component of these spaces and the quality of life that can still be derived from economically depressed family and community contexts. The social-scientific zeal that erases qualitative factors related to the basic human composition and to the social and cultural character of these spaces also makes it easier to impose policies, plans, and programs from the institutionalized "outside" or, in a more stratified analogy, from a hierarchically structured "above." Quite simply stated, the numbers do not tell the whole story of these social landscapes, nor do they account for the interactions and experiences that constitute their unique social character.

In the cultural output of black artists of the late 1960s and early 1970s, the ghetto was cast as an intense and complex urban spatial site, as "home" and the legitimate space of political and cultural fomentation simultaneously. Because every large American city has its own black or minority ghetto, ghetto consciousness was national in scope and was an essential influence in the shaping of black urban cultural identities throughout this period. The pro-black Afrocentrist ideologies and artistic expressions that ensued often mobilized the ghetto as a symbolic image of location and cultural struggle. This was certainly true of black popular music, in which the ghetto was the dominant spatial trope symbolically referring to an urban terrain that was recognizable to the majority of black (and white) Americans whether they actually inhabited ghetto spaces or not. It was associated with a common currency of meanings and values, motivating images of shared cultural experience within a popular vernacular central to the communication of black cultural struggles.

By the early 1970s the relative cohesiveness of the black power movement was eroding, and the promise of either radical political empowerment or economic progress was harder for many people to accept as anything more than rhetorical idealism. I say "relative cohesiveness" because despite a much wider base of sympathy and support, the discursive terrain of activism was, as now, highly fragmented. In more recent distillations, including numerous recorded rap tracks and Spike Lee's 1989 film *Do the Right Thing,* these differences have been reduced to the polarized political stances embodied by Malcolm X and Martin Luther King, Jr.

Addressing this period, Reebee Garofalo writes:

The Civil Rights Movement appeared to have run its course. Activists knew that the issues it raised would surface again in different contexts and new organizational forms, but for the time being the movement had been forcibly rendered dormant, its 20-year history of peaks and valleys, successes and failures, contradictions and divergent tendencies chronicled in popular music.   (Garofalo 1992, 239)

The decline of strong, progressive leadership and its by-product, "progressive politics" (West 1993, 45), along with a deepening economic debilitation among urban minority populations, contributed to a profound sense of social and cultural drift and widespread nihilism that have, over the years, gradually taken root among many black and Latino youths.

As the American ghetto has seen transformations of various kinds since the early 1970s, the discourses within which ghetto existence is defined have undergone corresponding transitions. Garofalo explains that the influence of politicized and culturally informed songs, which had been an important feature of the popular music landscape toward the end of the 1960s, was diminishing:

Reflecting the "quieter" mood of the early 1970s, the black popular music which came to the fore was the "soft soul" sound pioneered by the Philadelphia-based writer-producer team of Kenny Gamble and Leon Huff, and producer-arranger Thom Bell. . . . With the movement in disarray, civil rights themes were on the decline in popular music.   (Garofalo 1992, 238–39)

Although the heavy funk music in this period was anything but "quiet," it was generally devoid of any "real politic" and was geared more toward the unambiguous expression of pleasure and sexuality—which is to say, politics of a different nature.

There are numerous examples of the discourse of ghetto existence in the 1960s and 1970s—the coming-of-age era of today's parental generation. Donny Hathaway recorded "The Ghetto" on his debut album *Everything Is Everything* (Atlantic) in 1970; War's first album, *The World Is a Ghetto* (1973,

United Artists), featured a hit single of the same title; the Spinners released "Ghetto Child" (Atlantic), which charted briefly in the United Kingdom in 1973. Preceding these, however, was Elvis Presley's 1969 hit "In the Ghetto" (RCA). Although Presley's sentimental treatment of the Mac Davis song is free of explicitly critical commentary or spatial details, it is indicative of a trend toward foregrounding the existence of class and sociospatial differences that had been reshaping the composition of the nation's cities with particular intensity in the postwar period and that had achieved a new level of interest—and concern—across the social spectrum. The emphasis on the ghetto as a social realm (and a problem) was undoubtedly a response to the combination of effective urban political organizing (and the accompanying visual impact of such urban activists as the Black Panthers), ghetto-centered violence that had escalated throughout the nation with the assassination of Malcolm X and the Watts riots of 1965, the assassination in 1968 of Martin Luther King Jr. and a general awareness that America at large could no longer ignore the perils of a separate and unequal society.

In his exploration of rap's themes and what he terms "cultural authenticity," Todd Boyd writes that "this emphasis on the working class, using the ghetto or the 'hood' as the dominant metaphor, has been most vividly presented in rap music" (1994, 292). Boyd accurately identifies the central importance of the formal tendency among rap artists to conjoin class-oriented themes and spatial imagery but he erroneously asserts that "with the advent of west coast (primarily, Los Angeles) rap, the life of a young African-American male and his struggles to survive have become the recurrent theme in demonstrating one's firm entrenchment in the jungle-like setting known as the ghetto" (293). By placing this evolution in the historical context of the emergence of West Coast rap, Boyd locates this particular phenomenon in approximately 1987–88, roughly coinciding with the release of Ice-T's *Rhyme Pays* (1987, Sire) and N.W.A.'s *Straight Outta Compton* (1988, Ruthless). In fact, the developments he describes had already begun, haven taken hold by 1982 with the release of "The Message" (1982, Sugar Hill) by Grandmaster Flash and the Furious Five, and was relatively well established by 1988.

Boyd is basically correct in much of his criticism of rap's later "gangsta-ism" and the hypermasculinist sensibilities that identify the ghetto and, later, the 'hood as social spaces of black cultural reality, but in failing to give proper credence to musical precursors (such as "The Message" or the Rake's "Street Justice" [1983, Profile]), the temporal enunciation of a spatial discourse and its accompanying relationships to a discourse of urban reality is misplaced. The spatial emphasis in rap has, in fact, changed substantially through the 1980s and 1990s, announcing shifting perspectives

on the lived environments which many (though by no means all) rap artists call home, as well as providing astute commentary on the intensification of ghetto poverty that displays historically and geographically precise
characteristics.

For example, *What's on My Mind* (1995, Po' Broke Records/Relativity
Recordings), by the Dayton Family, a rap act based in Flint, Michigan, features several cuts that refer directly and explicitly to the socioeconomic
conditions of Flint. The city has been subjected to a serious downturn in its
local economy since the early 1980s owing to larger extraneous conditions
impacting the automobile industry and local employment. (Flint's economic
and social malaise was the subject of Michael Moore's scathing 1989 documentary film *Roger and Me*.) In this context there is a clear historical, geographical, and social matrix that multiply inflects the articulations of race,
class, and gender issues raised by Boyd. The symbols and implied values associated with social geographies forming the basis of rap's narratives and expressions within hip-hop have not remained static since its inception: the
changes in spatial discourse over time indicate that the repertoire of signs
and symbols has been transformed to a considerable extent with the evolution of the hip-hop culture.

Furthermore, reductionist assumptions implying that the spatial elements of rap narratives function as mere "metaphors" fail to consider the
crucial relationships between the spatial character of low-income areas and
the lived conditions of working-class existence. In practice, human experience is substantially influenced by the geographies of class difference as
well as by the geographic variations of race, gender, and age. The articulation of space- and place-based perspectives involves the process of translating micro-worlds of experience into language and making this experience
meaningful in social terms. As Ernest Allen Jr. explains, "Generally speaking, the core values articulated in a given rap message, no matter the origin
of individual rappers, tend to be socially rooted in the daily lives of marginalized African-American youth" (1996, 162). In much recorded rap, the
ghetto is portrayed as a symbolic center that anchors the narrative images
portrayed. The symbolic meanings of spaces and places both reflect and
affect the ways in which race, class, gender, generational identities, and so
on are constructed and understood (Massey 1994, 179), not only in the
ghetto, but outside it. Each configuration of variables reveals sets of relations that are geographically distributed and spatially varied. Spatial narratives and the discursive reproduction of ghetto sensibilities thus derive
their social meanings from the fact that ghettoes do exist as knowable spaces
and, as such, they constitute a real force of influence in human lives as part
of a dialectical interaction of mutual though unpredictable influence.

Space and place are never simply employed metaphorically in rap lyrics; they are also deployed discursively as part of a much more sophisticated project involving the ideological articulation of race-, gender-, and class-based interests, identity formation, and cultural critique. When bound in tension with other circulating discourses, they reproduce the form and shape of our social environments, providing maps upon which young artists and their wider audiences might trace patterns of dominant hegemonic power and locate spaces where alternative or oppositional potentials can cohere and thrive. As I have noted, these expressions can be cast in either conservative or radical ideological forms.

The ghetto, in all of its negative complexity, is still heralded as an idealized space for minority teens within rap's cultural discourses precisely because it is considered as being somehow more "real" than other spaces and places, leading Robin Kelley to the observation that "to be a 'real Nigga' is to have been a product of the ghetto" (1996, 137). Rob Shields offers an explanation for this phenomenon by citing spatial discourse and its capacity to inflect an affective sense of belonging:

People . . . ascribe to particular discourses about places as a mark of their "insider status" in particular groups and communities. This group affiliation through knowledge of discourses which locate places and areas as particular types of places, with particular relations to other places and people (outsiders) does not restrict the development of personal views of "the real situation." (Shields 1991, 25)

Blacks and Latinos, who were disproportionately affected by economic downturns through the 1970s and 1980s, continue to occupy the lower end of the nation's economic spectrum. These groups are also disproportionately represented in most major urban ghettoes in contemporary America. Yet black and Latino youths are also disproportionately active within rap, dominating the creative side of the industry and driving the genre's ongoing processes of innovation and reinvention. This results in a situation whereby the contemporary American ghetto can be easily identified in rap's popular narratives as a predominantly black realm, reinforcing the different status contexts that revolve around a structured logic of insider-outsider designations.

This is not always the case, however, as the urban working-class boroughs in many major cities reflect. For instance, in Boston the equalizing forces of impoverishment and class status have led to frequent racially motivated antagonisms between Irish American and black and Latino teenagers in the housing projects of Dorchester, Roxbury, and South Boston, or "Southie." As immigrants and refugees from Cambodia, Vietnam, Somalia, and Bosnia enter the low-income or welfare housing areas, the profile of authentic ghetto identities is further altered. The racial overlaps have also produced the cultural frame for creative amalgamations, such as that of the white Dorchester rapper Marky Mark (Mark Wahlberg, brother of Donnie Wahlberg, a member of New Kids on the Block) in the early 1990s. In Canada, Toronto's successful dance-hall reggae rapper Snow represents an example of the meeting between Irish and black Caribbean working-class cultures.[11] One outcome of the trend is that the conflation of the ghetto as a privileged sociospatial site and an idealized image of black authenticity within hip-hop discourse has continually threatened to override other possible images of lived cultural space among the hip-hop generation, regardless of one's racial identity.

Historically contextualized, rap's pronounced shift toward an expressive ghettocentricity occurred at the same moment that its popular appeal and commercial distribution experienced a phase of innovation and accelerated commercial growth, around 1987–88. The consequences of the pressure to attain ghettocentric authenticity were fully realized in the early 1990s with the rap artist Vanilla Ice's unsuccessful rewriting and publicization of his personal biography in a crass attempt to establish false ghetto credentials and reinforce his popular viability. Through what amounted to a forgery of identity conducted across a cultural and spatial divide, Vanilla Ice attempted to conceal his class and geocultural origins, recasting his background identity in a false composite: a white youth who emerged from the black ghetto. His LP *To the Extreme* (1990, SBK) became the fastest-selling rap album of all time upon its release, but his prospects for securing a place in the rap pantheon were dashed (his uneven skills and confused terminology notwithstanding) when the truth about his middle-class background and the schools and neighborhoods from which he actually emerged were revealed. It is this deception, and *not* solely the fact of his whiteness, that has made Vanilla Ice the symbolic antithesis of ghetto authenticity and caused him to be vilified. His skin color was undoubtedly an inconvenience among the hardcore hip-hop aficionados whose own preconceptions about authenticity and ghetto reality blinded them to the possibilities of white talent in the field. His arrogant attitude and deliberate deception—not keeping it real at all—were unconscionable in the eyes of the collective hip-hop nation.

In other cases, the legitimacy of the white New York rappers the Beastie Boys, Pete Nice and MC Serch (who formed the nucleus of the now-defunct Third Bass) and, more recently, of the Detroit artist Eminem is located in their documented connections with the black youth culture of the urban boroughs, housing projects, or high schools where they visited regularly or were raised and educated. Alternately, the contemporary Detroit rapper Kid Rock has vocally established his credentials by proclaiming his nonurban affiliations, invoking another spatial stereotype involving "poor white trash" and the accompanying imagery of trailer-park chic. These tendencies are no less significant for many black rap artists who, like Run-D.M.C. (as an early example), attempt to tap into the image of ghetto chic, seeking street credibility though they hail from more affluent neighborhoods that are slightly removed from the urban core. For black artists, the projection of ghetto associations is less difficult and less contentious, since the dominant social perspective "always already" (Althusser 1971) interpellates black youths, especially males, as ghetto citizens, if not ghetto thugs. The image and expression of ghetto authenticity in rap continue to succeed in the market. Still, while rappers seek to reaffirm their identities as qualified chroniclers of social reality and ghetto conditions, they also extend a plethora of negative stereotypes that ultimately hobble and restrict black youth in a white-dominated, systemically racist society.

The Spatial Logics of Rap and the Rise of the 'Hood

The shift in rap and hip-hop's emphasis toward a discourse introducing the 'hood as a new spatial trope delimiting an "arena of experience" can be viewed in relation to larger trends currently restructuring global and national economies, transforming national and regional workforces, and, often, devastating urban localities. The discourse of space encompassed by the term "'hood" may in this context also be interpreted as an articulate response to conditions of change occurring at a metalevel, far beyond the scale of the local (and the influence of those who inhabit it). As an analytical point of departure, I cite Paul Gilroy's observation that "today we are told that the boys, and the girls, are from the 'hood—not from the race, and certainly not from the nation" (1992, 308). The emphasis on localized patterns of spatiality is understood here as a displacement of older, more established discursive frames in which black cultural and political identities are formed.

Gilroy's concern is, importantly, that fragmentation into localized and particular patterns of identification reduces the expansive possibilities and enabling potentials of a mobilized cultural politics of race. His apparent anxiety stems from the likelihood that, by defending territorial spaces and regional identities, black youths will continue to lose a political motivation that might add convergence, if not necessarily unity, to the black cause in America as well as in the extended international African diaspora. By symbolically representing the 'hood as a relatively stable enclave where localized identities might cohere, however, hip-hop's creative practitioners also risk falling into line with the conservative patterns of various nationalist movements that attempt to "fix the meaning of places, to enclose and defend them" by constructing "fixed and static identities for places . . . as bounded enclosed spaces defined through counterposition against the Other who is outside" (Massey 1992, 12).

Those ensconced in the hip-hop culture, which is also commonly described as the hip-hop nation,[12] do not entirely ignore the earlier dominant themes of race and nation that were so central to twentieth-century black American intellectuals and leaders along a continuum encompassing W. E. B. Du Bois, Marcus Garvey, Malcolm X, and Martin Luther King Jr. (and which today includes Jesse Jackson and Louis Farrakhan). The exceptions are demonstrated, for example, in the rise of a pronounced Afrocentric cultural identity in the late 1980s and the resultant political stances of rappers such as Paris, who reflects a political discourse and cultural agenda explicitly modeled after the Black Panther party, or the Poor Righteous Teachers, Lakim Shabazz, Rakim, the X-Clan, and many others who display strong commitments to pro-black Muslim ideologies. In the absence of sustained institutional forms and coherent leadership, the often vague and abstract notions of "race and nation" (which suggest a much more unified and cohesive sociopolitical foundation than is often actually the case) are difficult for teens to imagine, having declined in relevance to many youths since the mid-1970s, as in the case of the NAACP.

It is at this stage, then, that the 'hood may be conceived as something more than a reactionary or conservative response to larger fluctuations. The progressive potentials of a discourse of spatiality rooted in the terminologies of urban locality and the specific concerns of young blacks and Latinos must also be considered an important topic for examination in the attempt to locate alternatives to the pervasive nihilism in black communities outlined by Cornel West (1993). The 'hood subsequently offers an immediate, local frame of reference and relevance. As Rose suggests:

Identity in Hip Hop is deeply rooted in the specific, the local experience and one's attachment to and status in a local group or alternative family. These crews are new kinds of families forged with intercultural bonds which, like the social formations of gangs, provide insulation and support in a complex, unyielding environment and may, in fact, contribute to the community-building networks which serve as the basis for new social movements. (Rose 1994a, 78)

The 'hood is constituted as a privileged realm of interaction and emerges through its connections to locality as a new "scale of analysis" for the definition of experience and identity in a world of diminishing opportunities and nonsustaining political and economic structures among minority youth. In its discursive constructions, it does not introduce an outright solution to the decentering of an expansive politics of race, but it is indicative of an alternative spatially oriented perspective that may be productive of other, new forms of progressive social movement.

Gilroy's further contention that "it's important that the 'hood stands [*sic*] in opposition to foreign things" offers an analytical approach to the eroding political discourses of race and nation that have, in the past, formed the bonds of black identity. The new emphasis on the 'hood signifies a transition that is part of "a shift away from the notion of the ghetto, which is eminently exportable, and which carries its own interesting intercultural history" (1992, 308). Yet, Gilroy's stated preferences for the ghetto trope notwithstanding, in a footnote to an article examining interracial relations, urban territory, and graffiti-writing practices among New York City youth, Ivor Miller relates that one prominent graffiti artist, Phase 2, "doesn't like the term 'ghetto,' because he feels it is pejorative. For people who live in poor barrios and projects, this is their home and their community and he calls it just that" (Miller 1994, 186).

The point here is that although ghetto regions and so-called inner-city neighborhoods frequently conform to the images and expectations of officials and the wider public, they also provide the site for a rich array of cultural creativity, social propriety, and nurture. As lived experiential environments, these spaces are invested with value and meaning by those who inhabit them. Seen in this light, a shift to an alternative discourse based on the 'hood's revised spatial frame introduces a potentially empowering conceptual transition for those who call its narrowly circumscribed parameters "home," which is recognized as a familial or community refuge as well as a political sanctuary in the contemporary American context. These spatial constructions formed within a discourse of the 'hood propose a departure from the historically sedimented meanings of the term "ghetto," which have, among other things, framed much of mainstream white America's preconceptions of black urban dwellers, regardless of their class status.

This still does not account for the "space" of the 'hood, however. The 'hood does not replace the ghetto but is, rather, a displacement of a more discursive nature. In many instances, spaces commonly referred to as "the 'hood" exist in the same physical locale and urban environment that has been described as "the black ghetto" by earlier generations for most of the past century. The ghetto has traditionally been understood within a deficit model as an unfortunate blight on the urban environment. Racialized and coded as "ethnic" by urban white ruling majorities for over 150 years, the ghetto as a geocultural enclave has always been cast as a spatial pariah, grudgingly ceded to ethnic or racial populations or, conversely, surrendered to them.

Commonsense understanding of the terms "ghetto" and "slum" is concretized through negative images pertaining to urban geographies and is based on previous usages and a spectrum of cultural norms and values amounting to a form of cultural shorthand. Mainstream *representations* of such spaces (including portrayals in newspapers, magazines, and literature, or on television programs) are closely aligned with the social construction of *reputations* that transgress the boundaries of the spaces and places in question and may overdetermine the actual daily practices of those who inhabit them. These "spatial myths" (Shields 1991), which also introduce a means of labeling according to a loose system of spatial values, not only are disseminated through media mechanisms but also are a feature of discursive patterns at the local level.

I want to argue that, as a discursive shift, the turn to the 'hood involves an intentional, engaged process of cultural recuperation of African-American- and Latino-dominated space enacted primarily by contemporary urban minority youth. Leonard Harris broaches this notion: "What actual space people are capable of usurping as a part of their identity becomes a function of resources and options under their control—and those resources or hindrances include racial identity" (1993, 38). The 'hood accommodates the general spatial image of the ghetto, but the term also allows greater flexibility when used by members of the hip-hop generation to describe and delineate locality—literally, one's neighborhood and the space to which one relates as a local home environment. Thus, where the ghetto has been culturally shackled to a negative symbolic configuration of images and ideas, the 'hood offers a new terminology and discursive frame that can simultaneously address conditions in all 'hoods everywhere, to individuated places, or to particular sites of significance. The 'hood "signifies" (Gates 1988) space differently, revising and rerouting the resonant precursors of the dominant discourses and images of the ghetto and displaying a new capacity to acknowledge, embrace, and extend the themes and concepts that the ghetto has traditionally encompassed as a representational term.

The 'hood, then, has a dually inflected meaning that refers inwardly to local sites and the specificities of place while simultaneously constituting a concept that isolates a real or imagined "here" from other places, from "there" (providing a relational basis for the establishment of a corresponding dichotomy between "us" and "them"). As Rob Shields explains, the discursive production of spatially inscribed values, achieved through the substantiation of "places and spaces . . . from the world of real space relations to the symbolic realm of cultural significations" (1991, 47), presents the means by which social hierarchies are achieved and maintained. The value ascribed to place is excised from actual terrains, sites, environments, and so forth and is consequently structured in and through discourse and concurrent symbolic images.

The spaces and places that form the foundation of rap and hip-hop's references to the 'hood are discursively produced from within a preexisting system of relational differences organized hierarchically and enforced through various institutional and cultural apparatuses. In hip-hop, "the 'hood" emerges as a meaningful term that is oriented toward, on the one hand, recognition of social and cultural idiosyncrasies of the artist's immediate environment and, on the other hand, recognition of differences (real or perceived) that identify other places, whether they be similar socioeconomic enclaves (i.e., other "'hoods") or external spaces comprising the spheres of middle-class comfort, upper-class affluence, or higher concentrations of racial "others."

Gilroy poses several relevant questions that revolve around the terminologies of the 'hood, indicating an attempt to understand the nature of the new historical conditions of youth, identity, and black cultural politics in contemporary America:

> But, if the 'hood is the essence of where blackness can now be found, which 'hood are we talking about? How do we weigh the achievements of one 'hood against the achievements of another? How is black life in one 'hood connected to life in others? Can there be a blackness that connects, articulates, synchronizes experiences and histories across the diaspora space? (1992, 308)

In response, it is useful to point to the dialogic character of rap and to its unique ability to focus conversation and debates within society in general and among black Americans in particular. Gilroy himself suggests this line of approach elsewhere (1993b) when he cites the progressive and "democratic" possibilities of "antiphony," or call and response, that is common to black musical forms and characteristic of a black cultural aesthetic. The call and response in rap, whether referring to what are termed "shout outs" (in the positive) or "disses" (in the negative), the use of sampled musical passages, or recordings that comment on or appropriate the work of other artists does in fact offer a cultural connection across time and space. So, too, do the physical confrontations of break-dance competition or the cross-spatial circulation of names and identities through graffiti art and tagging (the unsanctioned writing of names or crew logos on walls and other public surfaces). These are hip-hop's spatial communicative forms.

The existence of these myriad communicative cultural practices also supports the argument that there is sufficient dialogue and shared interaction to realistically discuss hip-hop in terms of a nation status. Rose points to the dialogical and communicative strengths of rap and hip-hop:

> Out of a broader discursive climate in which the perspectives and experiences of younger Hispanic, Afro-Caribbeans and African-Americans had been provided little social space, hip hop developed as part of a cross-cultural communication network. . . . And, characteristic of communication in the age of high-tech telecom-

munications, stories with cultural and narrative resonance continued to spread at a rapid pace.

(Rose 1994a, 60)

Today's prevailing articulation of home environments in the 'hood situates hip-hop-identified youth within an enunciative space (meaning the space from which they articulate their sense of self and their relationships to the world around them as they enter into various cultural discourses) that is often summoned "in opposition to foreign things" but not necessarily in a negative or defensive configuration. In both the affirmative and the negative configurations (i.e., "here" is good, "there" is less good, or bad), the discourse of the 'hood is still part of a pattern of communication and is more often than not part of an open and ongoing local, regional, and national dialogue, rather than a sort of punctuation signifying its end.

Still, Gilroy's line of interrogation is well founded, for it remains unclear precisely how such contextually specific expressions of experience are capable of establishing dialogue across the multivalent and shifting spaces of black popular culture. Further complexities arise when these dialogues cross into the extended cultural realm consisting of a huge audience of young, white, and nonurban hip-hop aficionados and rap fans. If rap can in any way be equated with the Cable News Network (CNN) as a communicative medium for black communities (as Chuck D of the influential group Public Enemy, among others, has asserted), then it is important to question the themes being communicated and to inquire how they might provide a foundation for grounded and informed dialogue among constituents of various dispersed localities.

Hip-hop offers an illustrative example of a set of cultural forms that emerge from the dynamic convergence of the global and the local. Its international reputation and popularity and its global distribution are enabled by the transnational entertainment industry, which is dominated by only a handful of major corporate labels. Yet hip-hop's connections to local contexts, social environments, and sites of significance are also entwined in local systems that form a foundation for its cultural production. These include street corners, basketball courts, schools, and neighborhood nightclubs and dance halls, as well as local or regional independent recording and distribution companies. These are often the sites unseen where youths, alone or in groups, hone their skills, practicing and developing their craft. They are, by and large, anonymous spaces (at least to outside observers and ethnographers) of little interest or relevance to the broader society and to much of the consuming public. Hip-hop, however, stands out for the urgency with which its creators address the urban environment around them, describing in often painstaking detail the activities that occur there or mapping the cultural byways that delineate their localities and give space meaning.

CHAPTER THREE

Old-School Geography
From the Disco to the Street

❄

Recounting their initial exposure to rap, Havelock Nelson and Michael Gonzales cite the music's integration into the lifestyles and practices of urban youth and its ability to alter the cadences through which they experienced the city: "After that black noise attack first invaded my earholes, my eyes were wide open to the changes rap music was causing in the neighborhood" (1991, xvii). As they note, rap produced a radical sensory experience while introducing a cultural form that was easily adapted to or absorbed by existing infrastructures and channeled into general social currents in the urban black community. From a more theoretically conceived angle, this corresponds with Elizabeth Grosz's perspectives on the "interface" between social subjects and their environments: "the form, structure, and norms of the city seep into and effect all other elements that go into the constitution of corporeality and/or subjectivity. It effects [sic] the way the subject sees others . . . as well as the subject's understanding of, alignment with, and positioning in space" (1992, 249).

This recognition of the reciprocal relations between space and self, or between space and one's social or subjective identity, is implicitly evident from Nelson and Gonzales's emphasis on the locality of their initial experience with rap, recalling that the spatial frame of the local comprises a territorial front line of contact. Their sense of locality is dually conceived, for, on the one hand, it summons place-based images of their own idiosyncratic experience with rap on the home front, yet, on the other hand, they imply that rap presented opportunities for expansive spatial identification with other localities where hip-hop was similarly lived and embraced. When it is framed within the twin coordinates of scale and value, however, the local as a structuring concept has a valid role in how we come to understand certain aspects of the world around us that may not be of our making: "the material landscape can never change as fast as meaning" (Sack 1992, 104). As a culturally influential force, rap music is seen here to be centrally implicated in the processes by which space is made meaningful—made into place—and the ways that locality is bound to notions of subjective experience and personal identification with narrowly demarcated zones of human existence.

Clearly, any music or cultural practice can be a factor in how individuals or groups experience a situation or a place, how they locate themselves in various contexts, and how they find meaning in them. But like any musical genre, rap is an expressive form existing within its own elaborate system of styles, codes, and images. The system foregrounds particular sounds and rhythms that can, in turn, affect one's sense of space and place. Rap and hip-hop have changed the ways in which particular places are perceived, whether it be a clothing store with rap on the sound system or a street where cars executing a slow cruise are blasting hip-hop beats at mega-volume through huge speakers.

In rap's formative stages, its impact was first registered at the micro-levels of an extremely local scale: it circulated primarily through informal social conduits such as house and block parties or school gymnasium dances, as well as through the important practices of cassette tape exchange between DJs and their burgeoning audiences (Toop 1991, 78). Its influence grew rapidly, and within a few years of its origins it was a dominant facet of the sound of young black America and could be heard in numerous social contexts as the backbeat to the practices of work and leisure among minority teenagers.

Locating Hip-Hop

Describing the early stages of rap music's emergence within the hip-hop culture for an MTV "rap-umentary" on the topic, Grandmaster Flash, one of the pioneering DJs of the early hip-hop scene, recalls the spatial distribution of sound systems and crews in metropolitan New York: "We had territories. It was like, Kool Herc had the West Side. Bam had Bronx River. DJ Breakout had way uptown past Gun Hill. Myself, my area was like 138th Street, Cypress Avenue, up to Gun Hill, so that we all had our territories and we all had to respect each other." The documentary's images embellish Flash's commentary, displaying a computer-generated map of "the Bronx" with colored sections demarcating each DJ's territory as it is mentioned, graphically separating the sites that comprise the main operative zones for the competing sound systems. This emphasis on territoriality involves more than just a geographical arrangement of cultural workers and the regionalism of cultural practices. It illuminates a particular relationship to space or, more accurately, a relationship to particular places. As Flash tells it, the sound systems that formed the backbone of the burgeoning hip-hop scene were identified by their audiences and followers according to the overlapping influences of persona and turf. The territories were tentatively claimed through the ongoing practices that went on within their bounds and were reinforced by the circulation and mobility of those who recognized and accepted their perimeters. It is not at all insignificant that the dominant historical narratives pertaining to the emergence of hip-hop identify a transition from gang-oriented affiliations (formed around their protection of turf) to music and break-dance affiliations that maintained and in some cases intensified the important structuring systems of territoriality.

Flash's reference to the importance of "respect" does not primarily address respect for the skills or character of his competitors (although he acknowledges it in the November 1993 issue of *The Source* [see George 1993]). Rather, his notion of respect is related to the geographies that he maps; it is based on the existence of circumscribed domains of authority and dominance that have been established by other DJs in the same way as he himself has done. These geographies are inhabited and bestowed with value. They are understood as lived places and sites of significance and as facets of a local market that involves a product (the music in its various live or recorded forms) and a consumer base (various audience formations). The proprietary discourse also implies, therefore, that the hip-hop cartography, even in its earliest stages, was influenced by a refined capitalist logic and the existence of spatially distributed market regions. Without sacrificing the basic geographic components of territory, possession, and group identity that play such an important role in the lives of the city's youth sector, hip-hop substantially revised the content of New York's urban spaces as the hip-hop culture developed a commercial and more broadly public profile.

Clearly, the boundaries Flash describes and that are visually mapped in the documentary were never firm or immovable. They were cultural boundaries, continually open to negotiation by those who inhabited their terrains and who circulated throughout the city's boroughs. As the main form of musical expression within the hip-hop culture, the early DJ sound systems featured a series of practices that linked the music to other activities such as graffiti art, tagging, and break-dancing or, as it is commonly known, b-boying. Together, these overlapping practices and methods of constructing place-based identities and of inscribing and enunciating individual and collective presence created the bonds upon which affiliations were forged within specific social geographies. Hip-hop's distinctive practices introduced new forms of expression that were contextually linked to conditions in a city composed of an amalgamation of neighborhoods and boroughs, each with its own highly particularized social norms and cultural nuances.

Still, the particularities of urban space are subjected to the deconstructive and reconstructive practices of hip-hop's cultural workers. Rap and the hip-hop culture have literally redefined and redesigned urban spaces and the ways they are inhabited or used as the cultural forms have been integrated into the lives and social practices of millions of people. Thus, when Iain Chambers refers to rap as "New York's 'sound system' . . . [and as] sonorial graffiti," with "the black youth culture of Harlem and the Bronx twisting technology into new cultural shape" (1985, 190), he is linking the corresponding strategies that give rise to the radical transformation of the sites where these cultures cohere and converge or the spaces that are re-imagined and, importantly, remapped. Hip-hop and the rap artists who give it a voice emerge in yet another guise, in this case as alternative cartographers for what the artists Boo Yaa Tribe have referred to as a *New Funky Nation* (1990, Island Records).

Rap has always been much more than a simple reflection of the urban soundscape, yet it is difficult to ascertain the complexities that lie between reality and the representation of the urban condition and the ways that the music itself has, in its perseverance and ubiquity, transformed the city as an experiential environment. Although the production of North America's major rap recordings is conducted exclusively in its larger urban centers and the city remains the dominant conceptual space in the music's thematic content, a complex spatial reciprocity is involved; rather than rap's being inflected by the city in a one-way flow of influence, owing to its sustained popularity and ongoing innovation, it has actually had a profound sensual impact on the urban environment. Hip-hop has evolved into an unavoidable facet of the contemporary city, and rap's pervasiveness has radically altered the character of urban soundscapes, affecting the social rhythms through which populations flow.

The Emergence of Commercial Rap

As hip-hop developed through its formative stages in New York's uptown region, its practices and, especially, its unique approaches to musical production and performance were slowly garnering attention and interest from outside the culture's central scene. *Billboard* magazine—the official trade journal of the music industry—first reported on the music in 1978, focusing on the early turntable technique called "rocking the beat" and describing Kool DJ Herc's growing acclaim in the Bronx and the role of the independently owned midtown retail outlet Downstairs Records in supplying him with the "obscure r&b cutouts" that formed the core of his extended outdoor and club performances. The story emphasizes the emergent "b-beat" or break-beat scene, which at the time was particular to the Bronx and was a rising influence among the borough's emerging hip-hop DJs. The popularity and expansion of Herc's innovative style was evident when Robert Ford Jr. (who later cowrote and financed Kurtis Blow's first charting single, "Christmas Rappin'," in 1979 on the Mercury label) reported that "other Bronx DJs have picked up the practice and now B-beats are the rage all over the borough and the practice is spreading rapidly" (Ford 1978, 65).

Almost a year later, under the headline "Jive Talking: N.Y. DJs Rapping Away in Black Discos," Ford described the rise of "rapping DJs" as an outgrowth of the mobile DJ business, simultaneously identifying rap's dominant sociospatial milieu as the black club scene. Profiling some of the more influential innovators of the style, he writes that DJ Hollywood "is now so popular that he has played the Apollo with billing as a support act. It is not uncommon to hear Hollywood's voice coming from one of the countless portable tape players carried through the city's streets" (Ford 1979, 3). With its focus on the mobility of the DJ, the relevance of the black dance club circuit and other performance venues, and rap's sonic dissemination through audiocassettes, this early coverage chronicles a crucial historical moment. Even at this stage it is evident that rap's capacity to develop and extend its influence was being cast in geographic or spatial terms, not simply in terms of popular appeal or commercial viability. Furthermore, this coverage provides information and documentation about who was making the music, who its audiences were, and what the primary contexts for the music's consumption and enjoyment were.

Perceived by industry insiders who had their "ears to the street" and by the artists themselves as a marginal "underground" phenomenon, the idea of rap's breaking out of the local scene in the boroughs of New York largely involved the extension of audience familiarity with the sounds and styles of individual DJs, although selling audiocassette mix tapes was a growing interest for budding hip-hop entrepreneurs. At this stage rap was generally diffused through live performances or informally distributed cassette recordings (i.e., sold from the stage at shows, out of briefcases or car trunks on the street, or, eventually, on the racks in small mom-and-pop record stores). Few innovators at the time expressed a clear sense of rap's potential. For example, Ford's coverage in *Billboard* reveals that in the late 1970s, before rap was a commercial recorded phenomenon, the pioneers

Eddie Cheeba and DJ Hollywood envisioned rap as a means of launching them on careers as radio DJs. They did not conceive of their musical contributions in business terms, nor were they focused on extending rap's popular appeal within the music industry, for they failed to see its potential as a recorded genre. When the music moved from small parties and nightclubs in the Bronx to larger and more prestigious venues in Harlem (known by many as America's "black cultural mecca") and elsewhere, it and the hip-hop culture associated with it underwent substantial transformation and growth.

While such disparate factors as technical advances affecting the quality and efficiency of DJ sound systems, the creative enhancement of DJ turntable skills, and the introduction of rapping MCs between 1977 and 1980 should be given their due, the influence of mobility needs to be stressed. It was crucial in facilitating the publicity and exposure of the early break-beat styles that gave birth to rap and carrying it outward to larger and more diverse audiences. Whereas house DJs helped to establish certain venues as bona fide hip-hop clubs that drew people toward them, the mobility of the various DJs and their MC crews simultaneously took the music out, enabling many more people to experience the burgeoning scene within the contexts of their own home sites, their own localities. In the city, territory and turf were (and remain) powerful elements of social identity and affiliation among urban youth. As DJ acts began circulating throughout New York and spawning a whole generation of DJs and rappers, there was a wave of localized adaptation as individuals and crews sought to develop their own styles, locally relevant but still true to an emerging hip-hop ethos and the scene at large. This adaptive tendency also enhanced the vitality of the scene by infusing it with new and hybrid elements that kept it fresh, interesting, and commercially attractive at these micro-scales.

According to a report in *Billboard* ("Rap Records," 1980), it was the appearances of the Bronx-born DJ Hollywood at the Apollo Theatre in 1978 that introduced the potential of the music to a wider segment of the black public, reflecting the enduring importance of Harlem as a barometer of black cultural taste. Significantly, DJ Hollywood's Apollo performance introduced Jerry Thomas (coproducer of the Brooklyn-based Fatback Band) to the music, which led to the band's recording and release of what some argue is the first single featuring rap elements, "King Tim III: Personality Jock" (1979, Spring Records). As this illustrates, by 1978 rap was already developing into a powerful cultural and commercial force among black and Latino teens in New York, following a trajectory from the Bronx to Harlem and then (via club and high school performances, audiocassette distribution, and community radio broadcasting) throughout the other New

York boroughs to New Jersey, Philadelphia, and beyond. Rap's spatial dimensions were consequently being widened as local artists and promoters introduced the genre as an emergent option for pleasure and leisure in public spaces catering specifically to the hip-hop scene, which later included clubs such as Danceteria, Disco Fever, the Latin Quarter, Negril, and the Roxy. All evolved into important rap venues.

As Kurtis Blow, the first rap artist to sign a major label contract, recalls, "A whole new cultural thing was growing up around rap. . . . The b-boy culture spread all over the city, and by early 1979 we were all working bus rides to Philadelphia and Baltimore. The whole East Coast was rocking" (George et al. 1985, xii). The Fatback Band's "King Tim III" entered the *Billboard* charts on October 6, 1979, at number eighty-eight, followed a week later by the Sugarhill Gang's "Rapper's Delight," which entered at number eighty-one and eventually reached number four on the Hot Soul Singles chart, number fourteen on the Disco Top 100 chart, and number thirty-six on the Hot 100 chart. After "King Tim III" and "Rapper's Delight" entered the Hot Soul Singles chart, *Billboard* noted that rap "has since escalated in popularity to such major cities as Detroit, Philadelphia, Baltimore, Washington, D.C., Chicago and Atlanta" (Joe and George 1979, 4). As reflected by its coverage in *Billboard,* rap rapidly gained national (and international) attention, and as it did so, consistent, reproducible elements of the hip-hop culture began taking hold in virtually every major urban American center. This spread was first facilitated by the human traffic between New York and other major cities and was later boosted by the influence of early hip-hop films, such as Tony Silver and Henry Chalfant's *Style Wars* (1982), Charlie Ahearn's *Wild Style* (1982), and Stan Lathan's *Beat Street* (1984), which helped to circulate many of hip-hop's stylistic and cultural underpinnings.

In addition, overlapping contact during this time between the gradually expanding hip-hop scene and the New York avant-garde art scene (with its own attempts at alternative or oppositional political and aesthetic articulations) extended the influences of rap, graffiti art, and break-dancing, introducing them to a larger and often more economically empowered public faction (i.e., white audiences). This led to wider exposure and produced some interesting alliances. For example, the British punk rock impresario Malcolm MacLaren was an early fan and supporter of New York rap, booking acts to open for his then-fledgling post-punk protégés Bow Wow Wow. The Clash, British political punk rockers, booked Grandmaster Flash and the Furious Five and the Treacherous Three to open for them on their New York concerts in 1981, although the rap acts were poorly received by the rowdy Clash fans. As rap grew in popularity, it seemed that its appeal was capable of successfully traversing many—though by no means all—ethnic, racial, and class boundaries. Rap was at this point generally perceived as a distinctly New York phenomenon, as opposed to being "simply" from the Bronx, and its audiences were becoming more diversified.

In New York, the gradual dissemination of rap, graffiti and break-dancing as the cornerstones of hip-hop culture involved the transgression of distinct social spaces that had historically been shaped by segregated cultural practices and were established well before rapping DJs ever picked up a microphone. As hip-hop branched out both stylistically and spatially, the mobility of people between different localized scenes, as well as the formal and informal cultural distribution apparatuses, facilitated communication across numerous cultural domains. There are several clear examples of cultural and musical cross-pollination in this period. In 1980–81, successful funk- and hip-hop-influenced tracks were released by the white New York bands Blondie ("Rapture," 1980, Chrysalis Records) and the Tom-Tom Club ("Wordy Rappinghood" and "Genius of Love," 1981, Island Records), whose members converged with hip-hop's pioneering forces in the nightclubs and galleries.

Performances by hip-hop DJs such as Afrika Bambaataa (who, with Soul Sonic Force, appeared in July 1982 at the third annual New Music Seminar, at which MacLaren was a keynote speaker) were common in galleries and clubs of the West Village, the Lower East Side, and the gentrifying Soho district. Bambaataa regularly peppered his repertoire of hardboiled electro-funk with snippets of rock, new wave, and punk musics, even encompassing the soul of James Brown, British progressive rock by Babe Ruth, and techno-rock by the German artists Kraftwerk. Bambaataa and many other early DJs displayed their vast storehouse of musical knowledge and an intimate familiarity with different styles, genres, and audience tastes, belying a persistent notion that rap was forged exclusively within African-American musical idioms. The breadth of creative influences can be further discerned in the Grandmaster Flash and the Furious Five release "It's Nasty" (1981, Sugar Hill Records) and Dr. Jeckyll and Mr. Hyde's "Genius Rap" (1981, Profile Records), both of which are structured around the Tom-Tom Club's "Genius of Love." The track's rhythmic and melodic characteristics resurfaced much later as a sample on Mariah Carey's top-charting hit "Fantasy" (1995, Columbia), with the Wu-Tang Clan's Ol' Dirty Bastard appearing on the remix.

Although white and black musical exchanges in America have a long history, the basis for such exchanges varies in different historical and musical contexts, with appropriative and recuperative strategies being exercised according to the needs and contextual possibilities of a given era. Hip-hop

DJs' conscious strategies, employing what George Lipsitz identifies as "bi-focality, juxtaposition of multiple realities, intertextuality, inter-referential-ity, and comparison through families of resemblance," can be regarded as part of the active "struggle to assemble a 'historical bloc' capable of chal-lenging the ideological hegemony of Anglo cultural domination" (1990, 152). In the late 1970s and early 1980s, the cultural geographies of a vibrant nightclub scene, a rising modern-art scene, and the accompanying media diffusion of relatively localized cultural practices provided context for the subsequent musical and cultural linkages. They introduce the mechanisms for transcultural interaction and exchange among overlapping subcultures, enabling affinities within casual or informal patterns that contrast with the institutional forces (such as the music industry) that traditionally follow more formally organized and economically rationalized patterns. The point to be taken from this is that even though hip-hop's myriad forms of cul-tural expression were exposed to the commercial potential of the art and music industries, their growth and development is not reducible to these factors; rather, hip-hop's expansion owes much to ongoing social practices within and between diverse cultural sectors.

The cumulative effect of this emergent cultural hybridity was the pro-duction of new zones of cultural contact, labor, and diffusion that, at least briefly, offered the possibility of interracial solidarity as well as a tentative commingling across class cultures. This was aided by the role played by white female promoters such as Cool Lady Blue and Patti Astor. Cool Lady Blue booked a weekly hip-hop event at the Negril club on New York's Lower East Side that brought "uptown kids downtown and rap music to white hipsters" (George 1992, 20). In 1981 Astor opened the East Village art space Fun Gallery, which displayed and sold graffiti "pieces" and publi-cized numerous hip-hop-influenced artists, including Fab Five Freddy, Keith Haring, and Jean-Michel Basquiat. In her documentation of the gal-lery's debut, Phoebe Hoban has cited the problematic commercialization of graffiti and the opportunistic maneuvering of artists and gallery owners alike who sought to exploit hip-hop's aesthetic output for capital gain. From the perspectives of many analysts, the collision of the market's ap-propriative commercial apparatuses with rap and hip-hop's perceived or-ganic innovation presented a dilemma of sorts. The question among more scrupulous gallery owners or cultural mavens was, how might artists and dealers profit without tainting the original, dynamic character of hip-hop —without selling out the culture?

While Hoban acknowledges the cross-cultural and intercity linkages that made the Fun Gallery's arrival relevant, she understates the impor-tance of the moment, suggesting that "like most of the East Village galleries, Fun seemed to spring overnight from some organic downtown spore" (1998, 152). Serendipity undoubtedly played a part in the gallery's initial success, but to claim a natural organicism fails to account for the assemblages of individuals from across a deep cultural chasm of race, class, and geographic differences. The increased activity engaging hip-hop and the New York art world was significant as a propellant force that elevated the music, dance, and graffiti as a commercially viable set of enterprises, repositioning them within new spatial contexts of the commodity market. As rap's discourses later acquired a more pronounced ghetto-identified edge, becoming more explicitly Afrocentric and exhibiting more pronounced black-nationalist themes, the loosely knit alliances between the art world and the hip-hop culture and between white and black cultural producers became somewhat more tenuous.

Hoban's uncritical perspective on the perceived organic origins of the expressive cultural energies emanating from both the art and hip-hop scenes is not uncommon. While rap cuts by Afrika Bambaataa and Soul Sonic Force, Grandmaster Flash and the Furious Five, Kurtis Blow, the Sugarhill Gang, and Felix and Jarvis slowly continued to chart on *Billboard*'s Hot Soul Singles and Disco Top 100 charts, many critics at the time seemed unprepared for its impact, describing rap as if it too had sprung from a vacuum or been disgorged from a deep, dark hole in the social structure.[1] There seemed to be little mainstream awareness of rap's roots or of the fact that its foundations were already well established in the local cultures in and around metropolitan New York. After the music first debuted on the *Billboard* Hot Soul Singles charts, however, *Billboard* acknowledged that "in New York the phenomenon is at least seven years old in its current form" ("Rap Records" 1980, 57), thus locating rap's roots in an earlier musical and cultural era.

Committing Rap to Vinyl

Writing in 1985, Nelson George noted the changes rap underwent as it gradually rose in popularity, observing that "what was once a fluid, quick-changing, live art is now defined by the recorded version. Where a live rap once consisted of a series of catch-phrases cleverly ad-libbed and strung together, today's recorded raps tend to be story-oriented" (1985, 18). With their emphasis on technological influences and aesthetic changes, George's comments correspond with Langdon Winner's perspective on technologies in general: "What matters is not technology itself, but the social and economic systems in which it is embedded" (1986, 20). Once rap was recorded for commercial distribution on vinyl in 1979, an array of accompanying implications became evident as the cultural forms of hip-hop were merged with new subsystems of social and economic activity.

The rise of professionally recorded rap and the music's commercial growth through the early 1980s introduced a new and expansive spatial dimension to the music's production and circulation and heralded new spatial facets in its lyrical content. Despite a cautionary skepticism, evident in the 1980 *Billboard* headline "Rap Records: Are They Fad or Permanent?," rap's entry into the recording studio and the commercial music stream extended the reach and influence of the rap scene that had developed in and around New York. The dimension of commercial recording introduced an alternative space for its production as well as means of consuming the music (via twelve-inch singles and record albums, radio, and later, music video broadcasting) in new ways and new places. The transition of rap's lyrical and narrative forms to longer or more "serious" raps also reoriented the relationship between artists and audiences, who occupy different sites of production and consumption. The trend signaled the emergence of a new musical product—essentially a new style of rap—that quickly distinguished it from disco and what Rickey Vincent (1996) refers to as "dance funk" and "monster funk," which remained strong on the black music charts at the time.

In rap's formative stages, prior to the introduction of the rapping MC (known variously as master of ceremonies, microphone controller, mic checker, etc.), the hip-hop DJ was regarded as the main attraction at clubs and parties. It was the DJ who initially rapped over the record tracks and break-beats with a series of simple shouts and phrases, akin to the style of boisterous radio DJs or the Jamaican dance-hall toasters who informed rap's early practices (Stolzoff 2000). A microphone mounted next to the turntables enabled the mobile DJ to connect with the audience while spinning disks, verbally cajoling them to dance, party, and otherwise engage in the event. This performative mode enhanced the live component of the DJ's work, adding an extra element to the overall entertainment factor: the DJ not only spun the records for the dancers but was also evolving into a showman in his own right. It was at this point in the music's evolution that *Billboard's* reporters first acknowledged that mobile DJs were a fixture in the unique Bronx party scene.

As the turntable mixing became more sophisticated and began to require more of the DJs' attention, MCs were hired to engage the audiences and motivate the dancers directly in a verbal call-and-response performance. It was they who developed a vocal style implementing simple rhyme schemes spiced with exhortations to the audience to "just scream" and "raise your hands in the air and wave them like you just don't care." As front men, the MCs projected personality and provided a new focus for audience attention during DJ parties, which were becoming more performance oriented. As handbills and promotional flyers from this period illustrate, the MC or MC ensembles, consisting of three or four members, quickly joined the DJ as headliners, altering the DJ's status. Throughout the 1980s the DJ's profile gradually declined as the MC or rapper attained greater popular recognition. This transition was also influenced by rap's entry into the professional music industry as rappers rose to the fore and were more aggressively promoted, illustrating the industry's capacity to appropriate and adapt new musical forms to existing commercial practices.

New York audiences proved receptive to the MC's direct modes of address, which had the effect of narrowing the distance and connective dynamics between performers and audiences. The emphasis in live DJ and MC performances was on maintaining the party atmosphere. This characteristic was sustained in the first recorded rap songs, which initially carried over the most familiar and conventional elements from the live performance setting. This also involved the important fact that rap was initially associated with dance music, although it did not hold the same kind of appeal for the hyperathletic, technically skilled break-dance crews that were emerging from within the evolving hip-hop culture as it did for the general clubgoing public (Holman 1984).

The musical forms, styles, and themes of the live setting set the basic standard by which early recorded rap was measured. This was reflected, for example, in the advertising for the first full-length album released by the Sugarhill Gang: it featured a photograph of the group onstage with microphones in hand, performing before an audience in a dance-club setting (see *Billboard*, Feb. 2, 1980). Likewise, the accompanying video for their hit single "Rapper's Delight" was set in a discotheque environment, with disco dancers arrayed around the group.

The space of the recording studio facilitates and demands certain musical production practices that render it distinct from the live performance mode. Exploring the relationships between performance and recording in rock music, Theodore Gracyk writes:

The recording creates a "virtual" space and time in which a performance is represented as taking place. . . . Realism may prevail for classical, jazz, folk, country, and other musics where fidelity to performance is still the goal. Under the conventions of rock the realist relationship between musical work, performances, and recording is moot; in part, thanks to rock's ongoing exploitation of the recording process itself. (1996, 53)

In rap, the DJ's turntable skills involve manipulating prerecorded tracks by scratching and cutting on the actual vinyl disks. Later the producer's involvement was enhanced through the use of digital sampling technologies, which lifted prerecorded sound segments and inserted them into new recordings, and by the early 1990s acts were relying on digital audio tapes for the rhythmic bed track in live performances. With both the earlier vinyl-record-to-master-tape studio process and the later digital sampling methods, the original performance and its vinyl reproduction are merged. Also included are audio imperfections that are in most standard commercial recording contexts deemed undesirable by artists and producers: the pops and scratches on the original vinyl recordings (which are often older and of varying quality) find their way into the rap studio performance and are incorporated into the recorded rap track. This functions as a testament to the authenticity of the original recorded product, with the patina or sheen of age being transferred to the newly recorded version. The space of the recording studio therefore twice mediates the relationship between the reality of the originary performance and the final rap product that is shipped to record stores for consumption.

With the move into the studio, rap artists and producers were able to exploit recording technologies in new ways, not the least of which included multitrack recording and studio editing techniques. The rationale and logic of the recording, engineering, and mixing processes also meant that songs could be more carefully ordered and structured in the studio than they were in the context of the informal street jam or the live club performance. Artists rather suddenly confronted the option of exploiting the technical attributes of the studio space not only to experiment and develop more complex beats and rhythms, but also to script the longer, more detailed lyrical narratives identified by Nelson George.

Like the radical reassignment of the turntable, which became an essential performance instrument among DJs (Chambers 1985; Hebdige 1987), the apparatus of the recording studio was exposed to entirely different expectations and demands by rap artists and producers. For instance, the drum machines of the early 1980s and the digital samplers that were available by the mid-1980s became basic studio tools that offered increased control over the recording process and enhanced cost efficiency by circumventing the need for extra studio musicians. Rap artists quickly appropriated and extended their technological possibilities into new and unforeseen realms, swiping and splicing beats and melodies from prerecorded material and simultaneously challenging copyright laws in unprecedented ways.

Rather than a case of technological determinism, the role of recording-studio technologies in rap's development offers an example of technology's enabling capacity, which allowed rap artists and producers to utilize these and other new technologies in the interest of creative innovation. Not only were the results aesthetically compelling, but also studio recording contributed to the better overall sound quality and consistency of the finished product, displacing earlier low-quality homemade or live recordings distributed on audiocassette. As studio recording became a more common and standardized rap practice, the creative processes were expanded to include new levels and forms of technical expertise. Among the considerations at this stage of rap's development, however, was how best to maintain and reproduce the general sonic qualities of live rap performance in the new studio contexts.

The question of space in early recorded rap can be taken up in several ways. Studio recording procedures permitted a relatively refined aesthetic; nonetheless, rap producers attempted to maintain the music's aural qualities and the sonic elements of club performances in tracks by early artists such as Kurtis Blow, the Sugarhill Gang, and Grandmaster Flash and the Furious Five. For instance, "Freedom" (1980, Sugarhill Records), by Grandmaster Flash and the Furious Five, features a continuous buzz of voices throughout the track that is audible behind the lead vocals and rhythm in the studio mix. "Freedom" communicates an important temporal perspective in its reproduction of the live discotheque atmosphere in 1980, since this was still the primary site in which to see and hear rap acts. Nelson George cites the transition to vinyl as a positive progression toward wider recognition of the form, but he acknowledges that the underlying skills and techniques "were developed and refined in basements and clubs around the Apple" since at least the mid-1970s (1992, 73). As an early example of recorded rap music, however, "Freedom" reflects the way that the public performance space of the discotheque functions as a dominant signifier of spatial authority at this stage in the music's development.

As on some earlier recordings—such as Marvin Gaye's "What's Going On" (1971, Motown), Willie "Little Beaver" Hale's "Party Down" (1974, TK Productions), the Fatback Band's "Mister Bass Man" (1974, Ace Records), and several Barry White tracks—the cacophony of voices in "Freedom" connotes a space other than the recording studio. In Gaye's "What's Going On," the background voices do not point to any particular space; rather, in keeping with the theme and content of the song, they confer a general sense of public space, a zone where dialogue and discussion take place, such as a bar, restaurant, or social club. Hale's "Party Down" and the Fatback Band's "Mister Bass Man," as well as Kurtis Blow's contemporaneous recording "The Breaks" (1980, Mercury), correspond more closely to the production effects underlying "Freedom": these selections display greater spatial specificity, evoking a party in a nightclub or discotheque and reproducing the atmosphere of a live performance in a medium-sized setting.

Referring to "a sense of musical space" in popular music, Simon Frith explains that most forms of rock and pop "bear the traces of their construction (of their ideal, imagined, construction, that is to say). Even on record a concerto means a concert hall, a chamber piece a drawing room, an opera an opera house; just as jazz means a jazz club, a big band a dance hall, a rock band a pub back-room or a stadium" (1996, 6–7). These built-in "traces" need not be explicitly audible in the recordings themselves; for instance, not all jazz recordings feature the occasional cough or the chink of glasses that spatially anchor the performance in the jazz club, although these attributes of the live recording do contribute to the listener's sense of location. Perhaps Frith's suggestion that listeners intuit the spatial orientations of the recorded music is more accurately a case of evolved conventional knowledge that includes a basic familiarity with and comprehension of the dominant contexts surrounding any given musical form. Much of recorded rap's "ideal, imagined construction" in this period bears the implied spatial character or traces of the public night spot or discotheque, deliberately constructed as primary referents in the music's production processes. The studio construction of a spatial aura is therefore based on a sense of performative space that is encoded as a sonic component in the recording. The spatial logic to which it adheres is known and understood by listeners.

The addition of an audience track reinforces the party-oriented themes of these recordings, enhancing the overall sense of space conveyed. This is achieved in other dance tracks as well (such as KC and the Sunshine Band's "Get Down Tonight" [1975, TK Productions]) through studio recording techniques that compress the lead vocals and other instruments or add an echo effect that creates a sense of an enlarged space, as if the song were being performed in a sizable club.[2] By replicating the sonic experience of a live show (albeit in a sanitized, perfected, and relatively distortion free form produced within a controlled studio environment), the spatiality of the track is foregrounded, but in virtually all of these examples it is more precisely the achievement of the sonic characteristics of a *successful* performance or a *good* party.

Disco, Studio, and Street: Convergent Spatial Sites

The release of "The Message" (1982, Sugar Hill Records) by Grandmaster Flash and the Furious Five introduced a radical element into the thematic focus and lyrical structures of rap music. Entering *Billboard*'s Black Singles chart on July 24, 1982, at number eighty-five, it eventually attained certified platinum status (over one million units sold), climbing to number four on the chart. It also met with substantial international success, charting in the United Kingdom, Canada, and Europe. More important than its hit status, however, is the fact that the song represented a bold departure from most other successful commercial rap releases up to that point, with their less complex rhyme patterns and playful party themes. Appearing on a BBC television documentary about rap titled *In Search of the Perfect Beat,* the track's, cowriter Melle, Mel recalls that "what started as a party movement became a protest movement, and the rhymes followed suit."

All subsequent rap recordings dealing with sociopolitical concerns or spatially oriented themes relating to black cultural frames of experience owe a debt to "The Message." As the first major example of the subgenre that became known as message rap, knowledge rap, or reality rap, the song altered the evolving genre through the urgent authority of its vocal presentation and its engaged social critique. Taken together, these factors introduced a new intensity and an alternative mode of address that stimulated a younger generation of rap enthusiasts. For example, referring to the authority of voice and conviction of the lyrics, Kid, of the rap duo Kid 'N Play, cites Melle Mel of Grandmaster Flash and the Furious Five as being the primary influence on his own decision to enter the music business (Rose 1994a, 54–55). The influence of previous rappers is commonly acknowledged in interviews and profiles in the pages of rap-oriented publications. Without sacrificing commercial appeal, "The Message" paved the way for youths who showed skill, talent, and a commitment to conveying what contemporary rapper and producer KRS-One has described as "ghetto street knowledge."

"The Message" shifted the rap form toward an incisive critical content, introducing what eventually became a standard and dominating rap discourse that maintained a pronounced ghettocentric sensibility. With "The Message," rap's discursive focus extended the genre's thematic boundaries, which up to this point had mostly been isolated in the conceptual loci of the party, nightclub, or roller rink. The innovation also alerted major-label executives and independent producers that rap music, still commonly perceived as a fad with limited market durability, had broader potential, and that it had substance—like folk music long before it, or rock at its best.

Rap's spatial discourse was also evolving toward a more intense and concentrated focus on the sociospatial character of the city in general and the ghetto or inner-city spaces in particular. In a literal sense, the street has been a consistent site for emergent hip-hop practices: block parties, breakdancing, and graffiti are all strongly associated with forms of expression that occur in outdoor or unsanctioned public spaces. This historical grounding in the authority of the street has had important implications for hip-hop throughout its evolution, providing a thread between contemporary practices and the formative practices upon which they are founded. Over time, however, the street as a physical locus has been mediated by the conceptual, symbolic, and mythical construct of *the street,* producing a unique hip-hop sensibility that might be understood through its comparison with the associative images of fields, farms, bars, and pick-up trucks in classic country music. The street within hip-hop and rap has emerged as a conventional construct that can be traced to the convergent factors of hip-hop culture's intensified commercial marketing (through film, recording, and media diffusion) and the shifting discourses spawned by the pronounced emphasis on ghetto imagery and themes. Negus (1999) further observes that rap's early independent status and its outsider—even outlaw—profile in the music industry also contributes to the mythic associations between rap and the street that endure to this day. Despite the introduction of a new, spatially oriented urban discourse and critical observations of city strife, the "party jams" did not simply disappear as message rap became established as a subgenre. The two styles flourished in tandem, providing an interesting—even sustaining—counterpoint as well as an indication of rap's capacity for growth and diversification.

As Roy Shuker notes, "Like much subsequent rap, while 'The Message' is lyrically negative it is set to a compelling dance beat" (1994, 161). His comment points to the often ironic disjunctures between lyrical and rhythmic structures or between texts and their uses by audiences, yet the naive fascination with the simultaneously funky and political orientations of "The Message"(based partly on rave reviews by critics in the mainstream music press, who publicized it to wider teen audiences) has its limitations. For instance, Russell Simmons recalls an incident in the influential Bronx nightclub Disco Fever where DJ Junebug was spinning "New York, New York" by Grandmaster Flash and the Furious Five:

This dude runs up to the DJ booth, smashed the record, then put a gun to Junebug's head, sayin', "if ya play that record again, I'm go'n kill ya. I don't wanna come in here *ever* and hear that record or you're dead." Junebug asked the brother if he was mad at Flash or something, and the dude said, "No. I'm just tired of hearing that ghetto shit." (Nelson and Gonzales 1991, 204)

Notwithstanding such reactions, "The Message" reinforced the legitimacy of the rap genre among critics and audiences. In both commercial and cultural terms, it announced a depth and substance that many critics and observers had believed were absent and ultimately unlikely.

This discursive transition generated an alternative means for the articulation of social critique and spatial analysis from a young black perspective (although the song's cowriter, Duke Bootee, was an older and more established musician who performed as a mainstay of the Sugar Hill label's famous studio band). The urban scene, which was centered in and around

New York in the early 1980s, provided the backdrop for the exploding hip-hop culture, but it was "The Message" that placed the emphasis directly upon the sociospatial structures within which this culture flourished. The condensations of African-American cultural traditions were consciously merged with the contemporaneous zeitgeist forged in conditions of urban existence, provide the informing elements of rap's varied discourses in this period. According to George Lipsitz,

> The popularity of hip hop reflects more than cultural compensation for political and economic domination, more than an outlet for energies and emotions repressed by power relations. Hip hop expresses a form of politics perfectly suited to the post-colonial era. It brings a community into being through performance, and it maps out real and imagined relations between people that speak to the realities of displacement, disillusion, and despair created by the austerity economy of post-industrial capitalism. (Lipsitz 1994a, 36)

The shifts in rap's discursive emphasis and the emergence of a new spatial sensibility throughout rap's relatively brief history should be seen as dialogical interventions in an ongoing, extensive dynamic of cultural interaction and cultural cartographic inscription.

Despite the fact that musicians such as the Last Poets, the Watts Prophets, Gil Scott-Heron, James Brown, Curtis Mayfield, and even the Motown crooners Marvin Gaye and Stevie Wonder had earlier deployed politicized cultural discourses by merging social commentary and explicitly urban perspectives within jazz, funk, and soul idioms, and that Brother D and Collective Effort had released "How We Gonna Make the Black Nation Rise" (Clappers), a "serious," politically oriented rap recording in 1980, "The Message" was distinctive. As for musical and cultural precedents, earlier soul artists had frequently displayed a radical sociopolitical focus and voiced poignant critical attacks on the injustices of American society. Their cultural sensibilities, however, were generally bound to an older counter-hegemonic political project founded in nationwide social struggle and traceable to the American civil rights movement of the 1950s and 1960s and to the black nationalisms that were pervasive throughout much of the 1960s and early 1970s.[3]

The distinction between Grandmaster Flash and the Furious Five and the above-mentioned musical predecessors is primarily generational.[4] Rising rapidly as one of the most prominent groups of the New York rap scene, Flash and his crew were able to articulate transitions in style and musical content by combining their ample skills and innovative abilities with a particular youth-inflected social perspective. The group itself was active in both the production and the consumption of hip-hop, reveling in forms of expression that were rapidly redefining the daily lives of young black and Latino teenagers and a scattering of young white interlopers in the 1980s. This was the new music of black urban youth, and as such it entered into the cultural antagonisms of difference whereby intergenerational distinctions, among others, attain particular meanings for young fans and consumers. Put quite simply, rap was for youth; the earlier jazz, soul, and R & B remained more firmly sedimented as adult music, although classic R & B, funk, and soul tracks culled from parental record collections and used record bins have had impressive longevity thanks to hip-hop's resuscitation and appropriation of these catalog materials. Along with Flash's taste in old and new recorded music, his turntable dexterity and technical inventiveness also propelled changes in the ways that hip-hop rhythms were organized and manipulated. For instance, it is he who is credited with perfecting and popularizing the precision needle-drop, phasing, and scratching techniques that later became standard facets of any DJ's repertoire of skills. His classic recording "Grandmaster Flash on the Wheels of Steel" (1981, Sugar Hill) is a historical benchmark and remains an important display of early DJ artistry. The MCs that made up the Furious Five—Melle Mel, Scorpio, Cowboy, Kid Creole, and Raheem—extended the scope of lyrical composition and forms of delivery, evolving into one of the more sophisticated MC ensembles capable of intricate ensemble rap performances.

"The Message" also generated a renewed interest in the rap genre within the black music industry. Although several small labels, such as Enjoy and Winley Records, were selling twelve-inch rap singles, as George (1992) indicates, the "across-the-board acceptance" of "The Message" was instrumental in the gradual erosion of Sugar Hill's market domination. The single's commercial and creative success produced favorable conditions for the rapid proliferation of competitive upstart independent labels catering almost exclusively to rap acts. Furthermore, Melle Mel's distinctive rapping style, which had a unique, recognizable tonal quality that diverged sharply from the less aggressive voices of party rap, touched a chord among music critics and the record buying public, similarly leading to a surge of interest. The commercial success of "The Message" drew renewed attention to the genre among the recording industry's corporate "majors," who had not, to this point, paid much attention to rap. Although slow to recognize the genre's commercial potentials, by the early to mid-1980s major record companies were beginning to explore rap as a commercial venture, and the smaller labels slowly encountered new competition.

A year after the release of "The Message," Grandmaster Flash and the Furious Five disbanded, owing to differences among the band members that, according to longstanding speculation, were rooted in dissatisfaction with the questionable accounting practices and other curious business procedures at Sugar Hill (Greenberg 1999, 30). Flash, Raheem, and Kid Creole signed with the major label Elektra, where subsequent releases failed to match their earlier successes with Sugar Hill. While the industry majors eventually acknowledged rap's market potentials by hiring savvy artist and repertoire (A & R) people and signing promising talent, their early involvement in rap mainly took the form of manufacturing and distribution arrangements with the smaller independents. This enabled both black- and white-owned production companies and record labels to maintain greater control and autonomy over their operations at various levels, including searching out new talent and expanding their label rosters while gaining access to an extensive national and international distribution system (Rose 1994a; Negus 1999).

The favorable consumer response to "The Message" was rooted in the appeal of the song's lyrical content and vocal presentation and in its adherence to and adaptation of a historically enunciated black aesthetic (Boyd 1997; Kelley 1997). The main element of innovation was in its lyrical emphasis on the portrayal of an ostensible ghetto reality. References to several specific cultural indicators (such as television sitcoms or well-publicized incidents) and to popularly documented social issues of the time help to locate the song in a historical present and added to its reality quotient by citing verifiable phenomena. The combined elements of geocultural and temporal locatedness were also important to the single's success and influence among the youth of rap's production center in New York, since nowhere was the human damage and social devastation of late 1970s and early 1980s America more evident than in the city's uptown boroughs where the hip-hop phenomenon originated.

Donald Warren's assessment of the social organization of ghetto environments has a particular resonance with the ghetto images in "The Message": "Ghetto means complexity of group structure. It refers to a series of cultures (subcultures) existing side-by-side. Ghetto, if it has any significance as an abstraction refers to a pattern of compression, the capacity of many status groups in a restricted physical environment" (1975, 26–27). Each verse constructs a sense of space where the desperation and stress of poverty is uniquely felt and lived within a contained territorial setting. The descriptive language conveys a graphic image of the underside of the urban environment, yet the organization of the verses also suggests that the pressures of economic disenfranchisement and urban stress are multiply inflected, affecting individuals differently in each social context and refuting the notion of evenly balanced or homogeneously distributed poverty.

Roy Shuker suggests that the evolving ghettocentric subgenre spawned by "The Message" also began to connote constrained mobility through its musical and lyrical structures. He writes that the "interplay of synth. and sharp percussion initially sounds merely bouncy and unobtrusive, but as it goes on and on throughout the song—some seven minutes in its extended play release version—it starts to have a more disturbing and irritating quality, becoming a metaphor for being trapped in the ghetto and tenement life" (1994, 161). In this interpretation, the rhythm and lyrical content combine in a mutually referential convergence while encoding a permeating tension within the track. As the repeated rhythmic loop produces this closed tension, each verse introduces a new conceptual or imagined space, generally fluctuating between representations of external, public spaces (the street and subway) and internal, private spaces (the domestic spaces of the home or tenement apartment and, in the end, the desperate loneliness of the prison cell).

The imagery presented in "The Message" correlated with what lay before a number, though certainly not the majority, of minority audiences and consumers every day. Its references to fractured families, drug abuse, unemployment and its attendant idleness, educational disenfranchisement, the strains of debt and poverty, and the often irrational responses that intense stress and pressure can provoke were all encapsulated and rounded out by the now-classic chorus:

> Don't push me
> 'cause I'm close to the edge
> I'm trying not to lose my head
> it's like a jungle sometimes
> it makes me wonder
> how I keep from going under.

The spatial impact of poverty and desolation taken up and rendered discursively in "The Message" cannot be denied, but even though the origins of the hip-hop culture and the music at its center are historically specific to the Bronx and New York's uptown areas, many social and cultural forces that negatively affect the spaces of the Bronx (or other "ghetto" environments) were not necessarily rooted there.

The articulation of a youth-oriented ghetto consciousness and social commentary by Bronx-based rappers was a reactive response that emerged in the late 1970s and early 1980s simultaneously with the downturn of black-nationalist political influence and the rise of the national economic discourse of Reagonomics. The lyrical references in "The Message" to "bum education and double-digit inflation" reflect failures on a grander scale. They point to the fact that prevailing promises of self-improvement and personal application that continue to form the cornerstone of "the American dream" (albeit with different inflections in white and black cultural loci or in native and foreign-born populations) had been all but exhausted in the midst of a more widespread structural erosion whose origins lay far beyond the cultural boundaries of the ghetto.

"The Message" reflects a keen social awareness and familiarity with the myriad localized manifestations of ghetto impoverishment that were being gradually intensified under the Reagan government's conservative economic agenda at the time. It thus communicates a particular social perspective, illustrating that urban minority youth were impressively aware of the routine outcomes of reduced spending on schooling and social services that produced economic and social disparities. They were not unattuned to the fact that assistance programs in American cities were being either slashed or eradicated completely, intensifying the damage for those of the economic underclass who were already most in need. The threat lobbed by the chorus of "The Message," which has become a cultural touchstone in the history of hip-hop, is not only leveled at the local scale, within the immediate ghetto environment, but also targets a wider, more amorphous American social system that reproduces the conditions of poverty and inequality on a larger scale.

Citing the Bronx's desolation, Rose writes that "depictions of black and Hispanic neighborhoods were drained of life, energy, and vitality. The message was loud and clear: to be stuck here was to be lost" (1994a, 33). This was powerfully reinforced and globally disseminated in other contexts as well, such as in the 1981 film *Fort Apache, the Bronx*, starring Ed Asner and Paul Newman, which negatively portrayed the borough as an embattled war zone and its inhabitants as little more than savages.[5] Despite the fact that "The Message" also reinforces negative portrayals by reproducing a particular place-image of the Bronx and other black ghetto enclaves, it also helped transform rap as a whole into a powerful cultural vehicle for the description of particular urban conditions of existence. "The Message" dropped into the midst of varied social contexts (at the level of private and public consumption and aural apprehension, whether through home listening, radio broadcast, or club play), but the link between the recording and its urban audiences is especially relevant. Its combination of engaged observation and palpable tension, frustration, and anger introduced a new means of highlighting social issues of direct relevance to the many city-dwelling teenagers who were active in the emergent hip-hop culture.

Characterized as dangerous and dilapidated in both myth and fact, the Bronx symbolized contemporary urban decay, its streets and vacant tenements being "central popular cultural icons" (Rose 1994a, 33) that signified the worst imaginable conditions of existence. Yet while the home environments of numerous rappers may have provided the inspiration behind "The Message" and other recordings in this period, the track is most compelling for its ability to reproduce an abstract construction of urban space, rendering a general portrayal or representational composite from an array of descriptive images. For instance, Steven Hager suggests that the lyrics reflect a "sharp, cinematic imagery," effectively communicating a sense of stratified, nonhomogeneous ghetto space. He further posits that "the persona in the song was that of a typical South Bronx resident pressured to the point of desperation by his environment. . . . Appropriately, the song that represented one of hip hop's finest moments described the South Bronx, the territory where hip hop began" (1984, 93). Despite Hager's assertions, however, the South Bronx is never explicitly mentioned. "The Message" does not present a picture of a specific place; rather, it reproduces an image-idea of ghetto space that is widely recognizable in the American urban context and that undoubtedly corresponds to many elements of the Bronx.

As a lyrical construction of urban imagery, "The Message" features a powerful, poetic story line comprising a series of gritty scenarios that describe the city from the perspective of the urban poor who inhabit it. The image of urban ghetto space is carefully organized through an amalgamation of embittered references to sites and characters: the housing project and the subway platform, the junkie, the prostitute, the homeless person, the pimp, the hustler, and the anonymous victim of violent crime. The characters imply a range of cultural contexts according to common typologies that ostensibly link certain social actors with discrete social spaces. This description of individuals of various castes produces a series of associations that imply particular spatial practices enacted therein. A sense of an elaborative political project is absent from "The Message," and there is no explicit appeal to collective action or to expansive processes of coalition building, although these exist and are essential organizing forces within the actual community spaces of the urban ghetto. The containment and enclosures of the ghetto space are framed as tensions affecting the lone human subject whose efforts to maintain a sense of self and to exercise authority over one's personal destiny are defined by spatial practices.

This construction of ghetto space corresponds to Shields's (1991) notion of "marginal places," which are constituted as "sites for socially marginal activities" or as "zones of Otherness." In the spatial constructions of "The Message," the ghetto is reproduced as a site of human devastation through the mobilization of specific representational images and signifying traits involving particular social milieux and urban environments. This is achieved with the concurrent deployment of a discourse of social spatialization that, as Shields notes, is formed within the tensions of spatial difference and the urban configuration of power, influence, and authority. According to Shields, place-images

> are the various discrete meanings associated with real places or regions regardless of their character in reality. . . . A set of core images forms a widely disseminated and commonly held set of images of a place or space. These form a relatively stable group of ideas in currency, reinforced by their communication value as conventions in a discursive economy. (1991, 60–61)

The accumulation of place-images consequently reinforces the foundation upon which socially accepted "space-myths" are structured, although such myths are a manifestation of historically specific phenomena and are constantly renegotiated, so that they remain in a continual state of flux.

Spatial Constructs and Urban Meanings

In "The Message," MC Melle Mel's chorus, with its reference to the jungle ("it's like a jungle sometimes / it makes me wonder / how I keep from going under"), mobilizes a common, even clichéd idea of urban dystopia. In fact, the jungle is a long-standing thematic concept that was expressed in popular texts from various eras throughout the twentieth century. For instance, Upton Sinclair's 1906 novel *The Jungle* portrays turn-of-the-century Chicago and the urban terrors confronting European immigrant labor; Sidney Poitier portrayed a troubled ghetto teen in the classic 1955 MGM film *The Blackboard Jungle*; in *The Autobiography of Malcolm X,* Malcolm recalls that during his days as a young hoodlum in the streets of Boston and New York, "for a hustler in our sidewalk jungle world, 'face' and 'honor' were important" (1966, 127).

Referring to music from the post–World War II era, Theodore Gracyk cites John Lennon and Mick Jagger, who have referred to early rock 'n' roll in terms of primitivism, tribal origins, and jungle rhythms. Gracyk notes that "the 'jungle label' must have been widespread, particularly in England with its colonial heritage. . . . But the jungle idea is not just a British perception. It dates back to the earliest days of American rock: witness Warren Smith's 1956 rockabilly classic 'Ubangi Stomp,' and Hank Mizzel's 1957 'Jungle Rock'" (1996, 130). Among other examples, Bob Marley and the Wailers created a popular reggae anthem of Rastafarian resistance with "Concrete Jungle" (1973, Island Records). The Four Tops' recording "Are You Man Enough?" (1973, Dunhill), which was featured on the sound track of the MGM blaxploitation film *Shaft in Africa,* also invokes the jungle metaphor with the line "It's like a jungle outside the door," a reference to the threat, danger, and paranoia of urban life.

The metaphor appears as well on the Melle Mel and Duke Bootee composition "Message II (Survival)" (1982, Sugarhill Records), released in the same year as its precursor, in which the chorus returns to the Darwinian ethic of the jungle with the suggestion that "only the strong can survive." Addressing rap aesthetics, Richard Schusterman explains that the genre "can be traced back to African roots, to jungle rhythms which were taken up by rock and disco and reappropriated by the rap DJs—musical cannibals of the urban jungle" (1991, 615). His argument then makes a questionable leap, shifting to a description of New York City ghetto spaces as if to close the circle between a more primitive Africa and inner-city America.

In the ghettoes of America's cities, the law of the jungle with its crude survival ethic remains a dominant trope that expresses a perception of the structuring forces influencing social existence. Invoking the concept of the urban jungle in music or literature is a strategic decision that seeks to question, expose, or otherwise comment on society's sense of civic order and social propriety. For example, with their debut LP release, *Straight Out the Jungle* (1988, Warlock), the Jungle Brothers are portrayed on the front cover emerging from an African terrain, while on the back cover they are pictured in a parkland marsh in the heart of New York. The title of the album also quotes N.W.A.'s *Straight Outta Compton,* altering the spatial coordinates, toying with the frames of reference, and indicating an arguably more progressive geocultural source of authenticity and identity that draws equally from each side of the hyphen in African-American.

The deployment of the discourse of poverty, struggle, and survival in the urban jungle succeeds in contexts such as "The Message" not because it reconnects rap with its African origins (which as Gracyk notes, is an enterprise of questionable ethnomusicological value). Rather, it succeeds because the jungle remains a familiar paradigm within which the song's elaborated vignettes make sense. Seen as a deliberate strategy, the implementation of the urban jungle metaphor effectively facilitates a broad, nationwide comprehension of the track's imagery and urgency. By operating within the discursive field of a social commonplace that has achieved unqualified status as a space-myth, the ghettocentric articulations are potentially rendered more acceptable, as a verifiable truth. The trope of the urban jungle has certainly not disappeared, yet over time it has been usurped by other powerful metaphors and descriptive terms as subsequent message-oriented rap songs have moved toward more complex and detailed formulations of the city.

Reflecting for BBC television on the impact and influence of "The Message," Grandmaster Flash states that "all the records prior to that were frivolous, happy-go-lucky, party, let's get down. . . . This particular record had to be created by somebody who lived in and understood urban America."

While the track's lyrics described specific characteristics of the U.S. ghetto, the images in the accompanying video further reinforced the connections, portraying the band in the heart of a run-down neighborhood with the group congregated on the street or the stoop of a brownstone apartment building. By intersplicing the group's performance with images of urban congestion or poor and homeless men in the streets, the message that the urban economic underclass is barely functioning under the pressure of civic neglect is ultimately enhanced.

Flash's perspective on subjective location and spatiality reveals a common attitude toward the relationships between people and places. It asserts an authority of voice that is spatially grounded and assumes that the speaking subject can accurately convey the underlying "truth" of the site of articulation. This perspective is echoed as well by Kristal Brent Zook when she writes, "What was immediately clear about this cultural movement (which came to be called hip hop . . .) was that it expressed certain sentiments that genuinely reflected the lives of working-class Black and Puerto Rican male youths in a way that the more romanticized disco scene, popularized by middle-class whites, did not" (1992, 257). These views, which persist among rappers, industry executives, journalists, and scholars, assume a bond between place and reality that requires continued attention and analysis (Kelley 1997). The sentiment persists even though it overlooks the fact that the lives and experiences of equal or greater numbers of blacks and Latinos (as well as most of rap's white consumers) are not, in fact, reflected in rap's discourses.

Citing "The Message" as her example, Zook asserts that "part of rap's streetwise edge came, undoubtedly, from the fact that most of its participants were from the ''hood,' that is, the neighborhoods of New York which required this edge for day-to-day survival, such as the South Bronx" (1992, 257). Although her terminology in reference to "the 'hood" is temporally misapplied, since it postdates the period she is addressing, she accurately acknowledges the dual relationship between actual physical space and rap's musical expressions of a spatial sensibility. Many artists loudly and proudly defend their position, claiming that they narrate true experiences that are produced within the social domains of black America. They claim that their very artistry lies in their ability to express an unproblematic and unambiguous reality of existence, as rapper MC Eiht illustrates when he states, "I just talk about the hood. That's just spittin' the real" ("Reality Check" 1994, 67). It is also true that they are producers of representational space and fictional narratives envisioned within actual environments and experiences and are thus within the realm of possibility. Sudjic supports this observation when he explains that images and representational articulations of urban space influence our perceptions and "help to convey a sense of what the city is, or can be" (1992, 301), as do Peter Jackson and Jan Penrose when they note that "the conceptual dimensions of place can be as important as its physical manifestations" (1993, 205).

These fictional representations cannot be segregated from real places and practices, for in their symbolic forms they are recirculated into the social realm, taken up, and made meaningful in collective contexts through sophisticated social engagements. The relationship between veracity and experience and their discursive articulation in rap and hip-hop are grounded in a complex array of deeply embedded cultural issues that is historically structured and can be identified and traced throughout hip-hop's cultural existence. By approaching what might be termed "the reality problem" as a historical facet of hip-hop and deconstructing its spatial meanings and values as an evolved tradition that has undergone transformations at numerous junctures, we can observe how it has become a cultural convention. Owing to convention, in hip-hop's cultural forms of expression and across a broad swath of the black cultural terrain the ghetto is elevated as the source of black authenticity, the stream in which both suffering and resilience flow in abundance. It is in this sense not necessarily any actual ghetto —or, later, 'hood—that is being appealed to, but the mythical and symbolically meaningful ghetto. None of this, of course, should undercut the fact that the social spaces of the ghetto and the 'hood are prevailing facets of the urban environment and that the structuring forces of poverty and its attendant ills inordinately affect African-Americans and Latinos, as well as continental Africans, Haitians, Cambodians, Vietnamese, Bosnians, and many other more recent foreign arrivals whose economic status locates them in some of North America's most depressed areas.

The appeals to geocultural reality are traditionally based in the dynamics and convergences of several forces that are themselves continually undergoing change, including the economic conditions of the Americas and of the world more generally, the social environments from which its innovators emerge, the specific and continually changing ghetto-oriented discourses and imagery, the changing audience formations and consumers that participate in hip-hop culture, and the use of ghetto-oriented themes in the promotion and marketing strategies devised by record labels and corporate distributors. None of these factors have remained static since "The Message" was released in 1982. We might ask why, then, the discussions about reality in rap approach the issue in such an unchanging manner, as if the reality being expressed had itself not also changed.

The commitment to the realistic representation of urban experience in "The Message" functioned as an important factor in promoting Grandmaster Flash and the Furious Five and their material. It helped establish their outlaw status upon its release, immediately winning fans across the color line who were growing increasingly disturbed by what many perceived as a political and aesthetic bankruptcy in American pop music and disco. This latter factor, however, also attracted the attentions of many critics who, observing rock's waning politicization, eagerly welcomed the arrival of "The Message" as an ostensibly authentic expression of racial and class consciousness. In the context of the period, Grandmaster Flash and the Furious Five took a bold step when they reintroduced a series of unwelcome images of contemporary America through their recording and video. The song's huge success, which as Zook suggests was unquestionably related as much to the apparent "reality" portrayed by the lyrical and visual representations as to the music itself, also opened new opportunities for others to exploit the trend or, in a less cynical view, to continue exploring the relationships between rap and reality.

After "The Message": The Rise of a New Subgenre

The ghetto imagery of "The Message" and its representation of urban space introduced a new standard form that rapidly evolved into a distinct rap subgenre, the resonant impact of which can be traced in numerous recordings that followed its release. Describing this development, Toop notes that a flurry of recordings of dubious quality were released in this period in the attempt to cash in on the trend initiated by "The Message":

The contradictions of a money-minded craze for gory social realism and criticism of the Reagan administration, with its callous cutbacks in social programs, are hard to resolve. The juxtaposition of protests about rape victims with rampant machismo or hard-times lyrics sung by kids in expensive leather outfits and gold chains can be hard to stomach. (Toop 1984, 124)

Toop raises an important point, for the separate agendas of political "conscientization" (defined as the elevation of a critical perspective and a honed cultural awareness of existing social conditions and their contradictions) and the commercial imperatives of the music industry are often in conflict. Negus (1999) refutes the notion of rap's ghetto-based reality, explaining that the strategies of independent record labels were frequently just as questionable as those of the majors: each sought to exploit hip-hop's potential by promoting an image of ghetto authenticity. Negus further challenges the commonly held assumption that independent rap labels were necessarily closer to the "street" and the ghetto, observing that middle-class black entrepreneurs and opportunists, together with their white peers, were mainly responsible for recording and promoting the hip-hop culture in the early 1980s. The cleavage between progressive political intent and commercial opportunism was made evident with Melle Mel and Duke Bootee's "The Message II (Survival)" in late 1982. An ill-conceived sequel, it clearly sought to capitalize on the original, but it was aesthetically and thematically redundant, contributing only marginally to the evolution of a new subgenre.

The release of "Street Justice" (1983, Profile Records) by the Rake the following year offers a better example of how the rhythmic and vocal aesthetics of "The Message" as well as its thematic content were further developed as the subgenre took root in the hip-hop culture. The Rake (whose real name is Keith Rose) had previously been a backup singer for Dionne Warwick, and the cowriters Marc Blatte and Larry Gottlieb, along with the producer J. Rifkin, were music industry professionals rather than ghetto upstarts. Their recording, which debuted on the *Billboard* Black Singles chart at number ninety on August 6, 1983, bore a considerable thematic resemblance to the scenarios and vigilante revenge themes introduced by the films *Death Wish* (1972) and *Death Wish II* (1982), starring Charles Bronson. While the influence of these films is evident, they are not the song's dominant referent. "Street Justice" can be more accurately regarded as a response to "The Message" or "Survival," displaying the emergent story-based style while addressing the potential consequences that can result if one is eventually pushed "to the edge," if a person does "lose his head," as "The Message" warned. The demarcation of urban space in "Street Justice" is more pronounced, illustrating an intensified attention to descriptive detail in what ultimately identifies the recording as an extension of the message-oriented subgenre initiated by "The Message."

Featuring a sinister, slashing rhythm track that builds an eerie suspension while an oddly melodic vibraphone riff provides a musical counterpoint to the lyrical flow, the tone of "Street Justice" is similar to that of "The Message." The Rake's deep voice, while similar in range to Melle Mel's, is characterized by a steady, menacing calmness that contrasts with the more boisterous, party-oriented rap of the Sugarhill Gang and with the sharp attack characteristic of the Furious Five's ensemble-style flow. This vocal quality is a crucial accompaniment to the theme of eruptive hyper-masculine violence, revenge, and retribution.

The track's theme is one of vigilante justice, the by-product of an ineffectual criminal justice system and the everyday stress and violence that regularly afflict the American urban underclasses. The lyrics tap into the discomforting reality of systemic racism and unequal treatment of blacks in the American social justice system and rhetorically appeals to the listener's understanding that in America the minority population is frequently at a disadvantage and must often circumvent the system on a local or personal level for justice to be served. Whereas "The Message" adopts the discourse of the jungle to critique the character of the urban environment, "Street Justice" deploys a more complicated (though similar) discourse of urban class war with the repeated refrain "Gotta meet the punks on the battlefront / gotta beat the punks / street justice." The battlefront is the undisciplined space—what the song refers to as a "no-man's land"—that has been taken over by angry and violent youths operating according to the unlawful codes of the street. In keeping with the song's general thrust, it is these very codes of power through aggression or of enforced authority and spatial dominance that must be enacted if true justice is to be attained. The lyrics also adopt the story-telling mode of "The Message" with a portrayal of common ghetto imagery. The distinction, however, is in the track's articulation of varying social activities that cohere in the American ghetto, establishing the normative image-ideals of controlled domestic and public environments that must be defended against the onslaught of violent and immoral thugs. As with "The Message" before it, the image of ghetto dilapidation in "Street Justice" is clear, but this particular construction has a pervasive emptiness that contrasts with the relative fullness and cacophony of the ghetto's multiple social settings.

Steve Hager's reference to the cinematic qualities of "The Message" notwithstanding, "Street Justice" is much more explicit in its cinematic structuring. It follows what amounts to a rational, ordered "script" leading from one spatial scene to another, as opposed to "The Message," which is organized around a series of self-contained spatialized vignettes. "Street Justice" maintains a much more coherent and unified narrative in a literary sense than that of "The Message," but it, too, builds on the description of several distinct social sites, demarcating cultural territories such as the home and the workplace and—of particular relevance to the song's title and theme—the contrasting spaces of the courtroom and the street.

In contrast to "The Message," the discursive tensions in "Street Justice" are produced through the juxtaposition of conflicting generational values and their associated spaces, establishing a dynamic of spatial polarities that isolate distinct social geographies and accompanying practices in a more clearly divisive manner. Describing the political shortcomings and a lack of unity or racial and class-based solidarity in the message rap subgenre, Ernest Allen Jr. observes:

Overall, the message tends to portray, in vivid and urgent terms, the contours of existing social breakdown, and in the best of cases may offer a vision of a new and more just way of life. But all too frequently these youthful assertions of social identity and envisioned social order degenerate into a malevolent disparaging of other groups. (1996, 160)

These tendencies are visible in the subgenre's earliest stages, and in "Street Justice" the contrasting sites are inscribed in stark definition as antagonistic zones of humanity that are fraught with the "malevolent" disparagement to which Allen refers: a relatively secure (and idealized) domestic sphere, the adult masculine domain of the workplace, the courtroom, and the comparatively lawless streets that constitute the war zone in the battle between adult respectability and unruly and indiscriminate teenage mayhem are all weighed against one another. The spatial depictions also conform to Shields's suggestion that "the social 'Other' of the marginal and of low cultures is despised and reviled in the official discourse of dominant cultures and central power while at the same time being constitutive of the imaginary and emotional repertoires of that dominant culture" (1991, 5). Each of the varied spatial images signifies dominant and subordinate characteristics, although a discomforting privilege is granted to the standard, traditional sites of authority and social domination that attain precedence in the track's spatial discourse. Curiously, the song's lyrics express perspectives associated with the threatened and embattled adult even though its primary listening audience at the time would almost certainly be represented by audiences that share age affinities with the opposing teenage antagonists—a factor that may be attributed to the age and perspective of the track's writers.

As critical commentary, "Street Justice" fails to fully engage with this intergenerational dissonance, opting instead for a spatially oriented commentary that is rooted in the distinctions between legitimate and illegitimate spatial practices and their attendant values. In "Street Justice" the ideal of mobility and escape from the ghetto is presented as an attainable goal that can be realized only through the traditional virtues of hard work and stable family relations. The conditions of ghetto society and urban youth that are so negatively portrayed in "Street Justice" consequently emerge as an ongoing threat to the normative forces of a capitalistic, parental, and patriarchal authority complex. There is no prevailing sense that joy and success can ever be achieved from within the ghetto itself, and "Street Justice" ultimately adopts a conservative formulation of cultural values and political ideology that rejects the potentials for positive personal or community attainment within the neighborhoods of the inner city.

The lyrics do more than just establish these settings and polarities, for they also enter into a stereotypical sociospatial discourse that attributes a repertoire of biased values to each space along the social spectrum. In this regard, whereas "The Message" constitutes an attempt to depict social disparities from a relatively critical and politically engaged position, "Street Justice" reflects a reactionary impulse. Like the *Death Wish* films, the tale in "Street Justice" appeals to the notion of urban frontier individualism. The Rake indicts both the unjust legal system and violent black ghetto youth as dual elements of threat and constraint, the former exerting its negative force from above while the latter arises from the outlaw underground. The constructed image is of the black working class, which is trapped between these twinned elements that, viselike, press in on it without relief.

"The Message" and "Street Justice" present two very different discursive constructs, each subscribing to distinct modes of articulation in the production of place-images and urban ghetto scenarios. They are exemplary of the emergent message-oriented rap that has become a standard facet of the genre, yet their divergent ideological positions reflect the differences in how space was understood and imagined across various rap subgenres at an early stage of hip-hop history. The tendency among many critics and commentators to herald message rap as a relatively progressive form at this early stage misconstrues the pronounced reactionary strands that were also evident at its inception. This ideological disjuncture between social critique and the conservative defense of traditional attitudes and institutions remains a complicated issue in hip-hop culture.

Rap's Emergent Specificity

As message rap evolved, the symbolic and discursive representation of ghetto space intensified, and artists articulated a ghettocentric sensibility at a further-reduced spatial scale. The shift involved an enhanced emphasis on the portrayal of actual social landscapes, departing from the description of broad, abstract urban geographies—"the ghetto"—by identifying specific sites and places by name. Before 1988 New York was still widely regarded as the true home of rap and hip-hop and the center of rap production. Grandmaster Flash and the Furious Five's "New York, New York" (1983, Sugar Hill) can be identified as one of the first recordings to identify geospatial terrains in a more detailed and nuanced manner, transforming space into place. Released in the spring of 1983, "New York, New York" was the group's final recording together. It eventually climbed to number seventeen on *Billboard*'s Black Singles charts and was, after "The Message," their most commercially successful single.

Already fully acknowledged as the source of the expanding hip-hop scene, New York was frequently cast as the backdrop or setting for much of the lyrical and thematic content in message rap. Again, Grandmaster Flash and the Furious Five influenced the trend, establishing rap's spatial conventions while further validating the group's identity as the consummate New York City crew. Notwithstanding its title, most of the track could refer to locations in any large city, since it adheres to the earlier discursive forms established with "The Message" by featuring an array of generalized scenarios and urban vignettes. Alienation and anomie emerge as the dominant themes of this dystopian place-image, and an accompanying world-weariness pervades the lyrics, which encompass descriptions of urban individuals, architecture and urban design, and the spatial practices of a complex and difficult city life. Yet despite the abstract and fictional images that underlie much of the song's spatial orientation, the title and chorus return the emphasis to New York itself, focusing on the city's pressure and the resultant sense in its inhabitants of isolation, paranoia, and powerlessness and reinforcing the source images of this particular urban landscape:

> New York, New York, big city of dreams
> but everything in New York ain't always what it seems
> you might get fooled if you come from out of town
> but I'm down by law and I know my way around.

The track reinforces the unique and privileged vantage of the bona fide New Yorker and establishes a distinction between inside and outside, implying that an insider's perspective is closer to the actual "truth" of the place. It advances the idea that outsiders cannot expect to see and know what lies behind New York's urban facade, situating the members of the Furious Five as field reporters (or, less likely, tour guides), each of whom "knows his way around." The discourse of reality evident in the chorus is a marker of reliability grafted onto the rappers, who, as the speaking subjects, know the "truth" of the city that remains invisible to those whose origins lie elsewhere.

The twinned factors of experience and location are introduced here in oblique terms, but they remain discernible. The assertion is that over time we become experts on our environment and are subsequently capable of having personal insights on the images and practices that comprise the popular terrains of everyday urban life, for, as Sack acknowledges, "being in the world is being in, and constructing, this personal sense of place, with ourselves at the center" (1992, 11). The strategy in "New York, New York" is to construct the terms upon which the speaking subject and commercial artist, who are one and the same, can be relied upon as a valid reference, as one who is capable of leading the listener toward a set of images that best represents his or her sphere of social reality. Although this discursive strategy has evolved as common practice in contemporary rap, it was not yet the norm when "New York, New York" was released, making it an overlooked benchmark in the development of rap's spatial discourse.

Specifically referring to Greenwich Village and Forty-second Street (before it was buffed, polished, and transformed into a Disneyfied middle-American destination), Grandmaster Flash and the Furious Five introduce images of actually existing or knowable sites already heavily coded with social significance—the very reference to them evokes certain images of their "social content" or of the practices that have earned them a reputation. They identify the transgender and transvestite culture common to the gay district in and around Greenwich Village, referring to it as a cultural fact of this particular locale even though it is only one facet of the area (albeit a highly visible one). Isolating this set of localized images as part of the representative or definitive place-image is a form of spatial labeling, with attendant risks of cultural stereotyping. It remains effective as a site reference in this context, however, because of its status as a verifiable image that conforms to the strategy of articulating reality-based messages.

Rap Music and Urban Economics in the 1980s

In the period leading up to and including the first wave of recorded rap, the music was highly influenced by the economics of the primary locales of its invention and production. Examining the growth of rap through a socioeconomic lens, Clarence Lusane observes that the impact in the 1980s of the policies of Reagonomics contributed to the urgency with which urban minority youth sought new avenues for financial enrichment. As he notes:

> For many of these youth, rap became not only an outlet for social and political discourse, but also an economic opportunity that required little investment other than boldness and a competitive edge. In a period when black labor was in low demand, if one could not shoot a basketball like Michael Jordan, then the entertainment industry was one of the few legal avenues available for the get-rich consciousness that dominated the social ethos of the 1980s. (Lusane 1993, 43)

Cornel West (1989) argues, however, that entertainment has long been an option of hope (within the triad of enabling cultural practices emphasizing "the persona in performance" that include athletics and the "sermonic practices" of the clergy) in the struggle for upward economic mobility among African-Americans, especially throughout the late twentieth century. Yet the options available and the means by which they might be accessed and exploited change across social spaces with the gradually fluctuating conditions of any given historical period. Thus, the effects of the transition to new global economies since the 1960s, combined with the constraints of conservative economic and social programs that emerged with particular intensity in the early 1980s, had a double-negative effect on America's minority (and nonminority) populations, especially those that were already economically disadvantaged by poverty.

As I have argued, rap music is an undeniably urban music emanating from city core regions that communicates many of the corresponding central themes of urban existence. In the functional logics currently guiding the evolution of modern cities (relating to, for example, urban planning and civic administration), urban black youth and minority immigrant populations generally constitute a vast labor resource for the ongoing operation and maintenance of civic systems and the service industries. Or, conversely, they are framed as a major factor contributing to the crises of the American city, which require additional allocations for basic services or for such budgetary items as urban policing. William Julius Wilson (1996) addresses the historical and contemporary impact on ghetto youth "when work disappears," citing the convergent forces of devastated urban economies, the rise of the crack cocaine–fueled drug scourge, and the unraveling of traditional community patterns. Against the notion of official unemployment and resultant teen idleness, the concept of "putting in work" in the underground drug or crime economy emerged as a prominent discourse within the hip-hop generation.

It remains true, however, that contrary to prevailing images of minority youth as class members of the economically dispossessed, the individuals who comprise these social factions also constitute an influential and necessary force in an active economy. Their limited earnings still allow them to contribute to the vitality of localized ghetto and nonghetto economies. It is both false and demeaning to consider individuals from America's so-called underclasses as noncontributing members of society. Owing largely to the ways that grim statistics tend to speak on behalf of individuals and social groups, their human presence and impact often remain unregistered except at local levels of interaction.

Furthermore, the existence of gray and black markets and the trade in contraband or illegal substances cannot be fully assessed for their local economic impacts. It is safe to assume, however, that the monetary flow from these sources constitutes an important aspect of many urban localities. Whites and blacks living in impoverished environments must continually confront the negative influences of prostitution, the street drug economy, and theft, which are common facets of local economies where people are faced with poverty or desperation, even as the revenues these activities generate help to sustain individuals and families and sometimes entire localized communities under hard-pressed conditions. It is crucial also to acknowledge this phenomenon as a facet of poverty that crosses all racial and ethnic boundaries.

The reductive representation of poor minority social formations based on biased measures of economic and consumer power devalues the struggles of those who, although financially hard pressed, continue to reproduce the basic threads that can weave the principles of community into local neighborhoods. Through much of the 1970s and 1980s, the widely documented "MacJob" syndrome was a common fact of urban existence. Increasingly, unskilled urban minority youths with a high-school education or less were told to expect little more than service industry work. This was in marked contrast with the mid-1980s affluence of young urban professionals (who, both black and white, often earned grossly inflated incomes) and their ability to purchase the material symbols of wealth and financial success. Although in the 1990s economic growth in most regions lifted all social classes, the distribution of wealth remains inequitable (Blanton 2000). It is this imbalance, fraught as it is with material and symbolic representations of difference, that continues to mark much of the tension among classes in larger American cities. The imbalance is further illustrated through phenomena such as neighborhood gentrification programs and various forms of civic rezoning and development that discriminate against low-wage earners, the unemployed, and those who rely on social assistance.

Against this bleak backdrop, "getting paid" or "making ends meet" emerged as common themes in the discourses of ghetto life and were clearly audible even prior to the message-oriented rap that began with the release of "The Message." For example, Jimmy Spicer's "Money (Dollar Bill, Y'All)" (1981, Rush Groove Music) was an ode to cash, weighing the expense of basic urban survival against the ideals of materialistic accumulation and unrestrained purchasing power.

The economic disenfranchisement of many young black urban Americans provided a grounding for the ideological articulation of class consciousness within capitalism and the symbolic representation of the experience of poverty, as well as the desire to transcend it. In the early and mid-1980s, for example, members of the hip-hop culture expressed their recognition of these material disparities through a semiotic appropriation of the signs of wealth. In sartorial expression within the hip-hop culture, the exaggerated symbolic depiction of material prosperity signaled a shift away from the "leather and feather" look of Grandmaster Flash and the Furious Five or Afrika Bambaataa's rap-funk units, which had been in existence since the late 1970s. It took the form of thick gold chains, twenty-four-karat-gold braided necklaces, and diamond-studded medallions—replicating, among other things, Mercedes-Benz hood ornaments—worn over the name-brand sportswear that characterized the b-boy style of the period. In terms of a developing rap discourse, "getting paid" can be heard as the expression of an agenda for transgressing restrictive economic boundaries and, in practice, of finessing the entertainment business in order to finance a departure from the ghetto. This is perhaps most notable on the LP cover image of Eric B and Rakim's classic release *Paid in Full* (1987, Island Records), which portrays the artists wearing name-brand sports gear and huge gold chains while flaunting stacks of twenty-dollar bills. In late 1997 Tupac Shakur illustrated his economic success in hip-hop in the inside sleeve photos of *All Eyez on Me* (1996, Death Row), which feature him holding wads of cash in hundred-dollar denominations. Similarly, Puff Daddy had an R & B hit with his single "It's All about the Benjamins" (1997, Puff Daddy Records), in which the title and chorus refer to Benjamin Franklin's visage on the U.S. hundred-dollar bill.

Lusane is critical of this development among rap artists, explaining that rappers' commitment to capital accumulation actually maintains a system of enslavement "that requires an economic elite and mass deprivation" (1993, 45). As he notes, these trends reproduce the ideals of the capitalist system within the ghetto environment by reinforcing an ultimately restrictive desire for material wealth and its trappings. Lusane's assessment notwithstanding, these changes can also be envisioned in a more progressive and optimistic light. The articulation of renewed optimism and vitality that mid-1980s rap carried in the context of ghetto existence also contributed to a partial (and often inconsistently applied) reversal of the dominant idea that the ghetto was effectively a dead end for black and Latino youths. On this point, Kelley notes that "the pursuit of leisure, pleasure, and creative expression *is* labor, and . . . some African American urban youths have tried to turn that labor into cold hard cash" (1997, 45).

The emphasis on economic accumulation through hip-hop's various cultural and performative practices intensified as artists, producers, and promoters realized the commercial potentials that hip-hop offered. As Nelson and Gonzales explain, the shift from free, impromptu performances in parks and other public spaces was largely due to the sudden commercial potential of rap:

Back in the day, before rap became a recorded artform, these live shows were the few outlets where neighborhood youth could enjoy this new music; once the hip-hop crews realized there were mucho dollars to be made (popular groups made about $150 per set), the street and park shows were limited.
(Nelson and Gonzales 1991, 204)

Interestingly, the general transition into the late 1980s, when rap finally attained a relatively stable position in the music business, also introduced a major contradiction in values within the hip-hop culture that has never been fully or adequately resolved. It involves attempts by commercially successful rap artists to maintain allegiances to their localized urban environs while in some cases generating multimillion-dollar sales and earning regal incomes that allowed them to move into more upscale neighborhoods.

Lusane points out that "since 1960, black youth suffered the largest decline in employment of all component groups of all races. In 1986, in the middle of the Republican years, black teenage unemployment was officially as high as 43.7 per cent" (1993, 43). Guided by budding young artists and entrepreneurs who often had little or no experience with promotions or production but who were actively seeking alternative ways (both legal and illegal) of generating an income, the rap scene began to "rise" from the underground in a culturally and spatially expansive way, merging with the wider music industry as individuals in and around the scene began to recognize a growing potential for financial reward.[6] Rap's trajectory from the street corners and parks into the clubs and studios was also leading into the boardrooms of small, mid-sized, and (more tentatively) major record companies as the business side of the hip-hop culture was exposed to its own micro-version of economic restructuring, which eventually contributed to the mainstreaming of various core facets of the culture. These developments had the effect of recasting the ghetto as new "milieux of innovation" (Castells 1989), and in the contexts of a transnational industry dominated by corporate entertainment giants with ravenous appetites for new commodity products, rap was elevated to a new plateau as a commercial form.

By 1984 hip-hop's stylistic and thematic trends had begun to change, as had its commercial prospects and profile in the entertainment industry. Hip-hop retained its emphasis on spatiality and themes of a grounded reality, although these characteristics were reworked as the culture was introduced to more aggressive industry influences and reproduced in regions beyond New York, reaching new geographically and culturally dispersed audiences.

CHAPTER FOUR

Growing an Industry
The Corporate Expansion of Hip-Hop

❊

As rap grew and expanded throughout the 1980s, the prevalence of geographical themes and spatial practices remained central to its evolution as a facet of contemporary popular culture. Rap was the newest and most influential form of black musical expression to emerge from this period and its development is relatively easy to track, yet the means by which its position in the music industry was established are more obscure. Much of the music industry is based upon distinctions that, to varying degrees, encompass geocultural considerations. Marketing or promotional strategies and sales monitoring were broken down into national, regional, and local sectors, and demographic data were geared to the production of character profiles and purchase patterns of consumers in the areas in which they reside. Additionally, rap's evolution has been marked by internal transformations in sound, style, and theme, changes that bespeak the rhythmic and lyrical languages of its origins. In many instances these can be directly credited to the commercial requirements of music corporations, both large and small, which seek to accelerate sales and dominate markets, or, on another scale, to localized cultural inflections that inform a sense and image of place, as pockets of production activity have proliferated across North America and throughout the world.

Rap's rise in the music industry has been influenced by diverse forces that at different junctures have either constrained or motivated the genre's expansive growth. For example, Tricia Rose writes that after the 1979 release of "Rapper's Delight," rap and hip-hop were exposed to the powerful appropriative mechanisms and insidious profit imperatives of the media and fashion industries, "each of which hurried to cash in on what was assumed to be a passing fad" (1994a, 3). Rose is only partially right on this point, since the industrial expansions of rap were just as frequently engineered from within the hip-hop culture itself. Rap was (and still is) co-opted and exploited in many cases by larger external corporate entities operating outside of hip-hop's proximate spheres, but it was also deliberately merged with the larger industrial operations of the media and fashion institutions by hip-hop-savvy entrepreneurs, many of whom were themselves participants and fans. In early 2000, for example, hip-hop fashion designer companies, led by Maurice Malone and Sean "Puffy" Combs, hosted elaborate shows that mirrored the more traditional presentations of established design houses, and the hip-hop impresario Russell Simmons has his own fashion line, as do the artists Master P, Jay-Z, and the Wu-Tang Clan. Owing to these maneuvers within the existing commercial environment and industry practices, rap and hip-hop have attained global recognition and international market clout and register considerable social impact through mass diffusion and easy audience access to images and commodities.

The geographic expansion of rap and the extension of its impact as a cultural force from 1983 to 1986 can be isolated in three distinct and related factors: the ongoing processes of institutional and entrepreneurial structuring of rap within the music business; transitions in rap's musical form and lyrical content; and the early success of large-scale rap tours. While each of these factors can be assessed individually, as is often done, their geocultural components are often insufficiently contextualized. Examining them together and in tension reveals the means through which rap and hip-hop rose as important cultural and commercial forces on a broader scale. What follows in this chapter is an attempt to add specificity to the general trends influencing rap's evolution and to isolate and assess several of the more pertinent factors affecting rap's industry growth and market expansion in a manner that illuminates the geocultural elements of the genre and provides a sociospatial analysis of its history.

Locating Sugar Hill Records

Following the initial success of the Sugarhill Gang's "Rapper's Delight" in 1979 and a wave of successful recordings by Grandmaster Flash and the Furious Five, Grandmaster Melle Mel, the Funky Four + One, Sequence, and the Treacherous Three from 1980 to 1984, Sugar Hill Records was at the forefront of the rap music industry. That it was the first label to successfully record and market rap suggests it was a crucial force within New York's hip-hop and b-boy scene at the time, functioning in a key role at the epicenter of the exploding culture that encompassed the triad of rap, break-dancing, and graffiti art. Yet the main force behind the label's foray into rap, Sylvia Robinson, was a middle-aged black businesswoman with a moderately successful past as a recording artist whose presence on the club and street scene where rap was tried and tested was marginal. This geocultural distance is evident in an early article on hip-hop featured in *Rolling Stone* (Carr 1983). Robinson is pictured in the opulence of her "twenty-two room home in Englewood, New Jersey," while the artists Grandmaster Flash, the Crash Crew, Sequence (who were all on the Sugar Hill label at the time), and DJ Starsky are pictured in nightclubs such as New York's Disco Fever and the Roxy, where rap had become a mainstay.

Robinson's experience and familiarity with industry operations and her marketing and promotional savvy proved to be indispensable to the label's rise as a force in rap production. With her husband and business partner Joe Robinson, she oversaw several minor black record labels, and the couple was well positioned to troll for unknown and untapped talent in the local music scene in and around the New York metropolitan area. The Robinsons quickly capitalized on rap's "fresh" quality by committing the emergent genre to vinyl on their Sugar Hill label, distributing "Rapper's Delight" in the commodity form most favored by DJs—the twelve-inch single —and marketing it through small and mid-sized record retailers and DJ shops in predominantly black neighborhoods in New York, New Jersey, and elsewhere. With the recording of "Rapper's Delight," Sugar Hill Records changed the trajectory of the New York–based hip-hop scene by introducing a new commodity form and commercial option that eventually lifted the music out of the localized cultural enclaves within which it had being gestating for several years.

Focusing on themes of locale in rap's outward growth, S. H. Fernando Jr. gives an account of Sugar Hill's opportunistic practices that, in various versions, is now a standard facet of rap's popular lore:

Rap's sudden explosion from the underground occurred quite accidentally, when Sylvia Robinson, a former singer and co-owner of the Englewood, New Jersey–based Sugar Hill Records, heard one of these bootleg tapes and decided to make a rap record. A club bouncer named Hank was rapping along to a performance by rapper Grandmaster Caz while working at a pizza parlor near Robinson's home. Immediately intrigued with what she heard, she approached Hank about being the third member of an outfit she was putting together called the Sugarhill Gang.

(Fernando 1994, 12)

This account reveals the disparities between generations and between sociospatial locations within the music scene itself as it grew into a more commercially lucrative form. Sylvia Robinson had previously heard about the underground hip-hop scene from her younger son, Joe Jr. As the narrative explains, she then stumbled onto rap in her own neighborhood and heard something that made sense to her in commercial terms. Following this initial exposure, which occured in an entirely informal context, she quickly mobilized her resources, assembling the artists who comprise the Sugarhill Gang herself rather than tapping into a preexisting and established performing group. This kind of corporate manipulation of talent is not unprecedented in popular music, extending from the male doo-wop groups of the 1950s through the Monkees, Menudo, the New Kids on the Block, and more recently, 'N Sync and the Backstreet Boys. In Sugar Hill's case, the exercise of control over cultural production reflects a pronounced lack of consideration for the integrity of the emergent form and for the pioneers who were nurturing its development in other localized enclaves, unaware that their cultural practices were being coopted for commercial presentation on a wider stage.

Robinson's "discovery," Henry Jackson (or Big Bank Hank, as he became known), was responding to sounds he was hearing on a regular basis while working and partying in New York's uptown clubs, although he, like Sylvia and Joe Robinson, was more of an interloper than an innovator. Between the Robinsons' and Jackson's positions were those artists in the uptown boroughs who were composing and performing the music without concern for or thought of its commercial potential or the broader appeal that rap might have. In fact, Grandmaster Caz, of the Cold Crush Brothers, is most frequently credited as the original author of the Sugarhill Gang's first recorded lyrics, and observers on the hip-hop scene at the time regarded "Rapper's Delight" as a case of unethical, if timely, plagiarism. Against the contrived construction of the Sugarhill Gang as a recording rap act, MCs and DJs in New York's uptown sections were actively carving out reputations for themselves in the streets, community centers, and clubs of their home boroughs and neighborhoods and within the limited spaces of leisure and pleasure that were available to them as teenagers.

These distinctly local geographies are, of course, interconnected through the mobility of performing artists, audience members, and producers and have overlapping influences. Still, there remains an undeniable effect of spatial variation that facilitates or encourages different practices within each separate domain. In this stage of its evolution, rap was highly influenced by its cultural ties to particular neighborhoods or to the boroughs in which it was being performed and enjoyed as an increasingly central leisure option. In terms of scale, rap was primarily a local phenomenon with corresponding local impact, but it was expanding in ways that linked diverse localities in a lively dialogic intercourse. It presented opportunities for the extension of a more cohesive, citywide hip-hop scene within deeply competitive contexts that were based in neighborhood and interborough combat among sound-system DJs, break-dance crews, and graffiti artists.

Sugar Hill Records attracted many early rap artists through its initial willingness to take a risk on the new music when few other labels would, and following its success with "Rapper's Delight," artists were drawn to the label as the biggest and most recognizable name in rap recording. The label's investment in recorded rap was soon rewarded. However, despite some commercial successes, many of the recording artists on the label's roster complained that they never received the royalties they were due and accused the Robinsons of various improprieties and deceits. Sugar Hill's allegedly unscrupulous management tactics and exploitative contracts generated considerable ill will among its contracted talent. The label's reputation was further sullied by its association with its most infamous financial backer, Morris Levy, "the 'Godfather' of the American music business," who "reverberated with the industry's street mythos" (Dannen 1991, 32–33) and ultimately met his professional demise following his conviction in May 1988 on mob-related extortion charges. These shortcomings, combined with the emergence of a growing field of similarly small and aggressive labels catering to the rap market, drew artists elsewhere and eventually diminished Sugar Hill's commercial hegemony.

The label's successes notwithstanding, Sylvia Robinson's professional distance from the scene worked in the end to her disadvantage and inhibited her ability to stay abreast of aesthetic and stylistic trends and of new and breaking artists and to knowledgeably assess the talents of DJs and MCs. Even Sugar Hill's New Jersey–based operation was a source of skepticism among many in the midst of the New York rap scene. In the early days, when the hip-hop culture was still isolated primarily in the Bronx and Harlem, New Jersey was perceived by "insiders" as being outside the loop or beyond the scene. Their spatial reasoning dictated that adult label executives based in Englewood could not possibly comprehend hip-hop's rapid changes as the music evolved from week to week in New York's uptown neighborhoods. Despite their initial surprise (and displeasure) at the fact that a rap song had been produced and released by individuals who were, at best, only peripherally involved in the burgeoning scene, many of the rap artists and DJs who were most active in the genre's development were impressed to hear "their" music on radios and in clubs in recorded form for the first time.

The struggle among rap artists and producers in cultural terms was not rooted in the issue of whether or not rap should be economically channeled or remade in commercial forms. It was already moving in that direction as early as 1978 through the entrepreneurial initiatives of local promoters booking multi-act shows throughout the Bronx and Harlem and of rap artists themselves, who, adhering to the do-it-yourself ethic, often enjoyed brisk sales of self-produced cassette tapes sold without the benefits of formal commercial merchandising or distribution apparatuses. Indeed, as Kelley explains, "a whole underground economy emerged, which ranged from printing and selling T-shirts advertising crews (Hip Hop groups), to building speakers, reconfiguring turntables, buying and selling records and bootleg tapes, even to selling food and drink at these outdoor events" (1997, 65). The issue, then and now, involves questions of artistic and financial control: who can legitimately represent the business side of the music, and what is that person's connection to the scene in general?

The first hip-hop practitioners displayed a certain proprietary logic that was ghettocentric in its geocultural composition and Afrocentric in terms of its generally applied core racial identity. In its earliest stages of development and emergence as a popular musical form, rap was situated as a black music, made for and by black (and Latino) youths who lived primarily in America's urban environments. As white label owners, producers, and musicians gradually entered the scene and the music was targeted toward new commercial markets and shipped to broader regional and national audiences, defining the music solely in terms of an African-American context became more problematic.

There is a latent connection here with the economic visions espoused in Harlem in the 1920s through the Garveyist movement, which was founded on a commitment to keeping wealth in the black community, although "community" in this contemporary instance does not revolve exclusively around race and a shared African heritage (or the family kinship ties to which Gilroy [1992] refers). After the funk and soul musics of the 1960s and 1970s had been diluted and mass marketed to both older and mixed audiences,[1] many black youths maintained that rap was theirs and, as such, was something worth protecting.[2] Addressing the threat of appropriation by the culture industry, Tricia Rose locates rap within a tradition of black musical forms and styles that were created according to African-American cultural contexts and later "discovered" by capital interests and the wider (i.e., white) public. Rather than assuming a singularly detrimental outcome, she suggests that these industry machinations have the potential to engender new, hybrid forms of cultural resistance:

The process of incorporation and marginalization of black practitioners has also fostered the development of black forms and practices that are less and less accessible, forms that require knowledge of black language and styles in order to participate. . . . In addition to the sheer pleasure black musicians derive from developing a new and exciting style, these black cultural reactions to American culture suggest a reclaiming of the definition of blackness and an attempt to retain aesthetic control over black cultural forms. (Rose 1994a, 6)

This notion of ownership and possessiveness in hip-hop is related to the particular logics of authenticity that slowly emerged in rap's discourses following the release of "The Message" in 1982 and numerous other commercial recordings in this period. As the ghetto was being articulated as the privileged site of authentic black experience, rap was gradually imbued with a similar character, as the authentic sound track to contemporary black *youth* experience. The thematic influences of ghettocentric signification traced along an axis of authenticity, experience, and cultural identity have, with few exceptions, proven difficult for white artists (and major record companies) to appropriate to the same extent as they did earlier musical forms such as R & B or rock 'n' roll. A similar pattern can be discerned in the development of reggae, which underwent an intensified Afrocentric shift in the early and mid-1970s when the Rastafarian religion rose as a culturally defining force in the music's aesthetics and discursive patterns.

Within the geographies of difference and exclusion that are informed by multiple relational factors, the protective stance expressed within hip-hop also reflected ingrained suspicions of outsiders, who were perceived as exploitative opportunists seeking to subvert the art and culture of ghetto youth according to their own corporate economic interests. This can be recognized as a product of geocultural "othering" that reverses society's dominant othering practices, which tend to position black and Latino youths on the low end of the scale as the undesirable others. The locale of the ghetto and the dynamics of age, race, and class initially cut the music and its primary producers off from the collective social mainstream. This had the effect of reinforcing the underground marginality of the music in relation to the wider industry while simultaneously contributing to pride and defensiveness among many ghetto and urban youth. Thus, while its designation as "street" music, later grafted onto rap by industry executives, had a certain marketing utility that was alternately derogatory and romantic, in the minds of many rap artists "the street" became the official source of the music's authenticity and cultural value. Marginality, therefore, functioned as a protective factor in hip-hop's formative phase.

David Toop describes eager middle-aged entrepreneurs, among them Bobby Robinson of Enjoy Records and Paul Winley of Paul Winley Records, who heard rap and, despite their disconnection from the core activities of the scene itself, were ideally positioned to witness its effects and gauge its commercial potential. Toop writes:

With Sugar Hill proving that there was a new market for streetcorner sounds, the old-time entrepreneurs dusted off the ancient contracts and moved in. . . . The early records are confusing, partly because they transferred a sound-system-based music onto disc and partly because some of the artists were recorded not so much for their talent but because they happened to hang out down the block from the record company. (Toop 1984, 100)

The initiatives of local record producers played an important role in this early developmental stage of rap. As Negus (1999) explains, deliberate strategies to identify new trends and innovations in hip-hop developed later, with companies assigning personnel to stake out the locales where youths congregated. But in the early stages there was a tendency toward capitalizing on more organic localized connections and social alliances.

Once displaced from the almost exclusively live contexts of streets, parks, house parties, and mid-sized club venues, rap remained inherently connected to New York's black communities, its revenues and returns circulating primarily within a contained social realm. Even after "Rapper's Delight" began attracting wider industry attention after 1979 (as the steadily proliferating articles in *Billboard* illustrate), most record labels working in the genre were black owned and operated. As the music developed aesthetically and expanded its range of public dissemination, it continued to be inscribed and shaped by a conjunction of localized cultural forces that were inflected by life in the black neighborhoods of New York City. The prevailing power in this sense of community both influenced rap's creative and innovative evolution and inhibited the speed and manner in which it was commercially exploited. David Toop suggests that "the lack of industry connections in the Bronx, the young age group involved in hip hop and the radical primitivism of the music itself conspired to produce an island of relatively undisturbed invention in a sea of go-getter commerce" (1984, 78). Keith Negus repositions this argument, however, noting that by approaching these developments with an understanding of deeper historical relations between major and independent labels and between major labels and black music in general, it is evident that "it is not as straightforward as this: the major companies have also allowed the minor companies to carve out such a niche" (1999, 495).

Before "Rapper's Delight" began its ascent on the black music and pop charts, it was spinning in the roller rinks, discos, and dance clubs in New York, which were the cornerstone of the night-life scene for young blacks and Latinos. The interconnections between nightclubs and music outlets catering to black neighborhoods and communities formed an important geoeconomic nexus that facilitated rap's rapid growth and dissemination among black and Latino teens and influenced the tastes of adventurous white teenagers (a group that has, incidentally, been underanalyzed in terms of rap consumption and listening patterns[3]). As a result of Joe and Sylvia Robinson's experience and longevity in the industry, Sugar Hill Records had a well-established distribution system in place at the end of the 1970s that serviced the black retail and consumer sectors. Their distribution network, which was later enhanced through a distribution contract with MCA

Records in the mid-1980s, was extremely important to the success of "Rapper's Delight," since the label served a limited but highly responsive consumer market. An advertisement for the Sugarhill Gang's eponymous LP, released in 1980, indicates their distribution reach: the thirty Sugar Hill distributors it lists span the nation from New York to Honolulu and from New Orleans to Milwaukee. Of further relevance was Sugar Hill's executive experience in the industry, which enhanced the company's capacity to meet wholesale and retail orders with relative efficiency, unlike many similar-sized labels. Shortly after its release, "Rapper's Delight" was heard throughout North America, and it soon appeared as a regular selection on *Billboard*'s "Disco Action" club-play charts, which featured the choice DJ selections garnering regular play in dance clubs across the United States and Canada.

There was little thought at this point of packaging rap in LP album format, since few acts had sufficient material to fill an album—and keep it interesting—and, as many industry insiders believed, the music was too "new" to the ears of mainstream America to warrant LP release. Sugar Hill's decision to release a full-length album by the Sugarhill Gang in 1980 was premature. Made up of an uneven compilation of singles, the LP seemed like an obvious attempt to exploit the group's only hit single and was commercially inert, appearing only briefly on *Billboard*'s Soul LPs chart. Even after the initial success of "Rapper's Delight," major record labels maintained a casual wait-and-see attitude toward rap; the LP's lack of success was a further indicator that rap's commercial viability was not yet established. In February 1980 *Billboard* ran an article under the headline "Rap Records: Are They Fad or Permanent?" The question was posed in terms of the genre's market sustainability. Though the article fails to provide a satisfactory answer, its overview of rap's cultural evolution and brief account of independent-label roster development indicate that the major labels were still not, at this stage, prominently involved in the genre.

Despite rap's steady commercial growth and geographic spread from 1978 to 1982, it was still primarily considered within the industry to be a regional phenomenon centered in the northeastern United States. While several releases reached the top of North America's DJ club play charts and attained gold record sales and hit status, there was still no strong evidence of a developing hip-hop scene beyond the East Coast. This is illustrated, for example, in a 1983 *Billboard* article that refers to Kurtis Blow's growing popular appeal and commercial success, noting that his rising profile enabled him to perform in California "where rap had never had that much impact" ("Rap Rocks" 1983, 50). Hip-hop's cultural influences were restricted by the fact that it was not yet fully integrated with the wider mass-media systems of dissemination: it developed regionally but did not exert much influence on a wider scale, sporadic hits notwithstanding. It is also worth noting that Blow was uniquely positioned within the rap industry at the time, having signed with a major label, Mercury Records. This provided access to a larger promotional budget, including expenses to cover his appearances throughout the country. While Blow's contemporaries were capable of building local reputations and slowly developing wider appeal through distribution of their singles, their careers were relatively constrained due to restricted promotional budgets and virtually no tour support. Major-label contracts were not a panacea for this dilemma, since they introduced their own constraining features. In its commercial infancy, rap suffered a dual displacement based on its marginality within the labels' already marginal black music divisions. This often meant that it was grossly undersupported and overlooked by executives who were pressured by their companies either to deliver huge hits or to develop artists with career and commercial longevity.

Billboard's reference to rap's minimal influence in California stands as an important temporal marker and helps to establish a more precise time line for its geographic expansion to dispersed regional markets. In some cases, rap was disseminated through patterns of migration between the East and West Coasts and other locales, with records, tapes, and the b-boy persona circulating as part of the regular human flow between different zones. Brian Cross's detailed study of the Los Angeles rap scene (1993) describes numerous interrelated factors that both constrained and slowly enlivened the Los Angeles hip-hop culture. Among these are the early influences of established New York hip-hop DJs who had permanently migrated to Los Angeles to work on various projects; the significance of an all-ages club, "Radio," that became the official home of the emergent LA hip-hop subculture; and infrequent appearances by important trend-setting New York acts. Cross explains that before 1983 access to new material was severely restricted on the West Coast:

Much of the early or old-school hip hop was recorded on independent labels (Uni, Sugar Hill, Enjoy, Tuff City) which were hard to find. This lack of access led to the development of a split in LA hiphop between those that had access and those who stayed with the electropop and West coast funk. Those on the street who had access generally had it through New York relatives or friends.   (Cross 1993, 21)

As this suggests, the informal mechanisms of social mobility and geographic peregrinations throughout the United States were still the primary means through which rap was disseminated. In its commercial infancy, it was still generally considered by major industry executives to be unviable for national distribution, which, as Cross suggests, stilted its growth while producing interesting cultural and stylistic cleavages that turned out to create a more diverse range of rap subgenres.

It was only with the advent of a more entrenched and established industrial infrastructure that rap and hip-hop's influence was gradually extended beyond New York and the northeastern seaboard. Sales of recorded rap sharply escalated in 1982–84, and rap appeared on *Billboard*'s black music charts with increasing regularity. In this phase, rap recordings periodically crossed over to the pop music charts, posting significant sales figures despite being perceived within the wider mainstream industry as an underground novelty. Additionally, during this period the general concept of crossover itself underwent a transformation, following the massive success of Michael Jackson's "Thriller" (1983, CBC/Epic) and, to a lesser extent, Prince's *1999* (1983, Warner) and *Purple Rain* (1984, Warner), which merged rock and funk aesthetics in new and exciting forms. Commenting on this general phase of hip-hop's evolution, Reebee Garofalo wryly states that "more than five years after the subculture had come into being, hip hop was 'discovered' in turn, by the music business, the print media, and the film industry. Though the first wave of the movement had long since peaked, hip hop was accorded all the flash of the new 'in thing'" (1990, 112).

On the same theme, but suggesting a subtle and pertinent geographic emphasis, Nelson George explains that a combination of separate circles of activity and enterprise and the overbearing rigidity of the corporate music world blinded the major labels and contributed to their slow acknowledgment of rap's artistic and commercial potentials:

The New York–based talent scouts were so office-bound, taking meetings with managers and listening to tapes from song publishers, that they failed to venture up the road to Harlem and the South Bronx where, in the middle of the nation's most depressing urban rot, something wonderful was happening. Because the big boys were asleep at the wheel, rap would spend most of its young life promoted and recorded by independent labels run by hustling entrepreneurs.

(George 1989a, 189)

The rapid proliferation of small independent labels (such as Enjoy, Jive, Profile, Select, Sleeping Bag, Streetwise, Sugar Hill, Tommy Boy, and Tuff City) catering to the growing rap consumer audience helped to establish the institutional structures within the hip-hop culture. They provided the more formal mechanisms for discovering and promoting new talent and for distributing artists' recordings, although this was eventually aided through the interventions of major labels, which provided the necessary distribution apparatuses to ship the music nationwide.

Headlines in *Billboard* reflect some of the developments influencing rap at the time. Covering the rap beat, Nelson George described the emergence of a new rap-oriented production sector (1982, 10), and the following month an article appeared under the headline "Indies Keep Rap Product Popping: Despite Sales Slowdown, Genre Maintains Steady Profile" (1982, 6). Both articles acknowledged that rap was almost exclusively under the purview of independent producers. In a special review on the state of the black music industry, *Billboard* later reported on the central role of independent labels in rap's artistic and commercial development through 1984 and 1985. Under the headline "Indies Stake in Street and Third World Music May Prove a Goldmine," the article described how "independent labels fathered rap, a genre whose timely arrival created a new piece of the market pie for indies when the majors stepped heavily onto the dance floor in 1983" (Freeman 1985, BM 2).

While various independent labels explored the developing genre, simultaneously capitalizing on its emergent popularity and nurturing its growth, the major labels continued to maintain a cautious distance. Even as late as 1985, there was surprisingly little direct major-label involvement in rap production. Profiling the success of the Boogie Boys' release "A Fly Girl" (1985, Capitol), *Billboard* reported on the irony that "the fact that this catchy rap record made the black top 10 is not as surprising as the fact that it's on a major label, Capitol Records." The article quotes Capitol's vice president for black music promotion, Ronnie Jones, who states, "Most conglomerate labels haven't gotten into rap because they don't have the tools—that is, street people with the knowledge of the market to work it properly" ("Major Label Rap Hit" 1985, 63). As Negus explains, however, the reference to "street people" who harbor an innate understanding of the hip-hop scene and rap market overrides the concurrent message that the corporate labels adhere to "organizational practices through which rap is confined to a specific 'position' within the industry and not accorded as much investment (economic, staff, time) as other types of music" (1999, 497).

The competition among small labels to push artists and recordings into the spotlight led to numerous skirmishes in the struggle to establish market superiority. Indeed, Sugar Hill's desire to dominate was so intense that, following its first brush with success, the label was accused of indiscriminately signing artists in an attempt to take the competition off the streets and corner the market on New York's most viable rap talents. From 1979 to 1982 Sugar Hill decimated a smaller rap label, Enjoy, by luring virtually all of its artists, including Grandmaster Flash and the Furious Five, with the promise of better exposure (Terrell 1999). Another example of market competitiveness can be seen in the 1983 dispute between Sugar Hill and Tommy Boy Records over Keith LeBlanc's "No Sell Out," an important track that linked rap and black militancy early on by incorporating the voice of Malcolm X in the recording. The rights to the recording were contested by Sugar Hill, which claimed proprietary authority based on the rationale that LeBlanc was then employed as a session musician at the label, most of the track was recorded at Sugar Hill's Englewood studio, and the label assumed that the executive producer, Marshall Chess, was actually recording the track for Chess Records, a division of Sugar Hill. In early December 1983 a court decision awarded Tommy Boy the rights to manufacture and distribute the single. The record's release subsequently boosted Tommy Boy's industry profile while challenging and diminishing Sugar Hill's dominance.

Among the artists themselves, the earlier forms of interborough market competition that were framed within territorial struggles between DJs and their sound system crews were rapidly being transformed as the competition came to be refocused on the studio and the record market. The desire to place a recorded single in retail outlets and clubs became a dominant motivation among artists, who sought to outdo one another. Signing a record contract or achieving club or radio play became a new symbol of rap supremacy.

The spatial dynamics of the rap scene were dramatically altered when the recording studio rose as a central site of cultural labor and production, displacing free, live outdoor parties and emerging alongside the clubs and concert stages as a prominent rap performance locale. Describing the impact of the shift toward recorded rap, Afrika Bambaataa states that "everybody was nervous. It took the excitement away. We didn't have the parties. Everyone could go out and buy the record." Grandmaster Flash also describes the transformation of the scene, noting that the emphasis on extended DJ performances was disrupted by the new celebrity status accorded to artists with label contracts and records: "The street thing flipped. Like one DJ would play eight different clubs in one night and not really have an audience anymore. You lost your home champion because there was nobody there. I personally would like to have stayed away from records a little longer" (George 1993, 50).

Flash's reference to the loss of a "home champion" reinforces the fact that with recording, rap's previous foundational structures, which were linked to neighborhoods or select nightclubs and organized around localized territorial affiliations, had begun eroding, undermining the connections between DJs and MCs and their originary locales. Artists became public figures on a broader, more extended scale, with responsibilities to a wider constituency. This contributed to the taxing demands of performing throughout the local club circuits in a single evening and, eventually, touring and performing a series of one-night engagements in distant cities. Such changes also reflect the lucrative economic dimension that quickly arose as rap's popularity expanded, with DJs and MCs commanding appearance fees from each club for their brief performances.

In the rush to capitalize on rap's commercial potentials, the short-lived hegemony of black-owned labels was also contested as numerous white producers, including Arthur Baker (Streetwise), Cory Robbins (Profile), Aaron Fuchs (Tuff City), and Tommy Silverman (Tommy Boy), entered the business. Although lingering resentments about this development prevail in hip-hop circles, in many instances the wider rap scene benefited from their involvement, since numerous white-owned labels became important players in rap's elevation in the music industry.[4] As Sugar Hill demonstrated, signing with a black-owned label did not guarantee that artists would receive fair and respectful treatment; many white label owners proved to be more scrupulous and attentive to their artists' concerns. It should also be stressed, however, that the systemic racism that was—and remains—rampant throughout the industry at large undoubtedly played a part in the white-owned labels' ability to gain a foothold in the industry and to secure distribution deals with the major labels.

Rush Productions and Def Jam Records

It is appropriate to focus on the emergence of Rush Productions (later Rush Artists Management) and Def Jam Records for their central significance as rap slowly underwent transitions within the music industry. While they are exemplars of activity taking place in a wider or more general way as rap became an integrated commercial aspect in popular music, Rush and Def Jam also demonstrate several unique elements that illuminate the complexities of race in America.

Under the guidance of the rap impresario Russell Simmons, Rush Productions played a constructive role in rap's establishment as a permanent facet in contemporary popular music. Recounting Simmons's introduction to rap, Fernando reconstructs the image of a twenty-year-old City College of New York student hearing the rapper Eddie Cheeba on 125th Street in the heart of Harlem:

He spent more time soaking up Harlem nightlife than at school. Disco was all the rage, but one night in 1977 at the Charles Gallery, a club on 125th Street, near the Apollo Theater, he got his first taste of something new. . . . Russell, like everyone in attendance, was completely bowled over, and as the coursing blood tingled in his veins he realized something that the hip uptown crowd already knew: A rapper is the life of the party. In the fall of 1977, with his crew at CCNY, he decided to throw a party of his own. (Fernando 1994, 154–55)

On first examination, this narrative follows the standard "great men, great works" approach to history, with the details of where and when Simmons first encountered rap being of central relevance. This telling reveals a double-faceted image of authenticity, organized spatially and temporally, that reinforces the point that Simmons was a participant and a rap "fan," a member of the evolving hip-hop scene "back in the day," before rap was a popular commercial form. What is most interesting, however, is the consistency of spatial detail with which the story is presented, indicating that geography, space, and place *mean something,* that they have an important bearing on the identities of the main figures involved and, beyond that, on our understanding of the evolution of the rap genre.

The *where* of this encounter manifests a deep sense of place that is structured through the citation of architectural landmarks, street names, and other sites of social significance. For example, it is pertinent that this revelatory moment occurs in Harlem and not in the Bronx (rap's birthplace) or Queens (Simmons's birthplace), since Harlem has long been both a real and an imaginary core of African-American cultural identification. It is a cultural crossroads, an urban space in which the cross-pollination of black cultural practices from various regions of the black diaspora (or, on a more localized scale, various city boroughs) transpires. Harlem's deep cultural importance and prominent cultural locales have a powerful and enduring effect on the constitution of individual and group identities in black America. In short, Harlem has symbolic value: 125th Street and the Apollo Theatre are similarly imbued with symbolic authority as familiar markers of black cultural tradition and affirmative cultural identity. These factors facilitate the elevation of Simmons as a legendary figure, locating him within a continuum of black cultural innovation and leadership that has traditionally emanated from Harlem and the upper boroughs of New York City.

Simmons began as a small-to-medium-scale concert promoter in New York, booking rap into high school gymnasiums, university fraternity houses, and various neighborhood community centers, forging citywide connections under the banner of Rush Productions. His reputation as a high-energy, fast-talking nightfly—hence "Rush"—preceded him, and his ubiquitous presence in the early hip-hop scene gave him an insider's knowledge of many of rap's unique characteristics, providing him with an advantageous perspective on the requirements for a successful event. Simmons was a rapid convert to rap and hip-hop, but as Fernando explains, his cultural background is incongruous with the prevailing assumptions about hip-hop and its relationship to the ghetto:

Russell Simmons's neighborhood of Hollis, in the reaches of Queens, was an area in transition while he was growing up. He saw Hollis go from being predominantly white when his family first moved there in 1964 to all black by the time he was in high school. Thus, from an early age, Russell learned to walk the line between the middle-class mentality of his parents, both college-educated professionals, and the mercenary activity of the streets, where you were either "down" or a "sucker."

(Fernando 1994, 154)

Fernando locates Simmons's background in a geocultural middle ground, implying that his origins positioned him between two dispersed poles of cultural experience from which he drew inspiration in equal doses, as a middle-class rap entrepreneur who at the same time had ghetto familiarity and street credentials. Simmons himself is quoted as saying that "in Queens you could hang out on the corner but there was safety in the house; in Queens, one could be part of a gang, but it was just part of a growing-up process—in the ghetto it's a lifestyle" (Nelson and Gonzales 1991, 203).

Implicit in this description of social space and cultural origins are a series of assumptions about class and racial influences. Indeed, race remains a core or determining element. Stereotypical representations of race, space, and place are mobilized when one enters the discourse of difference, and Simmons is cast as a by-product of convergent cultural influences and the interrelationship between the stable and resource-rich environment of the suburbs and the more volatile and, arguably, enriching organic forces of the ghetto. Yet this particular historiography suggests that, had either dimension of Simmons's geocultural background dominated (i.e., if he was too urban—"too black"—or, conversely, too suburban), he would likely not have become a "mogul of rap," as the *Wall Street Journal* described him (Cox 1984). It constructs an ideal image based on the convergence of the "best" elements of each sociocultural space, positioning Simmons as an entrepreneurial and cultural innovator who was able to transgress the borders of racial and cultural difference or, more to the point, to remake difference into a positive and productive force, to make it work for him.

The mythologization of Simmons's past and the particular manner in which his background has been articulated toward future successes remains virtually uncritiqued, a situation that allows the underlying logic of this story of racial and cultural hybridity to prevail as a determining factor in his ascendance in the rap music industry. This might be compared with the vastly different narratives associated with the Death Row Records executive Marion "Suge" Knight, whose alleged gang connections and violent, strong-arm business tactics position him within a radically different discursive frame that includes racial stereotypes of black male aggression and volatility. At a deeper level of analytical refinement, Simmons can be regarded as a contemporary embodiment of W. E. B. Du Bois's "double consciousness," which is frequently cited as a fundamental concept underlying the construction of the African-American identity. As Du Bois writes, "One ever feels his two-ness—an American, a Negro; two souls, two thoughts, two unreconciled strivings; two warring ideals in one dark body, whose dogged strength alone keeps it from being torn asunder" (1994, 2). Perhaps, at even closer range, Simmons is the embodiment of the hyphen that straddles cultural sensibilities—African-American—in terms of racial and class-based cultural identity.

Underlying the narrativization of Simmons's rise in the music industry is a more interesting tale of American social reality. Although he has been heralded for his accomplishments in the industry and for elevating rap music, he is also celebrated as an example of black American enterprise waged through an ability to finesse the rigid spatial definitions of difference and to fluidly cross over and pass through the traditional territories of white and black social interaction. Simmons's primary achievement, from the perspective of most early commentators, was his capacity to navigate both implicitly and explicitly enforced geographical boundaries, which are often also racial boundaries, and to merge the starkly divided cultural practices of hip-hop with the business practices of the music industry. In the 1990s these same attributes emerged in the megaproducer and hip-hop artist Sean Combs, who, like Simmons, moves in an elite executive sphere and the hip-hop underground with equal ease.[5]

From 1977 to 1982 Simmons was perhaps the most successful entrepreneur among a small contingent of agents and promoters who helped to establish a regular local circuit for New York rap acts, adhering to common small-scale promotional practices such as posting advertisements throughout New York's black communities and the blanket distribution of flyers and handbills. He established close connections with rap producers, artists, and consumers, surveying shifting tastes and demands among the young and often fickle audiences with which he was intimately familiar. As the rap scene itself became more coherent (demonstrating consistency in terms of frequency of performance events, developing a relatively loyal fan base, and spawning several local celebrity figures who regularly drew crowds), these practices developed into logical and efficient expressions of localized business savvy. As Simmons gradually improved his promotional skills, he (along with other local promoters operating on a similar scale) came to be identified as a force in the very construction of this consistency. The rap music scene and the spread of the hip-hop culture were spontaneous only up to a point; by the early 1980s they had entered a new phase that was more clearly commercial as young black entrepreneurs learned how, in the words of Robin Kelley (1997), to "put culture to work."

Exploiting his insider familiarity with both the uptown hip-hop scene and the midtown Manhattan nightclubs, Simmons successfully moved his parties downtown to the larger clubs and concert halls, which were more racially and culturally mixed. The effects of this mobility can be discerned in a 1983 *Billboard* article that posed the question, "Is rap music now as much a part of the new wave scene as pointy shoes and streaked hair?" ("Rap Rocks" 1983, 50). Simmons's dominance in rap promotion was partly due to the effectiveness with which he was able to position rap acts for maximum crossover with the predominantly white post-punk and new wave audiences. This proved to be a crucial move from a business angle. He accelerated this crossover trend through more concentrated marketing and promotional strategies on a larger commercial scale from 1984 to 1988, and his greatest successes were in fact based on his ability to facilitate the broadened appeal of Rush acts. The organized structure that Simmons and his competitors helped to instill in the New York rap scene was an important factor in the process of establishing the necessary conduits for rap to reach national and international markets, geographically expanding its listenership.

Noting rap's appeal beyond the narrowly demarcated black youth audience, Simmons stated that "the newer Rap artists have more in common musically with rock 'n' roll than any commercial r&b since the days when r&b *was* rock 'n' roll" ("Rap Rocks" 1983, 50). This evaluation, while expressive of a particular view of the history of American popular music, is clearly formed within the subtle and implicit articulation of racial and class distinctions. Simmons is speaking about music, but he is also speaking about audience formations and listening contexts that have much more to do with the dynamics of a racially diverse America than with musical genres per se. Afrika Bambaataa and others have also explained that their early fan base included white teens who were associated with the Manhattan punk and new wave scenes that converged around night spots such as the Mudd Club or Danceteria (the influences of which can be seen in photographs of Bambaataa's bands, bedecked in multihued mohawk hairstyles and elaborate leather costumes that later became the target of derisive commentary by Run-D.M.C.). By moving his acts into clubs other than those catering primarily to black and Latino patrons and steering rap toward venues with more racially and economically diverse audiences, Simmons was gradually laying the groundwork for rap's expansion and his own rising influence within the industry.

By 1984 Simmons had an established track record in the New York concert scene working exclusively with rap acts, and Rush Productions became the main booking agency for many of the top artists in the city. From about 1984 to 1987 the rap scene produced its first bona fide stars. Among them were Run-D.M.C., LL Cool J, Whodini, the Fat Boys, and the Beastie Boys, and they were all represented by Simmons.[6] When Brian Cross (1993) describes the impact and influence of New York acts, which carried the vestiges of the New York scene with them on their California tours throughout the 1980s, most of the groups mentioned were on the Rush roster. Indeed, the extent to which acts represented by Rush dominated the genre between 1983 and 1987 can be seen in the pages of *Billboard*, where scores of articles and columns on rap are dedicated to Rush protégés.

Simmons aggressively booked his acts into clubs and concert halls throughout the Northeast and also managed their recording contracts. He assigned the artist rights to various labels, most notably Profile Records, which had substantial success with its top recording act, Run-D.M.C. Record sales for Run-D.M.C., Whodini, and LL Cool J drew attention to Rush, while the agency actively reinforced the popular profile of its main clients. For example, Rush artists were prominently featured in the film *Krush Groove* (which was loosely based on Simmons's biography) and the Fresh Fest tours, and Simmons was involved in negotiating a commercial endorsement contract between Run-D.M.C and the Adidas sportswear company based on the strength of the hit single "My Adidas" (1986, Profile). Simmons consciously endeavored to bring rap more directly into line with prevailing practices within the industry's rock music sector. He confirmed his role as a dominant force in rap's creative and commercial evolution when he formed Def Jam records with Rick Rubin in 1984. The label's formation was a logical step in a rap enterprise that was structured on the belief that rap was not solely of interest to the black music-buying public.

Like that of Simmons, Rick Rubin's personal history is frequently conveyed with a strong emphasis on his geocultural background and the social contexts of his introduction to the hip-hop culture. Rubin had grown up in a middle-class home on Long Island where, as lore has it, he developed a love of heavy metal and punk music, and he even performed briefly in a New York punk band. But he is also described as having been a teen rebel whose tastes encompassed rap as an alternative to the mainstream fare that seemed to be identified with his suburban background and his racial and class origins (Farr 1994). When he met Simmons through the club culture of the New York hip-hop scene, Rubin was living in a student dormitory at New York University, which later briefly served as Def Jam's head office, and together they decided to form Def Jam as an outlet for the rap that they were hearing in the clubs. Rubin is also easily positioned along a continuum, in this case as a white teenager who, like his father, was fascinated and influenced by the "underground" black cultural practices that have traditionally emerged from New York's uptown boroughs. Describing his father's influence, Rubin states that "he grew up in Brooklyn and the Bronx and he listened to jazz. When he was growing up, he'd go to black jazz clubs and be the only white guy in the place" (Farr 1994, 119). Rubin is thus encoded as a hip white explorer who, like Simmons, bridged the culture gap between white and black spaces and between white and black cultural and aesthetic sensibilities. Together, Simmons and Rubin embody rap's expansive tendency; they represent the extent to which the genre had conceptually, if not yet altogether commercially, transcended the borders of ghetto neighborhoods in the Bronx and Brooklyn, extending into suburban and nonurban spaces and middle-class realms.

Harmonizing Rap and the Music Industry

With rap's continuing entrenchment within the industry there was a corresponding effort to define it in relation to the existing market categories. It was during this period that the dominant descriptive terminology developed around rap and the youth subcultures from which it emerged as a plethora of independent rap-oriented labels introduced new artists and material. For example, *Billboard*'s writers and other industry spokespersons often used the terms "rap" and "hip-hop" interchangeably when referring to the genre, eventually (by 1984) settling on the cultural-spatial descriptors "street music" and "street labels" to describe rap and its independent producers. The irony lies in the fact that the music was actually moving away from the production and performance domains of the street at the time, and merging more consistently with the studios and executive spaces of the music industry. Despite its spatial designations, the term "street music" was coined in the attempt to isolate and identify a particular subgenre of the wider catalog of black music (which was itself eventually designated as "urban music" in radio formats) and thus locate it within the core logic and practices of corporate production and distribution. As Keith Negus observes, hip-hop's self-motivated entrepreneurs have always existed alongside the MCs and DJs, placing rap "not 'outside' or bursting out from the 'margins' or 'periphery,' but central to the changing business practices and aesthetics of the contemporary music industry" (1999, 492).

Urban or black music generally encompassed a wide range of musical styles and musicians that included harder funk-based units such as George Clinton (and his various touring and recording units), Bootsy Collins, the Gap Band, Graham Central Station, Cameo, Fatback, and Kool and the Gang; mid-range funk, R & B, and soul artists such as the Ohio Players, Rufus and Chaka Khan, the Commodores, and Earth, Wind, and Fire; and pop-oriented artists such as Michael Jackson, Prince, Lionel Richie, and Tina Turner. The latter were crossover artists, but several white artists, including Culture Club, Hall and Oates, and Michael McDonald, also attained "reverse crossover" success, appearing on black music charts and black radio playlists with increasing frequency.[7] As a distinguishing term, street music as it was employed at this stage referred exclusively to rap.

Negus notes a spatial dichotomy when the market term "street" is presented in contrast with the domain of "the executive suite":

"The street" operates as a metonym for a particular type of knowledge which is deployed by executives throughout the music industry; a type of knowledge which legitimates an enduring belief that rap *is* and *should be* outside the corporate suite. . . . This not only maintains social divisions within the recording industry; it also contributes to the ongoing reproduction of broader economic, cultural and racialized divisions across which r'n'b and rap have been and continue to be made.
(Negus 1999, 492)

This accurate reading of the street's discursive significance shows a full grasp of the relational implications of the industry's structures in which senior black executives are rare and black talent is abundant—and lucrative. References to "the street" also encompass a secondary order of meaning that, in practice, formed the basis of the industry's public articulations of space and race. Its descriptive value draws on an economy of meaning focused around an image of the ghetto.

As an industry market designation, "street music" implicitly refers to elements of rawness and urban intensity that ostensibly constitute the "real" or true locus of cultural production for many black and Latino youths. It resonates with the problematic and arguably racist themes of authenticity that identify black youth exclusively with inner-city or ghetto environments. In basic terms, the industry's use of the trope of the street involves the recirculation of existing stereotypes and assumptions—what Negus (1999) refers to as "mythical" features—about urban experience while also demarcating the music in relation to other musical forms and genres. The fact remains, however, that in the early stages of its entry into the recording industry, rap was defined and typified through discursive processes of spatial othering that isolated the music and its creators, reproducing the exclusionary and biased sociocultural values that segregate minority youth from the social mainstream.

The term "street music" was used to simultaneously accommodate the racial and spatial dimensions of young consumer demographics, radio formatting, and the presumed taste distinctions upon which they were based. This emergent lexicon within the music industry also provided terms that reveal generational distinctions, since "black" and "street" also indicated certain consumer delineations: the former referred to a generally, though not exclusively, black audience and consumer formation (including adult soul, R & B, and funk audiences), and the latter primarily to a youth segment within the larger black music market. Such a lexicon is part of fragmentary discourse that segments urban and black constituencies from a larger mass consumer bloc while introducing discursive boundaries among black consumer audiences.

Foremost among the difficulties in harmonizing rap with dominant industry practices was the major labels' general unfamiliarity with the music and hip-hop's accompanying practices, their slow start in establishing distribution deals with the smaller labels, and their reluctance to sign contracts with new rap talent. The majors failed to fully comprehend the significance of rap's popularity among black and Latino teenagers, despite coverage in *Billboard* explicitly announcing to the industry that a new movement was afoot. Parallels can be drawn with several earlier moments in the history of the American recording industry at which the dynamics between major and independent labels merged with issues of race, class, and locality, as Lipsitz explains in his account of popular music in the 1950s:

Before RCA's purchase of Elvis Presley's contract from Sun Records in 1955, the major studios ignored the music emanating from working-class neighborhoods, leaving the field to the more than four hundred independent labels that came into existence after the war. Existing outside of corporate channels, the smaller firms in working-class areas produced records geared to local audiences, especially in minority communities. (1990, 138)

As Russell Simmons suggested in a special section of the music trade journal *Billboard* dedicated to his Rush Artist Management enterprise, "I don't think the major record companies understand this music. The a&r people there are old" ("Rap Visionary Russell Simmons" 1985). According to Simmons, the major labels missed the opportunity to exploit rap's potentials, allowing independents to initially define the market and its product. He also offers an interesting opinion on why older blacks rejected rap at the time:

Why don't some people like rap? It's too black for some people and too noisy for others. It's like the first wave of rock 'n' roll or like heavy metal today. . . . It just so happens that the best rap music is probably the most offensive to adults, especially black adults. Rap reminds them of the corner, and they want to be as far away from that as they can be. ("Rap Visionary Russell Simmons" 1985)

The geocultural logic underlying this explanation is compelling in its racial and generational assumptions, for the statement conflates youth, blackness, and the street into a symbiotic whole that is, again, representative of some innate authoritative identity. In this instance, it is not white folks who are excluded, but older blacks, folks whose age constitutes a territorial barrier that prevents them from savoring rap's expressive pleasures. Simmons's deployment of a mapped discourse of difference illustrates yet

another way the sites in which cultural tastes and aesthetic preferences cohere are problematically rationalized within terms of spatial exclusion.

The "corner" to which Simmons refers is also a metaphor of considerable weight, for it constitutes a socioeconomic boundary demarcating the
point from which middle- and upper-class blacks depart on their economic
sojourn of "getting up and getting over." In April 1985 a graphic representation offered a telling interpretation of Simmons's "corner." Appearing in
a *Billboard* special tribute to his Rush Productions agency was an image of
street signs reading "Rush Productions" and "Profile Records" with the accompanying copy "the corner, where the hottest sounds on the street,
meet." In this context, the corner is also a source of black identification and
ghetto authenticity, and a new site of vast commercial potential that facilitated Simmons's own upward economic mobility.

Rap introduced a marketing dilemma for the industry majors, which
initially avoided the genre en masse. Their reluctance to work with it was a
reflection of the tendency among major-label executives either to approach
rap as a passing fad or to consider its primary consumers—urban minority
youth—as an insufficiently large or economically empowered sector to warrant their investment. Most early rap was popularized through the informal modes of word-of-mouth hype, club play, and live performance. Sales
were often poorly tracked and monitored (allowing some labels to sell
records "under the radar" and avoid taxes and artists' royalty payouts), and
the circulation of bootleg tapes made it difficult to accurately gauge consumer interest from a commercial perspective. Furthermore, the persistence
of novelty recordings by comedians such as Rich Little ("President's Rap,"
1982, Boardwalk), Rodney Dangerfield ("Rappin' Rodney," 1984, RCA),
and Joe Piscopo ("Honeymooner's Rap," 1985, Columbia) did little to
strengthen rap's reputation as a legitimate and sustainable genre.

Pop radio remained largely cool to rap throughout this stage, and black
radio was indifferent at best, despite reports illustrating the growing appeal of "street music" when it was programmed on urban formats.[8] Prominent exceptions were New York's WBLS (and several low-wattage community or campus radio stations extending from Long Island to New
Jersey), which regularly programmed rap, and the Los Angeles AM station
KDAY, which shifted to an all-hip-hop format in 1984. In each of these
cases, rap programming helped to focus the local scene, fostering rap's further development and expansion by playing the newest records and helping to break local acts. MTV's presence as a staple of home cable television
services was growing (from roughly 2.5 million homes in 1981 to almost 30
million homes in 1986), but rap fell outside the network's narrow definition of rock programming.

Since the emergence of MTV on the American music and entertainment scene coincides with the intensification of rap's commercial industry development, it is appropriate to consider their relationship. According to Phillip Brian Harper (1989), the establishment of black artists, including Michael Jackson and Prince, as mainstays among white teen consumers was enabled by MTV's begrudging addition of their videos to its regular rotation. Run-D.M.C.'s video for "King of Rock" (1984, Profile), which features a humorous portrayal of rap's "bum rush" of an imaginary rock 'n' roll hall of fame, was accepted on the network largely because the track more explicitly conforms to MTV's stylistic and aesthetic parameters than did most of Jackson's material at the time. Harper describes MTV's reluctance to screen videos that failed to meet its rigid format requirements:

> Unlike "commercial" television, whose appeal to financial backers is based on its ability to "broadcast" programs to the widest possible audience, the MTV of the early '80s banked on its ability to target a sizable yet necessarily homogeneous viewership, an audience whose affinity for "rock music"—that difficult to define entity—is only one of its demographic traits; it is also relatively young—12–34, predominantly male, and overwhelmingly white. MTV's development of narrowcasting policy was *necessary,* to a large degree, because, as late as the early '80s, cable television was available primarily in white rural and suburban communities.
>
> (Harper 1989, 112)

A generation of white listeners who, as the network's popular ad campaign suggested, "wanted their MTV" remained generally underexposed to rap through the exclusionary practices of cable music television apparatuses at the time. Yet as the restrictive definition of rock was loosened after 1983 to include first black funk-rock, some R & B, and, later, rap, MTV also quickly became instrumental in the popularization of the genre among diverse audiences, enhancing the rate of its popular dissemination across geographical distances and cultural divisions.

As rap became more prevalent and more easily accessible through the mainstream media (including local cable-access television stations and, more slowly, the Black Entertainment Television [BET] network), its rhythmic and vocal nuances were also more frequently appropriated by numerous top pop acts (e.g., Michael Jackson, Chaka Khan, and Prince) that were standard on both pop and urban radio formats. As a result of the influences of "the beat box generation" (George 1985b), crossover patterns were often upended, with the more radio-friendly rap-oriented releases breaking on Top 40 radio *before* they received play on black or urban format stations. MTV was also influential in this pattern, as videos proved to be catalysts for the acceleration of interest among nonblack teen audiences.

Such a pattern reversed the normal trends in establishing hits by black artists, reflecting the effects of resistance to the genre that prevailed among radio programming directors and the black music establishment. As Nelson George explained in *Billboard:*

Until recently, there has been some curiosity, but little enthusiasm. A profound generation gap between the black promotion and a&r men at the majors and the younger people making this music has stifled its movement into the black mainstream—but, surprisingly, not its access to white buyers.   (George 1985a, 57)

Music industry executives at major labels—both black and white—were initially stymied by the rap market, which, from their perspective, was unpredictable and thus a less attractive option for development and the investment of time and resources. It was quite literally foreign to many of them, if not necessarily in a cultural sense, then in commercial terms. Negus's focus on the industry's internal classification system reveals the dynamics between commerciality and cultural character that complicate rap's status in the industry:

A genre such as rap, however, may be classified as a "wild cat" by industry analysts who are uncertain about its future aesthetic changes and "potential market growth" and by business personnel who are uncomfortable with the politics of black representation that are foregrounded by the genre, and anxious about the political pressure from the moral opponents of rap.   (Negus 1999, 493)

It was not only the future that was at issue, because the analysts and executives also failed to recognize the cultural patterns that inform rap's aesthetics. From their vantage point, rap had virtually no history to which they might refer and no clearly established commercial sales patterns that could be taken into consideration. Since they could not predict its commercial potentials or understand what motivating cultural forces were driving the market, they remained dormant.

Many successful black music executives were focused on the still-lucrative returns from more established soul and pop acts, or else they sought to develop new talent within these genres. Seldom was any substantial market research conducted that focused on rap's main consumer demographic or its locales and practices, though this was a standard practice in other youth-oriented music sectors and corporate divisions at the time. Yet, as Reebee Garofalo writes, generational difference was only one factor involved in black radio's stubborn refusal to promote rap:

Black radio has often been caught between "rock" and a hard place in the struggle for viable listenership. But in these instances, black stations were exhibiting a reluctance to play cuts that were clearly outselling other selections on their playlists. Beyond a simple generation gap, the split between rap and other forms of popular black music may also be an indicator of the increasing importance of class divisions within the black community.   (Garofalo 1990, 114)

Radio program directors acknowledged the success of rap and its sales potentials but argued that advertisers were generally less interested in the stations' ability to deliver audiences from the urban minority teen demographic. This demographic segment simply fell outside the radio and advertising industry's "preferred" audience profile. However, program directors' reluctance to playlist rap turned out to be shortsighted, for, despite having less economic spending power per capita, the black and Latino rap audience expressed sophisticated consumer tastes. Their active desire for and consumption of high-end commodities, in combination with their influential role as cultural trend-setters among the teen population, should have made them an excellent target demographic. It is only in more recent years that the advertising and corporate worlds have acknowledged this, providing another example of corporate misassessment of the hip-hop culture's potential impact.

With major labels servicing the priority requirements of the nation's mainstream radio outlets, independent labels had greater difficulty reaching them and introducing their product for consideration, which further reduced their material's exposure to wider markets. In addition, long before the late 1970s the majors had organized their operations according to a set of marketing principles that favored the rock and pop genres. Dance music was regarded as less durable, less "serious," and single-driven. By the early 1980s, album-length releases, which tend to have an extended chart durability, received greater corporate attention in terms of publicity and marketing support than did singles, which have less chart durability. Dance music was also more closely associated with the creative artistry of the producer than with musicians, and although rap featured DJs and MCs as the musical focal point of the genre, in its infancy there were simply too few notable stars for the industry to back. Rap, which fell between the rock and dance genres, subsequently blurred the definitional boundaries, and the major labels misperceived the contexts of its performance and use, which, until 1983–84, generally favored singles or cassette tapes. The resulting lack of certainty around the rap market and the desirability of either twelve-inch single or LP configurations was yet another contributing factor to major labels' and radio broadcasters' hesitation to embrace rap.

In a 1980 article appearing under the headline "Value of 12-Inch Single from LP Questioned," *Billboard* describes industry differentiation between dance-oriented singles for club play and those that were released for album promotion, mainly on radio. Citing a bottom-line economic rationale, company spokespersons explained that if an album was likely to sell without the additional support of a prereleased single, then the single was perceived as an expensive redundancy, especially since FM radio programmers often selected several cuts from an album and many DJs preferred choosing an album's hit songs themselves.

The combined factors of dance music's continued influence among black teenagers in the early 1980s and the emergent innovative role of hip-hop DJs reinforced the supremacy of the twelve-inch single in the rap genre, and consequently the earliest recordings were available *only* in this form. The twelve-inch single's advantage as the main commodity unit effectively coincided with the cultural practices of club DJs, who collectively constituted one of hip-hop's primary consumer groups. Their role in introducing and popularizing the emergent genre was crucial and with discos still being immensely influential in the establishment of dance hits, the club DJ occupied a central position in the flow between artists, producers, and audiences.

By the late 1970s most major labels had recognized that they had missed the opportunity to capitalize on the explosive disco craze, a lapse that allowed several independent labels, such as Henry Stone's Miami-based TK Records (featuring KC and the Sunshine Band) and Neil Bogart's Casablanca Records (which elevated Donna Summer to disco diva status), to dominate. Despite their early reluctance to work with rap, in the early 1980s the majors were gradually returning to the production of twelve-inch singles in an attempt to recapture market shares that had been lost to the smaller independent disco and dance-oriented labels. This resulted in a glutted market for twelve-inch releases and threatened the independent labels, whose product was also destined for club play and whose main sales volume was in that format.

In June 1984 a *Billboard* Spotlight on "The World of Black Music" noted that "twelve-inch disks continue to play a major role for black retailers. The big difference in '83 was the strength of 12-inch releases by the majors and in-roads by pop artists into the once exclusively independent, urban dominated configuration" (Goodman 1984b, BM 12). In a cover story the following month, *Billboard* reported a growing nervousness among independent labels as majors increased their production of twelve-inch singles: "A glut of product and increasingly conservative club DJs are combining to give major labels the upper hand in the 12-inch single market. . . . The street-sharp independents who invented the 12-inch game are finding themselves with a shrinking field" (Goodman 1984a, 1). Larger and more established independent hip-hop labels such as Profile and Tommy Boy, which had confirmed their status and their product (or, in traditional terms, their "street" *and* industry credibility), were not as vulnerable to the major-label onslaught despite having to offer greater incentives and more lucrative contracts to rappers. Nonetheless, these conditions led Tommy Silverman of Tommy Boy to voice his concern that the major labels' incursions could reduce the already minimal independent-label share of the twelve-inch market from approximately 5 percent to 2 percent.

Owing in part to the major labels' not entirely unreasonable perception that rap's popularity was grounded in highly specific localized or regional market domains, executives believed that the genre was inconsistent with the prevailing methods of handling rock or pop musics. For somewhat different reasons, rap was also thought to be inconsistent with the general industry approaches to mainstream black music or funk, which in fact reached many of the same audiences as rap. Prior to 1984 rap singles were generally regarded as isolated products—one-offs—that were marketed according to each single's saleability and commercial appeal. There was little effort or interest in developing artists beyond the next hit or of creating a commercial demand for an individual artist or group's extended work. The few rap acts that had established themselves as stars by the mid-1980s were still judged on their capacity to survive from single to single, although some, including Kurtis Blow and Grandmaster Flash and the Furious Five, had gradually transcended these constraints through the respectable sales of their recorded singles prior to 1984. It is relevant that even at the end of the 1990s, individual rap artists who could boast of a deep catalog of recorded material were few in comparison to their contemporaries in the rock or pop sectors.

Harper explains that *Billboard*'s influential "Rock Tracks" chart also revealed an implicit devaluation of black music's history and importance in relation to white rock:

The implication is that a "rock track," though technically a single song, is part of a larger artistic work comprised in an album and that, although for airplay purposes singles must be used to represent the whole work, the album ought not be dissected into its constituent songs if one is to appreciate the artistic integrity of the whole. This, apparently, is not true of the other categories for which singles charts are published, and certainly not for "Black" songs, which evidently do not cohere as conceptually integrated albums, and thus are easily charted as discrete "singles" whose rise up the charts is always contingent and anomalous.   (Harper 1989, 116)

This emphasis on singles and hits in the industry was both a benefit and a hindrance to rap: on the one hand, small labels could, with one successful release, generate substantial sales and revenues with which to finance future projects and expand their operations, especially since singles were much less costly to produce, manufacture, and promote. On the other hand, it constituted an obstacle against which independent labels and their artists struggled, since albums were regarded by the industry as an indicator of greater cultural value and importance.

An example of this dichotomy is illustrated by the case of Profile Records, which was founded in 1981. Dr. Jeckyll and Mr. Hyde's "Genius Rap" was produced in 1982 for $750, but the single sold over 150,000 copies and actually kept the label afloat through the following year. In 1983

Run-D.M.C.'s "It's like That/Sucker MCs" became the label's biggest seller and effectively underwrote the production of the group's first full-length album, *Run-D.M.C.* This benchmark in rap's history boosted Profile's industry status as well as the career of the genre's fastest-rising act. The label's release in 1984 of Run-D.M.C.'s second album, *King of Rock,* confirmed the group's star status primarily as a rock act and proved definitively that with proper handling rap could be successfully recorded and packaged in the LP format. This success, engineered by the production team of Rick Rubin and Russell Simmons, navigated the prevailing market and format demarcations and was formulated as part of a bid to elevate rap as a more serious and sustainable genre.

While headlines proclaiming "Independents Enjoy a Major Turnaround" (Pasternak 1987, 9); "Small Labels Maintain Street Sense" (Chin 1987b, 33); and "Rap Taps into Mainstream Market (Chin 1987a, 26) announced small-label activity in the rap genre after 1986, major labels such as Capitol and Columbia were purchasing double-page spreads advertising the release of catalog material by the Beatles, the Rolling Stones, and Pink Floyd in the new CD format.[9] The major labels were sitting on a gold mine of master tape recordings and in addition were heavily invested in their established rosters. Corporate value was rooted primarily in what the companies already owned, rather than in their vision when it came to capitalizing on new musical forms or developing new artists (despite stated intentions to reinforce black A & R units).

Motown Records, once the most important purveyor of popular music by black artists, also exploited its extensive catalog, as a *Billboard* special section on black music reported in September 1986. Motown had by this time already abdicated its influential leadership role as a black-owned and -operated label working almost exclusively with black acts, and Def Jam was on the verge of becoming the second-largest black-owned label operating in the United States.[10] By 1986–87, Motown was largely seen as being out of touch with street music, and its revenues were better guaranteed by CD reissues of established hit classics by proven stars, the sustained appeal of its main charting artists, Lionel Richie and Stevie Wonder, and a struggling stable of moderately talented performers. It was not until the mid-1990s, with the appointment of Andre Harrel to the position of president, that Motown attempted to reconnect with the youth market.[11] His efforts fell short of expectations, and Harrel was later hired by his former protégé, Sean Combs, at Bad Boy Entertainment.

At the same time intensive industry restructuring was also under way as transnational corporate mergers and buyouts extended patterns of industry concentration throughout the latter half of the 1980s. CBS (and its subsidiaries Columbia and Epic), WEA (Warner Brothers, Elektra, and Atlantic), PolyGram, RCA, MCA, and Capitol-EMI dominated the industry, controlling almost 90 percent of the popular market. In relation to their music divisions (as opposed to corporate involvement in other media and entertainment sectors), major-label reputations, wealth, and value were highly dependent on past pop- and rock-oriented archival assets as well as the capacity to continue turning out megahits by megagroups on an international scale. Indeed, the stage was set for major acts such as Aerosmith, Def Leppard, Michael Jackson, Madonna, George Michael, Prince, and R.E.M. to sign lucrative multiyear contracts that effectively bound them to their corporate labels (leading Michael and Prince into prolonged and ultimately career-damaging contractual battles to establish greater artistic freedom or to retain control over master tapes and release schedules of new material). The image of corporate behemoths staggering under their own weight with a roster of similarly "heavy" acts to manage while rap's independent labels made fast contacts with new artists targeting regional and national domestic markets is not altogether inaccurate.

As the catalog CD advertisements reflect, the major labels were seeking to exploit their vaults of recorded material and to reap the financial rewards with minimal overhead or financial outlay. CD sales increased as consumers adjusted to the new CD technologies, often repurchasing popular classics that they often already owned on vinyl or audiocassette. Reporting on the transition to the CD configuration, *Billboard* noted that "1991 seems to be shaping up as the year the reissue will reach its crest" (DiMartino 1991, 11). Although adults were responding to the technological shift from vinyl to CDs, teen music consumers generally lacked the capital to make the transition immediately once the new CD technologies became available. This was initially even more true among minority teen markets. As George Plasketes observes, mobility was another crucial element in the demise of the vinyl LP: "To a generation raised on 'boom boxes' and the Sony Walkman, music mobility is a necessity. And, vinyl does not travel. While the tendency is to attribute vinyl's decline almost exclusively to compact discs, cassettes have quietly been a contributing factor" (1992, 112). In rap, cassettes as well as vinyl were the two major selling configurations; CDs became a regular feature only after 1988. Indeed, the industry movement away from vinyl toward CDs caused considerable concern and debate among hip-hop DJs, who relied on vinyl releases for their livelihood.

Unfounded conspiracy theories occasionally circulated within the hip-hop culture. Among them was the claim that since they were not profiting from rap anyway, the majors were entirely unconcerned that their actions might destroy rap and the independent rap labels by forcing a change to

CD-based technologies. Still, the independent labels maintained a strong (if not necessarily controlling) presence in the rap market to the end of the decade, and the genre benefited in market terms from new access to the national and international distribution systems that the major labels provided —and profited from. Independents also maintained their connections with smaller, more localized sites of musical production and consumption by following the standard dance music practices of circulating album tracks to club DJs for remixing and rerelease in the twelve-inch format even after cassettes and CDs had become the dominant commodity configurations. In addition, they made positive efforts to improve the overall quality of LP releases (involving more coherence and, in Def Jam's case, more tracks on each album), which were perceived as being a better value for teen consumers with limited income.

Mobilizing for Crossover

Measured against rock and pop, rap was a minor commercial force, yet the industry as a whole was in dire need of new product. The market was still recovering from dismal sales through the late 1970s, and industrywide corporate restructuring efforts, despite the fact that black music divisions were introduced and black personnel were hired to staff them, also often resulted in inconsistent or reduced support for R & B, soul, and funk acts. By 1984 rap's commercial potentials were becoming clearer, and as the increased number and more optimistic tone of articles in *Billboard* reflect, there was a subtle turn indicating new interest in rap among the major labels. Rap's industry growth after 1984 signaled a transitional trend as it expanded from a relatively contained micromarket to a macromarket of diverse and dispersed consumers. Rap had already demonstrated the ability to grow and to enlarge its audience base while reinventing itself at several junctures in a process of ongoing innovation and development; much of this activity, however, was either unseen or ignored by the majors. Artists were developing more consistently applied professional skills in performance and recording contexts, and, crucially, the independent labels and agents were honing important business skills that allowed them to function more productively in the industry and market.

Because of rap's inconsistent exposure on urban or Top 40 radio stations and its virtual absence from MTV, live performance was still a crucial means of promoting artists' images and material. Among the more significant events in this period was the 1984 Swatch Watch New York City Fresh Fest Tour, which was booked into twenty-seven major urban centers and featured Run-D.M.C, Whodini, the Fat Boys, Newcleus, the Dynamic Breakers, Magnificent Force, Uptown Express, Dr. Jeckyll and Mr. Hyde, and T. La Rock, with Kurtis Blow as the host. Based on positive audience response to rap package concerts earlier in the year, the tour was organized by a consortium of promoters from Atlanta, Cleveland, Miami, and Houston (with artist representation by Russell Simmons's New York–based Rush Productions and national booking by Norby Walters Associates, which maintained offices in Los Angeles and New York).[12] The tour, which is commonly referred to as Fresh Fest, adhered to the general structure of major rock tours, harnessing the corporate sponsorship of the Swatch watch company. The national cooperation behind the tour suggests that rap was by this time becoming a recognizable force in regions beyond New York, New Jersey, and Pennsylvania, and regional promoters were beginning to witness the emergent traits of the hip-hop subculture in their own home markets. An additional but often overlooked detail of the tour was the organizers' decision to earmark five percent of the proceeds for donation to the United Negro College Fund in acknowledgment of the music's growing role and importance among black communities.

Billboard reported the tour's official announcement under the headline "'New York City Fresh Fest': Hip-Hop Heading for Huge Halls" (Weinger 1984a, 40). The article described the importance of rap's first full-fledged entry into major performance centers and concert halls on a national level. In it, Simmons is quoted as saying, "The industry has yet to realize that audiences are coming to hear the groups, not just the record. This is the next step for sure." In a similar vein, Mark Seigel, of Norby Walters Associates (which at the time had North America's largest roster of black artists), optimistically suggested that "now the companies will start believing" (Weinger 1984a, 40), in acknowledgment of continuing major label reluctance to enter the rap market.

Fresh Fest was an ambitious attempt to more fully gauge rap's audience base and the extent of interest and appeal in regions beyond New York and the Northeast, which, as the tour's full name reflects, was still identified as the genre's main center of activity (even though New York was not booked as a tour stop). The Fresh Fest tours of 1984 and subsequent years introduced the genre in a new, professionalized context, lifting it out of the narrowly defined ghetto terrains with which it was still predominantly associated. Fresh Fest also influenced a new generation of nationally dispersed black youths who, as the Compton, California, rapper MC Eiht explains, soon regarded rap as a realistic career option: "After I saw the Fresh Fest concert in 1984, it made me figure that maybe I could get paid for rhyming too. That's how I started making my way out of the gang-banging lifestyle" (MC Eiht 1995, 56).

The tour was deemed an organizational and financial success by industry standards, repeatedly selling out large venues (15,000–20,000 seats) and netting $3.5 million in total profits. Yet more important was the tour's success in introducing rap to diverse audiences across middle America, which, as Nelson George reported, was "highly integrated . . . as much as 35% white in some markets" (George 1985a, 57). In the tour's wake, releases by concert headliners the Fat Boys, Run-D.M.C., and Whodini all sold certified gold, with unit sales in excess of 500,000 each, while Kurtis Blow had unit sales in the 300,000 range. These figures served notice to the industry that rap's commercial potential was expanding. Rap quickly accelerated as a crossover force, coinciding with white and minority youth tastes simultaneously. In 1985 a second New York Fresh Fest tour was mounted with almost double the number of dates and an itinerary that included New York City as well as areas that, according to *Billboard*, "had been resistant to rap." The appeal of this second Fresh Fest Tour was evident when *Billboard*'s list of the nation's top forty concert grosses identified the tour's July 6–7 concerts in Philadelphia as the second-highest-grossing engagement of the month. At $12.50 a ticket, the concert was also listed as being the least expensive event in *Billboard*'s BoxScore column (July 20, 1985, 39). These nationwide arena appearances by rap's top recording acts also produced new contexts of exposure that offered the artists insights into regionally dispersed social practices and locally specific vernaculars beyond their own limited range of experience, introducing a dialogic component to the circulation of geocultural sensibilities.

Other events and performance contexts also extended the reach and influence of rap in this period. Among these were tours linking teen-oriented R & B acts with rap acts, such as a concert package featuring New Edition, the Fat Boys, and Whodini that was listed among the top-grossing tours in *Billboard*'s BoxScore column (March 9, 1985). Run-D.M.C., a late addition to the lineup for the internationally broadcast Live Aid concert on July 13, 1985, was the only rap act to appear at either the Philadelphia or London performance site, effectively presenting the group and the genre to an estimated two billion people worldwide; many in the audience had undoubtedly never seen or heard live rap. Finally, by the end of 1985 plans were also in place for the live satellite telecast to fifty-eight markets of the Krush Groove Party held at Madison Square Garden in New York. This was a carefully orchestrated concert tie-in with the Warner Brothers film *Krush Groove* (directed by Michael Schultz), which featured prominent Rush acts. In each of these contexts, rap's unique live-performance format and its varied aesthetic nuances were being rapidly popularized throughout North America and the world, enhancing audience familiarity with the genre while reinforcing artist recognizability among teen fans.

Concert Violence and Rap's Negative Social Stigma

Despite rap's bright sales prospects and audience enthusiasm for rap tours, from 1985 to 1989 hip-hop encountered a wall of negativity, complicating its growth and expansion. Spontaneous rap concert violence emerged as a dominating issue within the music industry, for muggings, stabbings, and shootings were part of a recurring pattern in the large arena venues across the nation. Among these incidents were multiple stabbings at the 1985 Krush Groove concert at New York's Madison Square Garden; a wave of street muggings in the aftermath of the Madison Square Garden stop of the Run-D.M.C. "Raising Hell Tour" in July 1986; and the infamous Long Beach Arena "riot" during the Raising Hell performance in August 1986. As the frequency and severity of incidents increased throughout the late 1980s, civic and industry attentions alike turned to the particular minority youth cultures that produced rap and comprised its primary audience. Moreover, the array of violent incidents also featured unavoidable geographic distinctions that indicated to many that the hip-hop nation was deeply divided and suffering inner turmoil.

Addressing the trends of concert violence, Tricia Rose isolates the September 1988 stabbing death of nineteen-year-old Julio Fuentes at a show featuring the headliners Eric B and Rakim at Naussau Veterans Memorial Coliseum in Uniondale, New York, as being of particular significance. While the Long Island incident was influential as a catalyst for change among the hip-hop community and others associated with the promotion and diffusion of rap, especially in New York, the earlier Long Beach riot can be more accurately identified as rap music's Altamont: it signaled to middle America hip-hop's apparent debauchery and heralded its decline during this period. Of all the incidents, the one at Long Beach was the most striking because of its scale: forty-two people were injured as marauding gang members cruised the venue, abusing other attendees and battling arena security, the police, and each other. The positive growth that the earlier Fresh Fest tours had engendered as the music expanded geographically was suddenly tainted by an image of ghetto ferocity that would continue to plague the hip-hop culture, even though the violence in Long Beach was later (and more accurately) attributed to deep-seated animosities between warring gang sets than to rap fans per se.

Mainstream media reports on the Long Beach Coliseum tour date failed to explicitly enunciate that the violence was gang related, nor did they clarify that, rather than somehow being the responsibility of the artists involved, the violence was spatially motivated, owing to a context in which rap fans of warring gangs converged within a compressed space. Mainstream media and critics also tended to focus on the stereotypical associations between rap music, black youth, and masculine aggression. Countering these reductive representations, the headliners Run-D.M.C. announced in a press conference the following day that they believed their concert provided a context for a "meeting" between warring gangs. They stated that the group "refuses to play Los Angeles until police or other authorities take sterner measures to protect Run-D.M.C. fans against local gangs. The gangs stand for everything rap is against. . . . Other cities don't have the problems that LA has. Run-D.M.C. isn't the problem, LA is the problem" (Morris 1986, 77). The group appeared on a live telephone call-in program on the Los Angeles rap station KDAY to discuss the incident and its implications for fans, the group, and rap music in general. Their decision to speak publicly with DJs and members of the public on KDAY also reflects the radio station's centrality in the Los Angeles hip-hop scene at the time, since it occupied a valuable connecting role in which relevant community issues were aired along with the broadcasting of new rap releases. Ironically, the incident launched much-needed debate on southern California's gang culture as well as on the ethical responsibilities of rap artists, who had emerged as influential public figures or, in a more complicated mode, as role models for impressionable teenagers.

The incident also announced to East Coast rappers that, for all their similarities, their teen peers in Long Beach and the greater Los Angeles area functioned according to drastically different codes and operated within highly structured spatial parameters that were quite different from those in New York and other cities along the eastern seaboard. Within two years, with the emergence of the gangsta rap subgenre, the spatial dynamics and implications of place-based social identification that shaped the Los Angeles youth environment would be widely publicized throughout the nation, producing even deeper rifts between black teens and adults, white and black communities, and East and West Coast rappers.

Many of the resultant phenomena that Rose points to (including the negative impact on future rap bookings, inflated venue insurance costs for rap concert promoters, and the circulation of public perceptions of mayhem or danger associated with rap), originated with the Long Beach Arena incident, which took place a full two years prior to the Nassau Coliseum killing. Commenting on the rapid rise of insurance costs for large-venue rap concerts after the Long Beach incident, the copromoter of the 1986 Run-D.M.C. tour noted that the insurance cost per paid spectator for rap shows had increased from 2.5 cents to 26 cents a head over a three-year period, resulting in higher ticket prices and making tours more difficult to mount. Under the headline "Venue Reads the Riot Act Following Melee: Run-D.M.C. Gig Spurs Arena Policy Changes" (Morris 1986, 7), *Billboard* reported that Long Beach Arena managers would more carefully scrutinize an act's performance record prior to booking but, they claimed, would not discriminate against any particular genre. This qualification was meant to encompass both rap and heavy metal, for the latter had also acquired a negative reputation, more because of venue property damage and self-induced injury than fan-on-fan violence.

The trend did, however, continue and intensify after the Fuentes killing in 1988 at the Naussau Coliseum, with *Billboard* reporting that the Trans-America insurance company had "canceled coverage in mid-term for G-Street Express of Washington, D.C., the show's promoter and a major player in the black music scene" (Hennessey 1988, 6). Subsequently, several other insurance underwriters closely examined the rap tour industry, citing perceptions of a high-risk insurance environment as a major inhibitor in extending coverage to venues and promoters. A year later, under the headline "Many Doors Still Closed to Rap Tours," it was reported that "venue availability is down 33% because buildings are limiting rap shows" (Haring 1989, 1).

The Naussau Coliseum incident galvanized the New York rap scene. Motivated rap artists along with, among others, the *Billboard* columnist Nelson George organized a coalition (the Stop the Violence Movement) and held public demonstrations and educational speak-outs against concert and community violence. Under its banner some of the top artists of the day, including KRS-One, Chuck D and Flavor Flav of Public Enemy, Heavy D, MC Lyte, Kool Moe Dee, Just Ice, and Afrika Bambaataa, recorded the twelve-inch single "Self-Destruction" (1989, Jive Records), which entered the Hot Rap Singles chart at number one on March 11, 1989, and eventually went gold. The movement's initiative raised an estimated $400,000 for the National Urban League for community antiviolence education programs targeting youths. In her self-reflective recollections on "Every Ghetto, Every City," Lauryn Hill cites the period in her life when the "Self Destruction record drops," attesting to the cultural import of the recording and the Stop the Violence collective's initiatives among hip-hop-identified teens at the time.

Whereas prior to 1988 rap headline tours had frequently been listed on the *Billboard* Boxscore chart for top concert revenues, after 1988 rap tours struggled to make money. Rap acts were more frequently added to mixed-bill engagements or package tours, appearing with R & B headliners in an attempt to circumvent the restrictive policies of insurance companies and venue managers. It soon became common practice for promoters to book rap and nonrap headliners together (something that had been common when rap was breaking into the mainstream earlier in the decade) in mixed bills that generally drew from a broader audience demographic and in-cluded more female attendees. The strategy at times stretched credibility and common sense, such as when KRS-One and his hardcore rap unit Boogie Down Productions were promoted as a reggae act because, as the promot-ers claimed, "he has a lot of reggae in his music" (Haring 1989, 1).

Although the previous Fresh Fest and Def Jam tours had been instru-mental in opening up middle America to rap and its constituent hip-hop elements, the repeated violence at rap shows had a reverse effect as venue management, local police forces, and civic administrators all acted within their authority to restrict live rap performances in larger public spaces. This often meant that the shows were undersold and frequently rebooked into smaller theaters or halls in predominantly black communities where fewer fans could afford ticket prices and into which young white rap fans were less likely to venture at night. Even though subsequent tours such as the 1987 Def Jam tour were still touted as financial successes, there was a discriminatory antagonism between promoters and authorities that iso-lated rap (and, for different reasons, heavy metal) from the general rock concert promotion business, containing and constraining rap concerts.

Because of the trend toward concert violence, various official spokes-people from cultural watchdog groups (including the police) began to speculate publicly that rap presented more than a context for violence—they claimed that rap was actually a causal factor in these outbreaks. Rap was discursively portrayed in these circles as a vector of a violence-inducing pathogen. There were ample cases to which the authorities could point as apparent evidence or proof of rap's capacity to incite violence, creating an oddly reminiscent link with the dominant responses to rock 'n' roll thirty years earlier.

The perception of civic threat, however, became more pronounced after rap's relatively new crossover appeal suddenly began attracting a large white suburban teen audience that was consequently considered to be at risk. Rap shows provided a common space where black and white teen music fans congregated, something that was generally less likely to occur with either R & B or rock shows, where greater audience homogeneity was the norm. Other public spaces such as high schools, movie theaters, and malls often offer similar contexts for multiracial interaction, but con-certs present a unique atmosphere for teenagers to mix and mingle, as they are held in the evening and generally outside neighborhoods where audi-ence members actually live. Furthermore, in concert settings, youth domi-nates, and a particular sense of teen liberty pervades the live event, con-tributing substantially to the "fun" factor involved. However, considerable tension can result when teen audience members collide with the institutional regulatory systems of venue security and a predominantly white police contingent that in many instances misunderstands or has little demonstrated tolerance for the cultural expressions of fun and pleasure at a successful hip-hop show.

Despite legitimate complaints that public venues should be free of danger to audiences, the conjunction between rap's crossover appeal to a growing white youth fan base and venue violence was an implicit factor underlying the intensification of calls for censure by civic authorities. By 1987 the emergence of new subcultural strands within hip-hop, most notably problack Afrocentrism and the aforementioned "gangsta" mentalities that informed the narrative imagery of gangsta rap, only reinforced the perceived danger quotient among white parents as well as among middle-class black adults. Rap was itself undergoing drastic discursive shifts that added a potent blend of politics and masculine aggression, changes that brought a more alert and sustained resistance to the musical form and its creators, with conservative cultural groups such as the Parents Music Resource Center (PMRC) mounting aggressive public campaigns against them.[13]

The multiracial composition of rap concert audiences was regularly cited in *Billboard* as an achievement that surpassed the corporate engineering of crossover. Yet in much of the mainstream reporting, rap shows constituted a new space of moral panic and were frequently the object of inflammatory attacks that stoked fear and concern among civic leaders and parents, effectively stalling ticket sales and overall attendance figures. In the summer of 1987 three major rap tours were crossing the country simultaneously: Together Forever, featuring Run-D.M.C. and the Beastie Boys; Def Jam '87, with LL Cool J, Whodini, Doug E. Fresh, Eric B and Rakim, Public Enemy, and Stetsasonic; and the Fresh Fest '87 Tour, featuring the Fat Boys, Salt 'n' Pepa, and Heavy D and the Boys. The tours were all deemed box-office successes, with the Def Jam tour averaging 10,000–12,000 fans per show and grossing in excess of $6.5 million (Moleski 1987, 34). By the middle of the 1987 summer tour season, Nelson George reported that the Together Forever tour was suffering from bad press and had repeatedly encountered civic resistance despite few actual disruptions, resulting in lower-than-expected ticket sales and damaging the "interracial good-will potential of the tour" (1987, 20). Further commenting on the media disinformation and surrounding civic resistance to rap tours at the time, Lyor Cohen, then the chief operating manager of Rush Artist Management, wrote a highly critical editorial in *Billboard* under the title "Run-D.M.C., Beasties Together: On Tour: A Dispatch from the Front Lines" (1987, 9). Among civic officials the rhetorical emphasis was on the reassertion of adult control and the maintenance of a structured authority within the social contours of law and order. Rap's commercial and popular success among teens drew it to the attention of white authorities, and it was subsequently subjected to closer surveillance and more stringent policing. In the discursive construction of social law and order, rap was acquiring an outlaw reputation as these and other incidents cast the music, the artists, and its core audiences as the product of a culture of violence.

Negative perceptions of rap's danger quotient were also complicated by moral stances and the sudden invocation of community standards among civic officials. Restrictions on venue access were also linked to a sense of outrage at the content of the performances. The Florida and California exponents of rap's more hardcore styles were singled out for special attention by police, civic officials, and venue managers. The 2 Live Crew, which was among the most consistently harassed groups in the rap industry, explicitly acknowledged its antagonistic and noncooperative stance when it adopted the slogan "2 Black, 2 Strong, 2 Live" as an unambiguous refusal of moral containment. In at least one case the containment they sought to overcome had pronounced spatial implications. As *Billboard* reported in 1990, 2 Live Crew's concerts met staunch opposition in New England and were twice canceled in Boston owing to civic "objections to the group's material." In an official appeal to the mayor, a Boston city councilor argued for the denial of the group's access to legitimate music clubs, suggesting "that the group's 'obscene, sexually explicit, and often racially provocative' act should be restricted to the so-called Combat Zone, 'the only area of the city where adult entertainment is legal'" (Flynn 1990, 3). The implications of the displacement are that in the view of civic officials, 2 Live Crew conformed more closely to the cultural category of pornography than music and should have been redesignated accordingly.

Tricia Rose explains that "the question is not 'is there really violence at rap concerts,' but how are these crimes contextualized, labeled?" (1994a, 133). As she notes, there are stakes involved in the processes of labeling rap concerts as danger zones and sites of violence and moral depravity. It therefore remains crucial to interrogate the interests involved and the means through which normative social morals and structures of social dominance are policed and maintained. This is especially so when the weight of authority is brought to bear on minority constituencies and cultural leisure practices that are in an expansive mode, as rap was in this period.

In 1991 Janine McAdams reported in *Billboard* that the authorities and the media still blamed the music and the artists, writing that rap was "still taking a beating for inciting violence" (McAdams 1991d, 31) after a shooting at a concert in Anaheim, California, on which Ice Cube, Too Short, and Yo Yo shared the bill. Rap's roots were undeniable: it was perceived by fans and foes alike as a black-identified cultural form signifying a black youth sensibility. But over the years, concert violence has continually been reframed in official discourses as a seemingly obvious outcome of any event that is attended by a sizable crowd of minority teenagers. Defined in these terms, the restrictive and ultimately racist apparatuses of authority that rap encountered—and continues to battle—in official public spaces of debate seem more clearly justifiable. They appear rational to rap's opponents, conservative cultural watchdogs, and disdainful observers.

CHAPTER FIVE

Crossover and Fragmentation
Rap in the Platinum Era

❋

Rap's commercial and critical successes in the mid-1980s, led by Run-D.M.C., the Beastie Boys, LL Cool J, Whodini, and a fluctuating array of less consistent but talented artists, demonstrated to the music industry that rap could have a sizable and sustainable market appeal. The evidence of hip-hop's influences was easily observable in the style and sensibilities of urban youths from across the racial spectrum who were active participants in the hip-hop culture. Once the appeal was established, rap and, more generally, hip-hop were amplified in new ways and with greater intensity through the appropriative interventions of capitalist investment. By 1985 rap and the b-boy/break-dancing phenomenon had provided the content for numerous print articles, television programs (such as *Miami Vice,* to which Grandmaster Melle Mel contributed the single "Vice" [1985, Sugar Hill]), and feature-length films. Even though the images and essence of the hip-hop scene were frequently diluted, the basic elements (music and dancing) reached white and black youths outside of the relatively close confines of New York's boroughs, where hip-hop was regarded as a way of life rather than as a series of unconnected practices. Despite—or, perhaps more accurately, because of—exploitative tendencies among entertainment industry executives in this period, the media diffusion of break-dancing and rap helped to establish new audiences in far-flung and, importantly, nonurban regions across the nation, further facilitating the music's crossover. This was especially true in the film industry, where the visual aspects of the hip-hop culture were most easily appropriated and re-presented.

As external players, including record executives and movie producers, attempted to cash in on what was slowly being recognized as the scene's lucrative potentials, many of the artists and some agents, managers, and executives in the rap music business grew increasingly wary. They complained that despite the opportunities offered by expansion into the commercial entertainment industry, the potential existed for a diminution of what they believed was the true nature of the music and hip-hop's raw energies, which were propelling rap as a facet of black youth culture. Some of these fears were realized with the release of *Flash Dance* (1983, directed by Adrian Lyne), Joel Silberg's *Breakin'* (1984) and *Rappin'* (1985), and *Breakin' 2: Electric Boogaloo* (1984, directed by Sam Firstenberg), which together exposed millions of American teens to rap, break-dancing, and the rudimentary facets of the hip-hop culture but at the same time stripped it of much of its informing vitality. Mainstream America was given a glimpse of the styles and practices of the hip-hop culture, but the often harsh conditions of the urban environment that comprised central and formative elements of the scene were either elided or exaggerated. In most cases Hollywood scriptwriters cobbled together some of the more superficial elements from the hip-hop culture together in a manner that conforms to the cinematic logics of representation and narration but fails to capture the range or intensity of hip-hop's social practices.

As rap demonstrated its staying power, commercial viability, and expansive potentials in regional markets throughout North America, the industry majors began strengthening the rap market through distribution deals with the independent ("indie") labels. There was already a concentrated effort in the industry to leverage black artists onto the charts and, crucially, to develop artists for careers (and LP sales) rather than expecting a string of hit singles. But the push for black crossover success on the scale of Kool and the Gang, Whitney Houston, Lionel Richie, and Prince led the majors to regard rap as a logical vehicle to extend the crossover thrust and expand into new urban markets. On February 11, 1984, under the headline "'Street Music' Label: Tuff City Rapping via Epic Tie," *Billboard* announced the unprecedented (and ultimately short-lived) distribution agreement between the independent "street label" Tuff City and the industry major Epic. The article defines the arrangement primarily in market terms that emphasize future growth and development in the genre. This would give indie labels a broader reach into diversified markets and reduce the constraints of labor-intensive localized marketing, which as the article suggests, at this stage still included selling records on the street out of the trunk of a car. The markets are also delineated along a conjunctural axis encompassing the overlapping variables of race, age, and musical tastes, suggesting a more complicated geocultural context for the deal. Tuff City is defined not simply as a comparatively smaller label, but rather as a company with a proximate relation to "the street" and the young black artists and audiences that inhabit the urban spaces the term evokes. The focus of the deal with Epic, therefore, was based on Tuff City's locus of operations and its connections to the hip-hop scene.

The enhanced distribution network meant that Tuff City would have the capacity to reach consumers in new regional markets and, crucially, to expand toward new audience groups, which in this context meant white teen record buyers. Spatially, Epic and the other corporate giants that followed were extending their reach into the urban locales where most of the production and innovation was based. By the end of 1985, two of the top rap indie labels, Tommy Boy and Def Jam, had also signed lucrative deals with major labels (Tommy Boy with Warner Brothers, Def Jam with Columbia), guaranteeing them access to substantially increased promotional budgets and broader distribution networks. In the Tommy Boy deal, the indie label maintained distribution rights over its twelve-inch singles, which allowed them to shop their product through established conduits including clubs, radio disk jockeys, and small, privately owned retail outlets. That these smaller labels sealed distribution deals with the majors at a point when prerecorded cassettes were the dominant configuration and rap LP sales were poised to rise (even though LP sales industrywide were slightly behind 1984 figures) is significant as an indicator that rap executives were strategically maneuvering within the industry to establish a greater market reach for their full-length album releases.

Additional organizational demands of the deals also necessitated the development of better marketing, promotions, and distribution structures within the independent labels in order for them to merge their operations with those of the majors. Maintaining talent, locating new artists, and ensuring that material was recorded, manufactured, and readied for distribution within the organizational practices of the larger labels introduced new standards to the still-evolving rap industry. This can be cited as an important factor in the continuing professionalization of the independent labels, which had, in a very short time, stepped into new industry relationships that gave rap unprecedented access to national and international markets. In an interesting development, in the aftermath of multi-platinum sales of Run-D.M.C.'s *Raising Hell,* the independent Profile label had attained sufficient capacity to sign production and distribution deals with eight smaller labels, working rap as well as rock product into the market while diversifying their business base.

Amid much talk of white consumer readiness for new-style R & B and rap, these deals between majors and indies were immediately touted for catapulting the Force M.D.'s single "Tender Love" (Tommy Boy, 1985), their LP *Chillin'* (Tommy Boy, 1986), and LL Cool J's *Radio* (Def Jam, 1985) onto the charts. Discussions of cautious optimism abounded, especially with respect to the majors' added clout and the renewed potential for rap to finally access black radio playlists, which commonly continued to dismiss rap. As one distributor suggested at the time, the Tommy Boy–Warner deal came as no surprise and quite possibly heralded "the wave of the future" (Chin 1985, 91). His words were prophetic: by the end of 1987 Cold Chillin' had signed with Warner Brothers, First Priority had a deal with Atlantic, Jive was working with both Arista and RCA, Uptown Records was linked with MCA, Uni was absorbed by MCA, and Ice-T's Rhyme Syndicate Records was in negotiations with Warner. The geographic distribution and increased market penetration realized through the Cold Chillin'–Warner deal led the chairman of Cold Chillin', Tyrone Williams, to note that since the distribution deal and the subsequent rerelease of MC Shan's *Down by Law* (1987), "we've been able to get product into places we'd missed before, such as the southwest and midwest" (George 1988a, 82).

Despite the announced intentions of most major labels to boost their commitment to black artists (with intensified marketing and promotion, videos, etc.) or to infuse their black music departments with more personnel and economic resources ("Learning Lessons of Prince Success" 1985), an air of caution still prevailed as they entered the street-music market. Rap was still regarded as a questionable musical and cultural force with an unproven capacity to sell records or produce bona fide stars in all markets with any longevity. The majors had demonstrated considerably more confidence in their strategic entry into the dance and crossover pop markets in 1983–84, reflecting their willingness at the time to develop their status in the black music markets. (It should be noted, though, that these markets continued to have a larger white consumer and audience base than did rap.) Seeking to reinforce their positions in the market, most of the more prominent black independent labels were at this stage all attempting to establish deeper rosters of hip-hop artists whose careers could be nurtured and extended and who could deliver consistent sales over an extended period.

Establishing Sustainable Crossover

By 1985 it was impossible for industry detractors to refer to rap in narrowly conceived terms, and by 1986 rap's sales were skyrocketing, led by Run-D.M.C.'s LP release *Raising Hell* (Profile), which, on the strength of the singles "Walk This Way" and "My Adidas," became the genre's first certified platinum LP. Released the same year, the Beastie Boys' *Licensed to Ill* (Def Jam) also attained platinum sales, eventually selling in excess of four million units, "a standard unsurpassed in rap until 1990" (George 1992, 27). The consolidation of rap in the business realm was only one dimension of the changes influencing the genre at this stage. Tricia Rose writes:

Like many groundbreaking musical genres, rap has expanded popular and aural territory. Bringing together sound elements from a wide range of sources and styles and relying heavily on rich Afrodiasporic music, rap musicians' technological in(ter)ventions are not ends in and of themselves, they are means to cultural ends, new contexts in which priorities are shaped and expressed.   (Rose 1994a, 95)

Her assessment accurately indicates the foundations of rap's sonic constructions, which have since its inception drawn widely from an array of sources, including Jamaican musical and cultural traditions, the archive of American black popular music recorded since the early 1960s, and the spoken words of politics and poetry, which are part of a rich oral tradition. Nonetheless, there is also ample evidence of more explicitly commercial motivations that informed the melding of musical sources in the construction of rap's hybrid styles.

In describing rap's crossover with white audiences, Rose voices her criticism of the music press, properly rebuking their paternalistic suggestion "that by using rock music, rap was maturing (e.g., moving beyond the 'ghetto') and expanding its repertoire." Citing the huge and unambiguously engineered crossover success of Run-D.M.C.'s "Walk This Way," featuring Steve Tyler and Joe Perry of the arena-rock band Aerosmith accompanying the rappers in the studio (and the video) with the familiar riffs of Aerosmith's 1976 hit release of the same name, Rose maintains that the song "brought these strategies of intertextuality into the commercial spotlight and into the hands of white consumers. Not only had rock samples always been reimbedded in rap music, but also Run-D.M.C. recorded live rock guitar on *King of Rock* several years earlier" (1994a, 51–52). While her initial assessment is valid—rock has, in fact, always been an audible element of rap—she does not explain *how* the intertextual nuances of rap were actually "brought" to white listeners, and she fails to fully explore the accompanying fact that rap had not, up to this point, been a consistent facet of white teen patterns of musical consumption.

Crossover success is never simply a commercial endeavor; rather, it involves the merging of signs and codes that are assumed to represent audience formations of different races. In rap's crossover movement, the images and aesthetic codes of urban black culture were carefully merged with the outlaw stances of white rockers. The timing of this engineered crossover is anything but accidental, for rock was also seeing a resurgence of interest and sales among white teen consumers—owing largely to intense exposure on MTV and the ongoing segregation of the airwaves—with groups including Bon Jovi, Def Leppard, Van Halen, Poison, Mötley Crüe, and Guns n' Roses gaining momentum and paving the way for an entire generation of hard rock acts. Heavy rock continued to show strong commercial activity from 1985 to 1988, as *Billboard* noted under the headline "Heavy Metal Bands Are Rocking Top 40 Playlists." Along with rap, it constituted one of the period's fastest-growing genres.

The more interesting question lies in how crossover was achieved and what practices and conditions facilitated it. Crossover success is, in a basic sense, transcultural. The very term carries racial and commercial connotations: Nelson George is unequivocal in his belief that "the test of crossover is how effectively popular black recordings can be sold to whites" (1989a, 157). Under America's persistent conditions of racial segregation, the connotations are also geographically delineated, encompassing social spaces such as points of purchase or primary locales of listening and leisure that are associated with the music. While most cultural analyses do emphasize rap's crossover to the white youth market, this demographic group constitutes only one segment of the wider audience formation reached through the genre's expansionist tendencies. For instance, it is also of supreme importance to acknowledge that not only did the commercial apparatuses position rap within white regional demographic markets with greater concentration, but they also ensured that it would reach a greater number of black consumer markets, coast to coast and border to border.

Analyses of rap's expansion in this temporal moment are so often focused on the implications of white crossover trends that the equally amazing saturation of the black teen market with increased product volume is too often overlooked. Rap was pouring into the black teen communities of America in a deluge of creativity and grassroots entrepreneurism. Mix tapes by local DJs were extremely important commodities in the hip-hop world, and the growing number of evening and late-night rap radio shows on campus and community stations provided a constant source of new material for home tapers. In 1985, the year LL Cool J's hit "I Can't Live without My Radio" (Def Jam) was released, sales orders of prerecorded cassette tapes surpassed those of vinyl recordings, although sales of prerecorded cassettes were leveling off as CD sales rose significantly. (Horowitz 1986). Homemade and pirate cassettes had been widely circulated among black and Latino youths within hip-hop circles for years, but their listenability was often hampered by poor reproduction quality. Tapes of this nature were cheaply reproduced and easily distributed, and they offered maximum mobility for consumers with battery-powered beat boxes. As rap gained industry support and independent labels established manufacturing and distribution deals with major labels, the flow of higher quality cassette products, along with vinyl twelve-inch singles, increased. In many cities, the beat box (at the time also referred to pejoratively as "ghetto blaster") was the medium of choice for mobile youths, who, to quote Public Enemy, "brought the noise" of rap with them as they navigated their urban environments. Simplified consumer access to a wider selection of rap recordings in multiple formats subsequently strengthened the transcultural appeal of the genre throughout the country.

Another issue warranting clarification is the common assertion that innovation and authority reside with the DJs and MCs themselves. This perspective overlooks the influential role of the various producers and label executives, who continue to have considerable impact on who and what gets recorded and distributed as well as on how these artists are positioned in relation to their genre and the broader system of generic musical categorization. Crossover is a manufactured or engineered phenomenon, and throughout the 1980s industry executives experimented with various black-white and generic pairings, seeking new and salable combinations (Garofalo 1997). For instance, the success of "Walk This Way," which also helped to rekindle lagging interest in Aerosmith—aging rockers who had been without a charting hit for the previous eight years—undoubtedly informed the Fat Boys' collaborations with the Beach Boys in 1987 ("Wipeout" [Tin Pan Apple]) and Chubby Checker in 1988 ("The Twist [Yo Twist]" [Tin Pan Apple]), both of which charted in the United States and the United Kingdom. These earlier rock and rap collaborations were also likely the inspiration for the remake of the classic 1968 rock hit "Magic Carpet Ride," featuring the original artists, Steppenwolf, with Grandmaster Flash and the Furious Five (1988, Elektra).

As *Billboard* interviews with industry executives from 1984 to 1987 illustrate, rap's crossover trend was engineered much more consciously than many scholars and critics acknowledge. A further expression of this can be seen in the means by which rap was introduced to North American audiences: through large-venue concerts and nationwide package tours and with promotional strategies that were entirely consistent with the music industry's established practices with respect to rock. The success generated by the deliberate merging of rock and rap aesthetics and promotions was so great that the dominant construction of the music and the accompanying scene underwent a substantial shift.

With crossover, at some point the sense of difference—with all of that term's spatial connotations—becomes blurred, permitting a weakening or collapse of constructed boundaries. Moreover, these boundaries are discursively established and maintained, and it stands to reason that their erosion is also a discursive project. Rap's crossover to sizable white teen audiences can therefore also be seen as a discursive process in which the socially invested values of rock and rap were articulated toward each other in such a way that they suddenly made sense to white teen listeners, who may have had only a passing familiarity with the genre based on the occasional crossover of single hits. This familiarity is important, since the more significant objective of sustainable crossover that had come about by 1986 was dependent on a certain prior awareness of rap as an option for consumption and enjoyment among the genre's new consumers.

While industry executives of independent and major labels aggressively marketed rap within an existing relational structure, the discursive construction of the genre as "black" music had the effect of distancing many potential white teen consumers, in some cases producing audience backlash against rap. This was seen as being consistent with the infamous "disco demolition" on July 12, 1979, in which the DJ Steve Dahl, of the Chicago rock station WLUP-FM, blew up hundreds of disco records at Comiskey Park, setting off pandemonium and outrage simultaneously. Rap, too, was exposed to the ire of rock fans who regarded the music, its producers, and its audiences with barely stifled racial disdain.

Within the industry, major label executives who were uncertain about how best to position rap in the market often wrongly regarded it as a natural extension of disco and dance musics. This was partly due to the fact that until 1983–84 (roughly coinciding with Run-D.M.C.'s eponymous debut LP) each of these genres was mainly club oriented, and were both distributed in the same twelve-inch-single format targeted toward black teen consumers. With the increased frequency of rap album production after 1985, releases had a better likelihood of being critically reviewed or prominently displayed in retail outlets and thus were positioned more closely to the rock market. Additionally, while *Billboard* reported (Horowitz 1986) that LP sales were down overall in the industry, rap album sales were relatively consistent. As the sale of singles fell off somewhat after 1984–85, rap labels were able to capitalize on shifting market trends.

Of further relevance is the fact that music is not always evaluated in terms of what it is (or what it is like), but in terms of what it is not. The rock-rap hybrid also therefore involved an aesthetic articulation away from the earlier disco-rap hybrid (characterized by much of the party-oriented subgenre represented by "Rapper's Delight" or "The Breaks"), which constitutes quite different assumptions that have been mapped onto the organization of audience formations and patterns of consumption and use. The acceleration of rap's corporate and commercial harmonization coincided with aesthetic transitions in the music's construction as rap's sound began to show the influences of heavy rock with greater frequency, a sound that is audible on Kurtis Blow's "8 Million Stories" (1984, Poly-Gram), Run-D.M.C.'s "Rock Box" (1984, Profile), or the Beastie Boys' "Rock Hard" (1984, Def Jam). In the case of Run-D.M.C.'s earliest efforts, including "Rock Box," the signature sound of the Latino guitar ace Eddie Martinez had a defining influence and provided yet another layer of cross-cultural interaction. The rhythmic drift away from disco (i.e., Chic's "Good Times," which had provided the bed track for "Rapper's Delight") toward a more pronounced rock backbeat made rap accessible to white teens in new ways while also introducing a new spatial reorientation of rap performance toward arenas instead of discotheques.

The guitar and drum embellishments displayed with the "new" rap reproduced many of the standard features of rock. Rap was, in effect, made more suitable for performances in the larger venues and arena spaces, which favored a mass audience forum, as opposed to its prior exhibition at the level of clubs and smaller concert halls. Rap's transformed sound—the tradition of bass-heavy volume of the Jamaican sound systems exemplified by Kool DJ Herc notwithstanding—literally filled space differently and in ways that made it more amenable to the arena venues, which up to this point had been primarily associated with rock. The achievement is isolated less in the hybrid constructions of rap's form or style than in its sonic capacities, its potential to have an aural impact in another kind of space where before it had been heard only infrequently.

The discursive and aesthetic distancing of rap from disco and its realignment with rock constructs a radically different sense of its character. This realignment also affected the attitudes of the record-buying public, which began to consider it in different relational terms and associated it with different listening sites and contexts. The tranformative sound was manifested through the merging of slashing rock power chords (or, as in Kurtis Blow's "8 Million Stories," the rare inclusion of a screaming guitar solo) and arena-rock postures accompanied by a deep funk beat, producing a musical hybrid that further facilitated a crossover effect and brought white teen audiences to the music in droves. In cases such as "A Fly Girl" (1985, Capitol), by the Boogie Boys, the rhythm owed more to rock than to funk, in this case successfully adapting the general sonic qualities and time signature of Queen's hit "Another One Bites the Dust" (1980, Elektra) (before the track had become a staple nationwide at sports venues). Still, the melding of styles and genres that attracted white listeners to rap should not be regarded as a simple, unidirectional feat. Numerous rap artists also acknowledge their fandom and familiarity with a generation of rock acts such as Aerosmith, AC/DC, Led Zeppelin, and Billy Squire, to name several guitar-oriented acts whose pronounced styles have been successfully integrated into rap. In the early 1990s the rock-rap collaborations continued, perhaps reaching their pinnacle with Ice-T's formation of the heavy metal group Body Count, and continuing toward the end of the decade with star acts such as Cypress Hill, Kid Rock, Limp Bizkit, and Rage Against the Machine.

Rick Rubin is frequently singled out by many rap historians for his role as the coproducer (with Russell Simmons) of Run-D.M.C's *Raising Hell* (1986, Profile) and for introducing the Beastie Boys as the first significant white rap act by streamlining their punk influences toward rap forms. Reflecting on Def Jam's market potential in relation to multiracial record-buying fans in *Billboard*, Rubin stated that "rap's appeal is mostly to black teens right now but it's getting bigger and attracting more rockers every day" ("Def Jam" 1985, R-6). It was Rubin who, as a producer for Rush artists and for the upstart Def Jam label, was mainly responsible for the intensified melding of rock and rap, leading David Toop to observe that "Rick's philosophy was that music should be hardcore" (1991, 159)—which was more in line with Rubin's own publicly confirmed taste affinities. Simmons and especially Rubin were central in redefining the rap aesthetic by foregrounding rock guitars and radically implementing developing technologies, including the Roland TR 808 drum machine.

Rubin's production and taste influences extended the hybrid tendencies that had been the trademark of artists such as Afrika Bambaataa by foregrounding the rock influences to the exclusion of everything except the hip-hop beats and rap's lyrical forms. The result was a sound that was the antithesis of mainstream commercial pop but that still appealed to a wide swath of black and white teenagers who were, like Rubin himself, seeking alternatives and buying from the margins, from the musical underground. These particular rock influences were more explicit and more relentless than previous experiments in hybridity, and although Rose and others have at times minimized the aesthetic implications of rock's influences on crossover, there is no denying that its conscious and strategic deployment more fully conformed to white teen male listeners' tastes.

The success of the most prominent example of the trend at the time, "Walk This Way," was achieved by more than the simple appropriation of a familiar chord progression or vocal chorus, and it involved more than the act of capturing a recognizable motif or sample upon which to expand. "Walk This Way" constitutes a textual site where two sets of musicians who unambiguously represented their respective genres met. Russell Simmons and Rick Rubin, among others, correctly speculated that the white teen consumer demographic would also support rap groups in the rebel mold of Run-D.M.C. or the Beastie Boys, isolating the marketing significance of their postures and mannerisms as elements that exceed the music and encompass more complex symbolic meanings. Run-D.M.C., the top rap act in the mid-1980s, was cast in an image of raw intensity that represented the image-ideal of the street-hardened b-boy (despite the group members' roots in Hollis, Queens).

As all of this suggests, the crossover success of black artists such as Run-D.M.C., LL Cool J, and Kool Moe Dee resides in more than the music alone; crossover always includes a cultural dimension. The carefully orchestrated posturing and posing and the much-circulated images of blue jeans, black leather jackets, and name-brand footwear combine to signify authentic ghetto-identified blackness. These sartorial expressions, along with the rock edge and funk beats, create an overall effect that taps into rock traditions and long-standing notions of teen rebellion to which white consumers have responded since at least the early 1950s throughout the rise of R & B and rock 'n' roll. These traces of a rock tradition are, furthermore, portrayed as facets of a predominantly male authority that functions through the primary signification of masculinity and the expression of heterosexual masculine desires. (It is significant to note that although female rappers have been active participants in the scene from its beginnings, from 1984 to 1986 their influence was comparatively minor. There were no female acts on the first Fresh Fest tours, and it was not until rap began its major crossover trend after 1986 that female rappers began to attain greater recognition and unit sales.) The new male rap acts were seen to embody an innate "badness" that fit white teen expectations of its rock stars. The argument might be made that rap's crossover movement signaled another confirmation of rock's masculine hegemony, since it was the codes of rock and its symbolic reproduction that, when grafted onto rap, finally boosted it into the upper echelons of the music charts.

Other changes were occurring as well: the vocal flow evolved, becoming more complex and less rigidly fixed on the beat after 1986, and several new styles of vocal delivery emerged. Lyrical content also revealed shifting thematic trends: message raps, love raps, party raps, and boasts could be found on the charts simultaneously. The rap genre's repertoire was expanding although the music's underlying "street" or ghetto sensibilities were still identifiable as a source of innovation. Major stylistic changes in the genre continued to take shape within smaller, more localized club settings before they emerged as elements of any larger trends. The sartorial b-boy image of Run-D.M.C., the punk-influenced image of the Beastie Boys, and the smooth lover-man image of Whodini and LL Cool J all combined to illustrate the widening breadth of styles that fell within the rap category. These shifts effectively rerouted the trajectory of rap and hip-hop.

Corporate Intervention and the Cultural Devaluation Argument

Rap's unprecedented successes, especially among artists recording on the Def Jam, Jive, Profile, and Tommy Boy labels, helped to stimulate sales in the entire black music market. Ironically, the genre's sales were lifted by the Beastie Boys, who, on the strength of their Def Jam release *Licensed to Ill*, had the first rap album ever to reach number one on the *Billboard* Pop Album chart, selling triple platinum (in excess of three million units) in less than eight months. The concept of a white act surpassing sales of other acts in a black-dominated genre was not unheard of in the history of American popular music, nor was it an accident in this case: Def Jam consciously positioned the album in the market to reach a white teenage market with substantial disposable income. The group's blend of rap and punk rock and their personae as hip urban "party animals" appealed to a cross-section that drew from several audience taste formations, especially on college and university campuses with alternative campus-based radio stations, where they received regular airplay. But even with the sales dominance of the Beastie Boys at this stage, rap did not succumb to an onslaught of white opportunists, and the white artists who have attained major prominence in the genre are few, although white hip-hop enthusiasts and entrepreneurs have frequently been influential in the production and executive sectors of the industry.

At the same time, black culture, identity, and musical expression remained central issues to community elders and national leaders who had fought long and hard during the civil rights and black power movements of the 1950s, 1960s, and early 1970s. In 1985 and 1986 discriminatory music industry practices attracted the attention and critical scrutiny of Jesse Jackson as well as the NAACP, and in January 1987 that organization released a report condemning the industry for racial discrimination throughout its ranks. The report also assailed the industry for racial exploitation based on its concentrated efforts to establish crossover sales by black artists. Thus, even as black music was reaching a commercial peak, it was perceived by many cultural critics as being in a morass, its cultural traditions threatened by industry interventions. Black cultural watchdogs and traditional activists, mindful of the powerful role that music had played in earlier social struggles, warned that major labels' commercial imperatives could diminish the music's capacity to mobilize political awareness or to provide cultural adhesion across generations. Although a younger generation of cultural commentators was heralding hip-hop's potentials and redeeming qualities, many older critics were less forthcoming, begrudgingly acknowledging that rap might offer a unique and valuable alternative to the industry manipulations of black music and talent that were still mainly concentrated in the R & B and pop music markets. Despite its multi-platinum sales and the now-standard distribution arrangements linking indies to major labels, rap was still largely free of mainstream industry meddling in A & R decisions and was considered by many of the artists involved in its production to be a pure expression of black cultural identity and youth experience.

Writing in *Billboard* in 1986, Nelson George retrospectively assesses rap's positive influence within a generally declining quality of black music over the previous ten years. He identifies the culprit as "corporate black music," which he defines as "product that had its raw edges rubbed off, that took the mellow side of black music as the standard by which all the music should be measured." Pointing to the increased number of black artists reaching the Top Ten charts and achieving gold and platinum sales, industry executives had what they considered reliable evidence that their support of black music was positive and reaching fruition. Success is measured monetarily in an industry context, however; cultural aesthetics, history, and tradition are of minor, if any, concern. Among the citizens of the hip-hop nation, rap was perceived almost universally as a bastion against the further erosion of black music's cultural relevance, leading George to state that "from its lyrics to its beat, it is as true an expression of the sensibility of urban black America as anything since soul" (George 1986b, 23).

In George's observation lies the affirmative logic gradually adopted by many rap artists themselves. The social consciousness and ghetto reality initially popularized by "The Message" was gradually emerging as a crucial element of the new rap as black youths continued to extend the project of reconstructing their social and political identities through hip-hop's expressive forms. Through a more pronounced ideological discourse and explicit cultural agenda, rap artists established strong and consistent links between issues of race, space, and youth identities, reproducing a facet of the genre that has had important consequences for youth of all ages and cultural dispositions.

Paul Gilroy addresses this phenomenon when he describes "a distinct, often priestly caste of organic intellectuals" (which he advances in a Gramscian sense of the term) who have actively maintained a sense of black cultural tradition while influencing cultural transformation and growth in and through their music:

They have often pursued roles that escape categorization as the practice of either legislators or interpreters and have advanced instead as temporary custodians of a distinct and embattled cultural sensibility which has also operated as a political and philosophical resource. The irrepressible rhythms of the once forbidden drum are often still audible in their work. Its characteristic syncopations still animate the basic desires—to be free and to be oneself—that are revealed in this counterculture's unique conjunction of body and music. (Gilroy 1993a, 76)

As this passage suggests, the capacity for music to communicate and disseminate more deeply known and felt elements of either subjective or collective identities that fall within what Gilroy terms a "cultural sensibility" is a central factor in the role of musical expression. Rap- and hip-hop-influenced styles are but the latest and currently most influential form in a lengthy tradition of black musical expressiveness that transmits the psychic materials upon which people of a shared but dispersed culture can draw as a sustaining force in their lives—as a resource. In this reading, then, the cultural functions of the music in relation to black cultural issues are at odds with the industry and market expediencies that sweep it up and into another realm, one that adheres to a quite separate (though not isolated) cultural sensibility of capitalistic materialism.

Yet, as Gilroy and others have remarked, there is rarely any kind of a cohesive blackness that serves to unite and bond blacks across the broad diaspora, let alone within a nation demarcated by cultural unevenness and geocultural variation. Noting the struggles over authenticity and cultural identities that have produced numerous ruptures within both the hip-hop nation and the more encompassing category of "black music," Gilroy states that "the fragmentation and subdivision of black music into an ever-increasing proliferation of styles and genres . . . has also contributed to a situation in which authenticity emerges among the music makers as a highly charged and bitterly contested issue" (1993a, 96). With the ongoing industrial appropriation of black music, rap's status as the next and newest form of black musical invention made it an optimist's repository for the ideals and values of black cultural authenticity. The ensuing struggles, which reached often deadly proportions by the mid-1990s, clearly involve issues related to the definition of a black identity within competing hip-hop cultural sensibilities as well as debates over what image of black identity should dominate.

As the NAACP study claimed, the thrust for crossover that brought many previously obscure black artists to a much larger and more culturally diverse social spectrum also had negative effects within the black musical community. For instance, while many pop and R & B acts willingly positioned themselves for maximum commercial market exposure, other black artists were frustrated by the major labels' push for crossover and were subtly encouraged to alter (or "bleach") their sound and style and make it more "palatable"—less black—in order to accommodate the tastes of a wider audience. As the NAACP correctly noted, the major corporate entities themselves were often responsible for assembling and grooming favored crossover acts that would transcend the Black Singles or Black Albums charts. This resulted in a two-tiered system within black music consisting of those who were targeted primarily toward the black charts and those who were positioned for crossover to the pop charts and the broader consumer base.

The crossover phenomenon was not unique to the period, having emerged as an established practice in the 1950s when R & B, doo-wop, and rock 'n' roll gained popularity and black artists and promoters actively pursued white teen audiences. In the 1980s the trend was much more aggressively driven owing to the higher economic stakes involved. Lionel Richie is one example of an artist who crossed over with relative ease: as a founding member of the successful R & B group the Commodores he was influential in achieving a string of Top Ten pop hits, but the group was more consistently represented on the R & B/Soul chart in the late 1970s. Richie embarked on a solo career in 1981, and as a result of careful orchestration by the label for which he recorded, Motown, he established himself as an adult contemporary and pop hit maker, following in the steps of Motown's earlier superstars Marvin Gaye and Smokey Robinson. Following his successes with the Commodores, Richie released four gold-selling records in the 1980s and reached platinum sales in 1981 with "Endless Love," a duet with Motown's soul/pop diva, Diana Ross.

Far too frequently, acts whose recordings reached number one on the black hit charts would languish in the mid-ranges of the pop charts, often because their labels failed to provide adequate market push for the release or the artist involved. The deeper cultural aesthetics and forms that were strongly associated with soul and funk in the 1960s and 1970s—the slap bass style, black vernacular, sly sexual innuendo, and politicized social commentary —were generally absent from the material of black crossover artists of the 1980s. This was thought by many to create a diluting effect, diminishing the connective and culturally sustaining role that traditional black popular music served in its prime. Top-charting recordings blending politicized content and soul or funk aesthetics—evident, for example, in the crossover Marvin Gaye hits "What's Going On" and "Mercy Mercy Me (The Ecology)" (1971, Tamla/Motown)—became increasingly rare as black pop was streamlined for mainstream audiences.

The plight of many black R & B and soul singers was further complicated by competition from talented white artists such as George Michael, whose style and repertoire often strayed into soul-tinged idioms. For example, several of Michael's releases were in high rotation on black radio and urban-format stations across the nation. *Faith* (1988, Columbia) reached number one on the Top Black Albums chart in May 1988, and the album single "One More Try" (Columbia) reached number one on the R & B Singles charts, earning him accolades and awards as a Soul/R & B artist. This white encroachment on a cornerstone of black cultural expression subsequently caused a furor within black musical and cultural debates, although this was neither the first nor the last of the issue.

Rap and (especially) black pop experienced a market surge in 1986–87. The period also saw the overall market decline of unexpurgated funk and with it the weakening influence of a particular musical and cultural era that had in part engendered rap. Despite the continued popularity of funk-oriented dance music and the ongoing funk influences that were central to Prince's compositions (and those of his Minneapolis protégés, the Time) or to Cameo, whose 1986 release "Word Up" (PolyGram) reached the *Billboard* Top Ten, many original funk-based mainstays, such as George Clinton and Rick James, gradually faded from the charts. Rickey Vincent describes the industry's actions from the 1970s disco era through the mid-1980s as a frontal assault in a "war on the funk." As he explains, "Major labels took control of every aspect of black music at the time, from management to distribution, promotion and *actual musical production,* leaving a perceptible void in the heart and soul of a people's collective identity" (1996, 213). He suggests that it was at the urging of the major labels that many funk acts first began to adapt their material toward disco in the attempt to catch the wave that swept much of the industry in the late 1970s and early 1980s.

Of course, neither industry manipulations nor technological innovation automatically produces conditions for cultural devaluation or resuscitation. Vincent does not elaborate on other, related factors, such as a growing conservatism among black middle-class consumers and deeper generational taste divides (exemplified by black radio programming), that were undoubtedly implicated in the changes that he observes. He asserts that "the funk" is and remains the fundamental element in contemporary black music, yet his argument displays a problematic understanding of black authenticity and cultural essentialism, which in his view is forged in the music itself and disseminated through rhythmic and lyrical forms. He claims that "in the 1970s it was first soul and then The Funk that maintained many of the values that were integral to the black community's sense of identity—but that all changed in the 1980s" (1996, 272). While this is true to an extent, he underemphasizes the intertwined relationships between commercialism, community, identity, and "the funk," which fluctuate according to shifting social and historical conditions. Having demonized the majors,

Vincent then points to the rise of black-owned independent labels as the saviors of black musical expression, positing rap as the new musical and cultural force shaping black identities despite a plethora of evidence of rap's own questionable commercial characteristics and decidedly mainstream (and unscrupulous) business tactics.

Additional influences, such as overreliance on digital synthesizer technologies, which deemphasized traditional funk aesthetics, also contributed to the erosion of the traditional soul and funk genres as the industry began favoring radio-friendly, dance-oriented pop. This is amply evident on the hit "Solid" (Capitol), by Nick Ashford and Valerie Simpson, or Kool & the Gang's "Cherish" (De-Lite)—both Top Ten pop hits that reached number one on the R & B charts in 1985. At the same moment traditional funk began to wane, it began to be appropriated by young rap producers armed with digital sound samplers who found in it a treasure trove of familiar sounds and beats. These formed the backbeat for some of rap's most exciting and important recordings. Digital samplers, which were emerging as a common feature of recorded rap by 1986, effectively maintained many of the earlier funk influences in black popular music, infusing select beats from recordings such as James Brown's "Funky Drummer" into myriad hip-hop tracks. Despite numerous legal copyright battles along the way, by the early 1990s several of the musicians—such as James Brown, the Gap Band, the Isley Brothers, and the late Roger Troutman—whose work comprised this deep sampling archive saw their careers reinvigorated. After a career derailment and bankruptcy, George Clinton launched a legal campaign to collect royalties on his sampled material, later going on to work with the Red Hot Chili Peppers, Ice Cube, and Prince. Clinton returned to regular touring and appeared on the much-hyped Lollapalooza alternative music tour in 1994 and at the 1999 Woodstock concert.

The Top Black Albums chart in mid-1987 provides an appropriate site for assessing the shifting terrains of black music and the competing strains within it at the time. Sharing chart space are artists from the lists of pop and R & B artists (Jody Watley, Luther Vandross, Smokey Robinson, and Anita Baker), funk (such as Prince, Cameo, and the System), and rap (including the Beastie Boys, Run-D.M.C., Kool Moe Dee, Salt-n-Pepa, D. J. Jazzy Jeff and the Fresh Prince, 2 Live Crew, and Public Enemy). As *Billboard* noted, as many as fourteen of the mid-year chart albums were by rappers (Chin 1987a, 26), although the list of rappers represented on the chart is also noteworthy for its diversity of forms and styles. Both white and black consumers in the over twenty-five age demographic were responding well to the soul-oriented sounds of Anita Baker, Maze (featuring Frankie Beverly), Freddie Jackson, and Luther Vandross, all of whom were prominently featured on the influential Quiet Storm radio format, which, like rap, matured in the mid-1980s, while independent rap labels reaped impressive sales among both white and black teens.

The Hot Black Singles chart of November 7, 1987, reflects a somewhat different phenomenon. Contemporary rap and pop artists were matched by recording mainstays from the 1960s and 1970s: the O'Jays, Michael Jackson, Marlon Jackson, the Temptations, and Stevie Wonder occupied five of the top ten spots. Clearly, black hit radio's rejection of rap is responsible for its poor showing in this list. As critics and independent label executives postulated, the older and middle-class interests controlling many black hit stations continued to seek a more upscale listenership to deliver to advertisers, demonstrating a continuing preference for the more familiar styles of established soul and R & B acts even after rap was firmly established on the record sales charts and had begun to display a broader stylistic range.

Cultural responsibility on the part of program directors seemed to be an underlying issue as rap struggled for consistent airplay on black radio. The prevailing discourse among independent label executives and artists cast recalcitrant programmers as insufficiently sensitive to their cultural role as black cultural advocates despite the counterargument that "an audience, not a musical form's cultural roots, dictates what a station should play" (Olson 1988). Black radio's lack of commitment to rap was a deep source of frustration among independent rap label executives, who had assumed that resistance to the genre would decrease after it had attained a critical mass in terms of popular recognition and market sales. They argued against rap's ongoing marginalization, suggesting that its market strength alone qualified it for inclusion on mainstream black radio stations, and rejected program directors' rationalizations that the genre was not commercially viable for radio. The failure of black radio programmers to give rap what label executives felt was its due was an important factor in the decision of many indie labels to merge their companies with major-label distribution networks.

After years of exclusion from black radio and in the aftermath of Run-D.M.C.'s enormous hits "Walk This Way" and "My Adidas," many rap labels turned away from black radio in frustration. Instead, they concentrated their efforts on Top 40 radio, which had been instrumental in breaking several rap hits and seemed better able to accommodate a flexible format. Ice-T's track "Radio Suckers," from the 1988 LP *Power* (Rhyme Syndicate/ Sire), castigates black radio program directors:

> Look, check out the sales charts,
> My record's kickin', I'm breakin' P.D.'s hearts,
> They banned me from their shows,

Because they said I'm too hard,
But no sell-out, I guess I'm just barred!
. . .
Radio suckers never play me!
"Tone it down" is what they said to me,
"The FCC will not allow profanity,
Your subject matter's too hard, make a love song,"
You better get real, come on,
I ain't no lover, I'm a fighter . . .
Radio suckers never play me!

The album liner notes also offer special thanks "to all the radio stations with brains and guts." Further defining his position in *Billboard,* Ice-T stated, "I don't think the negative propaganda about rap comes from the true black community—it comes from the bourgeois black community, which I hate. . . . The bourgeois blacks term Freddie Jackson 'good R & B' and rap as 'nigger music, too black.' The black bourgeois middle class don't want their kids to listen to this 'nigger music'" ("Artists on Image" 1988: R5).

Even with the negative examples of industry manipulation in pop and R & B, speculation abounded about the virtues of major-label participation in rap. The latent belief was that if the majors were to take a more aggressive role in rap, rather than functioning at arm's length from the scene, their considerable heft and influence would leverage rap onto black radio play-lists and give it exposure commensurate with its sales and market impact, enabling it to reach an eager multicultural fan base that spanned the national landscape. In retrospect, it is obvious that campus and community radio were leading the charge in rap broadcasting, fulfilling their license mandates to provide complementary and noncompetitive programming while "bringing the newest Hip Hop jams" to audiences in the nation's largest broadcast markets.

In New York, Los Angeles, and other major urban markets, key urban commercial stations (including Los Angeles's all-hip-hop KDAY and New York's WKSS and WBLS, the latter featuring the highly recognized and respected hip-hop DJ Mr. Magic) that regularly featured rap day-parts or that switched formats completely to accommodate a steady playlist of hip-hop music often had the best Arbitron "books," making sizable gains in ratings and listener shares among the youth demographic. As rap developed less aesthetically compromising and non-radio-friendly subgenres (exemplified by the music of Public Enemy, Boogie Down Productions, and N.W.A.) after 1987–88, campus and community radio also offered an important alternative public site in which to regularly hear "hardcore" rap, along with artist interviews and freestyle demonstrations, which were infrequently featured on commercial stations. As a result, urban black radio stations that refused to program rap were no longer perceived as cultural taste leaders among their core youth audiences, and teen listeners tuned out in search of more consistent rap programming.

Distinctions in the Hip-Hop Schoolyard: Old- and New-School Rap

Accompanying the many changes rap underwent from 1987 to 1990 were key aesthetic transitions that signaled a break from the popular rock-influenced sounds that had prevailed since 1984. Several influential albums — now considered classics in the genre — by new artists introduced a wider range of rap styles and represented a correspondingly wide range of regional activity. Among these are Eric B and Rakim's 1987 debut album *Paid in Full* (4th & Broadway/Island Records); Boogie Down Productions' *Criminal Minded* (1987, B-Boy Records); DJ Jazzy Jeff and the Fresh Prince's *Rock the House* (1987, Jive); LL Cool J's *Bigger and Deffer* (1987, Def Jam); Ice-T's *Rhyme Pays* (1987, Sire); N.W.A.'s *N.W.A. and the Posse* (1987, Macola); Public Enemy's *Yo! Bumrush the Show* (1987, Def Jam); Salt 'n' Pepa's *Hot, Cool, and Vicious* (1986, Next Plateau); and 2 Live Crew's *2 Live Crew Is What We Are* (1987, Luke Skyywalker). Commenting on rock music's cyclical patterns of obsolescence and renewal, Theodore Gracyk describes the phenomenon of "aesthetic fatigue," which necessitates either adjustment or death in a style or genre: "There aren't always pressing social forces driving change, and the 'problem' of generating the creation of artifacts need not be replaced by a fresh problem. We simply tire of our minor variations of the same old thing" (1996, 206). The artists listed are exemplary of a response within rap to the aesthetic fatigue that had crept into the genre by 1987.

The style, sound, and presentation of the industry leaders, Run-D.M.C. and the Beastie Boys, was, by late 1987, almost four years old, and despite their multi-platinum sales figures, continued chart placement, and concert drawing power, neither group ever regained the full momentum of their *Raising Hell* or *Licensed to Ill* phase. Yet over the course of roughly eighteen months, the impact of new, emergent artists altered the trajectory of rap and hip-hop. The rise of a new wave of talent with distinctive and distinctly fresh approaches to the genre creatively revitalized rap and motivated its growth in the market, making this an important phase in the geo-cultural expansion of hip-hop.

The rap scene's aesthetic diversification contributed to a need for the genre distinctions (or what Frith refers to as "genre labels") that were eventually implemented by the industry to identify the proliferation of new styles. These genre labels (knowledge rap, gangsta rap, reality rap, pop rap, etc.) were eventually standardized in industry discourses and the media as a form of marketing shorthand, deployed as an efficient means of description in the industry's larger marketing strategies aimed at effective product positioning. From a commodity perspective, the enhanced stylistic variety provided much-needed diversity for the genre even though older, more established artists, including Run-D.M.C., the Beastie Boys, and Whodini, among others, were still leading in terms of sales and exposure. Through its expanding distribution and sales apparatuses linking independent and major recording companies, the industry was better able to position new artists and their material for different listener groups representing nuanced market niches. This extended the range of options for rap consumers, whose numbers were growing and who inhabited diverse and farther-flung locales, and led to the development of a more sophisticated understanding of the rap metagenre.

At a certain point rap's temporal and spatial elements converge. The general stylistic and cultural disparities between early rap and that of the late 1980s led to the definitional distinctions between "old-school" and "new-school" rap. Not sufficiently substantial to be defined as genre distinctions, the differences between the old and the new schools were nonetheless relevant and meaningful in industry and audience circles. By 1988 rap had been a fully realized facet of black youth expression for over ten years, and many of its emergent artists had grown through their formative teen years with hip-hop as a standard cultural influence. Rap's impact at various junctures had provided the funky backdrop to an entire generation (and is now also doing so for another generation), spawning another wave of styles and artists with a diverse range of talents.[1]

Critical perceptions of a scene without focus (Toop 1991) failed to acknowledge that the apparent drift can also be explained as a realignment and changing of the guard. The older, established artists were challenged by up-and-coming talent displaying different skills from those of their predecessors. This was played out most prominently in the ongoing public battle between the old-school artist Kool Moe Dee, who cofounded the pioneering Treacherous Three (and who appeared in a cameo role in the 1984 film *Beat Street*), and LL Cool J, who personified the arrogant self-confidence of the mid-1980s new school. The issue sparking the combat was simple in principle: who is the baddest, freshest, deffest rapper in the business? LL Cool J set the tone by questioning the talents of old-school rappers, deconstructing their dominance and positing himself as the brash new rap leader. The battle garnered considerable attention among hip-hop fans and critics, however, for in the rap scene these are not trifling claims but the equivalent of throwing down the gauntlet.

The tension and antagonism between the two rappers in fact became a selling point, and both artists exploited the conflict as a means of generat-

ing greater consumer interest in their recorded output. With every new release, each artist boasted about his prowess while "dissing"—dismissing,
disparaging, or disrespecting—the other, continuing the cycle through calculated responses that were eagerly anticipated by audiences. The lyrical
blows were delivered in songs such as Kool Moe Dee's "How Ya Like Me
Now" (1987, Jive) and LL Cool J's "Jack the Ripper" (1988, Def Jam); the
cover image of the LP *How Ya Like Me Now* depicted Kool Moe Dee driving a Jeep over LL Cool J's trademark Kangol hat. Describing their mutual
antagonism, the liner notes to *Def Jam's Ten Year Anniversary* CD compilation package (1995, Def Jam Records) draws a parallel with the young
boxer Cassius Clay, who dethroned the "old bear" Sonny Liston in the
ring. Nelson George focused on the rappers' publicly expressed antagonisms in his *Billboard* column under the headline "Old School and New
School Rappers Battle for Supremacy: Kool Moe Dee, LL Cool J Get Busy"
(George 1988b, 25). While foregrounding the temporality of their competition, George also identifies a cartographic element that emerged as rap expanded from the narrow locales of its origins: "the old-school rappers are
those whose careers started in the New York boroughs of the Bronx and
Manhattan during the early '70s. The term 'new school' is applied to anyone outside that elite group, though it is usually meant to refer to successful young rappers from Queens or Long Island, N.Y., and elsewhere"
(George 1988b, 25).

The spatial context for Kool Moe Dee and LL Cool J's battle, waged on
wax over the course of several releases and on several occasions in front of
live audiences in concert settings, was, at its core, also directly influenced
by rap's commercial popularity. The dueling MCs were not protecting
local turf boundaries or audience loyalties associated with geographic
space in any traditional sense. Rather, by 1988 rap's commercial growth and
national appeal had altered the stakes and changed the form and forum of
the battles as artists engaged in struggles over *market* turf on a whole new
scale. Consuming fans expressed their loyalties to artists at the point of
purchase, since it was record sales that constituted the final measurable
gauge of rap superiority. This can be discerned in LL Cool J's derisive attack on Kool Moe Dee on the single "Jack the Ripper" when he states
"How ya like me now? / I'm getting busier / I'm double-platinum / I'm
watchin' you get dizzier." As this suggests, microphone skills were crucial,
but sales were the final determinant of one's supremacy. While Kool Moe
Dee was unquestionably a bankable talent and a bona fide rap star, LL
Cool J's sales far outdistanced him, a reflection of his victory in the MC
battle and the commercial terrains of the evolving rap music market.

None of these commercial developments fully eradicated the sense of geographic identification and localized turf affiliation that had been central to the scene from the start; the influence of local cultures and neighborhood influences remained strong. Numerous recordings addressed space and place explicitly, boasting about the virtues of the performers' home environment while dismissing or negating the relevance of other spaces and places to which opposing rappers pledged allegiance. This dynamic provided the underlying theme in another celebrated rap battle involving MC Shan and KRS-One. With his 1987 single "The Bridge" (Cold Chillin'/ WEA), Shan attempted to elevate the profile of Queens and the Queensbridge housing projects in particular, challenging the rap supremacy of the Bronx as the home and heart of hip-hop. Shan was a member of the Juice Crew, a production posse (including Marley Marl, the Real Roxanne, Biz Markie, and Big Daddy Kane) that recorded on the independent Cold Chillin' label and that represented some of the best rap from the borough of Queens. KRS-One and DJ Scott LaRock of Boogie Down Productions battled Shan on wax, releasing the devastating response records "South Bronx" and "The Bridge Is Over" (1987, B-Boy Records). With the lyrics "Manhattan keeps on makin' it, / Brooklyn' keeps on takin' it / Bronx keeps creatin' it / and Queens keeps on faking it," KRS-One attacked MC Shan and the entire Juice Crew for "lying" about rap's origins. Significantly, even the name Boogie Down Productions keeps the Bronx front and center, adapting hip-hop's cartographic designation: the Boogie Down Bronx.

In a special section on rap published in *Billboard*, Monica Lynch, then president of Tommy Boy Records, explained that "the way the New School of rappers dress, the way they rhyme is different from what's been going on in New York for the past four years. It's not Run-D.M.C. or an LL Cool J style. The New School doesn't have anything to do with the macho posturing or busting a gold chain" ("Artists on Image" 1988). Lynch is indicating the rise of yet another wave of talent, including DJ Jazzy Jeff and the Fresh Prince, Eric B and Rakim, and Public Enemy, who comprised the ascendant groups in the rap industry in this period. Her observation describes further transitions that were underway in multiple contexts and helps to isolate the point of the crucial shift between rap generations as the next crop of artists and styles emerged, establishing the patterns that were to dominate until roughly 1994.

The New Funk, the New Flow: Aesthetics, Style, and Content

After 1986 a new kind of "noise" emerged, a reorganization of sound and an altered sense of "flow" (Rose 1994a, 39) that challenged the dominant rock-oriented rap that had earlier swept the charts. From both the marketing and the consumer perspective, these aesthetic transitions suddenly made rap more interesting. David Toop reads these developments quite differently, citing the proliferation of subgeneric styles in 1987 as a negative result of rap's expansions. In his view, "the market had fractured and rap briefly lost a sense of direction, either looking for a marketing niche, looking for crossover sales in the opening created by Run-D.M.C. or temporarily withdrawing into the underground to compose rhymes loaded with serious purposes and music devoid of commercial sweetening" (1991, 175). His description defines the rise of new artists and influences primarily in market terms, and he views their efforts either as calculated gestures geared toward enhanced commercial success or as conscious strategies of a more cultural and political nature. Toop does not specifically address the aesthetic aspects of these transitions or the myriad elements that appeal to listeners and ultimately form the basis for their affective investments and subsequent audience formations. Whether calculated or not, what is not acknowledged about the music's changes in this period is that the array of emergent subgenres was intrinsically related to the remapping of the geographies of the rap music scene and that they had important implications for the evolution of the genre as it continued to grow outward and reach new audiences.

Rap's aesthetic transformations and fragmentation in 1987–88 produced several prominent stylistic subgenres that introduced a variety of listening experiences. Rap's cadences, which had been so closely linked to the rhythmic and vocal qualities of a rock aesthetic for the previous three years, showed a gradual return to funk influences (often through the use of digital sampling technologies and innovative production techniques), accompanied by a broader range of vocal styles and lyrical themes. The establishment of a new aesthetic and discursive framework was an achievement of major proportions as rap's appeal and cultural influences continued to extend not only beyond the confines of the Northeast, but also beyond the localized terrains of black cultural communities and other closely defined social settings. Growing numbers of consumers and fans were attracted to the music as its stylistic range expanded and regionally dispersed "home champions" more consistently established themselves both in their local settings and in wider regional markets, producing corresponding local and regional audience bases. Although the centrality of New York was not immediately at risk of being usurped, regional talents such as the Fresh Prince and Steady B (from Philadelphia), the Geto Boys (from Houston), Ice-T and Eazy-E (from Los Angeles), Luther Campbell (from Miami), and Sir Mix-A-Lot (from Seattle) were asserting their presence and gradually decentering New York rappers as the sole driving forces of the rap aesthetic. Curiously, despite harboring their own active rap scenes, prominent music cities such as Detroit, Chicago, and Washington, D.C., seldom produced chart-topping rap talent. Detroit's techno dance music is renowned, as is Chicago house and Washington go-go, but while these musics contributed substantially to the depth of hip-hop culture, the cities that spawned them remain lesser forces in commercial rap to this day. In considering how rap became a major musical and cultural force, it is therefore necessary to acknowledge the transformative aesthetics involved, for the changes have resonating implications for developments in other areas of activity, including industry categorization, product placement and marketing, and artist recruitment and development.

Rap's lyrical content shifted as well, as MCs including Ice-T, Just Ice, KRS-One, and Rakim frequently expressed their views and described various experiences (including criminal activities) from a first-person, subjective, ghetto-oriented perspective. They were not necessarily the first to do so: this was also a characteristic of the influential but less skilled Philadelphia rapper Schooly D, who emerged slightly earlier (and who deserves some credit for being the first gangsta rapper). In contrast to earlier forms of message rap or the place-specific references of Run-D.M.C., which explicitly identified itself with Queens, the descriptive imagery in the lyrics rendered place in a much more proximate sense.

Artists' common byways and everyday perambulations were given a new depth and detail. The tendency toward narrative self-awareness and a more clearly definable subjectivity effectively closed the distance between the story and the storyteller, and the concept of a place-based reality became more of an issue in evaluating an artist's legitimacy within the hip-hop scene. Perspectives on the detailed spatial terrains of an artist's environment were a new focus of listener attentions, evolving as a standard discursive element of gangsta or reality rap.

The proliferation of artists and new subgenres also reoriented rap in the market, producing a new series of marketable commodities. Defined by Simon Frith as "genre rules," the formation of subgenre differences and distinctions is part of a structuring of values in the segmentation of markets, which is relevant to fans and industry taste-makers alike:

It is genre rules which determine how musical forms are taken to convey meaning and value, which determine the aptness of different sorts of judgment, which determine the competence of different people to make assessments. It is through genres that we experience music and musical relations, that we bring together the aesthetic and the ethical. (Frith 1996, 95)

In the post-platinum period after 1986, rap's fragmentation into a multitude of identifiably distinct and interrelated subgenres adhered to the general rules described by Frith. As I mentioned, temporal distinctions between old- and new-school styles were insufficiently encompassing to function meaningfully as generic markers. But by instilling this aspect of temporality and an accompanying chronology of breaks and ruptures, critics, journalists, and rappers together were writing rap's history and building a sense of the genre's tradition.

The eventual naming of detailed subgenre distinctions provided a more useful set of terms for understanding categorical differences or similarities as they evolved across the temporal spectrum, whether the analysis is focused on beats, vocal flow, style and personae, or ideological, discursive, and thematic characteristics. For instance, while the distinctions between gangsta rap, knowledge rap, and Afrocentric-Islamic "message" rap are based primarily on discursive themes, the distinctions that define reggae hip-hop more accurately reflect a response to the music's formal characteristics. The major subgeneric distinctions were not initially identified and defined by the industry. Rather, they emerged as meaningful comparative references from within the hip-hop culture and rap scene and were of primary significance in the organization of audience formations and discrete taste groups that formed more or less spontaneously. It was not until 1988, with the combined ascension of a New York–based Afrocentric black-nationalist impulse (most clearly associated with Public Enemy and KRS-One) and the West Coast gangsta rap styles (initially embodied by Ice-T and N.W.A.) that the industry began explicitly and fully exploiting these generic distinctions as part of their marketing strategies.

Rap's aesthetic diversification and capacity for commercial growth was noted by the music industry elite. In June 1988 Mike Greene, president of the National Association of Recording Arts and Sciences (NARAS), officially announced a new Grammy Award category for rap. The given rationale was that the genre had proven its market durability and demonstrated commercial staying power, at the same time displaying a capacity for change and innovation. In his press release Greene stated, somewhat paternalistically, that "rap last year was an urban black music form, and over the last year it has evolved into something more than that. It has matured into several kinds of music, with several kinds of artists doing it. We felt there was enough product coming out to justify a rap category" (Terry 1988, 6).[2] Clearly, rap had always displayed a range of styles and aesthetic characteristics; Greene's statement simultaneously exposes his unfamiliarity with rap and expresses the industry's capitalistic ethos, which disconnects culture from commerce. With his announcement, however, Greene also articulates a much more biased perspective, one suggesting that as an "urban black music form," rap apparently does not warrant NARAS recognition; it is only with its market growth and geographic expansions into new social sectors that NARAS deems it worthy. The quote offers a classic example of the continuing devaluation of rap, and of black cultural expression in general, in the culture industries.

While Greene's comments imply that the genre's conformity to industry structures and market demands was a sign of its maturity, they also indicate the point at which industry executives fully acknowledged rap's sophistication and, more important, its enhanced commercial potential as an array of subgeneric styles. Rap's surge of diversification was regarded as a necessary factor in industry terms, offering more options for marketing and promotion to a wider range of consumers. With the NARAS stamp of approval, rap was eagerly embraced by the mainstream music industry after 1987, finding regular placement in record retail outlets, television, film sound tracks, and music and culture magazines.

CHAPTER SIX

Boyz N Girlz in the 'Hood

From Space to Place

❈

Say somethin' positive, well positive ain't where I live
I live around the corner from West Hell
Two blocks from South Shit and once in a jail cell
The sun never shined on my side of the street, see?
—Naughty by Nature, "Ghetto Bastard (Everything's Gonna Be Alright),"
1991, Isba/Tommy Boy Records

If you're from Compton you know it's the 'hood where it's good
—Compton's Most Wanted, "Raised in Compton," 1991, Epic/Sony

Reflecting on the intensification of regional rap activity during what might be defined as the genre's "middle-school" period, Nelson George writes that 1987 was "a harbinger of the increasing quality of non–New York hip hop," citing as evidence the fact that three of the four finalists in the New Music Seminar's DJ Competition were from "outside the Apple— Philadelphia's Cash Money, Los Angeles's Joe Cooley, and Mr. Mix of Miami's 2 Live Crew" (George 1992, 30).[1] In the pages of *Billboard*, he observed that despite New York's indisputable designation as the home of rap, Philadelphia rappers in particular (most notably, DJ Jazzy Jeff and the Fresh Prince) were making inroads into the scene and on the charts, making it "rap's second city." This expansion was facilitated by the emerging trend of artist-owned independent labels and management companies, which in some cases entered into direct competition with other non-artist-owned independent labels or with major music corporations.

After years of bogus contracts, management conflicts, and poor representation, a growing number of artists began dividing their duties between recording or performing, locating and producing new talent, and managing their respective record companies. By forming self-owned labels and publishing companies and establishing themselves as autonomous corporate entities, forward-thinking rap artists were also able to maintain creative control over their production while ensuring a greater percentage of returns on their sales. In rather excessive language, artists spoke of throwing off the corporate shackles of the recording industry, and they invoked the quite separate issues of building something of which one can be proud and being remunerated in a more equitable and lucrative manner.

Once several key start-up labels—such as Luther "Luke" Campbell's Skyywalker Records, on which recordings by his X-rated group 2 Live Crew were released, and Eazy-E's Ruthless Records, home to N.W.A.—were established and had proven their viability, the trend grew markedly as more and more artists followed their example.[2] For many recording artists, getting "paid in full," as Eric B and Rakim put it in their song of that title (1987, 4th & Broadway), suddenly also meant learning the production and management side of the industry and exercising entrepreneurial skills. As the trend expanded, small artist-owned and -operated labels rose throughout the nation, and another tier was added to the industry. With the rise of artist-owned labels came an increased emphasis on regional and local affiliations and an articulation of pride and loyalty in each label, its artist roster, and the central locale of its operation.

Rap is characteristically produced within a system of extremely close-knit local affiliations, forged within particular cultural settings and urban minority youth practices. Yet the developments in the rap industry whereby production houses or record labels might be identified by the artists or producers at the helm or on the basis of their regional and local zones of operation are not unique to this current period. Immediately after World War II, when independent labels were dispersed across the nation, many small specialty labels recorded local and regional artists while serving the needs of black music consumers within these regional markets. Attempting to track rap's position in relation to the history and traditions of black commerce in the music industry, George explained in *Billboard* that "regional music used to be the backbone of black music and—maybe—it will be again" (1986a, 23).

When one examines the history of black popular music in the 1960s and 1970s, the names Motown, Stax, and Philadelphia International Records (PIR) evoke images of composers, producers, and musical talent working within very specific studio contexts in Detroit, Memphis, and Philadelphia. The dispersed independent labels and production sites that operated from the 1950s through the 1970s are therefore culturally meaningful and relevant to descriptions of black music of the period, for they convey an idea of consistency and identifiable signature sounds or styles.[3] This trend has continued with rap, yet there is a more pronounced and explicit connection to specific locales and the articulations of geography, place, and identity that sets the genre apart from many of its musical predecessors. In rap, independent labels are valued and measured according to the skill and quality of the production team as well as the roster of artists who are recording and releasing material. Developing the collective assemblage of fellow artists is one of the primary duties of artist-owned independent hip-hop labels. This includes locating potential talent, often through informal social contexts, and nurturing their artistic development by providing them with opportunities to perform live with the headlining artists or to associate with them in the studios, where they may also be granted a guest spot on a track or a full-length CD. This common industry practice constitutes a professional system that is hierarchically organized, with the established artists themselves constituting the main draw as aspiring rap talent enters their orbit in the hope of being signed to the label.

Most of the smaller labels that had thrived in the 1950s, 1960s, and 1970s disappeared as musical tastes shifted, economic transitions evolved, or the industry majors swallowed them up or bumped them out of the market by introducing their own specialty labels. Toward the end of the 1980s, the larger industry was no longer even primarily American, as the trend toward huge transnational entities intensified. These entertainment conglomerates (EMI, Sony, Polygram, RCA, MCA, and Warner Brothers) operated from corporate offices based in several countries. Mergers and corporate buyouts have since changed the names and the corporate terrain. Against the placelessness of transnational capital and the global flow of information and cultural commodities, there was a resurgence of regional music production in the mid- to late 1980s and, with it, the resurgence of regionally distinct styles or "flavors." In the black music sector, these were exemplified by Minneapolis funk, a trademark of Prince, the Time, Jimmy Jam and Terry Lewis, and Jesse Johnson; the Washington, D.C., go-go sound of Chuck Brown, Redd and the Boys, and especially Trouble Funk; and from Chicago, house music, exemplified by DJ Frankie Knuckles. Rap production in New York, Los Angeles, and Miami also began to display geocultural idiosyncrasies as individual producers emerged with their own trademark styles and influences. Studios such as Chung King in New York (where many of Def Jam's acts recorded) also became associated with specific rap production styles and sounds.

Artist-owned labels must also define their sound and style in relation to other artists and labels in the market. Once artists have established themselves among audiences, critics, and peers, they commonly continue to mine the aesthetics with which they are already associated, reproducing a general sound that serves as a label signature and distinguishes them from the competition. Using Ruthless Records as a corporate home, Eazy-E helped shape and publicize the Los Angeles gangster aesthetic that was central to N.W.A. while providing a stable production center for Dr. Dre to work with additional talent, including the non-hardcore acts JJ Fad, Michel'le, and Po, Broke & Lonely. Eazy-E worked his product with the existing hip-hop radio stations, providing them with new material and establishing close relations with the localized rap scene in the attempt to build a strong reputation through effective promotions. He also at one point hosted a rap program on KDAY, which provided further exposure and located him at the center of a vibrant scene. Luther Campbell likewise established his Skyywalker label (later Luke Records) as a base from which to develop his porn rap subgenre. The bass-heavy production styles of 2 Live Crew were standard at Skyywalker, but Campbell also diversified, signing H-Town as a sensuous male vocal group.

In December 1989 a *Billboard* special section on rap featured advertisements for several new artist-owned labels that illustrated the regional expansions underway. Among these were ads for Ruthless Records (Compton, California), Skyywalker Records (Miami, Florida), and Ice-T's Rhyme Syndicate (South Central Los Angeles). Appearing alongside these were advertisements for the established independent rap labels Def Jam, Tommy Boy, and Jive, as well as ads for the newer "street" divisions of major labels, including Atlantic ("The Strength of the Street"), MCA ("Wanna Rap? MCA Raps. Word!"), and Epic ("Epic in Total Control. No Loungin', Just Lampin'"). The phenomenon has since evolved to the extent that artist-owned operations have become an industry standard. Artists and producers are now influential players within the same corporate forum as the dominant major label executives.

Homeboys and Production Posses

As Greg Tate explains, "every successful rap group is a black fraternal organization, a posse" (1992, 134). On the same theme, Tricia Rose writes that "rappers' emphasis on posses and neighborhoods has brought the ghetto back into the public consciousness" (1994a, 11). For Public Enemy's Chuck D, posse formations are a necessary response to the fragmenting effects of capitalism; "the only way that you exist within that mold is that you have to put together a 'posse,' or a team to be able to penetrate that structure, that block, that strong as steel structure that no individual can break" (Eure and Spady, 1991, 330). Each expression here isolates the posse as the fundamental social unit binding a rap act and its production crew together. It creates a relatively coherent or unified group identity that is rooted in place and within which the creative process is supported. It is not unusual for an entire label to be defined along posse lines, with the musical talent, the producers, and various peripheral associates bonding under the label's banner.

Collective identities are evident as a nascent reference throughout rap's history in group names such as the Sugarhill Gang, Doug E. Fresh and the Get Fresh Crew, the 2 Live Crew, X-Clan, or the Wu-Tang Clan. The term "posse" is today unambiguously adopted by rap artists such as California's South Central Posse or Orlando's DJ Magic Mike, whose group records as the Royal Posse. In some cases several recording acts align themselves within a linked posse structure, sharing labels and producers, appearing on each other's recordings, and touring together. This aspect of the posse influence, despite disclaimers to the contrary (Wood 1999), can be discerned in earlier amalgamations such as the Native Tongues, which at one point included A Tribe Called Quest, De La Soul, the Jungle Brothers, Monie Love, and Queen Latifah; the Blackwatch Movement, a Muslim-oriented rap posse made up of X-Clan, Isis, and Queen Mother Rage; the Brooklyn-based Boot Camp Click, consisting of Buckshot, the Cocoa Brovaz, Heltah Skeltah, Originoo Gunn Clappaz, and the Representativz; and, more recently, the New Orleans–based No Limit Army associated with Master P's No Limit label, which included C-Murder, Fiend, Master P, Mia X, Mystikal, Silkk the Shocker, and its marquee recruit, Snoop Dogg. As if to underscore just how pervasive the concept has become, the mainstream press has also employed the term: an article about Death Row Records and its CEO, Suge Knight, was published in the *New York Times Magazine* (Hirschberg 1996) under the headline "Does a Sugar Bear Bite? Suge Knight and His Posse."

Defined as "a strong force or company," for many North Americans the term "posse" summons up notions of lawlessness and frontier justice that were standard thematic elements of Hollywood westerns in the 1940s and 1950s. This is, in fact, the basis of the term as it is applied within rap circles, although its current significance is also crucially related to the ways in which the Jamaican posse systems have over the years adapted the expressive terminology and gangster imagery of the cinema to their own cultural practices. In her illuminating research on the sinister complexities of the Jamaican posse underworld, Laurie Gunst (1995) relates how the posse system grew under the specific economic, political, and cultural conditions of mid-1970s Jamaica, evolving into a stratified and violent gang culture that gained strength through the ganja, cocaine, and crack trade. As she explains, the Jamaican posse system has since 1980 been transplanted to virtually every major North American city.

The time line of the Jamaican posse expansion is important in this context, as it coincides almost precisely with the emergence of rap and hip-hop in New York's devastated uptown ghetto environments. This connection is strengthened when the common lore of rap's hybrid origins, which were forged in the convergence of Jamaican sound systems and South Bronx funk, is considered. Among reggae artists through the 1970s and 1980s, names associated with real or cinematic criminals, such as John Dillinger or the Outlaw Josey Wales, were common. The Jamaican "bad boy" character, which shares several common traits with black American icons such as Stagger Lee, constitutes the image-ideal of the outlaw posse member. It has been traced through various social mechanisms and discursive overlays upon many of rap's themes, images, and postures that take the forms of the pimp, hustler, gambler, and gangster in the music's various subgenres that evolved after 1987.

In certain instances, contemporary rap artists have also tapped into the well of black cinematic figures, resuscitating the cool, hard, dominating postures of the blaxploitation figures John Shaft (*Shaft* [1971, directed by Gordon Parks]) and Goldy (*The Mack* [1973, directed by Michael Campus]). Since roughly 1987, the hip-hop culture has also been influenced by alliances associated with West Coast gang systems, which are primarily centered around the territorial boundaries and practices of the Crips and Bloods. For instance, media speculation on Death Row's connections with the Mob Piru Blood set in Los Angeles has never been denied by Knight, and numerous album covers and videos in the rap genre feature artists and their posses "representing" their gang set and their local 'hoods by displaying hand signs and symbols. The practice reached such an epidemic that BET's *Rap City* video program now forbids explicitly gang-related hand signs in the videos selected for screening. Additionally, the New York Italian Mafia (the Gambino and Luciano families and the "Teflon Don," John Gotti) has emerged as a recurrent thematic model that has been adopted within the New York rap scene, including the late Notorious B.I.G.'s protégés, Junior Mafia, as have Asian Triad gangs, evident among the Wu-Tang Clan. Together these examples provide a series of image-ideals of "fraternal organizations" based in a symbolic economy of gangsterism, or what the vocal group DRS refers to as a "Gangsta Lean" (1993, Capitol).

Since its inception in the mid- to late 1970s, the hip-hop culture has always maintained fiercely defended local ties and a built-in element of competition waged through hip-hop's cultural forms of rap, break-dancing, and graffiti. This competition has traditionally been staged within geographical boundaries that demarcate turf and territory among various crews, cliques, and posses, extending and altering the spatial alliances that had previously cohered under other organizational structures, including but not exclusive to gangs. With the discursive shift from the spatial abstractions framed within "the ghetto" to the more localized and specific discursive construct of "the 'hood" occurring in 1987–88 (roughly corresponding with the rise and impact of rappers on the West Coast), there has been an enhanced emphasis on the powerful ties to place that both anchor rap acts to their immediate environments and set them apart from other environments and other 'hoods as well as from other rap acts that inhabit similarly demarcated spaces.

Commenting on rap's nationwide expansions in 1988, Nelson George writes: "Rap and its Hip Hop musical underpinning is [*sic*] now the national youth music of black America. . . . Rap's gone national and is in the process of going regional" (George 1992, 80). George was right then, as rap was rising out of the regions and acts were "hitting" from the South (Miami-based 2 Live Crew and Houston's Geto Boys), the Northwest (Seattle's Sir Mix-A-Lot and Kid Sensation), the San Francisco Bay area (Digital Underground, Tupac, and Too Short), Los Angeles (Ice-T and N.W.A.), and elsewhere. Indeed, the significance of the east-west split cannot be overstated; it has led to several intense confrontations between artists representing each region and has been the single most divisive factor within the hip-hop nation to date. Prior to the establishment of more stable and consistent rap labels throughout the nation, artists associated with cities in midwestern or southern states often felt obligated to align themselves with one region or the other, or else they attempted to deftly sidestep the issue without offending their peers on either coast. In the past several years, however, Atlanta, Houston, and New Orleans have risen as important rap production centers in their own right, emerging as powerful forces from what is termed in hip-hop parlance "the Dirty South."

After 1988 the emphasis was on place, and by the early 1990s groups were explicitly publicizing their home environments with names such as Compton's Most Wanted, Detroit's Most Wanted, the Fifth Ward Boyz, and South Central Cartel. Some also structured their home territory into titles and lyrics, constructing a new and internally meaningful hip-hop cartography. This is illustrated by the Flint, Michigan, group the Dayton Family, whose release *What's on My Mind* (1995, Po' Broke Records/Relativity) features the tracks "Flint Niggaz Don't Play" and "Dope Dayton Ave." It is also common practice in recordings and live performances for acts to explicitly refer to their home region's telephone area code or postal service zip code, as exemplified by the title of a release by the Boston-area act Ed O. G. and da Bulldogs, *Roxbury 02119* (1993, Chemistry Records/PolyGram). The explosion of localized production centers and regionally influential producers and artists has drastically altered the hip-hop map, and production posses have sprung up throughout North America. These producers have also demonstrated a tendency to incorporate themselves as localized businesses (often buying or starting companies unrelated to the music industry, such as restaurants or car accessory outlets, in their local neighborhoods) and to employ friends, family members, and members of their wider neighborhoods. Extending Nelson George's observation, it now seems possible to say that rap, having gone regional, is in the process of going local.

As a site of affiliation and circulation, the 'hood provides a setting for particular group interactions that are influential in rap music's evolution. In rap, there is a widespread sense that an act cannot excel in the market—"blow up"—without first gaining approval and support from the crew and the 'hood. Successful acts are expected to maintain connections to the 'hood and to "keep it real" thematically, rapping about situations, scenes, and sites that comprise the lived experience of the 'hood. At issue is the complex question of authenticity as rap posses continually strive to reaffirm their connections to the 'hood in the attempt to mitigate the negative accusations that they have sold out in the event of commercial or crossover success. Charisse Jones has noted a dilemma confronting successful rap artists who suddenly have the economic means to "get over" and leave the 'hood. Writing in the *New York Times,* she notes that successful artists such as Snoop Doggy Dogg and Ice-T were often criticized in the mid-1990s for rapping about ghetto poverty and gang aggression while living in posh suburban mansions (1995, 43).

Those who stay in the 'hood generally do so to be closer to friends and family, closer to the posse. While a common rationale for staying in the 'hood is familiarity and family bonds, in numerous cases artists also justify their decision to stay on a creative basis, suggesting that the 'hood provides the social contexts and raw resources for their lyrics. Others leave with some regret, suggesting that the 'hood may be home but the tension and stress make it an entirely undesirable place to live (this is even more frequent among rappers with children to support); there is no romanticizing real poverty or real danger. The 'hood is, however, regularly constructed within the discursive frame of the "home," and the dual process of announcing place-based pride in one's home place, or "representing" (which involves creating a broader profile for the home territory and its inhabitants while showing respect for the nurture it provides), is now a required practice among most rap acts. The posse is always explicitly acknowledged, and individual members are greeted on disk and in live concerts with standard shout-outs that frequently cite the streets and localities from which they hail. This continual reference to the importance of social relations based in the 'hood tempers the damning images of an oppressed and joyless underclass that are so prevalent in the media and contemporary sites of social analysis. Rap may frequently portray the nation's gritty urban underside, but its creators also communicate the value of places and the people that build community within them. In this interpretation, an insistent emphasis on support, nurture, and community coexists with the grim representations that generally cohere in the images and discourses of ghetto life.

As in all other popular-music genres, "paying dues" is also part of the process of embarking on a rap music career, and the local networks of support and encouragement, from in-group affiliations to local club and music scenes, are exceedingly important factors in an act's professional development. One way this is facilitated is through the posse alliances and local connections that form around studios and producers. For example, in describing the production house once headed by DJ Mark the 45 King, Fab 5 Freddy recalls that "he had this posse called the Flavor Unit out there in New Jersey. . . . He has like a Hip Hop training room out there, an incredible environment where even if you weren't good when you came in, you'd get good just being around there" (Nelson and Gonzales 1991, xiii).[4] This pattern is replicated in numerous instances and is also exemplified by the production/posse structure of Rap-A-Lot Records in Houston (home to acts such as the Geto Boys and Scarface, the Fifth Ward Boyz, Big Mike, and Caine), where the company was forced to relocate its offices because "artists were always kicking it there with their posses like it was a club" (James 1992, 18). By coming up through the crew, promising young artists learn the ropes, acquire lessons in craft and showmanship, attain stage or studio experience and exposure, and quite frequently win major record deals based on their apprenticeships and posse connections.

It is necessary to recognize that the home territory of a rapper or rap group is a testing ground, a place to hone skills and to gain a local reputation. This is accurately portrayed in the 1992 Ernest Dickerson film *Juice,* where the expression "local" is attributed to the young DJ Q. In one instance it suggests community ties and home alliances, whereas in another context it is summoned as a pejorative term that reflects his lack of success and inability to mobilize his career. In interviews and on recordings most rappers at some point refer to their early days, citing the time spent hanging out among friends—with their "homies" or crews—writing raps or perfecting their turntables skills, and getting onto the stage at parties and local clubs or dances. Their perspective emerges from within the contexts they know and the places they inhabit. These experiences are also mediated by the powerful influences of professional artists, whose forms and styles tend to establish dominant trends that, in turn, affect the practices of young artists who seek entry into the upper echelons of the music industry.

Few rap scholars (Tricia Rose and Brian Cross being notable exceptions) have paid attention to these formative stages and the slow processes of developing MC and DJ skills. There is, in fact, a trajectory to an artist's development that frequently goes unremarked. In practice, artists' lyrics and rhythms must achieve success on the home front first, where the flow, subject matter, style, and image must resonate meaningfully among those who share common bonds to place, the posse, and the 'hood. In this sense, when rappers refer to the "local flavor," they are identifying the detailed inflections that respond to and reinforce the significance of the music's particular sites of origin and that might be recognized by others elsewhere as being unique, interesting, and thus marketable.

The posse structures that privilege place and the 'hood can be seen, then, as influential elements in the evolution of new rap artists as well as relevant forces in the emergence of new, regionally definable sounds and discourses about space and place. For example, critics and rappers alike acknowledge the unique qualities of the West Coast G-funk sound, which defined a production style that emerged with Dr. Dre's work on the *Deep Cover* sound track and the release of his 1992 classic *The Chronic* (Death Row/Interscope), and arguably reached its apex with the 1994 release of Warren G's *Regulate: G Funk Era* (Violator/Rush Associated Labels). Warren G is Dre's half brother, and their extended posse had considerable chart success between 1992 and 1995.[5] Other local artists from the Los Angeles area, such as the Boo Yaa Tribe, Above the Law, Compton's Most Wanted, and DJ Quik, also prominently feature variations on the G-funk sound and reinforced its influence in the industry as a West Coast subgenre. G-funk characteristically employed standard funk grooves by artists including George Clinton, Bootsy Collins, Gap Band, and the late Roger Troutman and is recognized for its "laid-back" sensibilities and sonic sparsity, featuring slow beats and extended sample loops. Although it was regarded as a regionally distinct style, it was also often related specifically to Dr. Dre's production aesthetic and was categorized by its difference from the more cacophonous East Coast jams (recognizable in the early work of Public Enemy's production crew the Bomb Squad). As Cross (1993) notes, however, the impact of the G-funk style among California rap acts is also related to the extended influence of late-1970s funk in the Southwest. This was a consequence of limited access to independently produced and distributed rap product in the early 1980s, a circumstance that delayed rap's geographic expansion from New York to the Los Angeles area.

Explaining the Bomb Squad's production processes following the release of Public Enemy's *Fear of a Black Planet* (1990, Def Jam), Chuck D describes his production posse's familiarity with various regional styles and tastes and their attempts to integrate the differences into the album's tracks:

Rap has different feels and different vibes in different parts of the country. For example, people in New York City don't drive very often, so New York used to be about walking around with your radio. But that doesn't really exist anymore. It became unfashionable because some people were losing their *lives* over them, and also people don't want to carry them, so now it's more like "Hey, I've got my Walkman." For that reason, there's a treble type of thing going on; they're not getting much of the bass. So rap music in New York City is a headphone type of thing, whereas in Long Island or Philadelphia . . . it's more of a bass type thing.

(Dery 1990, 90)

These regional distinctions between the "beats" are borne out in the example of the Miami production house of Luther Campbell and Orlando's Magic Mike. In Florida (and to some extent, Georgia) the focus is on the bass—Florida "booty bass" or "booty boom," as it has been termed—which offers a deeper, "phatter," and almost subsonic vibration that stands out as a regionally distinct and authored style.[6] Within the hip-hop culture, artists and fans alike reflect an acute awareness that people in different parts of the country produce and enjoy regional variations on the genre; they experience rap differently, structuring it into their social patterns according to the norms that prevail in a given urban environment. Thus, the regional taste patterns in south Florida are partially influenced by the central phenomenon of car mobility and the practice of stacking multiple ten- or fifteen-inch bass speakers and powerful sub-woofers into car trunks and truck beds.

Add to these stylistic distinctions the discursive differences from the various regions (i.e., the aforementioned gangsta rap from the West Coast crews, the chilling, cold-blooded imagery from Houston's Fifth Ward and "Bloody Nickel" crews on Rap-A-Lot Records, and the "pimp, playa, and hustla" themes that were standard among Oakland crews in the late 1980s and early 1990s and are now common among New Orleans acts); the localized posse variations in vocal flow and slang; and the site-specific references to cities, 'hoods, and crews, and a general catalog of differences in form and content becomes evident. What these elements indicate is that while the rap posse provides a structured identity for its members, it can also provide a referential value to the production qualities and the sound of the musical product with which it is associated.

Spatial Discourse, the 'Hood, and the Nation

By 1990 what were defined as message rap and gangsta rap (or, as they were also known, knowledge rap and reality rap) had emerged as important rap subgenres that, more than other strands, adhered to relatively defined spatial discourses. Message rap is identified by its thematic bonds to Grandmaster Flash and the Furious Five's release "The Message" and a conscious engagement with the interrelated issues of race, class, and cultural identity. Gangsta rap portrays lifestyles of the young and edgy, replete with violent imagery of the seamy urban underside. In their different, contradictory, and even antagonistic approaches to the concept of space and spatiality, theses two subgenres more than others effectively reveal the extent to which issues of race, space, and place dominate the concerns of young rap artists and the various audience formations that comprise the hip-hop culture. Prominent message rap acts such as Boogie Down Productions (BDP), Paris, and Public Enemy maintained the centrality of traditional rap skills by basing their presentation on the established performative interrelationships between the DJ and the MC. KRS-One of BDP, who is also known by the moniker "The Teacher," has emerged as one of the staunchest defenders of traditional hip-hop cultural values, instating a cultural organization called the Temple of Hip-Hop that he promotes on recordings and in live performances as well as via the Internet. Their unique contributions, however, were in the promulgation of distinctly Afrocentrist and pro-black political and cultural ideologies, lyrical pedagogy, and often insightful analysis and critical commentary regarding contemporary social issues. The nationalist discourses in this rap subgenre consequently inform minority youths and challenge them to educate themselves and each other in order to mobilize real change within their collective communities rather than relying on racist social systems to provide their cultural knowledge (and their spiritual knowledge of self).

An important adjunct of this subgenre is the Islamic rappers of the Chicago-based Nation of Islam (or the smaller Five Percent Nation sect), in which Ice Cube, Paris, the Poor Righteous Teachers, Rakim (of Eric B and Rakim), Lakim Shabazz, X-Clan, and many others claim membership. Among this cohort the lyrical messages maintain a commitment (often inconsistent) to the basic tenets of the Islamic faith and remain sympathetic to the American Muslim heritage of Malcolm X as well as to the contemporary Muslim teachings of Louis Farrakhan.[7] These rappers frame the black cultural diaspora within the expansive reach of the faith and the religious discourses of Islam rather than articulating it in specifically spatial or racial terms.

As the heavy gold chains of one generation of rappers and b-boys gave way to the next generation's red, black, and green medallions featuring a silhouette of the African continent—a cartographic statement of cultural identity with extenuating nationalist implications—the general idea of a unified black youth culture acquired a clearer definition among hip-hop practitioners. By founding identity and shared history in an essentialized blackness, the pro-black messages introduce a collectively realized image of racial and cultural heritage while attempting to address issues of contemporary common struggle. Blackness—not urban environment or social space—determines the nationalist character of this position, fixing identity along a linear continuum with the past. Message rap, especially from 1987 to 1994, arose as part of a deliberate effort to forge links across the diverse social settings and urban landscapes that divide and separate black youth throughout the country. This process includes the communication of a series of hybrid black nationalist discourses functioning within an inconsistently applied and at times contradictory political agenda. The hybridity of these discourses is defined by the sweeping embrace of a variety of historical and political movements: antislavery and emancipation movements, the 1950s civil rights and 1960s black power movements, and current activist movements contesting social prejudice and police violence against young blacks are all discursively encompassed.

The rhetoric of black unity linking artists and members of wider hip-hop audience formations is invariably constructed in the form of an urgent appeal for greater political and cultural awareness. The aim is to resist and reorder the debilitating social conditions gripping black America. In attempting to communicate a sense of solidarity among black youth, the spatial differences between 'hoods, cities, and regions are generally downplayed, although they are not—indeed, they cannot be—ignored completely. In a manner reminiscent of the Black Panther party's initiatives in the 1960s, the different cities and the separate 'hoods are often conceived as self-contained cells that exist autonomously, working within the particular conditions of the local, but remain part of the larger hip-hop movement. Through recognition of shared conditions across the nation, the depressed environment of the 'hood emerges as a common spatial symptom of a larger systemic decay that has had an inordinate impact on black and Latino populations.

As the most dynamic act to rise within the message rap subgenre after 1987, Public Enemy and its frontman, Chuck D, have continued to outline an agenda for radical social transformation in its recordings through explicitly politicized terminology and uncompromising ideological commitment to political activism. For example, "Power to the People" (1990, Def Jam) invokes both the battle cry from the 1960s black power movement and 1970s funk, through explicit references to several James Brown songs, in the context of a 1990s rap mix. This strategy forges a sense of historical continuity within black cultural activism that, importantly, encompasses both men and women. The group's most recognizable anthem, "Fight the Power" (1990, Def Jam), adopts the title of a 1975 Isley Brothers hit and forms the musical underpinning of the director Spike Lee's 1989 film *Do the Right Thing*. On the track, Chuck D stresses the need for intellectual awareness and a learned attitude toward revolution and radical social transformation, referring to "mental self-defensive fitness" and the mission to "make everybody see / in order to fight the powers that be." The rhetorical appeal to collective revolutionary action describes the idealistic formation of a broad-based social coalition of conscious youth.

The Oakland-based artist Paris was even more explicit about his "plea for unity" on the track "Break the Grip of Shame" (1990, Scarface/Tommy Boy), in which he refers to black pride, revolutionary movement, and the Islamic faith, all presented within what he describes as "pro-black radical raps upliftin'." Paris and Public Enemy both identify a knowledge gap within the black nation that must be spanned in order to unite the black constituency as a coherent whole. Like KRS-One (especially on the track "You Must Learn" from the album *Ghetto Music: The Blueprint of Hip Hop* [1989, Zomba/BMG]), these artists articulate the need for black youths to inform themselves for the "revolution" that is already under way in the cultural war zones and in the depressed urban terrains of the 'hood. In these constructions, the 'hood is not conceived as a benign space in the urban landscape, nor is it portrayed simply as a localized zone of economic disenfranchisement or social depravity. Rather, it is depicted as ground zero in the imminent class war; a zone of urban unrest in which resistance is fomenting as the themes of renewal are promulgated through hip-hop's radical discourses.

In his inquiry into the cultural resonance and meanings of the term "the 'hood," Paul Gilroy poses the question, "How is black life in one 'hood connected to life in others? Can there be a blackness that connects, articulates, synchronizes experiences and histories across the diaspora space?" (1992, 308). He criticizes the idea of "nation," which has emerged as an important structuring concept in American hip-hop culture (mainly since 1987), and remains skeptical of the value invested in the discourses of "family" unity (communicated in the rhetoric of black brotherhood and sisterhood) when so much territorial antagonism is evident in the strands of rap that privilege the spatialities of gang culture and turf affiliation. Gilroy expresses his perplexity at the closed contours that the 'hood represents, suggesting that its centripetal spatial perspectives inhibit dialogue across divided social territories and cultural zones. He further argues that redemptive attempts to appeal to either the black "nation" or to the "family" of internationally dispersed blacks within the message rap subgenre are ill conceived and based in a particularly North Americanist viewpoint that harbors its own exclusive and hierarchically stratified biases.

Perhaps more in line with Gilroy's expansive transatlantic visions of rap's diasporic potential is the track "Ludi" (1991, Island Records), by the Canadian act the Dream Warriors. Based in Toronto, the group is part of one of the world's largest expatriate Caribbean communities. Like Gilroy's London, Toronto can be seen as an

important junction point or crossroads on the webbed pathways of black Atlantic political culture. It is revealed to be a place where, by virtue of factors like the informality of racial segregation, the configuration of class relations, the contingency of linguistic convergences, global phenomena such as anti-colonial and emancipationist political formations are still being sustained, reproduced, and amplified.

(Gilroy 1993a, 95)

In mapping a cultural "crossroads," "Ludi" utilizes an early reggae rhythm and a lightly swinging melody (based on a sample of the Jamaican classic "My Conversation," released in 1968 by the Uniques) that taps into a particularly rich moment in the evolution of the reggae style and revives a well-known Jamaican track while relocating it within the performative contexts of hip-hop.

"Ludi" (which refers to a board game) begins with the rapper King Lou stating that the song is for his mother—who wants something to dance to—and his extended family, to whom he offers the musical sounds of their original home environment. The family to which he refers is not, in the immediate sense, the family of black-identified brothers and sisters that cohere within nationalistic and essentialist discourse but literally his siblings. He then expands his dedication to the wider "family" of blacks with a comprehensive roll call of Africa and the English-, French-, and Spanish-speaking Caribbean islands, which inform (but by no means determine) his cultural identity. He makes no attempt to privilege an originary African heritage, nor does he make a nostalgic appeal to a Caribbean heritage. The extensive list recognizes Toronto's hybrid Afro-Caribbean community and refers directly to a locally manifested culture of international black traditions (rather than a single tradition of essentialist blackness) within which the Dream Warriors developed as young artists. The song's bridge more subtly reinforces the Caribbean connection by making several references to the turntable practices of Jamaican sound systems, which are mainstays throughout internationally dispersed Caribbean communities.

At one point in the track, King Lou's cohort Capital Q reminds him that "there are other places than the islands that play Ludi. Why don't you run it down for the people?" Here, employing a distinctly Jamaican DJ toaster style framed within a loose patois, King Lou provides a wider expression of black diasporic identification as he expands his list to include Canada, the United Kingdom, and the United States, countries where the Afro-Caribbean presence is the largest and most influential. He concludes by mentioning his international record labels, 4th & Broadway and Island

Records and, finally, names the influential Toronto-based independent production house Beat Factory, which first recorded the group. In this last shout-out to Beat Factory, King Lou effectively returns the scale to the local, closing the circle that positions the Dream Warriors within a global-local system of circulation.

There is no simple means of assessing the impact of this expansive global-local perspective, but within Gilroy's innovative theoretical oeuvre, the song can be celebrated for the ways in which its musical and lyrical forms reinforce the dispersed geographies of contemporary black cultures without falling victim to the conservative reductions of black essentialism. Cleaving neither to the rhetorical rigidity of black nationalist rap nor to the nihilistic vitriol of "niggaz with (bad) attitude," the Dream Warriors present an alternative path. As "Ludi" illustrates, the group unself-consciously articulates an evolving hybrid identity informed by transnational migrations that are actively manifested on local grounds.

Concurrently occupying another point along the rap spectrum were those artists who mainly operated within a discursive field featuring spatialized themes of intense locality. The expanded vision of black America evoked by the proponents of message rap contrasts with the ghettocentric visions of urban black experience that emerged in the genre from what is referred to as gangsta rap. Despite many shared perspectives on black oppression and systemic injustices, tension exists in the interstices between the expansive nationalisms of message rap and the more narrowly defined localisms of gangsta rap, with its core emphases on "the 'hood." This distance is widened by the unapologetic claim among numerous "studio gangsters," such as Ice Cube on the N.W.A. track "Gangsta Gangsta" (1988, Ruthless/Priority), that "life ain't nothin' but bitches and money." The two subgenres address common phenomena in their focus on black struggles for empowerment, yet they deploy spatial discourses and programs of action that do not fit easily together.

An intensified spatial terminology did not emerge suddenly, but by 1987, when Boogie Down Productions (featuring KRS-One), Eazy-E, and Ice-T broke onto the scene, the privileging of localized experience rapidly acquired an audible resonance. The New York group BDP released "South Bronx" (1987, B-Boy), a track that aggressively disputes the allegations of various rappers from Queens who, in the aftermath of Run-D.M.C.'s commercial successes, claimed that they were rap's true innovators. KRS-One's lyrics reaffirm the South Bronx as the birthplace of hip-hop, reinforcing the message in the now-classic chorus with its chant "South Bronx, the South, South Bronx."

Giving names to locations and to the artists who inhabited them anchors KRS-One's testimony. He attempts to prove the hip-hop dominance of the South Bronx by recounting the genre's formative stages, paying close attention to localized, highly particular details:

> Remember Bronx River, rolling thick
> With Cool DJ Red Alert and Chuck Chillout on the mix
> While Afrika Islam was rocking the jams
> And on the other side of town was a kid named Flash
> Patterson and Millbrook projects
> Casanova all over, ya couldn't stop it
> The Nine Lives crew, the Cypress Boys
> The Real Rock steady taking out these toys
> As hard as it looked, as wild as it seemed
> I didn't hear a peep from Queens . . .
> South Bronx, the South, South Bronx.

The references to people and places provide a specificity that is by and large absent from Eazy-E's important (but often overlooked) single release "Boyz-N-the-Hood" (1988, Ruthless/Priority) from the same period. With its plodding beats and Eazy-E's underdeveloped rap skills, the track is considered to have done little to advance the genre aesthetically. Yet, in its uncompromising linguistic turns and startling descriptions of homeboy leisure (involving beer, "bitches," and violence), it was riveting and offered a new hardcore funky model for masculine identification in hip-hop:

> 'Cause the boyz in the hood are always hard
> Come talkin' that trash and we'll pull your card
> Knowin' nothin' in life but to be legit
> Don't quote me boy, 'cause I ain't said shit.

Describing the LP *Eazy-Duz-It* on which the single first appeared, Havelock Nelson and Michael Gonzales explain that it "overflows with debris from homophobia to misogyny to excessive violence. And yet, anyone who grew up in the project or any Black ghetto knows these extreme attitudes are right on target" (1991, 81). The reality factor that Nelson and Gonzales invoke surfaced as a complex and troublesome aspect generally in rap and with greater frequency in gangsta rap, especially as it rose to prominence in the music industry, displacing other more progressive and inclusive forms of discourse. The theorist Michel de Certeau describes the intense emphases on the real as a relatively recent phenomenon, the product of a contemporary media culture:

The media transform the great silence of things into its opposite. Formerly constituting a secret, the real now talks constantly. . . . From morning to night, narrations constantly haunt streets and buildings. They articulate our existences by teaching us what they must be. They "cover the event," that is to say, they *make* our legends out of it. (de Certeau 1984, 185–86)

The appeal to the real is founded on the claim that hardcore rap is a legitimate vehicle for the expression of actual cultural experiences. The streets and the 'hood are generally conceived as the primary sites where the real coheres, and it is the street-oriented themes of gangsta rap that most often refer to "keeping it real," "representing the real," and the like. Indeed, in the mid-1990s, there was a gradual shift away from the potentially pejorative term "gangsta rap" as an increasing number of artists implemented the term "reality rap," which is today a more commonly employed subgeneric designation. MC Eiht of Compton's Most Wanted explains that "it's just like reliving the past, and I do it on paper. Things that I seen in my younger years that I know about. It's not just talking, it's realism. . . . Whether people think it's fake or whether people think I'm trying to be studio or whatever, muthaphukkas know the real" (DJ Zen 1994, 41). Elsewhere, the Oakland rapper Spice-1 offers another, more complicated, spatially inflected explanation when he states that "to white kids it's just music. To the black kids it's real" ("Reality Check" 1994, 68).

This latter proposition is perhaps a more accurate assessment of the term. Whereas the term "reality" in rap tends to be linked exclusively to the lyrical content and street-based narratives, rap taken as a whole is deeply connected to ongoing and ever-changing black cultural traditions that remain a central force in the daily reality of urban black teens. Within an essentialist cultural logic, the real is always located within the core culture; Afrocentrist proclamations, bolstered by emerging anthropological evidence attesting to the African continent as the originary source for all humanity, fulfill a similar function by other, more academic means. In this regard, reality within a hip-hop paradigm is more than "just music," and it is certainly more than the sum of the lyrics. It encompasses each of these aspects as they are situated within the lived contexts of black expressivity and contemporary cultural identity formations.

Clearly, the multiple realities that comprise life in the 'hood, like the multiple identity formations that accompany them, are not granted equal attention by either rappers or social critics. Much is absent, owing to the selective privileging of a limited facet of 'hood experience that has become associated with the real as an image construct. The focus is ultimately on a particular image of reality that, while existing in the streets and neighborhoods of numerous black urban sections, has been mobilized for numerous reasons, not the least of which is the calculated strategy to create a compelling and graphic product that appeals to a sizable audience (much like slasher films or contemporary gangster movies). Ice-T, Eazy-E, and the various members of the original N.W.A. provoked these debates and quickly established the terrain for the representations of an ostensible urban reality in gangsta rap, leaving critics to question their legitimacy and ethics from the cultural sidelines.

Eazy-E's "Boyz-N-the-Hood" reflects many of rap's earlier modes of spatial representation, conceiving of the ghetto landscape as a generalized abstract construct, as *space*. The terminology of the 'hood, however, also introduces a localized nuance to the notion of space that conveys a certain proximity, effectively capturing a narrowed sense of *place* through which young thugs and their potential crime victims move in tandem. Claims to the representation of authentic street life or 'hood reality emerged with startling frequency following the rise of Eazy-E, N.W.A. and the Posse, and Ice-T, who were among the first to communicate detailed images of closely demarcated space in this manner. This suggests that "reality," authenticity, and reduced spatial scales are conceptually linked by those who developed and sustained the spatial discourses of the 'hood. The main contribution of "Boyz-N-the-Hood" has ultimately been its influence on the popularization of a new spatial vocabulary that has spread throughout hip-hop from all regions as artists from the West Coast have gained market and media prominence.

By most accounts, the spatial discourse that coheres around the concept of the 'hood emerged with the greatest frequency and force in rap by California-based artists. But in the popular media as well as in academic treatises, the focus tends to be on the expressions of "gangsta" violence and masculine aggression to the exclusion or minimization of prevalent spatial elements. For example, David Toop writes, "the first release on Ruthless Records, launched by rapper Eazy-E and producer Dr. Dre in 1986, was like a tabloid report from the crime beat fed through a paper shredder" (1991, 180). The very term "gangsta rap" is more concretely concerned with the articulation of criminality than with any other attributes that may emerge from its lyrical and visual texts. Having become sedimented in the popular lexicon as the key or trademark term for the subgenre, it is difficult to critically challenge the primacy of criminality and to replace it with the spatiality that precedes the gangster ethos saturating the texts. The criminal activities described in gangsta rap's intense lyrical forms are almost always subordinate to the definitions of space and place within which they are set. It is, therefore, the spatialities of the 'hood that constitute the ascendant concept and are ultimately deserving of discursive preeminence.

Since rap's inception, it has become something of a convention for the MC or rapper to place himself or herself at the center of the world, as the subject around whom events unfold and who translates topophilia (love of place) or topophobia (fear of place) into lyrics for wider dissemination. As Robin Kelley explains,

Although the use of first-person narratives is rooted in a long tradition of black aesthetic practices, the use of "I" to signify both personal and collective experiences also enables gangsta rappers to navigate a complicated course between what social scientists call "structure" and "agency." In gangsta rap there is almost always a relationship between the conditions in which characters live and the decisions they make.   (Kelley 1996, 124)

Kelley's point is illustrated in Ice-T's "Intro" on his debut album, *Rhyme Pays* (1987, Rhyme Syndicate/Sire). Adapting a sampled version of Mike Oldfield's 1974 hit "Tubular Bells" (Virgin), the track displays none of the rhythmic norms of the period and is devoid of bass and drum beats. Similarly ignoring the standard rap flow of the period, Ice-T's vocals are influenced less by the dominant East Coast form than by the spoken-word delivery of the adult-oriented humorist Rudy Ray Moore (whose character, Dolemite, was featured in several low-budget blaxploitation films as well as the 1999 video for Ol' Dirty Bastard's "Got Your Money" [Elektra]). The pimp and hustler themes expounded throughout the album are also more reminiscent of the novelists Donald Goines or Iceberg Slim, from whom Ice-T took his name, than anything that had existed in rap up to that point, with the possible exception of the Philadelphia MC Schooly D.

As an introduction, the track allows Ice-T to present his hip-hop curriculum vitae, which is explicitly defined in spatial terms:

> A child was born in the East one day
> Moved to the West Coast after his parents passed away
> Never understood his fascination with rhymes or beats
> In poetry he was considered elite
> Became a young gangster in the streets of L.A.
> Lost connections with his true roots far away.

The description of the personal exodus upon which the young rapper embarks under conditions of extreme adversity is crucial to the construction of mystique and legend. Describing his entry into Los Angeles gang culture and the rap scene in the magazine *Rap Pages,* Ice-T identifies cities, neighborhoods, high schools, and housing projects that have meaning to him and to those familiar with these areas:

I went to a white school in Culver City, and that was chill, but I was livin' in Windsor Hills near Monterey Triangle Park. . . . When I got to high school all the kids from my area were gettin' bussed to white schools and I didn't want to go to them schools. So me and a few kids from the hills went to Crenshaw. That's where the gangs were.   ("The World According to Ice-T" 1991, 55)

In this narrative, place is a lens of sorts that mediates one's perspective on social relations. It offers familiarity and provides the perspectival point from which one gazes upon and evaluates other places, places that are "other" or foreign to one's own distinctly personal sites of security and stability (no matter how limited these may be). Ice-T may be *from* the East (Newark, New Jersey), but he is *of* Los Angeles, and it is the spaces and places of that city that provide the coordinates for his movement and activities.

In the same passage, Ice-T goes on to make the distinction between East Coast rap and the emerging Los Angeles gangsta style, noting that the latter developed out of a desire to relate incidents and experiences with a more specific sense of place and, subsequently, greater significance to local youths, who could recognize the sites and activities described in the lyrics. In this regard, rap offers a means of describing the view from a preferred "here," of explaining how things appear in the immediate foreground (the 'hood) and how things seem on the receding horizon (other places).

Adopting a boastful tone and attitude, Ice-T also locates his origins in the greater New York area, essentially fixing his own roots in hip-hop's cultural motherland. Ice-T is clearly centering himself, building his own profile. In the process, he relates a history that invests supreme value in New York as the first home of hip-hop, naturalizing his connections to the art form and validating his identity as a tough, adaptive, and street-smart Los Angeles hustler, the self-proclaimed "West Coast M.C. king." Ice-T's references to New York illuminate the spatial hierarchy that existed at the time, since the Northeast was still unquestioned as the dominant zone of hip-hop cultural activity. Battles among rap innovators were still being waged on the local, interborough scale in New York City, although New York gradually lost its monopoly on the form as various other sites of innovation emerged. The rise of the Los Angeles rap sound and the tremendous impact of the gangster themes after 1987 resulted in the first real challenge to New York's dominance. This development had the additional effect of polarizing the two regions as the aesthetic distinctions based on lyrical content and rhythmic styles became more defined and audiences began spending their consumer dollars on rap from the nation's "West Side."

"The West Side Is the Best Side": Representing Compton

The arrival of a pronounced West Coast rap style and hip-hop cultural traits was heralded by a deluge of songs that celebrated and glorified the street warrior scenarios of the California cities of South Central Los Angeles (with help from the 1988 Dennis Hopper film *Colors* and Ice-T's galvanizing title song on the sound track), Oakland, and, especially, Compton. Starting with N.W.A.'s "Straight Outta Compton" (1988, Ruthless/Priority), numerous recordings conveyed the narrative imagery of vicious gang-oriented activities in Compton, including the tracks "Raised in Compton" (1991, Epic) and "Compton 4 Life" (1992, Epic) by the group Compton's Most Wanted, and DJ Quik's "Born and Raised in Compton" (1991, Profile) or "Jus Lyke Compton" (1992, Profile). Appearing on the back cover of his album *Way 2 Fonky* (1992, Profile), DJ Quik poses alongside a chain-link fence topped with razor wire, sporting a jacket emblazoned with the Compton logo, proudly "representing" his home territory. Representing involves the artist's employment of numerous and often subtle communicative codes and cultural practices to define and articulate individual and posse identities, spatial locales grounded in the 'hood, and other aspects of individual and collective significance. Through these multiple means of signification, the city of Compton rapidly gained a notoriety framed by the image of tough and well-armed homeboys and the ongoing deadly conflict between rival gangs (the Bloods, the Crips, and the Los Angeles Police Department) operating with a near-total lack of moral conscience and an alternative ethical code—the code of the streets. This last point can be most clearly discerned in the ubiquitous refrain in gangsta rap that "Compton niggaz just don't give a fuck."

Tricia Rose and Brian Cross situate the rise of Compton-based rap in two quite different frames of understanding. Rose writes that "during the late 1980s Los Angeles rappers from Compton and Watts, two areas severely paralyzed by the postindustrial economic redistribution[,] developed a West Coast style of rap that narrates experiences and fantasies specific to life as a poor young, black, male subject in Los Angeles" (1994a, 59). Her assessment situates the phenomenon of West Coast styles and lyrical forms in an internally based set of socioeconomic conditions that are responsive to transitions within a complex convergence of global and local forces, or what Kevin Robins (1991) refers to as "the global/local nexus."

Cross locates the rise of Compton's rap scene within a wider and more encompassing cartographic relation to New York and other California locales:

Hiphop Compton, according to Eazy, was created as a reply to the construction of the South Bronx/Queensbridge nexus in New York. If locally it served notice in the community in which Eazy and Dre sold their Macola-pressed records (not to mention the potential play action on KDAY), nationally, or at least on the East Coast, it was an attempt to figure Los Angeles on the map of hiphop. After the album had gone double platinum Compton would be as well known a city in hiphop as either Queens or the Bronx.   (Cross 1993, 37)

The general lyrical content of "Straight Outta Compton" sheds little light on the city or its social byways and does not demonstrate any particular concern with the locality's economics and their impact on everyday life. Compton functions as a geographical backdrop, following the same standard constructions of abstract space heard in either Grandmaster Flash and the Furious Five's "New York, New York," recorded five years earlier, or Eazy-E's "Boyz-N-the-Hood."

Stating at the outset that "when something happens in South Central

Los Angeles, nothing happens. Just another nigger dead," Ice Cube establishes the track's general theme of spatially organized violence:

> Here's the murder rap to keep you dancin'
> With a crime record like Charles Manson
> AK-47 is the tool
> Don't make me act the motherfuckin' fool
> Me and you could go toe-to-toe, no maybe
> I'm knockin' niggers out the box daily
> Yo, weekly, monthly, and yearly
> Until then, dumb motherfuckers see clearly
> That I'm down with the capital C.P.T.
> Boy you can't fuck with me
> So when I'm in your neighborhood ya better duck
> 'Cause Ice Cube is crazy as fuck
> As I leave, believe I'm stompin'
> But when I come back, boy
> I'm comin' straight outta Compton.

Without detailed spatial descriptions of landmarks and environment, Compton does not emerge as a clearly realized urban space in the N.W.A. track even though it is the group's hometown. The California city is instead interpolated as a bounded civic space that provides both specificity and scale for the communication of a West Coast rap presence. The group is representing their home territory, and the song's release was their bold announcement that the "boyz" from the 'hoods of Compton were "stompin'" onto the scene and could not be avoided by anyone who paid attention to developments in the business. The Compton and South Central Los Angeles crews were not only serving notice to their neighboring communities that they were in charge, they were also serving notice to New York and the entire hip-hop nation that the new sound had arrived and that the balance of power (based on innovation and inventiveness) had tipped toward the West. This was, in fact, the beginning of a decade-long antagonism between East and West Coast rap crews that has too frequently proven that the gangster themes comprising the lyrical content are based in more than mere lip service or masculine posturing.

On "Raised in Compton" (1991, Epic/Sony), MC Eiht of the group Compton's Most Wanted explicitly racializes the urban spaces of the city, more fully addressing the specificities of its cultural character and providing a further sense of the place he recognizes as his formative home. He reproduces several of the general elements that N.W.A. had already imposed on Compton's representational repertoire, but for him the city also has a personally meaningful history that is manifested in his identity as a gangster turned rapper:

> Compton is the place that I touched down
> I opened my eyes to realize that I was dark brown

> And right there in the ghetto that color costs
> Brothers smothered by the streets meaning we're lost
> I grew up in a place where it was go for your own
> Don't get caught after dark roaming the danger zone
> But it was hell at the age of twelve
> As my Compton black brothers were in and out of jail

The attempt to historicize his relations to the city and the 'hood makes this cut slightly more complex than "Straight Outta Compton"; MC Eiht's bonds to the localized Compton environment are defined in evolutionary terms, as a child becomes a man. Subjective history, conveyed here in an almost testimonial form, and the experiences of space together offer relevant insights into the social construction of a gangster attitude or a gang member's raison d'être.

In his analysis of the sociopolitical importance of merging musical and nonmusical sources of inspiration and experience among California Chicano rock musicians since the 1960s, George Lipsitz offers an insightful overview of the detailed descriptive factors that communicate practices from below, the common cultures of everyday youth experience:

> As organic intellectuals chronicling the cultural life of their community, they draw upon street slang, car customizing, clothing styles, and wall murals for inspiration and ideas. . . . Their work is intertextual, constantly in dialogue with other forms of cultural expression, and most fully appreciated when located in context.
>
> (Lipsitz 1990, 153)

Like the California Chicano music Lipsitz describes, "Raised in Compton" explicitly highlights a culture of customized cars, urban mobility, and the sartorial codes of the Compton streets ("T-shirt and khakis"), all described within highly particular vernaculars. In its inclusiveness of the minor details that are, in practice, part of the daily norm for many urban black and Latino youth and those in the rim cities surrounding Los Angeles, the track accesses the spatial and racial characteristics of the city of Compton that have influenced and shaped the man MC Eiht has become. The closely detailed articulation of spatial specifics (places, place names, specific site references, etc.) is still lacking, but there is a rich description of some of the spatially distributed social formations, which reproduce the forces underlying the racialized teen gangster ethos with which MC Eiht and many others so clearly identify.

Maintaining the gang member's pledge to defend the set and the 'hood forever is the theme of MC Eiht's "Compton 4 Life" (1992, Epic/Sony). This track also offers a personal profile that ties MC Eiht into the neighborhood environment and inextricably links him with the deeper gang structures that prevail. Again, the prior history of place is invoked as a determining factor, and in a tragic example of fatalism, MC Eiht accepts the idea that the authority of the past is supreme and is therefore implicated in the reduced range of options available to many young black urban dwellers. From his perspective, his destiny, while not foreclosed in absolute terms, is highly influenced by the pressures of the past that have produced the social conditions in which he now finds himself.

Midway through the track he challenges outsiders to "throw up your 'hood cause it's Compton we're yellin'," in a calculated turf statement that is entirely consistent with the understanding of spatial otherness fundamental to Los Angeles gang culture. Eiht and other gangsta rappers speak of alienation and social disenfranchisement as negative factors compelling them toward criminal lifestyles, yet they also easily expound their own versions of alienating power, drawing on the imagery and codes of the street and entering into a discourse of domination that subjugates women, opposing gang members, and those who are perceived as being weaker (and thus lesser) than they. Framed in terms of gun violence and human decimation, these expressions are intended to diminish the presence of others who represent other cities and other 'hoods. This is the articulation of control through domination, ghetto style.

Spatial domination and geosocial containment in the threatening forms of "one time" or "five-oh" (both terms for the police) and other gang members are conceived as unavoidable forces of danger in the 'hood. Defeating the enemy forces is the ultimate goal. But in establishing this dynamic, MC Eiht cleverly acknowledges that even in victory the streets impose their own kind of incarcerating authority:

> Compton 4 Life
> Compton 4 Life
> It's the city where everybody's in prison
> Niggers keep taking shit 'cause ain't nobody givin'
> So another punk fool I must be
> Learn the tricks of the trade from the street
> Exist to put the jack down, ready and willin'
> One more Compton driveby killin'

There is a brief pause in the rhythm that hangs like doom, stilling the track's pace and flow and creating a discomforting gap in the track. When the chorus "Compton 4 Life" suddenly breaks in with the final echoing syllable, it becomes clear that the title is formed around a double entendre. On the one hand, this is an expression of spatial solidarity and loyalty to the 'hood; on the other, it refers to the pronouncement of a life sentence—eternal imprisonment in the city's streets and alleys.

As "Straight Outta Compton," "Raised in Compton," and "Compton 4 Life" illustrate, "our sensibilities are spatialized . . . [and] spatialities have always produced landscapes that are loaded with ethical, epistemological, and aestheticized meanings. Almost invariably these are contested" (Keith and Pile 1993, 26). In these examples, Compton's central significance is maintained through the lyrical representation of space-bound activities that are then discursively traced onto the identities of the rappers who "claim" Compton as their own. The issue of whether or not the songs refer back to a consistently verifiable reality is rendered moot by the possibilities they present as textual spaces of representation. Artists discursively locate themselves in an array of images and practices within the texts, constructing a relatively coherent identity out of the urban debris that is evidently a crucial aspect of the Compton they experience.

Despite claims by critics of gangsta rap, such as David Samuels (1991) or the folk musician Michelle Shocked, who with Bart Bull suggests that "Los Angeles as a whole and South Central specifically bear little resemblance to the cartoon landscape—the Zip Coon Toon Town—of gangsta rap" (1992, 6), the subgenre's narrative depictions of spaces and places are absolutely essential to an understanding of the ways in which a great number of urban minority youths imagine their environments and relate those images to their own individual sense of self. The spaces of Compton and other similar minority communities that emerge through their work are simultaneously real, imaginary, symbolic, and mythical. The question that should be asked is not "Is this real and true?" but "Why do so many young black and Latino men and women choose these dystopic images of spatial representation to orient their own places in the world?" Framing the question thus displaces the undeniable fascination with the grisly mayhem of the lyrical narratives and allows one to embark on a more illuminating interrogation of the sociospatial sensibilities at work.

Bangin' On Wax: Hip-Hop Perspectives from "Here" and "There"

According to Doreen Massey, the identity of place is "constructed out of movement, communication, social relations which always stretch beyond it" (1992, 14). Place acquires its significance in and through human interaction, and despite the various songs that may suggest otherwise, the cities or sites of significance that are encompassed by the term "the 'hood" never exist in isolation. Their unique significance for rappers and other members of the hip-hop culture is based on a structured relationship to other places, whether on the wider scale of the city or in the compressed spatial locale of the 'hood. This phenomenon corresponds with Keith and Pile's observation:

Any articulation of identity or object formation is only momentarily complete, it is always in part constituted by the forces that oppose it *(the constitutive outside)*, always contingent upon surviving the contradictions that it subsumes *(forces of dislocation).* In such a fragile world of identity formation and object formation, political subjects are articulated through moments of closure that create subjects as surfaces of inscription, mythical and metaphorical, invariably incomplete.

(Keith and Pile 1993, 27)

Indeed, the nationwide mobility of rap artists such as Ice-T and his DJ, Afrika Islam (who moved from New York to Los Angeles), Ice Cube (who briefly moved from Los Angeles to work with various New York producers), and Too Short and his entire production posse (who briefly relocated their base of operations from Oakland to Atlanta) introduces a range of contact and overlapping influences that is noteworthy in hip-hop. The influences can also be seen in one of rap's established conventions: artists' guest appearances on recordings, the volume of which far exceeds that of similar collaborations in other musical genres. Hip-hop has never been a static form; it has always been subject to change and hybridity owing to ongoing influences that are generated through multiple connections and contacts. Its practitioners continue to demonstrate a high rate of mobility, which extends the range of the culture and contributes to enhanced dialogue across the map.

In 1992 two recordings about Compton were released that reach beyond the prevailing representations of a city framed within localized boundaries and attempt to situate the phenomenon of Compton-based rap in a wider and more elaborative perspective. DJ Quik's "Jus Lyke Compton," from the 1992 LP *Way 2 Fonky,* adopts a unique perspective on space, place, and subjective identity formation that, in its emphasis on mobility throughout the American heartland, is relatively rare. Quik's capacity to navigate the spatial cartographies of hip-hop and to communicate the cultural importance invested in spatial difference sets "Jus Lyke Compton" apart from most recordings that maintain place-based perceptions of the 'hood. DJ Quik bears witness to various permutations of the gangster lifestyle that are enacted "in the field," and in so doing he motivates a process of self-reflection and meditation on the impact of his cultural labor.

The geographical and conceptual boundaries of any closely delineated zone are not impermeable, as DJ Quik observes on the track. He first locates himself as "local," a Compton native whose modest enterprise and 'hood-oriented entrepreneurial success on the home stage have enabled him to tour and travel throughout the nation:

> Finally out the motherfuckin' C.P.T.
> Off to other cities and shit
> No longer just an underground hit
> Movin' thangs, a local nigga made good
> And made a name off of making tapes for niggaz in the 'hood
> And now let me tell a little story
> About the places I been to and the shit that I been through

> Like fightin' and shootouts and bangin' and shit
> All because a nigga made a hit

Quik's strategy is to position himself at the threshold between local and national scales of success. While the boastful introduction is standard to the rap form, his equation of success with enhanced mobility illustrates a system of values organized around a celebrity's spatially expansive evolution from a local phenomenon to a more widely recognized artist on the national stage and in the commercial market. Identities forged in the 'hood are products of spatial compression and are deeply influenced by locally sustaining bonds cohering within the more narrowly defined social parameters of place. Since the song is a paean to his Compton roots, the means through which he links himself with the city are important and are also ultimately intended to elevate both his status and that of the hometown. By employing a spatial discourse to describe his success and outward growth as he excels in the rap game, Quik implicates his experiences at the local scale as essential factors in the construction of his enhanced profile as an emerging, nationally renowned rap star.

Quik's spatial narrative is structured along an expansive trajectory, moving from Los Angeles to the urban enclaves of Oakland, St. Louis, San Antonio, and Denver. The track is in essence a virtual reproduction of the concert tour itinerary, mapping performances in cartographic succession. The spatial descriptions shift as the track progresses, framing the city of Oakland within more proximate terms of familiarity and recognition, whereas the other cities he names seem much further away and, consequently, much less familiar. As his lyrical travelogue unfolds, one senses that DJ Quik's worldview is undergoing adjustment through new contacts with dispersed members of the hip-hop nation, and he expresses a touristic awe of middle America, revealing the provincial mindset of an untraveled individual with limited exposure to other distant spaces and places. What remains most perplexing to Quik, however, is not simply the differences that he experiences but the similarities between other cities and his home, Compton:

> Moving on to St. Louis, where the country is fucked
> With gold teeth in they mouth, but they still know what's up
> Where it's hot as a motherfucka, hot enough to make ya cuss
> That's why I kept my ass on the bus
> . . .
> That's when I started thinking that this wasn't like home
> But then they had to prove me wrong
> 'Cause later on that night after we did the show
> We went back to the afterset and wouldn't ya know
> Yeah, Bloods and Crips start scrappin' and shootin' . . . in Missouri?
> Damn, how could this happen?

> Now St. Louis, is jus lyke Compton
> Yeah, y'all, St. Louis is jus lyke Compton, nigga

DJ Quik attempts to account for the far-reaching impact of Compton-based rap, reflecting on his own incapacity to foresee that the violence and nihilism commonly associated with his home terrain could be so easily transported elsewhere. The passage conveys Quik's fascination with what he believes he and his Compton cohorts have begotten. More important, it illustrates his effort to comprehend the potential implications of the broader diffusion of images and elements of the scene he had evidently assumed were specific to Compton alone. Citing the gang signs and ubiquitous red and blue colors associated with Blood and Crip gang members seen at his various concerts, Quik reveals mixed emotions of pride and horror in his description of the multiple ways in which the California gang culture has been adapted and integrated into the daily practices or locally meaningful experiences of audiences residing throughout the American heartland.

Without implicating West Coast gangsta rap or his own musical output, he criticizes audience members across the nation for reenacting cinematic gang scenarios without comprehending the spatial contexts and their relevance to Southern California urban youth:

> I don't think they know, they too crazy for their own good
> They need to stop watchin' that "Colors" and "Boyz n the Hood"
> Too busy claimin' Sixties, tryin' to be raw
> And never even seen the Shaw
>
> But now, back to the story that I'm tellin'
> We packed up the tour and started bellin'
> When we arrived I saw red and blue sweatsuits
> When I'm thinkin' about horse dookey and cowboy boots
> I guess Texas ain't no different from the rest
> And San Antonio was just waitin' to put us to the test
> and before it was over the shit got deep
> A nigga got shot in the face and was dead in the street
> Then they came in the club thinkin' of scrappin'
> Yeah, we was puttin' 'em down and squaring the rest, shit,
> I even had to wear the bulletproof vest
>
> Now San Antonio, is jus lyke Compton
> Yeah, San Antonio, is jus lyke Compton, bitch

DJ Quik's perspectives and their articulation correspond with what Michel de Certeau refers to as traveling "enunciation" and the methods of inscribing the relational coordinates "near" and "far":

To the fact that the adverbs *here* and *there* are the indicators of the locutionary seat in verbal communication—a coincidence that reinforces the parallelism between linguistic and pedestrian enunciation—we must add that this location (*here—there*) (necessarily implied by walking and indicative of a present appropriation of space by an "I") also has the function of introducing an other in relation to this "I" and of thus establishing a conjunctive and disjunctive articulation of places.

(de Certeau 1984, 99)

With a reference to "home" functioning as an explicit context for the track's revelations, DJ Quik balances the "here" of Compton with a recurring "there" of the tour stops and social encounters along the way. Isolating a series of similarities and differences, the spatial logic and investment in place finally lead him to measure all other places against the neighborhoods and community spaces from which he emerges:

> After a month on the road
> We came home and I can safely say
> That L.A. is a much better place to stay
> How could a bunch of niggaz in a town like this
> Have such a big influence on niggaz so far away?
> . . .
> Now Denver, is jus lyke Compton
> Yeah, y'all, Denver, they wanna be lyke Compton
> And ya know that Oakland, is jus lyke Compton, bitch
> Yeah, y'all St. Louis, we made it jus lyke Compton, fools
> Uh-huh San Antonio, is jus lyke Compton
> Yeah, and Denver, the wanna be lyke Compton, punk ass niggaz
> I thought ya knew.

Quik's territorial identification with the home place of Compton is centered as the track's narrative constant, although its value is realized only through Quik's new perspective as a touring musician. The bridge hinges on the realization that while the "C.P.T." (Compton) and the 'hood comprise a refuge to which he can comfortably return, it is not nearly as insular or contained as he had originally believed. As a result, home acquires new meaning for the rapper once he has attained the profile and means to extend his territory and range of mobility beyond the home front, beyond the 'hood. Compton and South Central Los Angeles may well be "a much better place to stay," but in order for him to make this statement, the prior imperative of departure is required. This offers Quik a reflective point of view, gazing back at the locale from which he came and reevaluating it in terms of his own subjective criteria based upon the spatial concepts of "here" and "there."

Neal Smith and Cindi Katz's theoretical perspective on travel and identity helps to further explain this phenomenon:

The notions of travel, traveling identities, and displacement represent another response to the undue fixity of social identity. "Traveling" provides a means for conceptualizing the interplay among people that are no longer so separate or inaccessible one to the other. . . . The flow of travel not the putative fixity of space donates identity.

(1993, 78)

DJ Quik's movement is between stable points on the map—he is the mobile force linking these various spaces and places. Each arrival and departure, however, brings a realization of something bigger than himself and the Compton world that he knows so well. The track conveys an evolving process of identity transformation, which involves the remaking of the locally defined self into a nationally structured subjectivity, as Quik constructs a more expansive identity that exceeds his previous self-image as "just an underground hit . . . a local nigga made good." In achieving this, however, he lyrically constructs a spatial hierarchy that privileges Compton above the other city spaces described. This spatial authority is then folded back upon Quik himself as he affirms his identity as a legitimate representative of the West Coast gangster practices that he sees being reenacted across the country. In this manner, then, Compton and DJ Quik become inseparable symbols of authority and authenticity, the traveling embodiment of the "real" and the original product of the funky West Coast sound as well as the compelling gang lifestyles that have been copied in other locales.

In another example interrogating Compton's distant impact, the Bronx rapper Tim Dog's "Fuck Compton," from the 1991 release *Penicillin on Wax* (Ruffhouse/Columbia), stands as a prime example of spatially segregated bicoastal antagonism in hip-hop. A response to the meteoric rise of Compton acts and recorded homages to Compton gangsters that erupted after 1988, Tim Dog's release attempts to undermine the status of Compton-identified acts and their West Coast gangsta rap style (specifically its most acclaimed propagators, N.W.A.) and elevate the status of his home territory, the South Bronx. At the time of the single's release, the impact of West Coast gangsta rap had substantially altered the hip-hop scene. Tim Dog was reacting to the shifting patterns as the prior authority and innovative leadership of East Coast artists came under review.

On the surface, the track adheres to the basic mode of the recorded "boast" and "dis," presenting a challenge framed in aggressive confrontational language. Yet the terms of engagement emphasize location and position on the hip-hop map, including both geospatial locations and market positions in the music industry, entering into the overlapping discourses of turf, territory, and spatial identities. In this sense, the track is a culturally meaningful articulation of hip-hop's cartographies of difference, conveying what was at the time a growing mutual disdain between artists and production posses from the two coastal regions.

Tim Dog's verbal attack suggests that he is responding to the dominant set of spatial and place-based images emanating from Compton. He is lashing out at a representation of Compton by the hardcore gangsta rap acts that established the city's infamy. The members of N.W.A. and their extended posse are the explicit target, metonymically isolated as representatives of the larger West Coast gangsta rap phenomenon. Over a drum and piano sample from N.W.A.'s "Kommershul" (1991, Ruthless/Priority), the intro on *Penicillin on Wax* opens with an ad-lib "message to N.W.A.":

> No matter how hard you think you are
> This is what the whole world thinks about you
> Yeah, straight outta the motherfuckin' Bronx
> Lettin' everybody know that Tim Dog ain't takin' no motherfuckin' shorts
> And I stole your motherfuckin' beat and made it better
> To show the whole world that y'all ain't nothin'
> But a bunch of pussys

N.W.A. responded to the appropriation of "Kommershul" with a legal suit claiming copyright infringement; it was eventually settled out of court. In the video for "Fuck Compton," Tim Dog and his crew enact the mugging and immolation of N.W.A. in the streets and alleys of the Bronx, with lookalike actors standing in for Eazy-E and Dr. Dre. The visual and lyrical message involves an indiscreet statement of utter disrespect for and dismissiveness of the Compton rap scene and the symbolic annihilation of West Coast rappers by those from the East, in this case led by Tim Dog and his crew.

While Tim Dog's collaborations with the Ultramagnetic MCs on their 1986 single, "Ego Trippin'," lends him credibility as a rap innovator, "Fuck Compton" (which featured production by the Ultramagnetics) is an aesthetically unexceptional track. With its harsh transregional invective, however, it remains a benchmark in what has frequently been referred to as a civil war that raged within the hip-hop nation from about 1988 to 1998:

> Oh shit, motherfuckers, step to the rear and cheer
> 'Cause Tim Dog is here
> Let's get down to the nitty-gritty
> And talk about a bullshit city
> Talkin' about niggaz from Compton
> They're no comp and they truly ain't stompin'
> Tim Dog, a black man's task
> I'm so bad I'll whip Superman's ass
> All you suckers that riff on the West Coast
> I'll dis and spray your ass like a roach
> Ya think you're cool with your curls and your shades
> I'll roll thick and you'll be yellin' out "Raid"
> One hard brother that lives in New York
> Where brothers are hard and we don't have to talk
> Shut your mouths before we come out stompin'
> Hey, yo Eazy
> Fuck Compton! Fuck Compton! Fuck Compton! Fuck 'Em!

As a response to the popularity and commercial clout of gangsta rap, "Fuck Compton" exemplifies the dialogical element within hip-hop, displaying the battle stances between rappers that are standard to the genre. It forms one node of a national conversation, with representatives from one regional front addressing those from another. Tricia Rose explains that "hip hop produced internal and external dialogues that affirmed the experiences and identities of the participants. . . . Hip hop developed as part of a cross-cultural communication network" (1994a, 60). While this is true, her explanation also implies a more cooperative interaction than is always the case. Rather than a series of positive engagements (which are relatively common), many recordings, including "Fuck Compton," deploy deeply negative discourses, which have been termed "lyrical gang-banging" and verbal warfare. These dialogic articulations of animosity within hip-hop also often display a pronounced spatial character, reproducing the tensions of spatially nuanced difference that continually thwart the formation of a sustainable politics of unification or solidarity within the loosely defined hip-hop nation.

In his assessment of "Fuck Compton," Paul Gilroy suggests that Tim Dog's diatribe is actually one of "profound bewilderment" with the portrayals of gang violence and black-on-black crime that are the hallmarks of West Coast gangsta rap:

> Havin' that gang war?
> We wanna know what you're fightin' for
> Fighting over colors?
> All that gang shit's for dumb motherfuckers
> But you go on thinking you're hard
> Come to New York and we'll see who gets robbed
> . . .
> Fuck Compton! Fuck Compton! Fuck Compton! Fuck 'Em!

Gilroy reads the text as a defensive statement registering "disappointment that the idea of homogeneous national community has become impossible and unthinkable." According to him, Tim Dog's cross-regional expression of incomprehension and nonrecognition is evidence that the discourses of black sibling unity and linked diasporic or nationalistic identities are untenable in practice, based more in wishful thinking than in material or historical fact: "If Tim Dog is to be believed, Compton is as foreign to some blacks in New York as Kingston, London, Havana, Lagos, Aswan, or Capetown—possibly even more so" (1992, 308).

Writing from the United Kingdom, Gilroy acknowledges his own geographic displacement from the city spaces being addressed in the track. He notes that the potential meanings underlying the lyrical discourses are invariably open to diverse translations once they are encountered in other cultural contexts (across the Atlantic or among dispersed audience formations within the black diaspora). His assessment on this point is entirely accurate; in fact, it can be said that there is also frequently a strong foreign element alienating blacks from separate 'hoods within shared metropolitan areas in the United States. More than merely revealing the limits to these connective discourses, however, "Fuck Compton" also reminds us that otherness can form the grounds for hate, even within the rather narrow cultural formation of hip-hop. It is easy to hate or mistrust that which is foreign, strange, and unrecognizable (shared racial attributes notwithstanding), and this is clearly evident in Tim Dog's vitriolic and contradictory attack against rap originating on the "West side."

Representing the Extreme Local: The Case of Seattle

Rob Shields writes that "representations of cities are like still-life portraits . . . representations make the city available for analysis and replay" (1996, 228). Although he is referring to planning documents, maps, and other materials, he includes stories and urban myths as part of the repertoire of urban representation. Shields explains that the various forms of urban representation introduce a range of signs and metaphors that "are linked to normative notions of what are appropriate social reactions to each of the myriad of possible events and encounters" (229). From this vantage, it might be added that new sites and scales of spatial representation that are communicated through specific signs and metaphors introduce an altered sense of what may be considered "appropriate" in different contexts.

By the end of the 1980s, rap artists had provided an assortment of spatial representations of New York and Los Angeles that were both consistent with and divergent from prevailing dominant image-ideas of those urban centers. Rappers worked within the dominant representational discourses of "the city" while agitating against a history of urban representations as they attempted to extend the expressive repertoire and to reconstruct the image-idea of the city as they understood it. This proved to be a formidable challenge, since New York and Los Angeles exist as urban icons, resonant signs of the modern and postmodern city, respectively. They are simultaneously the products of a deluge of representational images and narrative constructions and of material existence and social interaction. Rap's emergence from city spaces unencumbered by a deep history of representational images, with less representational baggage, presents a unique opportunity for its lyrical innovators to imagine and represent their cities. As a traditional frontier city and a prominent contemporary regional center, Seattle might be considered an underrepresented city that lacks the wealth of representational history common to the larger centers to the southwest and the northeast.

In the mid-1980s the greater Seattle area was, to much of the United States, a veritable hinterland, best known for its mountains, rivers, and forests and as the home of Boeing's corporate and manufacturing headquarters. In the music industry, Seattle spawned such artists as Quincy Jones and Ray Charles; Jimi Hendrix was perhaps its most renowned native son. The city was otherwise not regarded as an important or influential center for musical production or innovation. Seattle's symbolic status changed with the rise of Bill Gates's Microsoft Corporation and the emergence of the Starbucks coffee empire. By 1990 it was garnering considerable attention as the source of the extremely influential (and commercially successful) grunge/alternative music scene that introduced bands such as Hole, Nirvana, Pearl Jam, and Soundgarden, as well as the independent Sub Pop label. The 1992 film *Singles* (directed by Cameron Crowe) was also set in Seattle and featured the grunge scene as a thematic backdrop. Music has since been an important element in the construction of Seattle's contemporary image, although the industry's rock predilections have not been as favorable to the city's rap and R & B artists.[8]

In the spring of 1986 the Seattle rapper Sir Mix-A-Lot's "Square Dance Rap" (NastyMix Records) entered the *Billboard* Hot Black Singles chart. The release failed to advance any radical aesthetic, nor did it make a lasting contribution to the rap genre. Its relevance lies more in its ability to reflect the diverse regional activity in rap production at the time as artists and labels attempted to establish themselves within the rapidly changing conditions fostering regional and local expansion. Sir Mix-A-Lot's emergence illustrates the fact that rap was being produced in relatively isolated regions and, as the track's chart status suggests, that it was selling in significant volume within regional "home" markets.

Nonetheless, an advertisement for Profile Records appearing six years later in *Billboard*'s "Rap '92 Spotlight on Rap" (November 28, 1992) portrays the proliferation of industry activity with a cartographic cartoon captioned "Rap All over the Map: The Profile States of America." New York, Chicago, Dallas, St. Louis, Vallejo, and Los Angeles are all represented with the names of acts and their respective regions and cities. The Pacific Northwest is conspicuously labeled "uncharted territory," which refers to Profile's inactivity there but also reproduces the dominant image of the region, in the view of those from the nation's larger or more centralized rap production sites, as a distant and unknown frontier. Perhaps of greater relevance, Mexico and Canada are even more sparsely depicted.

Regardless of the advertisement's insinuation, the fact that a Seattle artist was at this stage on the charts (and, in hip-hop parlance, "in the house") indicates that not only had rap's consumer base extended throughout the nation, but also new and unforeseen sites of production such as Seattle were being established. In an interesting spatial inversion that regards marginality as a positive factor, Bruce Pavitt, cofounder of the alternative-oriented Sub Pop label, states that "one advantage Seattle has is our geographical isolation. It gave a group of artists a chance to create their own sound, instead of feeling pressured to copy others" (Pike 1990, 30). The president of NastyMix, Ed Locke, reflected similar sentiments: "I'm sure there are advantages to being in New York or L.A., although I wouldn't know what they are. Seattle is a great place, and we operate on a more human scale, more sane. We're not trying to compete furiously with people in our own backyard, and we don't come from a position of muscle and money, so we can go to human qualities and the intangibles of quality of life" (Blatt 1990). Sir Mix-A-Lot slowly solidified his Northwest regional base, posting reputable figures on two albums recorded on the NastyMix label, which his sales helped underwrite. He later sealed a distribution deal that merged his self-owned Rhyme Cartel label with Rick Rubin's Def American label (a subsidiary of the Warner Music Group, later named simply American Records) and went on to release the widely acclaimed album *Mack Daddy* (1992, Rhyme Cartel/American). His single "Baby Got Back," a ribald ode to women's posteriors, reached the number one position on the *Billboard* Pop charts, eventually selling double platinum.

Displaying pride in his northwestern roots, Sir Mix-A-Lot provides an excellent example of the organization of spatial images and the deployment of a spatial discourse. In general terms, details that are sometimes overlooked speak volumes about space and place, presenting additional information about the ways individuals' daily lives are influenced by their environments and conditions of existence. For instance, the standard group photo on the CD insert of *Mack Daddy* depicts several members of the Rhyme Cartel posse wearing wet-weather gear consisting of name-brand Gore-Tex® hats and jackets. This is a totally pragmatic sartorial statement from the moist climate of the Pacific Northwest that remains true to hip-hop's style-conscious trends. It displays a geographically particular system of codes, conveying regionally significant information that once again demonstrates hip-hop's capacity to appropriate raw materials or images and to invest them with new values and meanings.

Of all the CD's tracks, "Seattle Ain't Bullshittin'" is exceptional for the manner in which it communicates a sense of space and place with clarity, sophistication, and cartographic detail. Establishing himself on the track as a genuine Seattle "player," as the original northwestern "Mack Daddy" (a term for a top-level pimp), Mix-A-Lot makes a claim to local prestige as a former Seattle hustler who shifted to legitimate enterprise as a successful musician and businessman. His braggadocio adopts a purely capitalist discourse of monetary and material accumulation, reproducing the terms of success and prosperity that conform both to dominant social values and to the value system inherent within the rap industry. Expensive luxury cars connote a certain masculine power and domination over the social landscape, but the image of cars and the motion they imply also metaphorically "drive" the cartographic portrayal of the greater Seattle and Tacoma region and the exploits of a highly mobile Rhyme Cartel posse.

As the title suggests, Seattle is the centerpiece of the track. This is clear from the beginning as Mix-A-Lot and one of the posse members, the Attitude Adjuster, ad-lib over a sparse guitar riff:

> Boy, this is S.E.A.T.O.W.N., clown (forever)
> Sea Town, Yeah, and that's from the motherfuckin' heart
> So if you ain't down with your hometown
> Step off, punk
> Mix, tell these fakes what the deal is.

As the bass and drums are dropped into the track, Mix-A-Lot lyrically locates himself as a product of Seattle's inner-city core, known as the CD (or Central District):

> I was raised in the S.E.A. double T. L.E.
> Seattle, home of the CD, nigga
> . . .
> It wasn't easy trying to compete with my homies in the CD

Seattle's Central District is home to a sizable concentration of black constituents who comprise roughly 10 percent of the city's total population. Mix-A-Lot's portrayal of the CD neighborhood is not explicitly racialized, yet the references to pimping and competition among "homies in the CD" easily fall into a common, even stereotypical definition of "the 'hood" that is pervasive throughout rap of the period.

The Attitude Adjuster states at one point that "it ain't nothing but the real up here in the Northwest," attesting to the hardcore practices and hip-hop cultural identities that are evident in Seattle as well as the rest of the nation. Unlike most major American cities, Seattle's black presence does not have a huge defining power on its urban character; black youths are a socially marginalized amalgamation within a geographically marginal city. The Attitude Adjuster's pronouncement may suggest a hint of defensiveness, but it also gives voice to the black hip-hop constituency that is, as the subtext implies, just as "hardcore" as those of other urban centers.

Having established his ghetto credentials, Mix-A-Lot expounds on several spatially oriented scenarios, shifting scale and perspective throughout the track with his descriptions of local, regional, and national phenomena:

> So even though a lot of niggas talk shit
> I'm still down for the Northwest when I hit the stage
> Anywhere U.S.A.
> I give Seattle and Tacoma much play
> So here's to the Criminal Nation
> And the young brother Kid Sensation
> I can't forget Maharaji and the Attitude Adjuster
> And the hardcore brothers to the west of Seattle
> Yeah, West Side, High Point dippin' four door rides.

Mix-A-Lot adopts the role of Seattle's hip-hop ambassador, acknowledging his own national celebrity profile while accepting the responsibilities of representing the Northwest, his record label and posse, and fellow rap artists from "Sea Town." Exploiting his access to the wider stage, he elevates the local scene, bringing it into focus and broadcasting the fact that hip-hop is an important element of the Seattle lifestyle for young blacks living there.

The perspective shifts again as Mix-A-Lot adopts an intensely localized mode of description, recalling the days when he "used to cruise around Seward Park," moving out of the bounded territory of the city's Central District, the posse's home base. Seattle is cartographically delineated here through the explicit naming of streets and civic landmarks that effectively identify the patterned mobility of the crew:

> Let's take a trip to the South End,
> We go west, hit Rainier Ave. and bust left,
> . . .
> S.E.A. T.O.W.N., yo nigger is back again
> . . .
> Gettin' back to the hood,
> Me and my boys is up to no good,
> A big line of cars rollin' deep through the South End,
> Made a left on Henderson,
> Clowns talkin' shit in the Southshore parking lot
> Critical Mass is begging to box
> But we keep on going because down the street
> A bunch of freaks in front of Rainier Beach
> Was lookin' at us, they missed that bus
> And they figure they could trust us.

With its references to the city's cross-town byways and meeting places, the track effectively communicates an idea of the everyday leisure practices of the Rhyme Cartel posse while also retaining a privileged local or place-based perspective that resonates with greater meaning for all Seattle or Tacoma audience members. This localized audience will undoubtedly recognize its own environment, and the track will consequently have a different and arguably more intense affective impact among Seattle's listeners and Sir Mix-A-Lot's home fans. Unlike Compton, which was popularized through a relentless process of reiteration by numerous artists, Seattle is represented much less frequently: "Seattle Ain't Bullshittin'" stands alone as a unique expression of Pacific Northwest identity. For example, there is no similar track on the Seattle-based Criminal Nation's *Trouble in the Hood* (1992, NastyMix/Ichiban), although references to the region are sprinkled throughout the lyrics on several tracks, and in a CD insert photo one group member sports a Tacoma T-shirt identifying his hometown.

It is precisely through these excessively detailed image constructions that the abstract spaces of the ghetto are transformed into the more proximate sites of significance, or places of the 'hood. The spatial discourse provides a language through which numerous social systems are framed for consideration. "Seattle Ain't Bullshittin'" is not solely about space and place on the local scale in Seattle; it is also about the ways in which these spaces and places are inhabited and made meaningful. Struggles and conflicts as well as the joy and love of place are represented here, as are the simpler facets of daily life, such as missing the bus. This is not a display of parochial narrowness but a much more complex and interesting exploration of local practices and their discursive construction in the popular media.

As I have explained, spatial language is flexible and can quickly encompass vast or minimal terrains, as Sir Mix-A-Lot and others demonstrate. The eponymously titled debut EP by the Lifers Group (1991, Hollywood Basic) offers an example of an even further spatial reduction that moves into entirely different social boundaries and reproduces a significantly different aspect of social experience. The Lifers Group consists of a collective of rappers who are incarcerated at New Jersey's infamous Rahway Prison, which is home to a segment of the Northeast's convicted criminals. Identified by both their names and their prison numbers, the group members represent a prison posse, one that is active in the Scared Straight program, which targets young repeat offenders convicted of minor crimes or youths convicted of more serious first offenses. With tracks titled "The Real Deal" and "Belly of the Beast," the EP provides an insider's perspective on prison life, lyrically constructing an image of space and place that is constrained by concrete walls and cell bars.

The Lifers Group's message challenges the bravado and street hustler images that pervade rap as it stresses the point that while the streets may be tough, prison is also a dangerous and frightening place to live. The Lifers Group represents the antithesis of "living large" and being mobile in the city; they introduce the sobering reality and negative consequences generally absent from gangsta rap's arrogant self-promotion. There is no celebrating their primary site of significance here, no glamorizing the world in which they dwell; the repeated theme is framed along spatial lines that continually reduce and compress the subjective self. For these men, the streets are part of a past life, and "walls, steel bars and mental scars" now constitute the defining boundaries of their spatial reality. Place is more than ever a defining element in their sense of self and identity. They can do little else but manipulate a spatial language.

By the end of 1992, the trend toward closely demarcated spatial parameters enunciated within a spatial discourse of the 'hood had become a common characteristic in rap lyrics and videos. Place, identified with the 'hood, was on the verge of becoming the preeminent signifier of ghetto authenticity and black identity. Rather than an expression of a narrow social perspective that celebrates the local to the exclusion of other wider scales, tracks such as "Seattle Ain't Bullshittin'" demonstrate a powerful method of representing the hometown local "flavor" on an internationally distributed recording. This allegiance to the sites of significance that constitute home and 'hood has evolved as a standard practice in rap representation, but it should not be overlooked that there are multiple messages being communicated to listeners who occupy different spaces and places and who identify with space or place according to different values of scale.

Hip-Hop Media
Dissemination throughout the Nation

❄

With the 1980s drawing to a close, rap was circulated widely as a major media wave popularized the style, language, music, and attitudes of hip-hop and further disseminated many of the culture's defining elements throughout North America and the world. In *Billboard*'s 1990 year-end wrap-up, the columnist Janine McAdams wrote that "1990 may well be remembered as the year when the biggest-selling albums were by rap artists" (McAdams 1990, 33). Rap posted top sales in the 1990 Pop Album category, with MC Hammer's *Please Hammer Don't Hurt 'Em* (Capitol) and Vanilla Ice's *To the Extreme* (SBK) outselling all other pop, rock, and rap artists. *Please Hammer Don't Hurt 'Em* sold over seven million copies in 1990, and *To the Extreme*, which sold five million copies in its first twelve weeks, was celebrated as one of the fastest-selling LP releases in the history of the music industry. It is interesting to further note that with the acceleration of rap sales came considerable diversity in the top sales listings, with multi-platinum figures posted by New Kids on the Block, Garth Brooks, Linda Ronstadt, Jon Bon Jovi, and Aerosmith. Defunct rock acts such as Creedence Clearwater Revival and Led Zeppelin also posted reputable figures through sales of CD back catalogs and boxed-set compilations.

Building on a momentum generated via major international market surges and concurrent growth in domestic regional and local markets that had not previously demonstrated strong rap sales, hip-hop's cultural profile grew to an extent that exceeded the 1986–87 multi-platinum sales period when the Beastie Boys, LL Cool J, Run-D.M.C., and Whodini dominated the rap music market. As rap's popular appeal expanded at the dawn of the 1990s, debates emerged around the articulation of spatially oriented themes and their relationship to notions of authenticity and reality in hip-hop. The topic of the subcultural roots of hip-hop came in for intense discussion within the extended hip-hop nation, and the internalized sense of cultural ownership among rap practitioners continued to collide with external corporate apparatuses—meddlers in the eyes of some hip-hop purists.

Despite factors such as the continued crisis in the rap tour and concert promotions industry, which contributed to restrictions on all-rap headline shows at large urban venues, and the ongoing pressures from the PMRC, Focus on the Family, and several other conservative action groups, rap was entering a phase of heightened activity.[1] This activity can be considered from competing perspectives, as either a result of hip-hop's dynamic and vibrant subcultural expressiveness or, in less optimistic terms, a product of the machinations of an opportunistic corporate culture. Each, in fact, has an element of validity, for even as talented artists continued to innovate and spur the rapidly expanding scene, hip-hop was also harnessed to a range of commodity marketing campaigns that many argue diluted its cultural strengths.

Hip-hop was saturating the media spaces of the mainstream press and, of greater consequence, television, gaining unprecedented attention throughout North America. At the end of the decade, rap emerged as a staple facet of advertising jingles, and hip-hop's stylistic codes offered a stock set of images that were incorporated into the marketing of name-brand soft drinks, snack foods, clothing, footwear, children's toys (including Mattel's Barbie® doll), and such products as Campbell's soup, McDonald's Chicken McNuggets®, and Pillsbury baked goods (with their trademark Doughboy recast as a conspicuously and literally white-bread rapping homeboy). Whereas in earlier stages of rap's evolution the music had primarily been associated with the city, as a mainstay among minority teen audiences and a culturally active and aware adult demographic (i.e., artists and clubgoers in New York's downtown scene), the genre had yet to achieve critical mass in terms of its penetration of the social mainstream. This changed drastically with corporate America's aggressive cooptive maneuvers in the early 1990s, which linked rap and the hip-hop culture with an array of common domestic commodities. The randomly applied hip-hop codes and signs and the rampant reproduction of decontextualized images of the hip-hop lifestyle were appropriated through what Elizabeth Blair (1993) describes as a process of "transfunctionalization," involving the reassignment of cultural objects, their uses, and their attendant meanings.

As Blair notes, the corporate intent was not to pay homage to hip-hop or to celebrate the emergent innovation of young black America; rather, the advertising campaigns were an obvious attempt to imbue standard name-brand products with urban chic, providing a new market gloss on otherwise banal commodities. These activities were also prominently targeted toward an adolescent and preadolescent demographic, introducing impressionable young minds to an ostensibly safe and palatable version of hip-hop. Artists themselves expressed divergent attitudes toward the trends, with MC Serch applauding the recognition of hip-hop's influences: "When the Pillsbury doughboy is kickin' a rhyme, you know you got rappers in the house." Luther Campbell, of 2 Live Crew, expresses another opinion: "When people turn on their TV and see the Pillsbury doughboy rappin', it's like anybody can do it. Why don't they get a real rapper? Everybody wants to [use] rap but they won't give real rappers a chance" ("Mainstream vs. Mean Streets" 1991, R-20). Neither Serch nor Campbell addresses the filmmaker John Singleton's appropriation of the name Doughboy, the character played by Ice Cube, in his 1991 directorial debut *Boyz N the Hood*. Marketing efforts in the entertainment industry were also influential in the mainstreaming of rap music and the hip-hop lifestyle, effectively circulating the more easily accessible symbols of hip-hop into new, dispersed social enclaves and more deeply instilling many of its base elements in the popular consciousness.

Having been carefully packaged and positioned for crossover, top pop rap stars such as MC Hammer, the Fresh Prince (Will Smith), Young MC, and Kid 'N Play eventually proved to be of benefit to the genre's commercial profile. For example, Young MC's biography emphasized his college degree and clean-cut lifestyle, which, combined with a Grammy Award for his debut double-platinum LP *Stone Cold Rhymin'* (1989, Delicious Vinyl), made him a suitable spokesman for companies and commercial products, including Taco Bell and Pepsi. Will Smith, the Fresh Prince, was awarded his own television sitcom, *The Fresh Prince of Bel Air,* in 1990 after gaining industry attention and commercial success with "Parents Just Don't Understand" and "A Nightmare on My Street" (1988, Jive). Today Smith juggles highly successful recording and acting careers. These and similar phenomena provoked a question among many in the hip-hop culture: Was the popular acceptance of rap evidence of an African-American cultural victory, or did it signal the ascendance of corporate America's authority over hip-hop and black youth expression? The dilemma again refocused discussion on the ambiguous line between "cashing in" and "selling out."

Tony van der Meer refers to the eventual emergence of "a lottery mentality among Black and Hispanic youth" (Toop 1984, 6), as many in their ranks were tempted to forsake local roots in community, rechanneling their hopes and dreams with new vigor toward "getting over" in the rap music business. Alan Light suggests another possibility, noting that "a dichotomy was firmly in place—rappers knew that they could cross over to the pop charts with minimal effort, which made many feel an obligation to be more graphic, attempt to prove their commitment to rap's street heritage" (1992, 229). Pop rap, which had always been a segment of the larger rap genre, emerged as the dominant subgenre, and its most successful purveyors, MC Hammer and Vanilla Ice, consequently became pariahs within some hip-hop circles. Neither artist showed exceptional talent on the microphone, but their production qualities were unassailable, and they excelled in live performances, with their elaborate dance routines and a full band. Hammer was as frequently associated with his trademark harem pants and energetic dancing as with his rapping, and despite the platinum sales of "Ice, Ice Baby" (1990, SBK) and gold sales of "Play That Funky Music" (1990, SBK), Vanilla Ice was never considered by hip-hop traditionalists to be much more than a melanin-challenged novelty.

The questionable status of Hammer and Vanilla Ice within the hip-hop culture became even more pronounced as their images virtually flooded teen magazines and, in Hammer's case, took the form of a plastic action figure and a Saturday morning cartoon, a dubious achievement briefly shared by the pop rappers Kid 'N Play in the wake of their success in the 1990 hit movie *House Party* (directed by Reginald Hudlin). The Seattle rapper Sir Mix-A-Lot offered accolades of hip-hop solidarity to Vanilla Ice ("ain't no beef") and Hammer ("keep gettin' paid") in the liner notes to *Mack Daddy,* but his gesture was atypical of rap's hardcore contingent. Hammer and Vanilla Ice were more frequently cast as the scapegoats for rap's slide into a commercial morass. In one of the worst imaginable accusations in hip-hop, both were regularly accused of selling out the culture and the art form. Even today Vanilla Ice is described in terms very similar to those used by defenders of "real" rock 'n' roll in reference to Pat Boone's —though not Elvis Presley's—presence on the scene from 1955 to 1962.

These divergent positions on hip-hop's new commerciality further heightened the perception within the rap scene that there existed a "real" or "authentic" hip-hop culture that was vulnerable to erosion by the "inauthentic" influences of exploitative capitalism. Janine McAdams articulated several of the more resonant factors underlying the issue of rap authenticity and the genre's pop derivatives in *Billboard,* framing it as a contrast in either content or geosocial origins:

The more rap may make it onto pop or urban radio and will continue to sell in record numbers in the years to come, "real rap" probably won't. What is "real rap"? Just think of where rap comes from, of the experiences and lifestyle and hardships that first fueled and informed rap music. The strong Afro-centric, street-level, urban political socio commentary call to action, call to party, tale of the 'hood rap lyrics and music are not likely to be recognized, heralded, or celebrated by the machine that is pop music. Because pop seems to accept only rap that cleans itself up, makes itself presentable, modifies its language and its intensity, and is devoted in part to pop video imagery. . . . Rap is the musical expression of revolution, of the anti-establishment. Real rap does not seek government approval; it is not meant to be mass-appeal.   (1991e, 24)

Despite a genuine concern for the topic, McAdams commits several errors in her critique that are representative of more widespread and prevailing assumptions about the music's past and its origins. For instance, she misrepresents rap's history by conflating distinct temporal movements, folding them upon each other in a manner that incorrectly posits an overly coherent teleological rap tradition. Adhering to a common misperception (but one that is not rare among rappers themselves), she suggests that a dominant defining characteristic of "real" rap is a modicum of sociopolitical content and, moreover, that political rap should not be considered in the same vein as pop rap, even if it sells platinum, as Public Enemy did. She creates the impression that, on the one hand, rap had been fiercely political and strongly inclined toward Afrocentric cultural conscientization from its inception (having been only intermittently so prior to 1987) and, on the other, the various subgenres are not differentiated by distinct and unique elements with their own informing histories.

While McAdams was partially correct in stating that the "pop machine" would not embrace "real" rap, her terms remain vague. Absent from her assessment is any clear acknowledgment of the music industry's role as an organizing influence that, among other things, is responsible for genre definitions and accompanying market demarcations that she herself relies upon. Evidence suggests that in fact the pop machine did warm to the real rap in numerous instances, exemplified by the emergence of a distinct genre of gangsta or 'hood films directed and often produced by black men which in turn provided the music industry with sound-track albums that frequently outdistanced the films in their commercial returns. Rather than critically examining the complexity of the music industry's involvement in market labeling, she simply offers examples of artists who conform to her loose definitions of "the real rap." None of this accounts for the popular success of the ideologically laden messages of Public Enemy or the fact that the hardcore gangsta act N.W.A. had topped the *Billboard* Top Pop Albums chart in the week following the release of *Efil4zaggin* (1991, Ruthless/Priority), joining the Beastie Boys, Tone Loc, MC Hammer, and Vanilla Ice as the only rap acts to ever reach the number one pop album position up to that time.[2]

Articulating a substantially different "hardcore" sensibility from N.W.A.'s, Public Enemy combined elements of what McAdams would define as rap "realness" with staged, even clichéd show-business flourishes (such as the group's "S1W" pseudo-military presence when they marched in place with toy weapons). They achieved crossover hit success and received widespread mainstream attention. Though they displayed unrelenting attitudes and politically charged discourses that were patently intended to grate against dominant social norms, Public Enemy and N.W.A. (among many others) both occupied positions that implied keen awareness of the broad range of popular consumer options. They consciously employed radical postures that turned their rebel images to commercial advantage. The groups were most dangerous, interesting, shocking, or entertaining from a cultural perspective precisely because they so evidently understood their relationship to pop music traditions and to the accepted norms from which they intentionally deviated. Rap's extension and growth at this juncture was predicated on the basis of the shrewd manipulation of media images and popular celebrity that the media engender. It is clear that enormous consumer response and headline popularity situates groups such as Public Enemy or N.W.A. within a popular phenomenon that escapes McAdams's limited definitions of "real" rap and pop.

Perhaps unknowingly, with their criticisms of hip-hop's increasing corporate adaptations, many hip-hop advocates were reflecting traditional mass-culture critiques (i.e., Theodor Adorno, Max Horkheimer, and the Frankfurt School), deriding patterns of commercial appropriation and mass production that depoliticized and divorced the product from the ostensible reality of its subculture. These attitudes were commonly founded in a nostalgia that maintained an image-ideal of a more unified, pure, or authentic set of cultural practices that have been lost or stolen. The debate had been smoldering for years, but as external high-stakes players continued to bring their commercial influences to the scene, the issue of authenticity and appropriation was reignited.

It was in this phase of hip-hop's evolution that the identification of a pronounced hardcore attitude, forged within the discursive articulation of the real, was firmly cemented in rap music. Staying "hardcore" and "keeping it real" emerged as part of the discursive reproduction of affirmative values that, in the wake of renewed commercial interest, were perceived as being at risk of cooptation or sanitization by forces displaying no commitment to or stake in the culture's tradition and continuance. Tony van der Meer explains the scope of the problem concisely in his introduction to Toop's *Rap Attack:*

There is nothing wrong with one community learning from the cultural forms produced by another, if it respects their specific shapes and meanings. There is something horribly wrong with a dominant community repeatedly co-opting the cultural forms of oppressed communities, stripping them of vitality and form—the heritage of their creators—and then popularizing them. The result is a "bleached Pepsi culture" masquerading as the real thing. This is what threatens to dilute the real feeling and attitude of hip hop, preventing its genuine forms the freedom to fully develop. The expression of Black people is transformed when it is re-packaged without any evidence remaining of the black historical experience.   (Toop 1984, 5)

From a historical perspective, the music industry's various stages of institutional appropriation of hip-hop provide a useful indicator in a chronology of rap's expansion into the American heartland. For instance, if rap was still perceived as being a strictly marginal music or an alternative to ordinary rock and pop fare, as it clearly was in the mid-1980s, its commercial appropriation would not have made sense from a purely business perspective by 1990. It quite simply would not have had sufficient recognition or appeal to warrant the attention it garnered from the major labels. In fact, though, despite a prevalent reluctance among commercial entities to embrace the full range of hip-hop practices, rap music was no longer being ignored as a cultural presence. Even black radio was programming rap more consistently by 1990–91, as radio playlists and singles sales indicate at the time, although it was the more palatable pop subgenre that was embraced.

Companies representing the aforementioned range of commodities subsequently attempted to absorb some of the attention that rap had won, grafting rap's popularity onto familiar consumer products in a desperate attempt to appear up-to-date or "cool," since, as a Campbell's public relations spokesman put it, "children love Rap. . . . It's very, very hip." Rap connoted a "fresh" identity, it was easily associated with youth, and in marketing terms, it had an appeal that was current. Yet, in most cases it was not rap or hip-hop culture per se that presented the desired object for appropriation, but rather the aura and the image appeal that they generated.

There also appeared to be an abstract value system in place among hip-hop aficionados that delineated acceptable and unacceptable incursions into the hip-hop scene. Major labels' practice of swamping the market with mediocre product was clearly regarded in the negative, but a similar surge in independent-label activity was deemed more acceptable within hip-hop circles, ostensibly because of the connections and benefits that accrued to local scenes. This was all the more true in view of the fears among independent-label executives that with the entry of major labels into the rap field, minor labels would not be able to compete. Appearing under the headline "The Majors: Marketing the Revolution down the Street, around the Corner, and around the World," *Billboard* reported on the concerns of indie executives:

They're heeere! Suddenly, the pie is getting smaller for indie rap label linchpins like Sleeping Bag and Tommy Boy and Profile and Next Plateau and Luke Skyywalker and Select and Tuff City. The majors are playing a favorite game: hardball. For the indies, it's a nightmarish fear—that the majors will glut the marketplace, leading to oversaturation and a backlash at radio, retail, and ultimately, with the consumer.

(Sacks 1989)

By 1990 the growth pattern of the rap industry had reached its apex, shifting first from a localized music with minor regional impact to a widely recognizable regional, national, and international cultural form. As the *Billboard* report notes, the majors were not only pushing into the domestic rap market, they were also positioned to leverage rap onto the international market, exploiting their established global distribution and retail systems. At this scale, the indies were certainly at a disadvantage unless they had established prior distribution contracts with corporate labels and could rely on the majors' systems to reach international consumers. Rap's spatial reach encompassed the entire North American market, and it was now also regularly extending to other continents within global market conditions.

Negus explains that a "pragmatic business judgment which affects the amount invested in rap is the assumption that it does not 'travel well'" (1999, 499). He cites industry executives who justify their minimal international promotions and distribution by pointing to rap's inherent identification with black cultural expressivity and localized "parochial" themes. Articles in *Billboard* between 1989 and 1992 reveal that independent rap labels (with major-label distribution arrangements) and majors *were* attempting to simultaneously break acts regionally (through exposure on campus or community radio stations and college concert dates) and internationally via extensive campaigns to introduce and promote the genre around the world. Having guided rap outward from its underground status and ghetto locales to the top of the charts, executives at both independent and major labels sought to open new markets where rap was still considered either a novelty or a minor alternative genre. As Janine McAdams describes the process, "Like an infant who must be fed pabulum before it can graduate to solid food, the mainstream audience had to be slowly introduced to a strained and diluted version of rap music first before it could graduate to the harder, full-strength stuff" (1991a, R-3). Her condescending discourse notwithstanding, international audiences too needed to be educated and oriented to rap's subgeneric distinctions, aesthetic forms, and quality.

On the strength of American responses to MC Hammer's and Vanilla Ice's recordings (and their fall 1990 tour together) and the crucial entry of MTV Europe, rap was finally breaking into the European market with significant sales. Despite the suggestion that language remained one obvious barrier to the development of the European or global rap market, *Billboard* (Sam Smith 1991, 9) revealed the standard perception that rap is equated with its lyrical content to the exclusion of its other salient features.

Though marketing executives repeatedly described the rapidly evolving slang and localized references as constraining factors, this assessment overlooks the fact that rap vocals could also be entirely impenetrable to English-speaking fans in North America. The majors could afford to throw rap out into the international market in the hope that some of it might catch the interest of international consumers, and ultimately some did, but attempts to develop a global rap audience were complicated by unenlightened assumptions about the music or about European audience tastes — and, as Negus observes, the tendency to regard rap as a cultural form that can be reduced solely to its lyrics. MC Hammer, Vanilla Ice, the Fresh Prince and Jazzy Jeff, and a growing crop of artists working in the pop rap subgenre provided the majors with some optimism, displaying their capacity as hip-hop ambassadors whose material was free of the political or gangster-oriented content that dominated much of the hardcore end of the rap spectrum.

Indeed, the major labels were unconcerned with replicating hip-hop's cultural foundations on an international scale; they were more directly interested in generating new consumer markets for the musical product. Pop rap opened the European market wide in a relatively short time. The question of how rap and the styles and expressions of hip-hop would be interpreted and adapted in foreign contexts was of little significance, nor could it be predicted. The major labels especially had an atrocious record of trying to read the North American market; their capacity and resources to do so in foreign contexts was even further reduced. *Billboard*'s suggestion that "while MC Hammer and Vanilla Ice have a pop appeal, pure rap may prove too hardcore for Southern European tastes" (Sam Smith 1991, 9) highlights the industry's aesthetic and generic distinctions as they attempted to position the music in the foreign market. The implicit coding between "pure" and "pop" coyly articulates a racial sensibility that is more strongly associated with U.S. cultural politics than with Europe and, accordingly, introduces a spatialized order of difference that is primarily comprehensible in U.S. terms. Pure rap refers to either Afrocentric or gangster themes that emphasize life in the 'hood, although it could also encompass tracks that feature greater rhythmic originality and less reliance on extended sample loops of popular mainstream songs. In the commercial logic of the market, the emphasis is placed on disparities in sales and financial returns; "pure" rap may be truer to hip-hop's U.S. ghetto sources, but in the executive mind and on the accountant's spreadsheet, it is ultimately less remunerative in the international markets.

The processes of hip-hop's geographic expansion in the global music market did, however, introduce important new contexts for transcultural cross-pollination as youths throughout the world adapted rap to their own heritage languages and locational contexts. In many cases young innovators merged rap's forms with the indigenous music of their nations, producing what are today common mélanges such as hip-hop-merengue or hip-hop-salsa in the Dominican Republic, Venezuela, Cuba, Puerto Rico, and major U.S. cities. The wide circulation of the discourses, signs, and symbols of hip-hop throughout the 1980s was amplified when pop rap landed on DJs' turntables in European discotheques and nightclubs or on commercial and pirate radio stations where it was mixed alongside indigenous recordings.

In the same period, with the rise of powerful iconic imagery embodied in the style and music of artists such as Public Enemy, N.W.A., and KRS-One, rap also emerged as the mode of choice for minority youths to express political and cultural resistance to their particular conditions of urban existence. Rap, like reggae before it, was taken up with unavoidable ferocity and commitment by poor and minority immigrant and refugee youth, and graffiti, break-dancing, and rap emerged with new force among North African Arab teens in Paris and Marseilles, Turkish youth in Germany, young Caribbeans in Britain, and Surinamese teens in Amsterdam.[3] The independent New York concert promotions company Joint Venture Music America (Da Joint), headed by Roy Cormier and Michael Fisher, tapped directly into hip-hop's countercultural appeal in foreign markets by booking concerts throughout Europe and Brazil where demand was growing but exposure to live rap remained limited. As the only black-owned promotion agency working the overseas market, Da Joint capitalized on the rising international interest in rap. Describing the agency's Public Enemy tour in Brazil, Fisher observes that

Brazil is a country larger than the continental U.S. with a population of 120 million, more than 80 million of whom are of African descent. Most of the African-Brazilians are dirt poor, so PE's appearances and message made a great impact on the 20,000 people who saw them perform.   (McAdams 1991b, 27)

Though collaborations between North American and international artists ensued—a notable example being the meeting of the Paris rapper MC Solaar and Gang Starr's MC, Guru, on the latter's *Jazzmatazz, Vol. 1* (1993, Chrysalis)—they have sadly remained infrequent. U.S. hip-hop generally remains the touchstone for many foreign expressions of hip-hop identity, though it is always filtered according to conjunctural influences and localized cultural innovations. In Canada's cosmopolitan urban center, Toronto, the Indian crew Punjabi by Nature unambiguously coopted the name of the New Jersey rap act Naughty by Nature, turning it toward their cultural identities while merging the beats and rhyme styles of North

American hip-hop with traditional Indian banghara rhythms, featuring digitized tabla drums, samples from Indian "Bollywood" movie sound tracks, and North American–style hip-hop beats.

A later illustration of the continuing U.S. influence emerges in 1999 from the Caracas rap crew La Corte, which lays claim to representing the "real" hip-hop culture in Venezuela. The group's rapper, MC Bostas Brain, is explicit about his ties to the United States and the fact that he lived there "for many years." The insinuation is that by virtue of his U.S. connections, he is closer to the rap source and therefore has a more legitimate stake in *hip-hop venezolano*. As he explains, "We make true hip-hop and we identify with its culture and in particular with the groups from the [U.S.] East Coast. Of course, we make our own contributions, like the salsa fusion, which is very different from those ugly flirtations with merengue" (Lebon 1999).

Today a "hardcore" rap aesthetic based on funky beats and solid microphone skills that are perceived as being "rough, rugged, and raw" (to quote EPMD's "Crossover" [1992, Def Jam]) and a corresponding discourse of 'hood-based authenticity suggest a certain defensiveness against the taint of pop ephemera. If hip-hop is a way of life, as many rappers suggest it is, then the discourse of a deep and enduring commitment to the scene and its cultural underpinnings arises as a crucial attitude that can and must be woven into rap practices. Even MC Hammer, when faced with a serious decline in his commercial status, underwent a transparent—even desperate—identity transformation, emerging in the image of a thugged-out Oakland gangster with his LP *Funky Headhunter* (1994, Giant). There seems to be little question that Hammer and Vanilla Ice were not judged solely on the basis of their rap talents but were in essence victims of a backlash against perceived inauthenticity. The integration of images, stylistic nuances, and thin traces of a hip-hop sensibility was, in fact, most often guided by the hands of others operating exclusively in the corporate and commercial realms. Despite insider criticism, many black entrepreneurs and artists managed to maintain close and, more important, respectful ties to hip-hop's cultural communities, since charges of selling out could lead to a career obituary. These businessmen and performers were forced to negotiate the contradictory terrains of a competitive industry that sought to maximize the commercial uses of hip-hop at home and abroad, in the local market and the international forum.

The portrayal of narrowly defined spatial milieux and the cultural practices associated with the 'hood continued to emerge as a fundamental facet of rap in the 1990s, confounding many critics who either hoped or expected that rap would lessen its place-based emphases as it reached a new status in the domestic and international markets. Attacks on rap's parochial focus were not always without merit, but they seemed to ignore the historical importance of place in hip-hop's evolution, as a crucial force in subjective identity formation and as the root of the idealized conception of "home." The independents, whose artists tended to display a more spatially conscious sensibility, were capable of serving the domestic market, but they lacked the capacity and clout to fulfill international market demands without major label distribution. The mainstream commercial marketers, however, were unfamiliar with such a high degree of spatial identification, and they lacked confidence and experience in handling it. As Benny Medina, then vice president of A & R at Warner Brothers, noted, "When we sign with an indie, we look for expertise beyond our own vision" (Nelson 1991, R-18). Complicating the matter was the fact that the rap market was inundated with product, and competition among independents and, rapidly, between indies and major labels continued to intensify. Major labels consequently showed a preference for less spatially aligned rap content, seeking to reproduce the pop forms that had catapulted MC Hammer and Vanilla Ice onto the international charts. The major labels, in effect, sought to accentuate a placeless rap form that they could more easily market within nonurban domestic markets and on an international scale.

This strategy shares several aspects with media theories of placelessness that surfaced in the late 1970s and throughout the 1980s. The communications theorist Joshua Meyrowitz, for example, argues that the impact of global mass media has had a leveling effect across social sectors, noting that the "unified backdrop of common information" and "the homogenization of information networks" (1985, 134) subtracts from the significance of place and undermines place-based identities:

Physical location now creates only one type of information-system, only one type of shared but special group experience. Electronic media begin to override group identities based on "co-presence," and they create many new forms of access and "association" that have little to do with physical location. . . . The homogenization of regional spheres is, of course, only a matter of difference. Different places are still different, but they are not as different as they once were. (143–45)

Edward Relph describes similar phenomena:

An inauthentic attitude towards places is transmitted through a number of processes, or perhaps more accurately "media," which directly or indirectly encourage "placelessness.". . . They have reduced the need for face-to-face contact, freed communities from their geographical constraints, and hence reduced the significance of place-based communities. (1976, 90–92)

Meyrowitz and Relph both place the responsibility for the deterioration of spatial integrity and place-based identification on the integrated mass-media systems that make up the institutional apparatuses of the music and entertainment industries. Their isolation of a widespread social condition provides an interesting perspective on contemporary postmodern phenomena and social trends that deprivilege the status of the local as a site of significance.

With access to efficient media distribution conduits since 1990, hip-hop culture has been greatly affected by global and local dynamics in the aftermath of its expansive growth. However, rather than rap's being placed at risk of sanitization or deterioration, as earlier supporters feared, it was confronted with the problem of losing fundamental connections to localities that have traditionally provided the proximate contexts for the genre's impressive capacity for innovation and creative reinvention. Pop rap is, in many ways, a placeless product that, despite its transnational commercial character, still maintains formal ties to hip-hop traditions and locally nurtured music scenes. The point is that with its spread to international markets, the connections to these local or regional sites become more tenuous.

As industry executives suggested in 1990, "The rap market is venturing into brave, new territory, and the majors are going along for the ride. The rap market, some industry insiders say, is limitless" (Donloe 1990, R-18). This statement actually carries two distressing messages: first, it is clear that the industry mainstream (made up of major corporate labels) was willing to get a free ride on the labor of black artists and entrepreneurs who had toiled in the business for years trying to build something that straddled the line between commercial viability and culturally redeeming value. When long-term major label ambivalence toward rap suddenly started to shift, considerable resentment appeared among those artists and entrepreneurs whose locally and regionally applied efforts had established rap as a stable facet of the national and international music industry. Describing what he considered a deplorable situation at the time, Russell Simmons noted that the majors involved themselves with rap "solely for the market share and not for the music. Majors hurt us developmentally. . . . In six months every major has put out more rap than I have in six years. That tells you something" (Donloe 1990, R-14).

Furthermore, the rhetoric of limitless boundaries and unconstrained potential is actually quite closely related to colonial discourses that regard marginal or "lesser" cultures as easily accessible sites for capitalist intervention and commercial exploitation. There is no sense of history in this pronouncement, no acknowledgment that rap is connected to the spaces and places from which it emanates through long-standing social patterns of production and consumption. These historical patterns encompass the practices of musical creation and performance as well as audience leisure activities, which, in hip-hop, are less a matter of consumption at concerts or clubs than of an active cocreation of the event. In contrast, major labels are virtually unanchored, stateless and placeless behemoths.

The intensification of debates and conflicts around the issue of rap's mainstreaming created a serious rift within the hip-hop culture. Hip-hop essentialists responded to pop rap's ascendancy in three major ways: they consciously attempted to maintain the foundational pillars of hip-hop, which include break-dancing and graffiti spray art and, in rap, freestyle microphone skills and DJ scratch and mix techniques (i.e., KRS-One); they initiated an urgent pro–black nationalist discourse that deployed rap as a communicative medium to reach and educate a youth constituency (Public Enemy and X-Clan); and they mobilized a spatial discourse emphasizing locality in order to reinforce their connective links with neighborhoods and place-based communities that were often in sharp contrast with the barrens of corporate industrial culture (Ice-T, N.W.A., and Compton's Most Wanted).

The Emergence of the Hip-Hop Press

As hip-hop turned toward new markets for records and promotional tours, a new array of ancillary media targeting an eager, multicultural teen market was also emerging. In the special section on rap in *Billboard* on December 24, 1988, there appeared a small advertisement for the rap-oriented teen magazines *Word Up!* and *Rap Masters*. Ad copy claimed that the magazines, published by New Jersey–based Word Up! Publications, together reached over 500,000 teenagers each month. Joined by similar teen-oriented hip-hop magazines, including *Rappin', Spice,* and *2 Hype,* as well as more journalistically inclined publications including *The Source, Rap Sheet,* and *Rap Pages,* the rap press created new sites for the expression of rap fandom while capitalizing on the sensational commercial and cultural growth of hip-hop. These magazines extended rap's range of circulation and enabled many of hip-hop's internal codes to reach a youthful and ever more style-conscious hip-hop audience. Over time, the high-gloss magazines have also been supplemented by an array of lesser-known and less professional efforts that include homespun fanzines, video magazines of varying quality, electronic 'zines, and a multitude of rap Web sites on the Internet.

Conforming to a basic fan-magazine format that follows traditions first established by Hollywood movie magazines in the 1930s and 1940s, the first teen-oriented hip-hop and black music magazines that were prominent from 1989 to 1992—*Word Up!, Rap Masters, Rappin', Spice, 2 Hype, Right On, Black Beat,* and *Black Sounds*—focused on "an image of the way stars live" (Dyer 1979, 39). These particular monthly magazines are most directly influenced by such teen-oriented publications as *Tiger Beat* and *16 Magazine,* which dominated in the 1960s and regularly featured casual coverage of popular trivia. Like traditional pop music publications, early hip-hop magazines continued to mediate fan desires as they relate to popular musical celebrity. This is especially true for audience members who were too young to attend concerts, regularly afford recorded materials, or otherwise participate as active consumers.

Teen music-celebrity magazines provide a general overview of either the entertainment industry as a whole or a particular musical genre, allowing magazine readers to boost their own sense of knowledge about celebrity lives and to increase their overall cultural capital (since the "better" or more serious fan is usually the one who knows the most—and the most current —information about an artist or group). For the youthful fan, this trivia helps to establish a more proximate relationship with the stars, facilitating a stronger sense of fan identification with a given celebrity by portraying the star's personal side and providing the material basis for the intensification of what Lawrence Grossberg has termed the "affective" relations of individuals and aggregate audience formations to a given musical scene. Grossberg's explanation situates this as a form of subjective cartography that adheres to the ever-changing and often subtle "mattering maps" upon which fan allegiances are inscribed: "The notion of *affect* points to the fact that there is more to the organization of our everyday lives than just a distribution or structure of meaning, money, and power; Some things *feel* different from others, some matter more, or in different way, than others" (1987, 186). At the level of affect, fans make the appropriate personal "investments" in the set of images, statements, or styles that "feel" the best, that seem to be best suited to the full range of an individual's interests or desires and the conditions within which they are experienced. They circulate within a self-defined terrain of popular relevance, overlapping most frequently with others who navigate similar cultural terrains and share common maps of meaning. Consequently, conventional teen magazines function as additional indicators of important detail, conveying the minutiae upon which fans might also base their subjective connections or structure their affective relationships to the music and the artists who achieve success, who "make it."

The spatial dynamic involves two distinct loci of celebrity and fan. They are separate but mutually dependent for their sociocultural definition. The organization of photos and interviews is part of a calculated attempt to breach the gap between celebrities and their young fans, providing what appears on the surface to be access to the inner sanctums of the celebrity milieu or conveying the sense of access to inside information about the men and women who comprise the hip-hop scene's upper echelons. As the celebrity's private domain is turned inside out and made public through photographic and interrogative probes (as in a *Rap Masters* photo feature on Biz Markie's newly renovated condominium that shows a photo of the star posing on the toilet), the perception of distance is drastically reduced, and readers acquire a proximate sensation of a more intimate relationship to the stars they admire and desire.

With the emergence of bobby-soxers in the mid- to late 1950s and teeny-boppers in the 1960s, teen fan magazines established themselves as being geared primarily toward young female readers. As Chambers (1985) points out, romance is the operative element of most pop music, and images generated in its musical performance as well as in teen magazines actively construct a preferred female audience. In their formal construction, earlier, conventional teen magazines promised their female readers a package of celebrity images and profiles, providing a cultural space within their pages where young girls could engage in the fantasy of romance within the safety and enclosure of their own bedrooms. This symbolically completed the cycle in which an artist's private life might be transformed into a public quantity and then, through audience consumption, returned in a new commodified state to the private domestic realm of the individual fan. This is also true of early hip-hop fan magazines, where the imbalanced ratio of photographs to written text indicates that these magazines are more to be looked at than read and the articles rarely concentrate on issues or problems that may be pertinent to a young girl's daily material experience. For example, an article in *Spice* dedicated to the topic of date rape is an anomaly that stands out precisely because of its intended seriousness and urgent relevance to teenage girls.

Simon Frith's suggestion that "the starting point for an analysis of the sexual differentiation of leisure must be that girls spend far more time at home than boys do. . . . The women's world is the home" (1983, 225) provides a context for the ways that rap teen magazine pin-ups might be used. Pin-ups are primarily intended for young teenagers' bedroom walls or possibly school lockers, areas closed off from the outside world and contained in the private domain of pleasure and fantasy. As Frith observes, "The relationship between music and the bedroom continues. Their public use of music might be much the same as boys (for background and dancing), but girls' home use remains different, with continued emphasis on personalities" (1983, 227). Hip-hop magazines can be situated in a common group with other teen music and entertainment magazines that are primarily (though not entirely) oriented toward a female audience. The format of the magazines and the composition of the photographs (characterized by head shots and close-ups of celebrities in carefully posed stances) adhere to the conventional teen-magazine mode of presentation. But it is the additional advertisements for jewelry or contests offering celebrity dates or phone calls and such as prizes that most clearly contribute to the gender-specific structuring of these publications. In the case of *Rap Masters* and *2 Hype*, the female editors function as mediators in the dialogue between the artists and the fan readership. Posed in friendly embrace among various male rap artists, including Ice Cube, who wears a jacket emblazoned with the slogan "bitch killa," these women occupy the position ostensibly most desired by the female readers, communicating the fun and excitement of participating in the parties and gatherings of the apparently bustling rap scene.

Ultimately, the capacity for teen-oriented rap fan magazines to portray or represent the full spectrum of rap practices is limited by the magazine format itself and the separate public and private economies of gendered desire and its expression. The more aggressive lyrical strains and the hardcore political ideologies that frequently comprise rap's discourses do not conform to the generally mild and apolitical content of publications geared toward a young, primarily female readership. Hip-hop teen magazines infrequently feature articles exploring rap's articulation of black-nationalist politics, the social conditions underlying gangsta rap themes, obscenity in rap lyrics, and issues pertaining to female rappers, including single motherhood, family commitments, and the negotiation of a male-dominated music industry. Despite these expansive themes, the constraints of addressing a teen readership and the minimal inclusion of hardcore rap sensibilities produces a tension between the magazines' covers. Teen-oriented hip-hop magazines must negotiate an often contradictory cultural terrain, navigating the complexities between pleasure and politics or between frivolity and substantiality that more traditional pop-oriented music and entertainment fan magazines need not confront.

By adopting this particular format, hip-hop magazines targeting younger readers have created a difficult project for themselves as they struggle not only against the ways that youths consider race and gender issues but also the ways that they might understand and use the medium of the conventional teen magazine. By employing a standard generic format and implementing its common discursive patterns, these publications put at risk the political projects advocated by rappers such as Chuck D or KRS-One while failing to adequately analyze and critique the conservative, racist, or sexist tendencies of others in the industry. Although teen rap magazines introduce a more radically inclined set of discourses than do most mainstream teen entertainment magazines, their printing of diluted political arguments that must vie for space with quite unrelated articles on style and fashion weakens their overall impact within the textual spaces of the publication and trivializes their importance as potentially transformative discourses. It is also true that although in some cases the various artists' stances and their cultural and political beliefs can be seen as stylistic gestures in the strategic construction of their public images, the critical mechanisms for assessing this possibility are not easily accommodated within the teen-magazine format itself. The conventional structure and content of teen hip-hop magazines are ever-present and overbearing, resulting in a banality that is subsequently imposed on the social and political critiques posed by rap artists in their recorded work.

Paralleling the rise in popularity of teen fan magazines, a more engaged rap music press emerged that sought to convey the complexities of rap and hip-hop's internal elements. *The Source, Rap Sheet,* and *Rap Pages* were the most influential, although *The Source* quickly established a market preeminence that continues to this day. *Hip Hop Connection (HHC),* which was published in Britain, was also widely available and provided consistent coverage of the hip-hop scene while introducing a valuable international perspective.

Rap Pages emerged from the publishing company of the porn baron Larry Flynt, premiering in October 1991. In its first issue, the executive editor, Dane Webb, describes his mission: "to present a magazine that helps define the Hip-Hop phenomenon and assists in its survival, instead of just riding the coattails of its success." But the magazine, which in terms of genre fell somewhere between the teen-oriented fan magazine and the conventional music magazine, lacked focus. The first issue featured articles on Marley Marl's studio production techniques and his approaches to rap recording in a regular section called "So You Wanna Be a Record Producer" and on John Singleton's experiences as a young black director in Hollywood alongside an article titled "Latin Hip-Hop Popster Gerardo" and a fan contest to "spend Halloween night hanging out at Knott's Berry Farm with rap's scariest new crew, KMC." The magazine had found its direction by 1994 but ceased publication in October 1999 and was put up for sale despite consistent growth in advertising revenue. *Rap Sheet* premiered in July 1992 in a tabloid format reminiscent of *Rolling Stone*'s first incarnation. The editor, Darryl James, explained that "with Rap Sheet . . . we deal with hardcore and gangsta rap. . . . We'll also take a listen to some new music, and try to give you an idea of what's good, and what's too booty to spend money on." The format was a liability given the competition, but it maintained its presence alongside the other, more attractive options available at the time.

Stretching across racial and cultural factions, *The Source* was started in 1988 by two Harvard University students, John Schecter and David Mays, whose interest in and affinity for hip-hop culture led them, in an example of low-profile enterprise recalling Rick Rubin's early forays into the music industry from his New York University campus dorm, to produce the magazine's first issues from their Ivy League campus dorm. Having started as an amateurish, photocopied publication produced for and by hip-hop enthusiasts, *The Source,* which defines itself on its masthead as "the magazine of hip hop music, culture, and politics," gradually evolved into a glossy-cover magazine that showed greater commonality with rock magazines such as *Rolling Stone* and its competitor, the 1985 start-up *Spin,* founded by Bob Guccione Jr., son of the publisher of *Penthouse. The Source* moved to a monthly publication schedule in December 1990. Its innovations included its "Unsigned Hype" column promoting rising rap artists, its "Fat Tape" column of selected singles, its "Source System" hit list of full-length CDs, a regular photo feature on global graffiti, and a pronounced emphasis on both youth and race politics and hip-hop fashion. One of its most enduring contributions is its microphone CD rating system, which accompanies reviews of new releases. The top rank of five microphones had, as of 2000, been awarded only eight times, and it remains the holy grail of hip-hop standards and achievement.

The journalistic hip-hop magazines featured lengthy artist interviews, learned record reviews, and general insider information that, taken together, provide a relatively concise update on industry activities as well as the more subtle makings of the hip-hop culture at local, regional, and national levels. The real contribution of the hip-hop press was the agenda-setting role it played nationally and its influence in defining the issues, themes, and discourses of analysis that surfaced around hip-hop. It focused the discussion of hip-hop's history and cultural importance in a new, more serious manner, adding depth and substance to the coverage of the music and its related practices through the genre's history. They also established themselves as important arbiters of taste through their reviews and highlights, making them valuable to consumers, club DJs, and industry executives who sought insights into the rap and hip-hop scenes in major urban centers throughout North America.

The hip-hop magazines also exhibit a more explicit emphasis on the political and social structures of the hip-hop scene as a foundation for rap music's production. This can be discerned in the in-depth articles tackling complex social issues, such as government legislation on violent youth crime or welfare policy, organized conservative campaigns against rap, and overviews of political policy initiatives that specifically affect hip-hop's primary innovators within black and Latino communities. The content and issues featured in the magazines target a slightly older or more mature readership than does the teen entertainment press: for example, *The Source*'s primary audience demographic is comprised of "mostly young men, 16–24, half of them white, the other half mostly black" (Sengupta 1996).

In feature interviews, artists frequently address their backgrounds (prior to their entry into the music business) and recount their patterns of daily interaction within highly localized zones of activity. It is in this mode that the 'hood and the spatial coordinates of lived experience are most clearly defined in the press. Place is an unambiguous factor in the themes and discourses of the music, and the rap press provides an important textual space for the explanation and elaboration of artists' relationships with their neighborhoods and local posses or crews. In *The Source* and *Rap Pages,* monthly photo features of graffiti spray art from across America and around the world were intended to display the ongoing practices of one of the cornerstones of the hip-hop culture. The features' specificity—that is, their practice of naming the aerosol artists and their zones of operation—acknowledges both the global and the local scales of hip-hop's influence.

Rap Sheet initially went the furthest in emphasizing geographic activities in the hip-hop nation with its regular feature sections: "Regional Rags," which reported on small and mid-sized hip-hop publications from across the United States; "Local Streets," featuring reports by locally identified artists on different aspects of their hometown scenes; and "A Day in the Hood," in which a *Rap Sheet* reporter meets the artists on their home terrain, visiting their familiar haunts and being introduced to the accompanying crews or posses. This last section is structured on the premise that there is an informing relationship between a group or artist's 'hood and his or her music. Coverage is intended to provide context for and insight into the artist's daily circulation and experiences while reinforcing the general and related themes of "reality" and "authenticity" through first-hand observation.

Rap Sheet's "A Day in the Hood" section also adopted a geographic or spatial theme in its profile of local urban neighborhoods. It is tacitly acknowledged that "the 'hood" is a generic term that describes minority ghetto spaces in contemporary American cities. But by featuring profiles of nationally dispersed 'hoods and nominating the 'hood as a definable territory that is demarcated through a subjectively experienced sense of place (evoked by the host rap artists featured in the articles), *Rap Sheet* attempts to see each 'hood as a unique spatial construct and to discern what the host artists consider to be locally meaningful phenomena. Distinctions of mobility and stasis and other characteristics mediating the relationships with various urban sites and local neighborhoods are often the most pronounced characteristics to emerge from the 'hood profiles each month, with some localities fostering a constrained and limited sense of place-based identity and others being more expansively conceived by their inhabitants.

For example, in *Rap Sheet*'s premier issue (July 1992), "A Day in the Hood" foregrounds the Cypress Hill posse's neighborhood, from which the group's name is derived. In this article, the compression of locality is a pronounced and influential factor in the sense of place that the artists have of their home turf. The intersection of Firestone Boulevard and Cypress Avenue is roughly at the center of the 'hood, and the Cypress Hill crew's family homes are spread throughout the immediate vicinity. They lived in this neighborhood throughout their formative teen years, before they were rap artists, and the interview reveals a sense of personal history that connects the members of the group to their 'hood as they recount stories and relate anecdotes about the area while moving easily through it.

Their comments communicate the importance of local tradition and the remembrance of past events, but in isolating them an explicit connection is made between a temporal past and place that allows the crew to point to a house or a street corner as they recount a story. Michel de Certeau writes that "there is no place that is not haunted by many different spirits hidden there in silence, spirits one can 'invoke' or not" (1984, 108). Events may be long since past, but the places where they transpired remain and in an almost mystical way continue to harbor a shimmering residue of the given event that can only be seen in memory by those who live there and experienced it firsthand. The members of Cypress Hill reflect this as they point out various sites to the accompanying journalist, completing the stories by "invoking" the "spirits" that make these places significant to them.

In general, the Cypress Hill posse seems sedentary, rooted in place (in contrast to their roles as nationally acclaimed rap stars with a demanding national and worldwide tour schedule). They live close to one another and walk rather than drive between each other's homes and the locales where they gather. A photograph portrays two band members, Sen Dog and B Real, settled on "the wall"—a low brick abutment on a neighbor's front porch—and conveys a standard image of "hang time" in the 'hood and the productive leisure practices that reinforce posse bonds (which, as the article suggests, usually involve smoking marijuana or drinking beer together). An additional emphasis on spatial compression described by the visiting *Rap Sheet* reporter conveys the concept of the 'hood as a bounded territory: "I roll with the Cypress crew up the street towards the railroad tracks—'the border.' . . . We get to the tracks that divide Cypress Ave., signifying the end of their hood. They don't like to go past the tracks" ("A Day in the Hood: Rolling With Cypress Hill" 1992, 20). Without further elaboration, the implication is that the 'hood is a relatively secure, bounded home environment beyond which the combined variables of risk, threat, and danger increase.

Quite another sense of the 'hood emerges in the October 1992 "Day in the Hood" feature on Houston's Fifth Ward district, known as "the Bloody Nickel," in which landscape and terrain are meticulously described. The reporter establishes an image of the zone that downplays the widely reported dangers of the neighborhood: "the landscape—green grass and thick groves of trees everywhere, wide two-lane streets and an occasional creek—made it hard to imagine massive drug trafficking and crime. It's there, but it's happening on quiet street corners under overgrown willow and oaks as much as in alleys or burnt-out buildings" ("A Day In the Hood: The Bloody" 1992, 19). This pastoral description is intentional: it dilutes the potency of lyrical descriptions of the ward in songs by the Geto Boys, Scarface, and the Fifth Ward Boyz, providing an alternative set of images for readers who are familiar with the discursive constructions of space and place in their music. The article later reiterates a common image of the 'hood as a depressed and potentially dangerous social environment in a reference to a "descent" into the Bloody Nickel area.

The Fifth Ward is compared along racial lines to other Houston wards (the black wards, the Hispanic ward, etc.), although Willie D of the Geto Boys is quoted as stating that "we're not really into that neighborhood stuff, we're all from Houston. We have it bad enough. We take pride in our individual neighborhoods, but we all run together" ("A Day In the Hood: The Bloody" 1992, 20). His sentiments reflect the fact that while Houston consists of an arrangement of interlocking sectors, the 'hood as a social construct is always identified only as a minority zone where race and class are the leveling factors. Willie D also reflects Cypress Hill's general attitude when he suggests that while each individual claims home territory in his or her 'hood, the allegiances are relational, based on personal background and history as much as on urban structure and spatial cartography. It is not just that the 'hood exists as a named or definable section on city maps or in urban designs, but that it is a known and lived place with affective values invested in it by its inhabitants. In the example of Houston and the Bloody Nickel, central markers on the landscape, such as recording studios, nightclubs, restaurants, and public parks (for example, Tuffly Park, "where Rap-A-Lot sometimes holds its artist meetings out on the grass"), resemble community commons in which members of the local hip-hop scene congregate. These are the sites of central significance that individuals collectively consider important to their daily reality as they actively remake anonymous spaces into particular places in an ongoing process of cultural production and transformation.

Contrasting with Cypress Hill's use of 'hood space, transportation and mobility among the Houston rappers also function in the production of a sense of place and identification with local landscapes, again reinforcing the relatedness of the dispersed neighborhood zones and territories. This might be a result of the Rap-A-Lot crew's nonhomogeneous roots in place. While the members of the Cypress Hill posse are all from the immediate neighborhood where they have grown up together and now own homes, the Rap-A-Lot crew represents several different city wards and sections and thus identifies itself with (or "claims") several different 'hoods. The wider range of city highways and streets represents passages that cross through more abstract (i.e., foreign or unfamiliar) transitional spaces surrounding the various sites of significance that comprise their various 'hoods. Consequently, the Rap-A-Lot crew seems always to be on the move, getting in and out of vehicles, arriving and leaving various sites, moving in unison as a posse. The crew members' sense of the city and of the 'hood is intensely informed by a degree of motion that resists narrow spatial constraints without ignoring points of territorial transgression and boundary crossings.

Rap Sheet's "Local Streets" column in the September 1992 issue features a guest reporter, J. T. Money of the Miami-based act Poison Clan. His focus is on the unique quality of the South Florida "bass sound" in hip-hop. Briefly citing several of the key labels, producers, and acts that make up the local scene, he describes the region's emphasis on bass-oriented mixes, comparing it to other regional styles in the United States and tracing out the cultural particularities of Miami and South Florida that give birth to the regionally distinct style. Money explains how the multiethnic and multiracial social context of the entire southern Florida region (especially Miami) is a product of the confluence of Caribbean cultures, with a convergence of musical influences from Cuba, the Dominican Republic, Haiti, and Jamaica. These musics, along with American R & B, funk, rap, and rock, provide the musical background for hip-hop artists working in the area. For Money, Miami's cultural hybridity is its strength and underlies the hip-hop lifestyle there.

In December 1992 Seattle's Kid Sensation profiled his local scene in a similar manner, but in his article the city's cartography is defined in considerably closer detail. While he names locally active artists, clubs, important local hip-hop radio programs, and record stores that stock rap and hip-hop, Sensation also provides a description of the proximate geographic relations between the adjacent cities of Seattle and Tacoma, the city's Central

District (the CD, "home for most of the hardcore rappers in South Seattle . . . the rougher ghetto area"), and the Seward Park area ("the spot where people like to gather and pump their stereos. . . . It's almost like a social club"). His descriptions are much livelier than Money's, and he isolates several important sites of significance that not only shape his own sense of space, place, and belonging but are also significant in a broader social sense as zones of social interaction and congregation among the local hip-hop contingent. In this mode, particular places are deemed crucial factors in the circulation of black youth and the organization of the hip-hop scene in Seattle. These places are also rendered as site markers that arise in the music itself—for example, providing the backdrop and the setting for Sir Mix-A-Lot's "Seattle Ain't Bullshittin'," with its particularized spatial references to the Seattle CD and Seward Park neighborhoods and the explicit mention of streets linking the two.

Despite these regular portrayals of sociospatial sensibilities and localized patterns of habitation and habituation, *Rap Sheet*'s "A Day in the Hood" displays several revealing assumptions about the composition of the 'hood as a socially constructed place in hip-hop culture. One assumption is founded in the notion that there is a "truth" about subjective identities that can be revealed through witnessing the featured artists in their home environments, which also harbor an essential "truth" quotient. Artists are elevated in the magazine's pages as rap celebrities but upon their return to the 'hood are resituated in order to better connect them with their foundational roots in a perceived process of artistic revitalization. This is part of how the artists claim to "keep it real," maintaining their legitimacy by not growing too distant from the 'hood that initially formed them and that in many cases continues to provide a grounding for the lyrical themes they write, perform, and record. The 'hood may be either a zone of threat or of nurture as the artists develop their skills and rise through the music industry; but once they have established themselves as prominent acts, the 'hood is almost invariably described as a well of sorts, providing spiritual, social, and artistic replenishment.[4] Understanding the 'hood in such terms is crucial to understanding its spatial resonance in hip-hop's discourses.

The *Rap Sheet* articles are also implicitly structured upon the belief that the broad popular profile of music celebrities produces a spatial displacement (whereby artists become touring and performing nomads whose images and recordings are available to consumers "everywhere") that has the capacity to affect and erode their locally constituted identities. By revisiting the 'hood, the artist is able to shed the false skin of pop celebrity and recapture the sense of self upon which his or her "true" identity is founded. The prevailing logic would have it that when artists achieve national or global status they lose their sustaining bonds with place, essentially making them placeless subjects. This logic posits the local as a site of positive virtue, whereas the vast and frequently anonymous spaces of the global communications complex are contrastingly portrayed as soulless and undifferentiating in their potential to destroy subjective identities. The further operative assumption here is that although the apparatuses of the mass culture industry transform individuals in negative ways, the authenticity of the home place, defined in hip-hop as the 'hood, functions as a mitigating force against the displaced identity of mass-media celebrity. Therefore, the interviews and reporting of "A Day in the Hood" are also concerned with a certain image of power that isolates artists in places where their strengths are most recognizable and most easily affirmed within the close encounters of neighborhoods and communities.

These elements merging self and place are conjoined through the overarching notion that the 'hood is a relatively self-evident, exposed, or transparent social space. A *day* in the 'hood is presented as an adequate allotment of time in which to see the local landscapes and the ways in which the featured artists use their space, and to glean a basic comprehension or feel for the places on display. Clearly, however, one day is not long enough to adequately assess much of anything substantial about the cultural norms and social patterns that may make a space into a place for rappers and their posses. Does this render the column irrelevant? No, or at least not entirely, for its main value is in its capacity to provide context for hip-hop's ongoing internal processes of defining and refining the many discursive patterns that involve articulations of space and place.

In the fall of 1995 the hip-hop press leader, *The Source,* responded to *Rap Sheet*'s feature with the introduction of its regular section "In the Hood." Whereas *Rap Sheet* provides insights and detailed impressions of the 'hood as an artist's home turf, *The Source* has, since the section's inception, maintained a more distant, objective journalistic style, presenting an overview of the local scenes throughout the nation rather than a specific view of one or two artists dwelling in their home neighborhoods. The 'hood is not actually represented as a locale of reduced scale and locational particularity; rather, it is the nation's cities that are foregrounded, with monthly coverage citing each city's most prominent rap acts and labels as well as hip-hop format radio stations, used record and rap CD retail outlets, clothing stores, clubs, and restaurants. "In the Hood" has greater utility value than most other magazines' features on geographically diverse hip-hop scenes, orienting readers toward urban venues in a manner that corresponds more fully with travel writing in the mainstream press.

Vibe magazine, founded by the entertainment impresario Quincy Jones in 1993, weighed into the hip-hop and black youth market as a high-profile joint venture with Time Incorporated Ventures before emerging as Vibe/Spin Ventures under the corporate banner of the Miller Publishing Group. Miller also produces *Spin* and the hip-hop magazine *Blaze* (which premiered in the summer of 1998 under an editorial "manifesto" proclaiming that "this is as real as it gets"). With its coverage of black popular culture, encompassing R & B, soul, and funk music as well as prominently featuring articles on film and television celebrities and hip-hop artists and producers, *Vibe* is a contemporary lifestyle magazine geared toward educated, upwardly mobile young consumers. Posting circulation figures of an estimated 600,000 copies per month in 1999 (S. Baker 1999a), the magazine is a powerful advertising vehicle for blue-chip companies such as Ford and Volkswagen, fashion clothing brands including Versace, Gucci, Calvin Klein, and Levi's, and numerous black-owned fashion design companies such as Maurice Malone, Ecko, Fubu, Karl Kani, and Phat Farm, as well as major and independent record labels. Although *Vibe* as well as *Blaze,* which sponsored the extremely successful 1999 Hard Knock Life tour featuring DMX, Jay Z, Method Man, and Red Man, were profitable and magazine circulation was increasing, each was put up for sale in 1999.

Introducing the magazine *XXL* in 1997, the editor-in-chief, Reginald Dennis, who, with the executive editor, James Bernard, had formerly been on the editorial board of *The Source,* scripted a mission statement that derides the transformation of hip-hop culture into a mere leisure option and fashion statement:

Hip-hop is both a defense mechanism and the ultimate manifestation of our survival instinct. It is an expression of Black genius, pure and simple. It is about starting with nothing and somehow, someway doing something worthwhile. The way we've done it since the times of slavery. . . . The b-boys and b-girls of the 70s, 80s and 90s are maturing. And since we will never outgrow our culture, we must force it to grow with us. . . . Welcome to the revolution. Welcome to XXL.

(Dennis 1997, 14)

Despite lofty intentions to the contrary, *XXL* adhered closely in form and content to *The Source,* which was its main competitor. Dennis and Bernard left the magazine and were eventually replaced by the former music editor at *The Source,* Elliott Wilson. The magazine initially premiered as a quarterly, but plans were underway to accelerate the publishing schedule to ten issues by spring of 2000, which it achieved.

As the proliferation of hip-hop magazines illustrates, the cultural forms and expressions of hip-hop have steadily evolved from the early DJ, MC, graffiti artist, and b-boy heritage to the point where it is now a fully integrated facet of music, film, and fashion promotions and advertising. Indeed, media forms have also been merged by independent entrepreneurs who are usually rap fans themselves; for example, video magazines have surfaced for sale in small hip-hop-oriented music shops and clothing outlets. The vid-mags feature interviews with artists and, of greatest interest to hip-hop aficionados, the inclusion of spontaneous freestyle performances captured on hand-held video cameras. Hip-hop as a "whole way of life" is, through these multiple media, more than ever on display, sharing or competing for shelf space with standard, mainstream cultural commodities and vying for advertising dollars, audience members, and consumer attentions with unprecedented vigor.

Mass Media Dissemination: Music Video and Television

Whereas rap's steady growth over the decade was achieved without substantial programming at either black or pop radio, its massive sales thrust in 1990 can be directly attributed to a new access to television, primarily through cable music video programs. Rap had appeared sporadically on television but beginning in late 1988 was finally embraced by the medium's program directors to an extent commensurate with rap's commercial impact and reception among teen consumers. It was during this period that the top-selling rap artists MC Hammer, Tone Loc, Vanilla Ice, and Young MC swept the pop music industry as cable music video programming boosted the genre's exposure and audiences' familiarity with its visual styles.

Television's role in hyping audience interest and motivating consumption of popular music is not at all a recent phenomenon: Elvis Presley's 1956 appearances on *Stage Show,* hosted by the Dorsey Brothers, *The Steve Allen Show, The Ed Sullivan Show,* and *The Milton Berle Show* were major cultural events that amplified his allure and cemented his celebrity status. In a similar vein, the Beatles' 1964 appearance on *The Ed Sullivan Show* helped to establish the group in the U.S. market and opened the door for the British Invasion. Following its debut in 1981, MTV was a crucial medium for introducing new acts and increasing their commercial prospects and formed a catalyst for the second British Invasion to sweep the nation.

By 1983, when the network finally entered the high-volume New York and Los Angeles cable markets, artists including Culture Club, Duran Duran, and other so-called video bands emerged as top pop stars in America, often well in advance of major tour exposure or radio play. Sales of Michael Jackson's *Thriller* were unquestionably aided by the sheer dynamism of his performance in the "Billy Jean" video, the artfully cinematic style of the "Thriller" video, or the Broadway-inspired production of "Beat It," and Madonna and Prince, each of whom developed a compelling visual persona, owe much of their career success to MTV. The network also raised the commercial profile of American alternative acts with distinct local and regional followings, such as R.E.M. (Athens, Georgia) in the late 1980s and Nirvana, Soundgarden, and Pearl Jam (Seattle) in the early 1990s.

Despite a quarter century of Dick Clark's *American Bandstand* and *Soul Train* with Don Cornelius, it is unlikely that television ever played such a crucial role in crossing black American artists and recordings over to white teen audiences as it did in the late 1980s and early 1990s with rap. As they had with funk and soul music before it, MTV executives based their initial exclusion of rap on the dubious claim that it did not conform to the station's rock format, the major exceptions being video clips by rap's leading acts such as Run-D.M.C., LL Cool J, or the Beastie Boys. Among the most important videos to emerge from the hip-hop scene was the Stop the Violence movement's "Self-Destruction" (Jive/RCA), which was a substantial success upon its 1988 release. The quality of the music and superb video production, the appearance of roughly a dozen rap celebrities, and the video's formal similarities to the popular charity videos "Do They Know It's Christmas" (BandAid [1984, Mercury]) and "We Are the World" (U.S.A. for Africa [1985, Columbia]) contributed to the video's acceptance among viewers and MTV executives. As rock videos had already proven, MTV exposure amplified audience interest and generated sales, and the "Self-Destruction" video helped push the single toward sales of a half million units.

The introduction of *Yo! MTV Raps* in September 1988 had the single greatest influence on rap's enhanced exposure despite the fact that the station had consciously resisted rap's regular inclusion in its video rotation since it began broadcasting. As Nelson George explains in hindsight, "*Yo! MTV Raps* didn't just pull in viewers—it sent seismic waves through the whole music industry. By giving hip hop dances, and gear a regularly scheduled national platform, the broadcast was integral in inculcating hip hop's distinctly urban culture into the rest of the country" (1998, 101). Following its premiere, the ratings for *Yo! MTV Raps* soared, making it the highest-rated program in MTV history to that point. Initially hosted by the hip-hop pioneer Fab Five Freddy and later by Dr. Dre (of the group Original Concept) and Ed Lover, the program gained serious street credibility thanks to the hosts' well-established connections within hip-hop circles. Their respected status among rap artists and MTV's considerable clout also gave them relatively unimpeded access to the hip-hop scene and its top talent, which was crucial to the program's immediate success. Once its ratings were revealed, *Yo! MTV Raps* was deemed a hit among the network's teen viewers, and its programming schedule expanded rapidly from a half hour weekend spot to screenings at 10 A.M. and 10 P.M. on Saturdays, eventually leading to a one-hour block of daily rap programming in the coveted midday after-school slot. Once rap had gained a foothold on the network, crossover video programming increased, and rap videos, as well as hip-hop-influenced R & B by artists such as Bobby Brown, began to be added more frequently to MTV's general rotation and thus to reach a wider segment of the viewing audience.

Prior to 1988 there is little mention of video production in relation to artist promotion or image construction; at the time it was perceived as a useful but marginal promotional tool. Rap had no substantial television presence, and as a result, labels were often hard pressed to develop the public images of their artists in a manner consistent with established procedures for handling rock and pop talent. In the aftermath of MTV's foray into rap (and concurrent initiatives by other cable networks), independent-label executives regularly voiced their desire to develop their artists visually by exploiting rap's sudden television access. The reason was obvious: a popular, well-received video by an independent label could add 200,000–250,000 unit sales nationwide to a recorded single that, prior to video, might have sold only 400,000 copies. Still, with their larger coffers and a more elaborate and established system for artist development, the major labels had a distinct advantage over independent labels. They were better able to budget for video production for their rap acts, often leveraging them onto video rotation and the charts simultaneously. Working in the independents' favor was rap's comparatively low studio production costs —substantially less than those of mid-range rock acts at the time. This freed up a larger percentage of the overall budget for video production and other promotional endeavors.

With the new option of reaching a wide and diverse audience via MTV, independent rap labels and major labels with active "street" divisions began investing a larger portion of their promotional budgets in video production, with no guarantee that they would in fact be screened. As the president of Profile Records, Cory Robbins, admitted in 1989:"What's really changed in the rap business is video. The fact that MTV has two hours of rap videos a day has been an incredible help in breaking artists for us. The way we're developing artists now is making more rap videos. We're making three, four videos on each album now" ("Album Deals, Video Promote Longer Careers" 1989, 78). As Robbins suggests, artist output was no longer conceived as a series of one-off singles but as a more integrated and fully realized body of work that demonstrated consistency in the overall product. With video production demanding greater financial outlay, the pressure on establishing career artists also intensified, and the emphasis on artists' images rose as a more central factor in promoting and positioning them in the market and extending their career shelf life. Tommy Silverman of Tommy Boy Records echoes these sentiments, stating in 1989, "The visual medium is 200% more important to us than radio" (Nathan 1989, R-13). The excitement for video among the indie-label executives illustrates their sense that black hit radio's longtime dismissal of rap was a less worrisome factor with the consumer access that video allowed.

Noting MTV's questionable record in handling black acts, Nelson George commented in *Billboard* that after its introduction *Yo! MTV Raps* instantly became an essential medium in breaking new acts and introducing the huge and crucial MTV teen audience to hip-hop:

> Where R & B failed, rap has made major inroads on MTV. . . . The long-term impact of this on the marketing of rap (and all black music) is yet to be determined. It is clear, such as in the case of Tone Loc and Living Color, that MTV has been crucial to their success. Its recent involvement with nontraditional R & B, particularly rap, puts MTV ahead of most black radio and the black press, which, considering MTV's beginnings, is quite ironic. (George 1989b, 20)

The benefit of Tone Loc's video exposure is a case in point, since the release of his hit singles "Wild Thing" and "Funky Cold Medina" (1988, Delicious Vinyl) coincided with the premiere of *Yo! MTV Raps*. After going into high rotation on the program, the songs accelerated up the charts. By April 15, 1989, his album *Loc-ed After Dark* reached the number one position on the Top Pop Albums chart. This was unheard of for a first album by a rap artist (although Vanilla Ice was soon to repeat the feat). Looking back, the unforeseen response to *Loc-ed After Dark* appears to have been a harbinger of things to come, and in this regard it stands as a benchmark in rap: it constitutes the first real indication of how sustained and regular exposure through music videos would affect rap sales in the future.

MTV also capitalized on the teen consumer awareness of *Yo! MTV Raps* with the release of *Yo! MTV Raps: The CD* (Jive) in 1989. Featuring a majority of tracks representing the lighter, pop-oriented end of the rap spectrum (including "Parents Just Don't Understand," by DJ Jazzy Jeff and the Fresh Prince, "It Takes Two" by Rob Base & DJ E-Z Rock, and "Gittin' Funky" by Kid 'N Play), the CD presented a new marketing tool to maintain the network's popular profile among its youth market (for example, the CD sleeve included a merchandise order form for a *Yo! MTV Raps* T-shirt) while further advertising the music and artists that appear on the program. The CD also reflected the network's aesthetic content restrictions and its tendency toward mainstream adolescent audience formations: although tracks by BDP ("My Philosophy"), Ice-T ("High Roller"), and Too Short ("Life Is . . . Too Short") were featured on the disk, they were "clean" versions, free of obscenity and explicit sexual lyrics. Of greatest interest is the inclusion of extended club remixes that introduced alternative versions of the recordings, ones that deviated from the standard album or radio edits on MTV's video rotation. Curiously, considering how visual a medium MTV is, the CD is free of images of either the artists or the video disk jockeys (Vee-Jays), with only a stylized faux graffiti image of the program's Roy Lichtenstein–influenced pop art logo on the cover. Over time, the cross-marketing of rap developed as a standard commercial facet of the industry, and by 1997 even the Grammy Awards rap nominees and *The Source*'s top hits were available for purchase in CD form, with *The Source* exhibiting an evolved and aggressive merchandising strategy on its liner sleeve (marketing the magazine, additional *Source* CD compilations, and clothing merchandise).

Other cable channels also introduced regular rap programming in this period: the *Video Soul* program on Black Entertainment Television (BET) had featured rap alongside R & B and dance-oriented fare for several years when in 1986 it had a run-in with Profile Records. BET accused Profile of denying them access to new videos by Run-D.M.C. at the height of the group's popularity and allowing a competing network—MTV—exclusive access to the videos upon their release. Although Run-D.M.C.'s manager, Russell Simmons, was also implicated in the decision to bypass BET, BET executives argued that the exclusives granted to MTV were unfair and neglectful of the black media and audience support that had provided the act's foundation from the start. The conflict blew over, yet its irony was not lost on rap industry executives, who had been trying for years to boost their artists' videos onto MTV after being spurned by black radio. As this episode indicated, the television airwaves, like radio, were segregated, and issues of race were not absent from the decisions being taken as the networks attempted to establish a niche for rap in their regular program schedules.

BET introduced its popular *Rap City* in 1989, and like *Yo! MTV Raps* before it, the program shot to the top of the network's ratings. Since MTV surpasses BET in terms of total viewership and budget, the production strategy at *Rap City* has consistently involved building links to the diversity of localized hip-hop scenes throughout the United States, establishing credibility and market equity through its connections to the urban 'hood and the portrayals of rappers hood life. As a producer of *Rap City,* John Tucker, explains: "When we go to a city, I want the viewers to be there living the life of the artists. I want them to see where they hang out, where they get their ideas from, where they dwell" (Baker 1999b, 114). This production strategy mirrors that of the *Rap Sheet*'s "Day in the Hood" column, which identifies place and the 'hood as a site of potentially greater truth and value in relation to the expressive communication among hip-hop artists. The approach reflects further similarities with the stance of independent record companies, which maintain that their size and scale of operations offers them a privileged contact with artists and audiences within the rapidly fluctuating dynamics of hip-hop culture. Extending its reach, *Rap City* widened its distribution, and it eventually screened in syndication on Canada's Much Music video station.

In 1989 MTV decreased its daily time commitment to rap by half "in response to complaints from record companies that rap had become too dominant a force on the station" (Nathan 1989, R-13). This claim, while distasteful, was more justified in the case of the Video Juke Box (later known simply as The Box), a pay-per-view music network that reached twenty-seven major urban markets when it debuted in 1989. Playing requests based on viewer call-ins to a 900 number, the station was criticized by music executives for reportedly programming rap as almost 75 percent of its total content. These criticisms of the Box's playlist were often based on rumors within the industry that unscrupulous promotions managers affiliated with both independent rap labels and major-label "street" divisions commonly hired teenagers to dial in requests for specific tracks or artists in order to generate market buzz. Owing to the inordinate demand for rap videos, the alleged practice was perceived by some in the industry as a motivated strategy rather than a legitimate expression of viewers' musical taste preferences and eventually became known in hip-hop parlance as "jackin' The Box." The Box and the Fox Network's relatively short-lived *Pump It Up* program entered into the everyday media diets of millions of teenagers, many of whom were nonurban, nonminority viewers with limited prior exposure to the styles and characteristics of hip-hop.

Fans of the genre and the mildly curious (as well as undiscerning or grazing television viewers) had easier access to hip-hop's visual forms and gradually became familiar with both individual celebrities and the subculture's nuanced signs—both of which were essential to the popularization of the genre. The quality of early rap videos was spotty, however; whereas mainstream rock and pop videos had developed more consistent standards and were more likely to be better funded, many rap video directors had neither history, resources, nor industry support behind them. Lower budgets often necessitated nonstudio video shoots, outdoor group performances, and a pronounced reliance on local folk as extras. This was not necessarily a problem, since the streets and neighborhoods of the urban environment had been, since the dawn of hip-hop, a cornerstone of the thematic representations of black youth cultures. Indeed, the inventive collaborations conjoining video directors, rap artists, and the promotions executives of the record labels produced an altogether new video aesthetic.

Rap artists and young video directors alike have proven to be extremely adept at communicating their sense of locale, visually representing the places of significance which they inhabit and delineating different social settings and different regions through rap videos. The set of images presented portray the scene and setting in which the rap narratives unfold, graphically conveying information about an artist or group's home front in order to provide a vehicle for the representation of their city or urban neighborhood. Rose succinctly encompasses the breadth of the phenomenon when she writes:

Over most of its brief history . . . rap video themes have repeatedly converged around the depiction of the local neighborhood and the local posse, crew, or support system. Nothing is more central to rap's music video narratives than situating the rapper in his or her milieu and among one's crew or posse. . . . This usually involves shots of favorite street corners, intersections, playgrounds, parking lots, school yards, roofs, and childhood friends. (Rose 1994a, 10)

References to local sites in both videos and rap lyrics are not ambiguous; the whole purpose of representing the local is to be explicit. From 1988 to 1994, however, the emphasis on detail and geosocial sites of significance was pronounced among West Coast rappers, whose daily lives are more strictly organized around turf and territory than are those of their East coast counterparts (the phenomenon has since evolved as a standard component of hip-hop's symbolic systems).

Rap's availability on a widespread and daily basis in the homes of urban, suburban, and nonurban teenagers across America altered the nation's cultural landscape. Tricia Rose observes, "Rap music videos have animated hip hop cultural style and aesthetics and have facilitated a cross-neighborhood, cross-country (transnational?) dialogue in a social environment that is highly segregated by class and race" (1994a, 9). The impact of *Yo! MTV Raps* and other rap video programs on youth and teen culture became evident almost immediately as, for example, general youth styles in nondescript suburban and rural enclaves began reflecting hip-hop's sartorial patterns. For many white youths, the insights into rap came as a revelation of sorts, but the same can be said of rap's increased and intensified exposure across black youth communities, which produced a new sense of the similarities and differences in hip-hop aesthetics across the nation. Teenagers from coast to coast increasingly adopted the loose and oversized sportswear that was popularized in the videos, resulting in record sales of name-brand and team-logo attire as well as the emergence of an entire industry of hip-hop-influenced clothing, including the now-defunct Cross Colours, Karl Kani designs, the successful FUBU line, and artist-owned fashion lines such as the former "IV Play" designs by rapper Play of Kid 'N Play, Naughty by Nature's "Naughty Wear," Chuck D's "Rapp Wear," the Wu-Tang Clan's

"Wu-Wear," Jay-Z's "Rocca Wear," and most impressively, the Phat Farm clothing line, originated and overseen by the hip-hop impresario Russell Simmons.

Seeing the impressive impact of home cable music video programs, Tommy Boy, Def Jam, Priority, Warner Brothers, and Atlantic also attempted to diversify their promotional thrust, capitalizing on audiences' interest in videos by introducing home videocassette packages to the commercial rap market. Heavy-metal home video packages had proven to be a successful commodity, and it was assumed that rap would also fare well among teen consumers. Public Enemy's debut video package, *Fight the Power—Live,* was released by Def Jam in 1989 and sold in excess of 25,000 units (which is certified gold for video), and Tommy Boy was pleased with the sales of its 1989 video compilation *Monster TV Rap Hits,* also released in 1989. But in comparison to record and CD sales, these figures were considered insufficient to justify the production expenses involved in the home video packages and their promotion, although marketing executives were often convinced that the disparity between CD and home video compilation sales was a result of ineffective promotions and unfocused market positioning, not a lack of consumer interest. The rap home video market, they argued, was an unexploited field. Independent label executives also expressed concern that by delivering the visual elements of rap to domestic viewers, live concert appeal among fans might dwindle as they became more inured to the acts' visual presentations. Tepid consumer interest in the home video package configuration owing to regular viewer access to new videos on daily music television programs more or less halted the industry's attempts to develop it as a major commodity; video compilation packages are still produced, but only infrequently.

In 1991 Priority released a home video package titled *Straight from the Hood.* With the cover claiming that the video featured "11 slammin' music videos & interviews from rap's most dangerous acts," the package included videos by N.W.A. and individual members MC Ren and Eazy-E, Ice Cube, the Geto Boys (plus a solo video by the group's Willie D), W.C. and the Maad Circle (featuring Coolio before he launched his solo career), Low Profile, O. G. Style, and 415. The moniker 415, which is also the telephone area code for the San Francisco Bay area, reveals an important characteristic of the package, since the majority of artists represented are from either the West Coast or Houston and are exemplary of the gangsta aesthetics at the time. Not all the videos take up the 'hood theme explicitly, though they tend strongly to film the groups and their collective posses in naturalistic urban sites, reinforcing the dominant representational space that remains standard in the portrayal of gangster "authenticity" and hardcore rap. MTV's authority at the time, as well as a sense of its content restrictions, is also reflected in the package's accompanying warning: "Caution: This video contains raw and uncensored behind the scenes footage of N.W.A. plus unedited video that MTV wouldn't play!" As with black hit radio, the more lyrically and rhythmically aggressive recordings were not welcomed on the video network, making the domestic home video configuration a viable alternative for those artists whose material was deemed inappropriate for both radio and music television.

Other, ancillary video formats also emerged, most notably vid-mags. One of these, *Real Magazine*, was produced independently in Boston, billing itself as "Da True Voice of Hip Hop Music." Featuring interviews, video clips, live concert footage, and freestyle sessions, the vid-mags presented an alternative to both hip-hop publications and mainstream television's video programming, falling between the two in content and focus. The vid-mag configuration often suffered, however, from inconsistent sound and image quality and lack of focus in the artist interviews. For example, *Real Magazine* provided coverage of Boston-area acts and artists connected with New York, establishing a local and regional presence that was also reinforced by the vid-mag credits citing "our homies" or "real Gs" in Boston, Cape Cod, Providence, and New York. By the late 1990s rap concert videos and feature films released straight to home video, such as Snoop Doggy Dogg's *Murder Was the Case* (Death Row) and *Da Game of Life* (No Limit Films), Master P's *MP Da Last Don* (No Limit Films), and Jay Z's *Streets Is Watching* (Roc-A-Fella), are widely available in most major video rental outlets and in select, privately owned neighborhood stores.

Despite resistance to rap from rock programmers and audiences, the significance and lucrative potentials of unprecedented rap video exposure were evident to industry insiders within a year. Rap's expansion through cable broadcasting on MTV, BET, and other cable networks was actually hindered by the fact that home cable access had not yet reached total nationwide saturation, though its growth was rapid. Cable hookups were often beyond the financial means of many urban poor—a highly motivated segment of the rap audience—and as a result, the cable medium expanded more slowly in zones characterized by high rates of impoverishment among the residents. Broadcast networks had much better market penetration, and as rap gradually became more common (if not exactly a staple) on the major television networks, it reached an even larger audience base throughout North America. Rap label strategies for navigating the different television options involved placing videos on MTV or other cable rap programs, since they had a higher rotation rate (albeit among a smaller and generally younger audience base), while attempting to book artists onto the major network talk shows.

Following a thirteen-week stint replacing Joan Rivers on Fox's *Late Show* in 1987, Arsenio Hall attracted the attention of Paramount Television executives, who recognized potential in his brash and, to their sensibilities, unconventional style. Premiering in early 1989, *The Arsenio Hall Show* (which was produced for syndication by Paramount) was for five years the most consistent vehicle through which rap acts gained access to mainstream network television. As the only late-night talk show with a black host, *The Arsenio Hall Show* competed with *The Tonight Show,* hosted by Johnny Carson (and, later, Jay Leno), and *The Late Show with David Letterman* in the same general time slot. Hall's program claimed to be the link "between viewers' homes and the 'hood." This coy racial coding hinted at the "who's who" of prominent black actors and hip-hop artists on the nightly guest list, implying a spatial and cultural divide between black America and the program's large white teen viewership.

In its first year on the air, the program featured many top rap and R & B musicians, helping to break new acts and new releases while attracting viewers of the desirable and profitable eighteen-to-twenty-four-year-old demographic, which also was rap's most active consumer group. Hall's hosting style, often either uncomfortably ingratiating or hip, offered a successful blend of mainstream talk television and b-boy cool. This was best exemplified, for instance, in appearances by MC Hammer, who was asked about the central role of the church in contemporary black music, and Will Smith (the Fresh Prince), who exchanged "snaps" and engaged in spry wordplay ("playing the dozens") with Hall in a display of black discourse and male interaction that was virtually unknown on television at the time. Capitalizing on his sudden popularity, Arsenio also recorded the novelty rap track "Owwww!" (1989, MCA) under the alias Chunky A, which reached the Hot Black Singles and Hot Rap Singles charts in December 1989.

Of greater importance, Hall was in tune with developments in the rap scene and the wider black community, making him an important arbiter of many cultural issues. When a coalition of West Coast rappers (including Digital Underground, Ice-T, MC Hammer, N.W.A., Tone Loc, and Young MC) replicated the Stop the Violence Movement's peace initiative with the release of *We're All in the Same Gang* (1990, Grand Jury/Warner), Hall hosted the record launch on air and provided a forum for discussions about youth gang–related violence and the June 15, 1990, "Peace Weekend." In the winter of 1991 Hall hosted artists from the Black Women in Rap tour (which included Queen Latifah, MC Trouble, MC Lyte, and Harmony), providing advance promotion for the tour and exposure to underrepresented female rap artists. In a major coup, Hall also featured then–presidential hopeful Bill Clinton as guest saxophonist with the program's house band, elevating the status of both men among the young viewing audience.[5] Finally, as sections of Los Angeles burned in the aftermath of the Rodney King verdict in April 1992, Hall invited civic leaders, community activists, and concerned actors and musicians (among them the city's mayor, Tom Bradley, and the actor Edward James Olmos) onto his program to address the issues and to engage in dialogue toward comprehension and a resolution. It was riveting television, and the serious and compelling social debate that unfolded confirmed Hall's unique role as a late-night television celebrity and black cultural icon.

In August 1989 *Billboard* reported that *The Arsenio Hall Show* was having a noticeable effect on commercial sales and consumer recognition of black musical talent. While researchers acknowledged that it was difficult to determine what the cumulative effects of cable video programming and Hall's show were, the show's direct clout was evident when urban radio in the same midnight time slot was examined. Urban radio stations had noticed that their late-night numbers dipped when Hall's show aired, leading programming directors to either work around the program, forge tie-ins, or slot artists appearing on the Hall show into their regular playlist rotation ("TV's 'Arsenio Hall' Having an Impact on Urban Radio" 1989, 1). In this regard, Hall was a boon to rap and contemporary R & B music while he was on the air. Notwithstanding his successes, however, Hall fell victim to transitions in the late-night talk show landscape, and *The Arsenio Hall Show* went off the air in 1994, leaving a gaping hole in the active representation of contemporary black musical cultures in the mainstream media.

In the midst of Arsenio Hall's late-night television tenure and in the wake of enhanced television exposure, rap radio suffered a major loss when the all rap–format station KDAY in Los Angeles permanently signed off on March 28, 1991. Citing insufficient advertiser revenue, the station owners abandoned rap entirely, shifting, in an ironic move, to an all–business news format and leaving several of Los Angeles's urban-oriented stations to cover rap as a part of their programming mission. The KDAY decision was consistent with a general trend away from all-rap or high-rap-rotation formats across the country, although rap's increased exposure through television and video may also have had a negative influence on the trend. The visual component of television added much to the image and sensationalism of the genre, and it is entirely likely that one of the unacknowledged results of rap's rise in mainstream media, along with other economic factors, was the demise of stations such as KDAY.

Rap's exposure on television during this period more firmly aligned the genre with the mainstream music industry, since television was the last media bastion restricting rap's expansion. Once its viability was proven for television consultants and viewing audiences, the basis was established for the genre's top-selling artists to enter into the popular flow of television programming. Yet rap's access to television and its full-fledged entry into the transnational media matrix produced a curious schism in hip-hop as the 'hood-oriented gangster themes of the reality rap subgenre gained prominence in this same general period. The divisions between more palatable, easily mainstreamed elements of pop rap and the often hostile localized imagery and discourses that were merged with gangster themes led some artists to more explicitly reject the pop spectrum of hip-hop, dismissing it as the symptom of unabashed commercial opportunism. Responding to the placeless and flaccid pop subgenre, Eazy-E, Ice-T, Ice Cube, Too Short, and KRS-One, among other artists, adopted the role of self-defined "underground street reporters."

Underlying these performers' self-appointed roles as 'hood journalists who communicate through rap's expressive conduits is the basic premise of journalistic objectivity and facticity, which, in Ice Cube's view, is based on personal observation: "We just tell it how we see it, nothing more and nothing less" (Mills 1990, 39). Rappers, then and now, claim that they developed their ideological and theoretical perspectives on race and class in America on the ground, at street level, drawing from earlier analytical modes that were also crucial to the sociopolitical agendas of the Black Panther party and Malcolm X as well as to earlier musical precursors such as the Watts Prophets or Gil Scott-Heron. Rap "reporters" articulate the widespread sentiment among minority youths that unless there is a body count, society deems their stories irrelevant. Hardcore rappers conceive of themselves as legitimate street reporters for disenfranchised blacks and Latinos who actively sustain the community infrastructures through which they circulate but whose access to public means of communication is denied or whose messages are either contained by or incorporated into the social and media mainstream.

Asserting control over the means of representation—if not the conduits of dissemination—rap artists tend to construct powerful images of the scenarios that they know best and are most familiar to them. They are careful not to divulge where the line between fiction and reality is drawn, however, often refusing to state where their experience ends and images of hypothetical ghetto conditions are inserted. Rapidly shifting visual and lyrical metaphors are implemented as a method of illumination or critique, challenging audiences and society at large to find meaning within the multiple and complex codes at work in the texts.

The notions of "street reporting" and a of national black news voice consequently rely on a conceptual construct linking local experience to more widely networked media representations. Chuck D employs a similar but more expansive analogy with his widely quoted (but underanalyzed) statement that rap is "the black CNN that we never had" (Eure and Spady 1991, 336). Tricia Rose suggests that

Chuck D . . . is right on at least two counts: rap is a highly accessible, quickly incorporative cultural form that gathers and presents information from multiple, black, (usually inaccessible) sources, *and* it is a highly mediated corporate-dominated product that tends to produce homogenized and deeply problematic representations. (Rose 1997, 269)

After 1989, as rap video was becoming established fare on television and the genre's strength was evident on the pop charts, the rap-CNN analogy seemed reasonable, if imprecise. Rap does not really resemble CNN in any direct way, but the analogy offers an interesting perspective on rap's social relevance in relation to issues of locality, since CNN reconstructs the local in a global context, raising the particularity of events and occurrences to national and international scales with stunning immediacy. The basis of the analogy lies in the dynamic conjunction of local and global sensibilities and practices. Rap, however, is widely listened to by urban minority and nonminority youth alike, and as such it provides a kind of connective tissue spanning a broad cross-section of the American sociocultural body.

During Public Enemy's most productive years (roughly 1987–91), the group's political and cultural agenda required a major media base to distribute the images of black resistance to U.S. racism and messages of expansive ideals of cultural nationalism. In other examples of hardcore rap, most notably the gangsta rap subgenre, access to the mass media provides a means of "representing" the local posse or crew and its home environment, depicting their members' methods of survival in the 'hood. Rap's descriptions of social spaces and the articulation of cultural identities forged within lived environments across the nation function, in effect, as a series of local reports providing regular updates on the struggles and victories of black America, which are rarely featured in unexpurgated form in the mainstream media. Viewed in this light, Chuck D's rap-CNN analogy is particularly astute.

CHAPTER EIGHT

"The 'Hood Took Me Under"

Urban Geographies of Danger and the Cinematic 'Hood Genre

❋

Now I'm of age and living in the projects
getting paid off the clucks and the county checks
I'm telling ya, fresh out of high school, never did I wonder
that the motherfucking 'hood would take me under
—MC Eiht, "Streiht Up Menace" (1993, Sony Music)

Teen Violence: Wild in the Streets. Murder and mayhem, guns and
gangs: a teenage generation grows up dangerous—and scared.
—*Newsweek*, August 2, 1993

Race, Identity, and Space: Black Cinematic Perspectives

Interviewed in the mid-1990s, Richard Price, author of the novel *Clockers* and, with Spike Lee, cowriter of the screenplay for its cinematic adaptation, addresses the social basis upon which black youths are represented in the film:

The reality is that these kids don't give a fuck about stuff like preying on your own people. They don't think of themselves as political or sociological. . . . They are thinking about how to get visible. Plus they are teenagers, and teenagers think of nothing but themselves, not whether they are black or white or rich or poor.

(Quart and Auster 1996, 16)

But there is substantial evidence contradicting Price's notion of black youth, identity, and collective cultural awareness. In practice, prevailing institutional forces make it difficult for many black and Latino teenagers to ignore either their racial or their class-based status. This is made clear, for example, in Mike Davis's detailed descriptions of the racist practices of the Los Angeles Police Department's enforcement of curfew laws and the spatial policing of "sumptuous playgrounds, beaches and entertainment centers," which have as a result "become virtual no-go areas for young Blacks or Chicanos" (1992, 284). These teen groups are continually isolated as visible minorities and are subsequently demonized as a mobile threat, leading Henry Giroux to note that "the racial code of violence is especially powerful and pervasive in its association of crime with black youth" (1996, 67).

In the economy of danger of the late 1980s and 1990s, black teens were inordinately wealthy, and they had a deathly concise comprehension of how they are perceived by the parent culture in their daily circulation through the urban landscape. Take, for example, a conversation I overheard when leaving a suburban cineplex after a screening of the film *Friday* (1995, directed by F. Gary Gray), starring the popular rap star Ice Cube. The film was not a blockbuster advertised with the accompanying slogan "on screens everywhere" (although its cost-to-revenue ratio made it one of the most financially successful films of 1995). Its appeal lay with the young minority audiences who identify most strongly with hip-hop, and the film was marketed accordingly, screening mainly in neighborhoods with high-density working-class minority populations. As the crowd of mostly black and Latino teenagers shuffled out of the cineplex, one young brother mentioned that "the 'hood films" are always screened in the same theater, the one closest to the entrance/exit. His understanding of this practice was that the management was uncomfortable with the idea of a crowd of minority youth traversing the full length of the lobby and potentially intimidating other paying customers.

On several subsequent occasions I corroborated this: the films that tended to draw a predominantly black and Latino teen audience from the surrounding neighborhoods were, in fact, consistently screened in theaters close to the doors. The additional presence of a "rent-a-cop" in the cineplex lobby when such films such as *New Jersey Drive* (1995, directed by Nick Gomez) were shown further confirmed his observation. Giroux (1996) points to the existence of a generational divide that is especially evident where black youths and white adults are involved, suggesting that the perception of teenagers as "indeterminant, alien, and sometimes hazardous" leads to practices of social regulation that are often exercised in precisely the ways the young theatergoers had experienced. Selective exhibition and segregation in theater spaces is nothing particularly new; it can be traced to the practices of theaters' either excluding blacks or banishing them to the "nigger heaven" of the movie house's upper balconies in the 1920s and 1930s, and to the booking and screening of blaxploitation films at inner-city theaters that, by the early 1970s, had been all but abandoned by white patrons, who had fled to the suburbs. Today it is common practice to isolate those films that are thematically focused on the lives and experiences of contemporary black youth from the 'hood.

And what, or, more precisely, where is the 'hood in cinema? Differenti-ated from the displaced construct of the ghetto that formed the dominant spatial configuration of such early 1970s blaxploitation films as *Shaft* (1971, directed by Gordon Parks), *Superfly* (1972, directed by Gordon Parks Jr.), *Cleopatra Jones* (1973, directed by Jack Starrett), and *The Mack* (1973, directed by Michael Campus), the 'hood offers a generational variant on the term "inner city" and the landscapes of urban oppression that prevail there. In the blaxploitation film, ghetto space is often rendered as a vast, abstract ex-panse of urban dilapidation. Its topography functions mainly—though not entirely—as background, providing a setting of urban decay in which ac-tion unfolds. Reporting in a *Newsweek* cover story on black movies that was published as they approached the height of their popularity in 1972, Charles Michner suggests that the depiction of ghetto spaces did commu-nicate a spatial specificity in certain contexts that helped to extend their recognition factor among localized audiences:

Unlike most white escapist fare with its never-never landscapes of purple sage and alpine luxury, the strongest of the new black films are firmly rooted in the audi-ence's own backyards—"Super Fly," "Charleston Blue" and "Shaft" in the squalid, decayed slums of Harlem, "Melinda" in barren, bleached-out Watts. The spectacu-lar Eldorado Cadillac driven by Priest in "Super Fly" gets quick recognition from some of the audience because it actually belongs to "K.C.," a well-known Harlem pimp who plays himself in the film.   (1972, 78)

In comparison to the dominant images of black cultural experience and everyday life portrayed prior to the 1970s—in which A-list actors such as Sidney Poitier and Harry Belafonte were often saddled with the burden of black representation—blaxploitation films presented images that resonated with a recognizable or familiar sense of ghetto authenticity among black audiences. Despite divergent opinions on the social value of the blaxploita-tion action films within black communities (Michner 1972, 1978), many black urban audiences initially responded favorably to the enhanced profile of black writers, directors, and actors who were deemed to be more adept at cinematically representing the ghetto than their white counterparts.

In 1970s blaxploitation films, ghetto space, constructed as a swath of human and architectural devastation, provides a rusty container to be filled by the cinematic exploits of John Shaft, Priest, Goldy, Foxy Brown, or Cleo-patra Jones. Furthermore, they reveal prevailing spatial and racial tensions between ghetto-dwelling blacks and urban whites, who are also frequently Italian and invariably associated with organized-crime syndicates in one form or another. Whites are cast as the inferior other in the majority of black action films of the period and are frequently represented as sexual fodder for the lusty appetites of the black male "superspades," as inept buffoons, or as icons of evil, each of which makes them suitable targets of the justifiable violence and brutality of the black protagonists.

Despite their popularity and profitable returns, both blaxploitation films and the proliferation of black filmmaking were relatively short lived. As Ed Guerrero (1993) has indicated, the blaxploitation era was in decline by 1974, and Hollywood studios, realizing that black audiences constituted a sizable market, attempted to reach white and black audiences simultaneously through films with greater crossover appeal. He explains that the strategy was largely successful, owing to the emphasis in the mid-1970s on white-black buddy films and on "one black comic 'superstar,' Richard Pryor, as even the featured black actors of the boom years found themselves in bit parts and increasingly shuttled into oblivion by the film industry" (110). Pryor's rise was also crucial in establishing a Hollywood precedence that allowed his successor, Eddie Murphy, as well as the female comedian Whoopi Goldberg to rise through the ranks in the 1980s and become the next generation's comedic black film superstars.

As I have explained, with the rise of hip-hop culture, the discursive dominance of "the ghetto" has been challenged and transformed. The range of spatial images and terms through which it has traditionally been defined has been superseded by the alternate youth discourse of the 'hood. In contrast to earlier cinematic representations of the ghetto, the 'hood is a more compressed construct, more tightly bounded and closely demarcated as a place. It emerges in the late 1980s as a spatial effect of the increasingly common social patterns of localization and particularity, which contrast with concurrent trends toward globalization and transnationalism (Robins 1991; Gupta and Ferguson 1992). This suggests that the 'hood is an expression of social scale situated along a spectrum of relationships spanning the local, regional, and global. Scale is thus a representational determinant in the visual and narrative portrayal of the 'hood.

Hip-Hop Cinema: The First Wave

With its strong visual appeal and pronounced physical expressiveness, hip-hop was well suited to the full-length cinematic productions that it spawned. Charlie Ahearn's *Wild Style* (1982) was a low-budget independent production that drew on experiences culled from New York hip-hop enthusiasts. It featured graffiti artists, rappers, and breakers from throughout the city with strong ties to the local scene. One of the enduring influences of the film is its fidelity to the geographic sites and scenarios from which hip-hop emerged, with the Bronx remaining the spatial focal point throughout the film. Not quite a documentary, *Wild Style*'s lasting reputation for authenticity is also based in the inclusion of key personalities who claimed the Bronx and uptown boroughs as their own. This includes the renowned graffiti artist Lee Quinones; hip-hop's early ambassador to the downtown art scene, Fab Five Freddy; and the MCs Cold Crush Brothers, Grandmaster Caz, Double Trouble, and DJ Grandmaster Flash. Although novelty films such as *Breakin', Breakin' 2: Electric Boogaloo, Rappin',* and *Break Dance* soon followed, often faring marginally well with teen audiences, they traced narrow spatial arcs through the urban environment and did not succeed in capturing much of the lived experience of hip-hop. They were by all accounts minor films, less directly related to hip-hop than to the cinematic genre that includes *Fame* (1980), *Flashdance* (1983), *Footloose* (1984), and *Dirty Dancing* (1987). After this quick flurry of formulaic releases, the early 1980s style of hip-hop-themed films faded away. In retrospect, these films are often regarded as relatively overt attempts at industry appropriation of hip-hop's cultural forms, though they did manage to disseminate surface images of the growing movement more widely into the social mainstream. Released in the same period, *Beat Street* (1984, directed by Stan Lathan) was not necessarily greeted within hip-hop circles as a more authentic representation of the culture, but the musical involvement of the producer Arthur Baker lent a degree of credibility to the project, which featured contributions by Grandmaster Melle Mel and the Furious Five, Afrika Bambaataa with Soul Sonic Force and Shango, and the System. Still, despite a formidable musical pedigree, it was not *Beat Street* that heralded the future importance of hip-hop sound tracks, but *Breakin',* the sound track of which entered the *Billboard* Top Ten LP chart on July 14, 1984, and remained there, alongside the *Footloose* sound track, for three weeks.

Krush Groove, released in 1985 by Warner Brothers and directed by Michael Schultz, displayed a more conscious attempt to reflect the hip-hop culture by employing actual rappers (the Fat Boys, Run-D.M.C., and LL Cool J) and featuring inside perspectives on their lives and struggles to rise in the music industry. *Krush Groove* also represents an interesting attempt to develop marketing synergy: the film's release coincided with a major concert at Madison Square Garden that was also telecast in the domestic market through pay-per-view. The 1988 release of the neoblaxploitation film *Tougher than Leather* (directed by Rick Rubin), produced by Def Jam's CEO, Russell Simmons, and starring Run-D.M.C. as young urban avengers, was aesthetically and thematically inconsistent with the earlier hip-hop films, since it shifted toward an emergent harder-edged image. Critical praise for the film was in short supply, and it was publicly regarded by many, including the *Billboard* journalist Nelson George and the filmmaker

Spike Lee, who both publicly dismissed it, as final proof that Run-D.M.C. was no longer part of rap's avant-garde. Run-D.M.C.'s two-year contract dispute with Profile Records, which had kept them out of the studio in the interim, clearly had taken its toll, and although their LP *Tougher than Leather* (1988, Profile) sold platinum, it failed to revive critical interest or mobilize new audience support for the group. The major site of innovation in hip-hop's visual representation was proving to be the rap video sector as budding young directors, among them Albert and Allen Hughes and F. Gary Gray, honed their skills on small budget projects of three or four minutes' duration.

At around the same time, the Dennis Hopper film *Colors* (1988) proved to be a much more influential vehicle for the hip-hop culture in commercial terms, exposing young audiences across the nation to a selective and sensational cinematic representation of Los Angeles's gang culture. Whereas *Tougher than Leather* looked like a B-movie update of the black gangster film of the early 1970s, *Colors* was touted as a realistic portrayal of the deadly conditions that pitted black and Latino youth gangs against police and against each other in South Central Los Angeles. The implicitly racist and paternalistic assumptions that informed the script were not easy to ignore, yet, for all of its shortcomings, the film seemed to offer insights into the southern California gang problem and the deadly consequences of turf warfare. The images managed to both revile and glorify California teen gang life, leading the rapper DJ Quik to later criticize the film's role in popularizing and facilitating the spread of Crip and Blood organizations throughout the midwestern United States on the track "Jus Lyke Compton." Outbreaks of violence—not all of it gang related—seemed to validate the film's message that the police were fighting a losing battle against young black and Latino outlaws who outnumbered and outgunned them.

Ultimately, it was the *Colors* sound track on the Warner Brothers label that brought the film its most pronounced connection to hip-hop. Featuring tracks by Eric B and Rakim, Big Daddy Kane, Salt 'n' Pepa, MC Shan, and especially Ice-T, the sound track album became an instant classic in the genre. Ice-T's title track was the vehicle that catapulted him into rap's front lines and helped to forge his gangster persona. Ice-T later emerged as an accomplished actor; while his first major cinematic role was in the 1991 *New Jack City* (directed by Mario van Peebles), he had also appeared in a minor cameo role, typecast as a rapper, in the 1984 film *Breakin'*. *Colors* was perhaps most important for its dual role in exposing a gangsta rap aesthetic within an accompanying representational array of West Coast gangster images, even though Ice-T's contribution to the album was the only track that remotely conformed to the gangsta rap style. *Colors* emerged just as rap was itself undergoing substantial thematic and aesthetic transitions, and it can be argued that the film was a catalytic force in the film industry, paving the way for a deluge of gangster-oriented films set in the 'hood and characterized by their rap and hip-hop sound tracks.

New Jack City capitalized on the success of *Colors* by casting Ice-T in a supporting role as a vengeful, street-smart cop, consequently reinforcing the strong links between hip-hop and new black cinema. Van Peebles could also lay claim to an earlier connection to hip-hop: he had been cast in a lead role as a break-dancer and street hood in the 1985 Joel Silberg film *Rappin'*. With major studio distribution from Warner Brothers, *New Jack City* was aggressively marketed to an urban demographic and attracted the attention of youth who, already cognizant of hip-hop's potential, were willing to spend their money on cultural forms that coincided with their hip-hop sensibilities. The sound track, featuring a clever blend of R & B and hip-hop tracks by artists such as Color Me Badd, Guy (featuring Teddy Riley), and Keith Sweat as well as another powerful performance by Ice-T in "New Jack Hustler," reaffirmed the strong commercial potential of marketing gangster movies with a 'hood orientation and hip-hop-inflected sound tracks to eager audiences. It is fitting that the son of Melvin van Peebles, whose 1971 film *Sweet Sweetback's Baadasssss Song* instigated the blaxploitation trend of the early 1970s, should have been influential in the later 'hood film genre that the industry touted in the early 1990s. As S. Craig Watkins explains, the film industry's response to new economic opportunities and shifting audience tastes and cultural sensibilities led to a new exploitative trend, one that "fueled an imitative cycle that eventually produced over twenty similarly packaged feature-length films between 1991 and 1995" (1998, 172).

Establishing Spatial Conventions: Do the Right Thing

Referring to the confluence of representational images that cohere in "black male ghetto films" and rap videos, Tricia Rose (1994a) points to the pronounced presence of the contemporary urban terrain. She explains that in rap and much of the hip-hop culture, place-based identity and location are important core themes. Crucially, the 'hood is visually coded and communicated in black cinema of the early 1990s as a zone of chronic danger and risk, a spatialized social landscape defining the practices that occur within the zone's representational domain. It is the primacy of this spatial logic, locating black urban youth experience within an environment of continual proximate danger, that largely defines the 'hood film.

While not ostensibly a 'hood film—that is, a film that is primarily structured upon a visual and narrative spatial discourse of the 'hood—Spike Lee's *Do the Right Thing* (1989) establishes a number of industry standards and cinematic conventions that warrant its examination as a precursor to the 'hood genre. Lee, a skilled cinematic auteur, was a central figure in the resurgence of black filmmaking in the early 1990s and led the way for numerous black directors to enter the industry's mainstream. He encountered industry resistance to his scripts, which were about cultural themes focused on contemporary black social existence, and he struggled against restrictive production and distribution budgets that constrained his films' revenue potentials in the wider mainstream market (Watkins 1998). Although he had moderate popular success (but showed impressive profit margins) with his earlier films, *She's Gotta Have It* (1986) and *School Daze* (1988); had directed music videos for artists including Grandmaster Flash and the Furious Five, Miles Davis, Anita Baker, and Branford Marsalis; and had produced the impressive Nike Air Jordan television commercial casting himself alongside "his airness" Jordan in the role of Mars Blackmon, his character from *She's Gotta Have It,* it was *Do the Right Thing (DTRT)* that confirmed his status and reputation among critics and audiences.

Lee's age and his thematic concerns also situate him in an important position as a link between young members of the hip-hop culture and an older generation of cultural workers and artists that preceded him, each of whom inflected and influenced his work in noticeable ways. His contract work for Sugar Hill records on the Grandmaster Flash and the Furious Five video "White Lines" and the Nike Air Jordan commercial spot, as prominent examples, link him directly to two powerful icons among youths of the hip-hop generation. Similarly, the diversity of musical forms that are sewn into his sound tracks illustrates an expansive comprehension of black expressive idioms, encompassing classic and contemporary jazz (Branford Marsalis and Terrence Blanchard in particular), the feel-good soul of the 1960s and 1970s, and the go-go, reggae, and hip-hop of the 1980s and 1990s. The repetition of Public Enemy's "Fight the Power" (1989, Def Jam) throughout *Do the Right Thing,* for example, was an important directorial decision that acknowledged and appealed to the young hip-hop crowd. The song ultimately went on to have considerable success and influence as a benchmark in rap music and became Public Enemy's most widely recognized release.

Set in one city block of New York's Bedford-Stuyvesant district, *Do the Right Thing* portrays the interactions of the local community on the hottest day of the year. The heat is clearly a factor in terms of the scripted violence that ensues, yet the site of a community locked in place also suggests a cauldron that continually threatens to boil over in the midst of heated social conflicts. The space of the neighborhood becomes much more prominent in terms of the story line itself: Lee's production journal (which was published following the film's release) opens with an architect's rendition of the neighborhood street plan spanning the block of Stuyvesant Avenue between Lexington and Quincy Avenues. According to the line producer John Kilik, the financing studio, Universal Pictures, had suggested that the film be shot in California at its studio facility to reduce production costs and permit more proximate studio control over the project, an idea that Lee adamantly rejected. Lee notes that as he prepared the script and considered the location, he simply rode his bicycle throughout Brooklyn and Bed-Stuy, scouting possible shooting sites. This informal approach not only adds a sense of familiarity and personal investment in Brooklyn but also remains consistent with Lee's well-documented commitment to the city borough he calls home.

As the production journal reveals, Lee's emphasis on location also takes into account interborough differences that basically segregate various ethnic and racial groups into separate regions of the city. The neighborhood portrayed in *DTRT* is not one of easy harmony; rather, it is a community in tension, informed not by a gentle tolerance but by intergenerational dissonance and a simmering racism that produces dislike and mistrust among its various inhabitants. His production notes convey the complexities of representing racial identification with localized places (such as Bed-Stuy or Bensonhurst) as he develops the central theme of displacement and conjunction among numerous groups within one block.

Lee's Bed-Stuy is in many ways representative of most major American cities populated by a diversity of cultures, and he remakes this block into a community through the spatial organization of individuals within the geography of the neighborhood. On one corner is the Italian-owned pizzeria; facing it is the Korean-owned market. Roughly next to the pizzeria is the local low-watt community radio station, WE LOVE, and the block is anchored at the far end by the apartment of the central character, Mookie (played by Lee himself). Between these poles are the buildings and front stoops where the other characters, both young and old, live and congregate. Mookie, a pizza deliveryman, constitutes the meandering thread connecting the characters and their domiciles, meeting the neighbors on the block as he makes his rounds.

The element of community is also constructed from within a real, existing community that lives on this block of Stuyvesant Avenue and gives the space a sense of vitality that precedes the film's production. Referring to the intrusive presence of the film production crew and actors, the location manager, Brent Owens, describes the preproduction meetings with the local homeowners, noting that the closing of a neighborhood crack house was a galvanizing moment for the crew and the community:

> One crack house, which was on Lexington Street, was notorious. The place was foul: crack vials, dead animals, used condoms, and feces everywhere. The straw that broke the camel's back was seeing a woman with two children no older than three, and an infant in a carriage, go into the crack house and stay for twenty minutes or so. We sealed the place up the next day. (Lee and Jones 1989, n.p.)

Notwithstanding this particular episode, however, drugs and issues of ghetto poverty on a major scale are absent from the script of *DTRT,* as they fall outside the terrain of racial tension and violence on which Lee is more narrowly focused. Critics argued that Lee had deliberately and perhaps irresponsibly excised the image of a crack-riddled community; he responded by addressing the theme of the community drug scourge and crack addiction in his 1991 release *Jungle Fever.*

Although the block portrayed in *DTRT* is not what might be described as "deep ghetto," where the damage of economic decay is often visible in the building structures themselves, neither is it a neighborhood of evident prosperity. It is a depressed neighborhood where the community members strive to maintain their dwellings, in the process exhibiting an alternating tension between stress or anxiety and humble dignity, the latter being most evident in the characters of the community elders, Da Mayor (Ossie Davis) and Mother Sister (Ruby Dee). The real danger of the neighborhood —economic oppression and resentment of entrepreneurial intruders of other ethnicities—is complex and difficult to convey cinematically. Yet Lee's script and Ernest Dickerson's careful cinematography construct the film's tensions, which are narratively informed by spatial relations. Danger is introduced as a manifest element in the images of plain, unadorned brownstone row houses and through the portrayal of listless and mainly idle youths; tension and the potential for danger might consequently be inferred without explicit definition, although the sense of danger will be interpreted differently by those who see the environment portrayed as a home place (the 'hood as a site of security, inviting topophilia) or as a space of otherness (evoking a sense of unease or topophobia).

Giancarlo Esposito (who plays the role of Buggin' Out) remarks on another aspect of the crew's involvement with the existing community:

> Most Hollywood films, even in independent films, don't give a goddamn about the neighborhoods they film in. . . . I know for sure that the crew and cast of *Do the Right Thing,* from the craft service people on up, cared about the people on Stuyvesant street. We organized a clothing drive, we gave away food, we hired people from the neighborhood. In a very concrete way, we did what we could.
> (Lee and Jones 1989, n.p.)

The combined and overlapping realities of need, want, and danger are articulated in a manner that implies a community in distress. This corresponds with John Adams's assertion that "a setting becomes a symbol of its function —an index of the kinds of narrative event which habitually (and literally) 'take place' there." Adams goes on to describe the ways in which "territorial oppositions are established through the mise en scene, where the deployment of actors within the space create specific spatial metaphors for attitudes and relationships" (1994, 183). Lee's direction carefully nurtures the portrayal of a placed or sited community, establishing characters such as Da Mayor and Mother Sister, who portray the patriarchal and matriarchal cornerstones of the neighborhood and who, with other common "types," perform the daily task of place making within the community. By slowly constructing the image of community as a situated social achievement with an evolved local history, Lee illustrates the problematic issues that can ensue when individuals with neither awareness of, interest in, nor concern for those histories buy their way into them.

Sal's pizzeria is portrayed as an anomalous fortress in the middle of hostile territory. This juxtaposition, which locates Italian entrepreneurs in a predominantly black neighborhood, also places the characters Sal (Danny Aiello) and his sons Vito (Richard Edson) and Pino (John Turturro) in the path of a quickly swelling danger. They are outsiders or aliens not just in the strictly spatial sense; they are also outside of the established rhythms and flows of the community itself, unfamiliar with the codes and rankings of status and identity that are so important to the locals with whom they interact through their business. The inner-outer spatial dynamic of threat and danger is extended by the roaming presence of the white police officers, who throughout the film display undisguised grimaces of distrust and dislike for the youths who live on the block. When tensions break the surface and Sal erupts by smashing Radio Raheem's (Bill Nunn) powerful portable stereo—which at the time is aptly playing "Fight the Power"—the police arrive like latter-day cavalry troops. As they attempt to neutralize the situation, they inadvertently kill Radio Raheem, setting off much greater violence in the form of a riot that destroys the pizzeria and shatters relationships between the different ethnic groups of the community.

Lee's script notes stress his desire to capture this fluctuating element of risk, threat, and danger and his attempt to render cinematically an image of the blurred boundaries between victim and aggressor and between subordinate and dominating social forces. Stephen Haymes describes these relations in terms of hegemonic authority:

The social geography of urban space is characterized by public spaces in the city that are positioned unequally in relation to one another with respect to power. The concept of power is key to interpreting this positionality, to understanding how public spaces relate to one another in the context of the urban.   (1995, 113)

Resentments felt by the black characters of the film are directed toward the apparent prosperity of racial others who also, centrally, come from other places, whether they be boroughs or neighborhoods in the city or other cultural locales: the Italian pizzeria owners, the Korean market owners, and a Waspish yuppie homeowner whose cultural allegiances are signified by a Boston Celtics basketball jersey prominently bearing the number of the white basketball star Larry Bird. Yet the very prosperity and success of these others and outsiders place them in the path of potential danger as neighborhood resentments rise, especially among the disenfranchised black youth whose own restricted social prosperity anchors them in the block with few apparent options for advancement or mobility.

When the prevailing community agreement collapses and the tenuous balance among the diverse groups is transgressed, the police respond. The danger threatening Sal and his sons is suddenly reversed, turned toward the neighborhood's black youths, who are muscled to the ground by the burly officers as they reassert authority and effectively return the power to the hands of outsiders. This set of images, which includes the arrival of a small army of riot police, corresponds with Michael Keith and Steve Pile's comment that "for those who have no place that can be safely called home, there must be a struggle for a place to be" (1994, 5). Here the discursive priorities of Public Enemy's "Fight the Power" are fully realized, for in the struggle to assert one's place against the force of the city's structured institutional authority, race and place are inherently summoned together. *Do the Right Thing* reinforces the notion that, community histories notwithstanding, many urban blacks live in bounded neighborhoods that are spatially maintained through policing and the frequently coercive expression of law and order. Place is consequently a primary site of struggle.

The Spatial Authority of the 'Hood in Cinema

Paula Massood asserts that it was the director John Singleton who, with his 1991 film *Boyz N the Hood,* "first mapped the 'hood onto the terrain and into the vocabulary of the popular imagination" (1996, 90). In fact, it was the release of the recording "Boyz-N-the-Hood" in 1986 by Eazy-E and the core members of what eventually became N.W.A. that established "the 'hood" as an emergent term in the spatial discourse of young urban blacks and Latinos—and eventually other youth as well—across North America. The track vividly portrays the 'hood as a space of violence and confrontation, a zone of indiscriminate aggression where threat and danger are commonplace, even banal. N.W.A.'s pioneering album *Straight Outta Compton,* as well as early recordings by Ice-T, introduced a situated "place-image" (Shields 1991) of danger that characterizes the subgenre of West Coast gangsta rap and is a literal presence in 1990s 'hood films such as *Boyz N the Hood* and *Menace II Society* (1993, directed by Allen and Albert Hughes).

With the coemergence of gangsta rap and 'hood films, previously marginal urban geographies were repositioned at the center of civic attention and public debate. N.W.A.'s *Straight Outta Compton* and the scenarios describing ostensibly natural and everyday occurrences of violence and mayhem were, for many listeners across the country, their first real exposure to the city of Compton. Just as rap tracks about Compton present the city as a bounded civic space, the representation of localized cultural geographies —the 'hood as a lived environment—in Singleton's *Boyz N the Hood* portrays these spatial zones as an array of fragmented areas, with each 'hood existing in isolation from the others. As Watkins (1998) observes, this produces a symbolic image of entrapment, although he is careful to point out that the experience of entrapment is not felt or expressed homogeneously throughout the 'hood, since individuals develop their own sense of space and the threat or opportunity that it might promise. In *Boyz,* Compton's dangerous reputation, promulgated in Los Angeles gangsta rap, is reinforced in the scene where Furious Styles (Lawrence Fishburne) takes his teenage son Tre (Cuba Gooding, Jr.) and his friend Ricky (Morris Chestnut) into the depths of the Compton 'hood. The boys' discomfort is evident as they look over their shoulders at the intimidating teens standing on the corner drinking beer from forty-ounce bottles, and their nervousness reflects the notion that they are in foreign territory, out of their element and off their own turf: they are in Compton. Later, when Tre and Ricky encounter Ricky's brother Doughboy (Ice Cube), he asks them, "Y'all come from Compton? I thought you was scared of Compton?" to which Ricky responds in the affirmative. Rather than challenging the prevailing symbolic representations of Compton as a highly threatening urban enclave, Singleton reinforces them through a "spatial labeling" (Shields 1991, 47) that conforms to the stereotypical images and hegemonic discourses of West Coast gangsta rap. The connections are drawn more tightly together with the casting of Ice Cube in his first major film role and a sound track (1991, Sony Music) that features, in addition to several R & B cuts, hardcore contributions by Ice Cube, Yo Yo, Compton's Most Wanted, Kam, 2 Live Crew, and Too Short.

The general conjunction between rap and the new black cinema of the early 1990s can also be seen in *Menace II Society,* in which the rap artist MC Eiht is cast as A-Wax, a street hustler and O.G. (original gangsta) in his early twenties who is described as being slightly older and more battle worn than the teenage members of his crew. The character is "down for the 'hood," a tested street soldier who scrapes by with his wits and a gun, selling crack to hapless "cluckheads" and doling out retribution to adversaries who cross him and his posse—a role not at all unlike that MC Eiht himself adopted at the age of thirteen ("Reality Check" 1994, 67). Adding his rap skills to the sound track with the song "Streiht up Menace," Eiht recounts and elaborates on scenes from the film, emphasizing the progression of threat, violence, and danger that form the basis of what many rappers refer to unproblematically as the "reality" of "growing up in the 'hood"—which is also the title of the contribution to the *Boyz N the Hood* sound track by MC Eiht's group, Compton's Most Wanted.

It is productive—even necessary—to maintain a sense of this reciprocal influence between rap and the 'hood film, for the two media maintain a relationship of cross-pollination and mutual invigoration that extends beyond the range of narrative and visual imagery. It includes the enhanced public exposure of rap artists on the movie screen (most notably the West Coast artists Ice-T, Ice Cube, and the late Tupac Shakur through the early 1990s, the New Yorkers Queen Latifah and LL Cool J in the late 1990s, and Philadelphia native Will Smith before them all) and the importance of commercially successful sound track recordings to the careers of rap artists as well as to the films' overall earning power. Through the 1990s film directors demonstrated a proclivity toward casting rap artists in either cameo or secondary roles: EPMD appeared briefly in Ernest Dickerson's *Juice,* Too Short in *Menace II Society,* members of Onyx in *Clockers,* and Yo Yo, briefly, in *Boyz N the Hood* and *Menace II Society.* This artist participation suggests an overlapping circuit of activity between young cultural workers in the film and music sectors and strengthens the bonds between rap music and the 'hood film, creating a symbiotic relationship that comprises both a new cultural site for the expression of and engagement with hip-hop images and discourses and a cultural commodity for sale in the popular-entertainment market.

Gangsta rap's graphic description of space, place, and danger has its correlative in contemporary 'hood films, as is evident in *Menace II Society*'s opening narration by the protagonist, Caine (Tyrin Turner):

Went into the store just to get a beer. Came out an accessory to murder and armed robbery. It was funny like that in the 'hood sometimes. You never knew what was gonna happen or when. After that, I knew it was gonna be a long summer.

The 'hood is the informing space in which the narrative action is framed; the film's timeline follows the evolution of that "long summer," beginning with Caine's high school graduation and ending with his violent death in a drive-by shooting as he, his girlfriend, and her young son prepare to leave South Central Los Angeles's mean streets. His trajectory throughout the film is not linear, however: he swerves between the roles of victim and victimizer, in one instance getting carjacked and shot in the shoulder, in another pointing a gun at the head of an unfortunate teenager whose gold wheel rims he covets. In the end, his summer sun is blotted out in a final act of payback and one-upmanship when he is shot dead in response to his vicious beating of a teen from another 'hood who has encroached on his home environment. The element of risk and surprise are fused in his statement that "you never knew what was gonna happen or when," and the narrative reinforces a sense of the 'hood's capacity for imminent danger through random incidents of gradually escalating violence that also emphasize the centrality of turf and bordered enclaves within the social systems of the 'hood in urban southern California.

A core element of both rap lyrics and contemporary black cinematic narratives is the conflation of youth and danger with life in the 'hood. Manthia Diawara explains that this often follows a geosocially specific coming-of-age theme:

> Just as in real life the youth are pulled between hip hop life style, gang life, and education, we see in the films neighborhoods that are pulled between gang members, rappers, and education-prone kids. For the black youth, the passage into manhood is also a dangerous enterprise which leads to death both in reality and in film.
> (Diawara 1993, 25)

Youth—or, more precisely, male youth, as the majority of 'hood films focus on the rites of passage of young black men—is represented as a heterogeneous formation, and its highly stratified composition is emphasized, with the distinctions between juvenile and twenty-something status playing a decisive role in character construction and plot. Films such as *Menace II Society, Boyz N the Hood,* and, somewhat later, *Fresh* (1994, directed by Boaz Yakin) and *Clockers* (1995, directed by Spike Lee) effectively portray the often subtle differences that separate and complicate the lives of youths in the thirteen-to-twenty-four-year-old demographic at the same time as they portray a range of reactions and responses to the dangers that young black men (and, to a different and lesser degree, women) routinely confront. This contrasts sharply with the age coordinates of the male and female heroes of the earlier ghettocentric blaxploitation films, who were generally much older and were accordingly more empowered in their roles as urban action characters.

In *Boyz N the Hood,* for example, when the preadolescent Tre, Dough-boy, and Ricky wander the periphery of their 'hood and encounter a gang of older teenage thugs, they cross the railroad tracks into a relatively hostile danger zone. There they dispassionately stare at a decomposing human corpse; then, moments later, when the teenagers steal their football, Dough-boy is beaten for trying to retrieve it. Spatial constructions of danger in the scene are consequently organized within accompanying boundaries of age, which indicate a pattern of interlocking constraints that define the 'hood for children. The processes by which youth negotiated localized neighbor-hood space and its associated dangers at different stages of their develop-ment and growth to which Diawara alludes are vital for an understanding of the narrative core of the 'hood film.

The spatial logic informing representations of the 'hood also intervenes in the process of identity formation inherent in the nexus of youth and race and present as an underlying current in Spike Lee's *Clockers*. Within a system of place-based values, the 'hood is fetishized as the unqualified site of what R. A. T. Judy (1994) refers to as "nigga authenticity," which, as she explains, is an existential and ontological conundrum confronting black youth today. The "real nigga" of the 1990s is, in the perception of many black teens as well as mainstream Americans (i.e., older, middle and upper class), young and "deadly dangerous."[1] For example, in the opening se-quence Strike and his drug-slinging cohort debate the danger quotient of various rap artists, discussing their "hardness" in terms of whether or not they have ever killed anyone. As this scene suggests, the rise of a discourse locating the danger-ridden 'hood as a realm of authentic black identity and experience also invalidates a substantial segment of black culture and black experience that exists in other locales and cultural milieux, including rural and suburban environments. Suburban and middle-class black constituen-cies are frequently reviled or dismissed within a discourse of the 'hood on the basis of their fundamental disconnectedness from the 'hood itself as the privileged space of authentic blackness. Whereas John Jeffries (1992) asserts that black popular culture and images of urban "cool" are crucially intertwined, it is more precisely the extreme inner city, or the 'hood, that is the primary locale of cool for contemporary teenagers.

This can also be seen in the television program *The Fresh Prince of Bel Air*, starring the rapper-*cum*-actor Will Smith (a.k.a. the Fresh Prince) and pro-duced by Benny Medina under the imprimatur of Quincy Jones's enter-tainment corporation, Quest. The sitcom's rap theme song, by the Fresh Prince, which sustains the vocal flow and content of Smith's early hits such as "Parents Just Don't Understand," establishes the scenario: As a basketball-playing teen in a West Philadelphia 'hood, Will (Smith's homeboy charac-ter) is bullied by a gang of local thugs. His mother, sensing the danger to her son, sends him to live with wealthy relatives in the posh community of Bel Air, California. Danger is thus the underlying motivation upon which the program's entire context is predicated, a factor that is rarely raised once the final strains of the theme song have ended but that cannot be ignored. Uprooted from his place of origin, Will remains an icon (albeit somewhat lightweight) of authentic ghetto cool, a fly brother for whom the 'hood will always be home.

The program's humor lies largely in the conflict of youth, race, and class, portrayed as a series of disjunctures. Carlton (Alfonso Ribeiro), Will's ultra-preppy cousin, constitutes the ironic foil to Smith's character.[2] Carlton is the image of what black youth is supposed to be, cast in negative relief: He has no street smarts, no sense of street style, and, importantly, despite being articulate he demonstrates no verbal dexterity. Carlton is the stereotypical "oreo"—black on the outside but white at the center. The scenario corresponds with Gilroy's earlier noted observation that "today we are told that the boys, and the girls, are from the 'hood—not from the race, and certainly not from the nation" (1992, 308), for if the 'hood, with its accompanying dangers, inscribes the contemporary black male as "real," then Carlton has no hope of ever being real, let alone black. Carlton's evolving buppie (black urban professional) character, like Will's homeboy, conforms to a relatively unambiguous identity position rooted in social space and place-based logics. Whereas Will's character bespeaks the inner city and, ostensibly, the 'hood, Carlton bespeaks some problematic netherland situated between cultures and poles of identification, producing a character that is hybrid in its construction and reflects a complex identity composite that is forged in what Homi Bhabha (1990) calls "the third space," which defies reductive essentialism. Bhabha's optimism for a progressive third space of cultural hybridity cannot be found in Carlton's character, however, since Carlton is scripted as the butt of the joke, the drifting social subject lost between his cultural blackness and the lure of a professionalized whiteness.

In *The Fresh Prince of Bel Air,* the 'hood is a structured absence, its effect and influence exerting themselves from the edges of the scripted narratives as an implicit danger lying in some distant beyond, outside the security that wealth can buy. In the rare instances where the 'hood explicitly resurfaces, it tends to be coded as a rupture along points in the script at which external danger breaks through the atmosphere of gentility pervading the Bel Air mansion where most of the action is set. The 'hood generally attains intensified access to the upper-class refuge of the mansion through the arrival and subsequent upheavals introduced by Will's longtime compadre from Philadelphia, Jazzy Jeff, as Jeff and Will revert to what is portrayed as a comparatively vulgar and unsophisticated set of identity positions: boys from the 'hood. In a way that reproduces social stereotypes and sustains the alienating images of black youth, danger or its primitive principles are carried on the backs of teenagers who depict the uncouth and undisciplined mannerisms of the 'hood, which, in the context of the sitcom, is intended to heighten the sociospatial distinctions between Carlton, Will, and the authentic zones of black experience that are commonly identified with the 'hood in hip-hop's cultural logic of representation.

Just as the demographic subset "youth" and the cultural designation "black" should not be conceived in singular terms, neither should the 'hood be approached as a homogeneous space or unified geocultural terrain. Paul Gilroy's (1992) critical interrogation suggests that while the discourse of the 'hood has emerged as the sociospatial dominant for North America's black teens, in its implied localism it problematizes the potential for expansive diasporic identification and collective political movement among black youth. His concern for and careful attention to the divisiveness of the 'hood discourse is, in fact, fixed on the dynamics between race, experiential space, and represented place that lie at the crux of identity and sense of self for a generation of young black men and women. Indeed, the distinctions between *this* 'hood and *that* 'hood, or, more precisely, between *our* 'hood and *their* 'hood, have crucial, often life-threatening implications for those who inhabit them and live in and by their territorial codes.

By extension, however, the cinematic representation of different 'hoods and of different modes of habitation also allows for an elaborated understanding of what the 'hood is in American society and how its social dimensions are constructed. According to Milbrey McLaughlin,

the experiences of youth growing up in one urban area can and do differ in many important ways from those youngsters growing up in another urban environment that may be only two blocks away. Most important in these differences are not the status and character of individual institutions but the collective determination of the environment in which local youth develop and mold a sense of identity.

(1993, 37)

The diversity of localized cultures, neighborhood patterns, and modes of existence does not necessarily negate the capacity for teenagers living within these distinct zones to communicate in meaningful and connective ways across their various differences. The strong tendency toward cultural dialogue, despite local or regional differences, establishes and maintains a sense of cultural commonality that is formed within the conjunction of race, class, and urbanicity. For example, while Massood's analysis examines the means through which contemporary black filmmakers "map the 'hood" as a previously concealed space on the American cityscape, her exclusive focus on films set in South Central Los Angeles does little to illuminate the manner in which the 'hood is represented in films set elsewhere. As a reminder of the implications involved, John Jeffries has noted:

In thinking about what the urban is, we have some preconceptions. . . . For those of us living on the East Coast, especially considering the way L.A., with its urban conflict and gangs, has been described to us in the newspapers, some of the images that were most shocking in *Boyz N the Hood* were the shots of low-density housing. Many of us in East Coast audiences either subconsciously or unconsciously asked, "Where's the city?"   (Jeffries 1992, 213)

Set in New York's high-rise housing projects and their adjoining neighborhoods, Matty Rich's *Straight Out of Brooklyn* (1991), with its title harking back to N.W.A.'s "Straight Outta Compton," Ernest Dickerson's *Juice* (1992), and Spike Lee's *Clockers* portray a different kind of 'hood that is constructed much more vertically than California's horizontal 'hood, with its wide boulevards, neat single-family homes, and low-rise public housing units.[3] In these films, the sense and image of danger are intensified by a pervasive spatial compression that fuels the stress and tension of the various characters. The twin elements of constraint and restricted mobility (to name two points that Massood foregrounds) are signified through a visual tightness that is only rarely alleviated, as in the scenes where geographic distance and cultural difference are communicated in *Straight Out of Brooklyn* through Dennis's (Lawrence Gilliard, Jr.) wistful gaze across the river toward the towers of Manhattan.

In *Juice,* the four protagonists—led by the late Tupac Shakur as the rapidly unraveling Bishop (whose name suggests a nod toward Ron O'Neal's character, Priest, in *Superfly*) and Omar Epps as the optimistic hip-hop DJ Q —are continually framed against buildings and brick exteriors. Theirs is a world of architectural height and institutional might that by contrast diminishes their own stature as black teenagers in the city. Throughout the film they are defensively positioned against the multifaceted dangers of the city: a rival gang, the school truancy cop, the police, and in the end, one another as Bishop's fear and paranoia turn to desperation and he hunts his friends down. Both before and after committing their murderous crime in what is supposed to be a straightforward robbery of the local Asian-owned corner store, they are shown scurrying through derelict buildings, alleys and back streets. Here, the narrow and constricting architectural contours of the city evoke danger lurking around the corner as *Juice* confronts the navigational dilemmas of avoiding violence and death in the 'hood. Unlike the 'hood films set in South Central Los Angeles, there are no broad spatial expanses depicted here, but rather a maze of connecting pathways. In the film's portrayal of urban density, knowledge and cartographic familiarity with the 'hood are conveyed as being informing facets of urban youth survival strategies.

Despite Spike Lee's denial that *Clockers* is a 'hood film, it fails to fully escape its allegiances to the genre, maintaining a tightly bounded spatial perimeter within which the central protagonist Strike (Mekhi Phifer) operates as a street-level drug dealer in the projects. According to Lee,

hood films are kind of over. This was one of the reasons I was hesitant about doing it. Audiences, black and white, are getting pretty fatigued of that genre. Rightly so, they want to see some different stories coming out of black culture besides a shoot-em-up hip-hop film. . . . I thought we could transcend the hood genre and make something greater.   (Wallace 1996, 12)

In *Clockers*, the 'hood is portrayed as a space of extreme limitations, constructed as a profile of density that is nonetheless replete with human intercourse thriving and faltering in intense proximity. Lee's construction of the 'hood fully acknowledges the magnification of danger under such tight conditions and the inherent threat engendered in the stratified arrangement of power, authority, and territorial contestation. Unlike most films in the 'hood genre, however, he leavens his assessment of the 'hood by encompassing positive, even liberating images of hope that also inflect the experience of urban existence. For example, Strike is portrayed not as a menacing gangster figure but as a teenager who, by virtue of his social positioning, is subjected to the magnetic pull of "the street." His hustler image is diluted by a closeted fascination with trains, which, as Richard Price observes, are "a symbol of mobility and the desire to break out" (Quart and Auster 1996, 17).

Lee's New York setting constructs Strike's zone of operation meiotically: his landscape is cramped and circumscribed in ways that correspondingly amplify the dangers that inform his actions and options. Strike is constantly under surveillance, watched by competing forces (the police and his criminal mentor), effectively frozen in place on the bench at the center of the low-rent housing complex where he lives with his mother. Yet spatial compression increases the intensity of relations among the primary characters, particularly Strike and the various males (a local drug entrepreneur, a police detective, a beat cop, and an elder brother) who inflect his sense of self and identity; whose push and pull combine to produce a hybrid composite replacing an absent father figure. The transcendent element Lee refers to may inhere in the unique means through which danger is narratively structured, for it is not solely the danger of inner-city violence that Strike must overcome but also the danger of failure in the eyes of those whose respect he most desires. Complexities of identity and respect function as crucial codes of the street. They must be renegotiated through ceaseless attention to profile, status and reputation.

With *Dead Presidents* (1995), Albert and Allen Hughes more successfully circumvent many of the common traits—and clichés—of 'hood cinema alluded to by Lee while maintaining the fundamental spatial sensibility characteristic of the genre. Set in the late 1960s and early 1970s, *Dead Presidents* returns to the Vietnam era and the general period from which blaxploitation films first emerged. *Dead Presidents* is an example of strategic genre blending, merging elements of various generic forms and conventions in a manner that produces a new, hybrid composite that can neither be reduced to nor equated with any single genre to which it may refer. Its themes suggest a retro war film crossed with a conventional heist film, yet its narrative and visual construction also resonate with contemporary 'hood films in ways that indicate an attempt to reach across the intervening years and to establish a dialogue with earlier black cultural cinematic forms.

The locality within which the central figure, Anthony (Larenz Tate), and his two "homeboys," Skippy (Chris Tucker) and Jose (Freddy Rodriguez), circulate is established with subtitles identifying the area as the "North East Bronx," an urban locale consisting of tightly packed single-family domiciles that challenges the dominant contemporary place-images of the South Bronx, with its high-rise or dilapidated low-income city housing. The trio is introduced working as milk delivery boys who, on the cusp of their high school graduation, can envision only two options: staying in the neighborhood and hustling for a living (Skippy is adamant in his desire to fill the role of neighborhood pimp), or going to Vietnam. In this regard, *Dead Presidents* shows common traits with the Hughes brothers' earlier feature film, *Menace II Society,* while also maintaining the male coming-of-age theme that is conventional within the 'hood genre. Upon graduation, Anthony shows his ghetto survival skills as a low-stakes pool shark and numbers runner in a small-scale racket operated out of the back of the neighborhood pool hall.

The sense of the 'hood is conveyed most forcefully in this segment as Anthony scrapes a living out of the local area, greeting men and women casually as he strolls through his home environment, where he is known well and appears entirely comfortable in his local identity. He is initially portrayed as being marginally connected to criminal activity, and the dangers he confronts are correspondingly minimal. The escalation of his criminal involvement is depicted in his ascension to the rank of getaway driver for his loan-shark boss, reflecting the 'hood's negative authority over many young black men. Skippy and Jose are drafted into the military soon after their graduation, an indication of the relative powerlessness of many young minority males to chart their own destinies or to map their own geographies. Anthony is different, portrayed as more focused and self-guided; he purposefully enlists in the military as a means of escaping the 'hood, of expanding his range of circulation and perspectives by following in his father's footsteps while capitalizing on the enhanced opportunities that military training and experience might offer.

In a clever and visually exciting segue, the Hughes brothers invoke the jungle analogy by conjoining the tough Bronx landscape and the Vietnam battlefield, with Anthony providing continuity through the scene. He is depicted leaping fences and sprinting through alleys as he escapes the wrath of his girlfriend's mother, shouting neighbors, and vicious attack dogs; then, through a seamless edit, he is running for cover in the middle of a tense, fast-paced firefight in Vietnam. Anthony is the connective figure forging the links between the spatial locations of his Bronx 'hood and the Southeast Asia war zone, and the narrative element of danger is simultaneously extended. He is positioned between two landscapes and two corresponding images of danger that demand similar survival strategies and similar options: fight or flee. Escaping these twinned threats, Anthony has little choice but to keep running, for, both symbolically and physically, stasis has grave and possibly deadly consequences.

As Anthony and Skippy relax in the American military compound in the aftermath of one battle sequence, Skippy says, "This ain't our war, man. Shit, our black asses should be back in the Bronx where we belong." The statement reveals the limits of his geocultural cartography as he maps himself permanently into the neighborhood he knows best, a neighborhood of predominantly black urban infrastructures. McLaughlin writes that "the city sets the broad context for youth. But within urban communities, neighborhoods are 'home' and are the most immediate and salient environments for young people" (1993, 44). From Vietnam, Skippy and Anthony refer to their corner of America as being "back in the world." The expression is intended as a comparative distinction between home and the hellish war zone, but it also attributes an enlarged or glorified sense of spatial importance to the constricted urban terrains of their neighborhood in the North East Bronx.

Skippy's statement also reveals his limited ability to process the complexities of an emergent black nationalism, hinted at in his reference to racial difference and the war effort. Excluding the dangerous terrains of the war theater, he has little experience of the world beyond the boundaries of his home environment, so his sense of black culture and a black cultural politics is framed almost exclusively within the images of home that he is most familiar with, affirming McLaughlin's further observation that "for inner-city youth, their neighborhood and the context it provides are all they know" (1993, 54). In fact, the black power movement of the period was in some ways mobilized through the meeting and interaction of young black soldiers who represented diverse regions and urban locales from across America but who, like Skippy, had had only limited exposure to other "worlds" of black (or white) experience. There is no narrative attempt to harness the political activism that defined a crucial facet of black life in the era; the directors do not expand on this aspect of the black G.I. experience except in an oblique reference to Viet Cong propaganda campaigns that attempted to appeal to black soldiers' own sense of their cultural and political struggle with America and to cleave a division between white and black troops.

Nor do the Hughes brothers capitalize on the narrative potentials of the black power movement as it constituted a connective force on the home front. Although historically the expansion of the Black Panther party across the United States, as well as that of other black social and political groups, provided a national network that linked communities and urban settings from coast to coast, in *Dead Presidents* this factor is neutralized, reduced to little more than a simple plot device. Delilah (N'Bushe Wright) is the revolutionary soul sister. She most clearly articulates the movement's political discourse but in the end is represented alternately as a sexy radical or as a female avenger stoked in black rage. She is subsequently killed in the midst of the poorly executed heist, and the notion of expansive American black power politics or the national uprising of ghetto blacks in the film's narrative dies with her. This is not to suggest a severe shortcoming of the film; rather, the directors' avoidance of these issues serves to deepen the localism and constraining limitations of a neighborhood perspective that, in the context of the narrative, blinds inhabitants of the 'hood to other, wider potentials that might align distinct urban geographies in a collective unity.

Compression and constraint finally undo the hopes and dreams of Anthony, Skippy, and Jose who, upon returning to "the world" from Vietnam, find that little has changed for them. Anthony is the figure of the emasculated male, unable to adequately support his girlfriend and their infant child. They end up living in a small apartment in a rundown housing tenement while he works at a menial job as a butcher, surrounded by lifeless flesh and blood. When he eventually loses this meager source of income, he is driven to design a plan for an armed truck robbery with his friends from the neighborhood. Danger and desperation are mingled as it becomes clear that escape from the constraints and dangers of the neighborhood require aggressive measures. Despite meticulous planning, however, the heist goes awry, and the deaths of several armed guards and a police officer lead to an intense search for Anthony and his crew throughout the neighborhood.

In the end, Jose, Skippy, and Anthony each fall victim to the effects of spatial compression. Jose's grisly demise is a clear metaphor for a loser's dead end when he is pulverized against a brick wall by a speeding police car in a chase down a closed alley. Skippy is discovered by police alone in his tiny, disheveled apartment, his dead eyes glazed into the cataracts of a heroin overdose, the needle still protruding from his arm. The profoundly melancholic moment is accentuated by his earlier optimistic references to home as "the world"; the police find him seated in front of a flickering television screen that features the bittersweet strains of the soul man Al Green performing "I'm So Tired of Being Alone" on *Soul Train*. Anthony's capture is filmed with a crane shot that foregrounds the sense of containment and enclosure; his arrest takes place in the narrow hallway of the pool room, where he is literally squeezed between two police phalanxes. The film ends with Anthony's courtroom appearance before a judge who sentences him to life in prison, finalizing the constriction and the danger that have framed Anthony's life throughout the film.

In *Dead Presidents* the geographic and architectural constraints are ultimately confirmed by the inability of the characters to think expansively and to project self-images that transcend the boundaries of their immediate social contexts within their 'hood. Their restricted imaginations (which, for all of its limitations, still displays a thin sheen of hope and optimism that something better exists just beyond their reach) further reduce their ability to "get over" by lifting themselves up and out of the localized geographies of danger that inscribe their daily existence.

If, as is often suggested, parody is the ultimate tribute, then *Fear of a Black Hat* (1993, directed by Rusty Cundieff), *CB4* (1993, directed by Tamra Davis), and *Friday* (1995, directed by F. Gary Gray) offer tributes to the images of gangsta rap and the 'hood film genre respectively. Both *Fear of a Black Hat* and *CB4* parody gangsta rap's stylistic and attitudinal excesses in the fashion of the parodic "rockumentary" *This Is Spinal Tap* (1984, directed by Rob Reiner) by framing them as a series of overwrought clichés that are widely recognizable as such within popular culture. Of the two films, *CB4*, a Universal Pictures release, reached the widest audience, although in many instances the creative insights and instincts of *Fear of a Black Hat* are superior. Each suffers, however, from a narrow topicality that isolates one temporal moment in hip-hop's evolution. Nelson George, *CB4*'s coproducer, describes the difficulties of working in the film genre:

Because film lacks the immediacy of music videos, any film on (hip hop and its effects) is, on some level, dated by the time of it release. Because hip hop moves so rapidly, any aspect of the culture—the clothes, the slang, the dances, the music— can make a film seem a bit behind the times.   (1998, 108)

By focusing on the gangsta rap genre as the films' comedic core, the parody really only makes sense in relation to this limited facet of the overall hip-hop scene. Referring explicitly to *CB4*, George laments that despite its virtues as comedy and the star's (Chris Rock) hilarious send-up of a diminutive rap poseur (almost certainly modeled on N.W.A.'s lead figure, Eazy-E), *CB4* emerged just as gangsta rap was in a transitional phase and the ascendancy of N.W.A., which was the obvious basis of the jest and had recently disbanded, was, in fact, over. With the release of Dr. Dre's title track to the Bill Duke film *Deep Cover* in 1992, West Coast rap and, in fact, the entire sonic character of hip-hop was instantly affected. Dre's title track introduced the world to Snoop Doggy Dogg, and the full-length release featured an impressive array of new talent, much of it signed to a then little known record label called Death Row. The *CB4* sound track (1992, MCA), however, showed greater depth and versatility than did the film, featuring three "parody" tracks based on samples (including N.W.A.'s "Straight Outta Compton") with humorous vocals (by Daddy-O of Stetsasonic, Hi-C, and Kool Moe Dee) and nonparody tracks by artists including Public Enemy, BDP, and MC Ren, as well as hip-hop and R & B tracks by Blackstreet and Tracie Spencer.

Friday exceeds the scope of *Fear of a Black Hat* and *CB4* by parodying localized patterns of everyday life and portraying the dangers of the 'hood in a humorous vein. Cowritten by Ice Cube and DJ Pooh, *Friday* affirms the bonds between 'hood and home environment in a display of exaggeration and camp excess. The spatial construct of the 'hood comprises the film's core, but the screenplay simultaneously sustains conventions of the 'hood film while exposing them to irreverent critique. Ice Cube plays Craig, a teenager facing a personal employment deficit, who with his blunted neighbor Smokey (Chris Tucker), spends the day sitting on the front porch of his family home. The compression and constraint common to the 'hood film are reduced to an absurd scale of minimal mobility; Craig and Smokey never wander more than one or two houses away from their roost. Yet their stasis resonates with elements of noncomedy films such as *Do the Right Thing, Menace II Society,* and especially *Boyz N the Hood,* with its porch posse scenes, in which Ice Cube also figures prominently. All of these films feature images of men of various ages sitting idly and bantering as they survey the 'hood around them.

The unmoving, localized site of action provides an amusing motivation for the film's narrative flow as various characters circulate through the 'hood, coming and going from the front porch where the young men sit. Their vantage offers them a window on their small world, yet for all its limitations, it is a rich and full world of drama and suspense. Danger is encountered in the menacing character of Deebo (Tiny "Zeus" Lister, Jr.), a slightly cross-eyed and slow-witted bully. Deebo's approach is announced by music similar to that which heralded the shark attacks in the movie *Jaws* (1975, directed by Steven Spielberg). Undercutting this intertextuality, however, is the accompanying sound of his squeaking bicycle, which neutralizes the threat he presents by infantilizing him. Where other 'hood films portray vicious carjackings, *Friday* portrays the neighborhood thug stealing a bike. In another scene depicting a drive-by shooting, the bravado and machismo that imbues the male characters in most 'hood films are parodied as Smokey quivers and cries in total fear. *Friday* consequently remains true to the conventions of the 'hood film by foregrounding the ever-present risk and dangers that arise for young blacks, but by inverting and exposing them to exaggeration and humorous critique it situates itself uniquely in relation to other 'hood films. In 1999 Ice Cube produced a sequel to *Friday,* titled *Next Friday,* which, despite withering critical reviews, debuted at number one on the box-office charts. In this latest contribution, Ice Cube shifts the setting from the 'hood to the suburbs, where the danger and stresses are improbably portrayed as being even more intense than those of his home turf. The conventions of the 'hood film have also been scathingly parodied in *Don't Be a Menace to South Central while Drinking Your Juice in the Hood* (1996, directed by Shawn and Marlon Wayans), which, with its exaggerations of 'hood film stereotypes, failed to fully capitalize on the 'hood film market. The film emerged after the genre had largely expired, but it still posted an impressive box office–to–budget ratio, making it one of the more profitable films of 1996.

This chapter began with a description of spatial segregation and of a pattern of exhibition of 'hood films that discriminates against young minority audiences. The incidents of real violence that did erupt at movie theaters screening youth-oriented films, including *New Jack City* and *Boyz N the Hood,* upon their initial release, however, make it difficult to ignore or dismiss the concerns of theater managers and the police. As a series of precedent-setting occurrences, this violence seems to validate the association of danger with 'hood films. In its variegated character as a discursive construct, a representational cinematic space, and an array of actually existing places, the 'hood is *constitutive of* a powerful image-idea of young urban black experience. At the same time, it is *constituted by* the multiple ways these images and experiences are merged and rearticulated daily within North America's urban geographies. Understood from this perspective, the portrayal of ubiquitous danger in the 'hood film also forces society to reconsider the means through which representation and reality often bleed together.

CHAPTER NINE

Industry, Nation, Globe
Hip-Hop toward 2000

❄

Globalization of our culture is our mission.
—Russell Simmons, *The Source*

Black music always used to go straight to the people. . . .
Big business speaks on that music now, before it gets to the people.
Start on the streets? Shit don't start on the streets,
it starts in the boardroom.
—Chuck D

With rap and hip-hop firmly established as artistic and cultural forces, the music, styles, and symbolic representation of hip-hop as a whole way of life were merged more consistently with prevailing practices of the culture industries, involving promotions, marketing, and distribution. The application of professional strategies that was evident by the early 1990s intensified throughout the decade, contributing to unprecedented sales and tremendous impact among youth cultures across ethnic and class spectra as well as, globally, across national and cultural boundaries. As the decade wound down and the hip-hop nation entered late adolescence, its citizens also encountered a period of extreme turbulence. This produced dramatic outcomes that reached deep into the social mainstream, spanning cultural and racial geographies. Foremost among the developments that amplified hip-hop's cultural influence were the reinforcement of hip-hop imagery and its stylistic character on a global scale through mass media diffusion; corporate label transitions and new accommodations for rap in the mainstream music industry; the rise and establishment of several crucial new independent record labels, especially in the southern United States; and the intensification of regional antagonisms, leading to a raging civil war across the hip-hop nation.

Throughout their short history, rap and hip-hop had been marginalized in the popular and mainstream media. Hip-hop's status and image as the industry underdog, the rebel sector, or even the exotic and dangerous other had been invoked by black music executives and artists as they sought a place in the larger commercial market. After more than a decade of underrepresentation, by the mid-1990s rap was making noticeable inroads on commercial radio, constituting a more consistent presence in the broadcast mediascape. In this period it was frequently "reality" rap and recordings by artists including Cypress Hill, Dr. Dre, Ice Cube, Onyx, or Snoop Doggy Dogg that were emerging on radio playlists in larger urban centers, with programming directors citing the need for their stations to both respond to the taste and consumer patterns of their teen listenerships and to compete with video stations such as The Box, where hardcore rap was a mainstay. Dr. Dre's *The Chronic* (1992, Death Row), and the single "Nuthin' But a G Thang" in particular, catalyzed the trend, for Dre's soul-tinged G-funk rhythms were highly regarded by radio programmers, while his lyrical themes communicated a compelling hardcore sensibility that had been largely absent from mainstream commercial radio, even among stations that regularly programmed rap alongside R & B. The president of Priority Records, Bryan Turner, noted the shifting media climate, commenting on the transition from radio's experimentation with the genre to a more consistently inclusive playlist: "Radio definitely was the big breakthrough. They're certainly taking more chances and playing a lot more things than they ever did before" (Nelson 1993e, 31). While it is unclear what the "chances" Turner refers to were or what the repercussions might have been for the radio stations in question, it was evident that the shifting character of urban radio playlists provided new opportunities for rap artists to access marginally interested or curious listeners, expanding rap's mainstream cultural influence.

As *Billboard* reported, industry executives cited "the popularity of rap video, an increasingly competitive radio landscape, and the musical blends that characterize many recent releases" as the major influences in radio's new acceptance of rap (Nelson 1993c, 10). A further influence is the fact that reality rap artists who gained a foothold on either pop or urban radio were often also associated with a white college audience demographic, among whom elements such as pro-marijuana themes or proven affinities with rock-oriented projects (such as the annual Lollapalooza summer shed tour) were well received. Other artists, especially those from the West Coast such as Dr. Dre, Snoop Doggy Dogg, Too Short, or Tupac, were aesthetically linked to R & B or funk traditions which were deemed more "melodic" and radio friendly, despite the lyrical content which was often more difficult to accommodate within the constraining regulations of mainstream radio. From New York, artists signed to Sean Combs's Bad Boy label—most notably the Notorious B.I.G.—fared well with radio programmers.

Modern rock stations continued to display flexibility in their formats, playing rap by the Beastie Boys, Disposable Heroes of Hiphoprisy, and a range of what was often termed "alternative rap" acts, including Arrested Development and US3. Programmers coined the term "Channel X" to name the evolving format, which took MTV's free-form, non-genre-specific playlist as its main model. Radio executives and programmers also observed that efforts such as the Lollapalooza tour were effective in preparing the market for greater acceptance of an integrated approach encompassing alternative rock and rap while it facilitated long-standing label strategies to cross rap acts over to a more adventurous white teen consumer demographic group. In marketing the film sound track to *Judgment Night* (1993, Immortal), executives sought to exploit the converging tastes among various teen demographics by returning to the rock-rap mix pioneered by Def Jam and Profile in the mid-1980s. The full-length sound track release, featuring hybrid rock-rap tracks by such artists as Mud Honey and Sir Mix-A-Lot, Living Colour and Run-D.M.C., Pearl Jam and Cypress Hill, Faith No More and Boo Yaa Tribe, Slayer and Ice-T, and Biohazard and Onyx, was promoted heavily among college audiences and on alternative and urban radio stations. On MTV, the host VJs of *Yo! MTV Raps* and *Headbangers Ball* introduced the material together, cross-promoting it among their respective viewing audiences. By mid-1995, however, many of the connective threads that were initially seen as linking rock and rap audiences together were unraveling. The Channel X format, for example, struggled to compete in its primary trial markets (Jacksonville, Seattle, and Detroit) as programming directors realized that rap and modern rock, once thought to be convergent forces, were in fact on vastly different trajectories, with "modern rock reaching out to mainstream listeners, while rap was turning inward" (Boehlert 1995, 19). Despite this vague directional reference, the "inward" actually involved a discursive and thematic intensification of 'hood-oriented imagery and a fierce attention to the locality of artists and their labels; it was, however, amplified, made more public precisely on account of the enhanced and unprecedented access to the mainstream commercial mediascape among black-owned independent rap labels and rap artists.

The growing acceptance of rap radio in larger urban markets in this period was demonstrated in the Arbitron ratings "books" in mid-July 1994.

The ratings clearly reflected the growth of the urban radio format, with New York City's WQHT/Hot 97 (touting the slogans "the place where hip hop lives" and "blazin' hip hop and r&b") rising from number seven to the number three position in the market, although in Los Angeles, which was dominated by the Spanish-language station KLAX, hip-hop did not perform as strongly. Hot 97 had altered its previous mix of R & B and rap, pushing forward with a format more heavily weighted to rap, working more closely with rap record labels in positioning their material, and collaborating with club and mix-tape DJs to ensure that the artists and records played were consistent with audience tastes "in the street." As one radio programmer from a southwestern station claimed, Hot 97 "is the mecca of rap right now," and programming directors from other markets began scrutinizing the station's successes, hoping to replicate them in their own market regions.

Among Hot 97's innovations was their hiring of established celebrity rappers and DJs (including, at various times, Afrika Bambaataa, KRS-One, LL Cool J, Funkmaster Flex, DJ Red Alert, and the indomitable morning team Ed Lover and Dr. Dre, who also hosted MTV's *Yo! MTV Raps*). The further open-door policy of inviting local and touring artists to drop into the station to spin records, chat, or rap freestyle, live on the air, further reinforced the sense that Hot 97 was a "home" for hip-hop and strengthened its profile as a purveyor of "authentic" rap and hip-hop in the city in which it was spawned. The Hot 97 format was reproduced in other markets with varying degrees of success, continuing hip-hop's outward expansion and solidifying its status within the mainstream mediascape. As of 2000 Hot 97 remained a cultural force in the hip-hop nation, with the current morning hosts (and full-throttled "player haters"), Star and BucWild, and the late-afternoon celebrity host, Angie Martinez, gracing billboards and posters throughout the city (but especially in the New York subway system, which many members of the hip-hop culture use for transportation), touting the station's appeal among a predominantly high school teen demographic with the slogan "another reason to hate getting up in the morning."

While rap was more fully embraced by commercial radio through the mid-1990s, rap performances remained largely absent from the home television screen, though hip-hop's cultural forms and character were commonly displayed, often on situation comedies. Even as television gradually embraced hip-hop-oriented themes, discourses, and styles with greater frequency, these tended to be in either exaggerated or diluted forms. Under the headline "TV Eyes Rap for Ratings" (Rosen 1993, 7), *Billboard* cited television networks' plans to introduce Hammer, Queen Latifah, and Tone

Loc to the nation's viewers in nonmusical roles, following in the footsteps of the Fresh Prince, Will Smith. Rap artists continued to prove their legitimacy and clout at the film box office, and television executives sought to capitalize on the recognition factor and the performers' celebrity status among youth audiences and popular-culture consumers. Entertainment industry executives and managers speculated that increased visibility on the domestic medium could prove beneficial to an artist's career, though primarily in a complementary capacity; nonmusical television appearances were deemed unlikely to motivate musical success in the absence of charting recordings and an active touring schedule. In Will Smith's case, a hectic acting schedule (involving taping for his weekly program as well as embarking on the early stages of a film career) had noticeably impeded the artist's first career as an MC, reducing his commitments to touring and studio recording.

Although mainstream commercial television was important for raising the public profiles and facilitating career diversification among a select few established artists, "underground television" in the form of community access cable programming also proved to be an increasingly viable avenue for less established hip-hop artists. Cable access television emerged as a new source for a diverse range of music, including reggae dancehall, African ju ju and highlife, "alternative R & B," hip-hop, and rap, geared toward local audiences. This array of genres, which encompassed a wide swath of the African diaspora, benefited in a minor capacity from exposure in small, isolated markets, sometimes with estimates for weekly shows of as few as a thousand viewers (*Russell* 1993, R-12). Unrestricted by the commercial imperatives of corporate or nationally syndicated shows on cable video outlets such as MTV or BET, these local stations continue to display a refreshingly free approach to their programming, which has little overlap with existing music video programming. Commonly hosted by earnest but inexperienced hip-hop fans, the programs also provide a space for the screening of videos by local artists with minimal video production budgets and lower production values, qualities that disqualify these videos from airing on the mainstream commercial networks.

In mid-1997, the debuts of the talk shows *Vibe* (hosted by the comedian Sinbad) and *Keenen Ivory Wayans* created hopes among black music executives that the programs would provide much-needed exposure for their acts on the small screen, something that had been lacking since *The Arsenio Hall Show*'s demise in 1994. Magic Johnson was also recruited to host the talk show *Magic's Hour,* which was critically panned. None of these shows survived long in the competitive talk-show market, yet with their regular inclusion of black artists they revealed the importance of television access for both rising and established R & B and rap acts. Some industry marketing and promotions executives had been optimistic that even after their cancellation, the programs might serve as a motivating influence for David Letterman's or Jay Leno's top-rated shows to book more R & B or rap acts, despite the tendencies for these programs to book mainstream, charting pop or rock acts. HBO's *Chris Rock Show*, with the former *Billboard* rap reporter Nelson George as coproducer and old-school pioneer Grandmaster Flash as musical director, showed more durability, emerging as a regular television option for black acts. Although it surpassed its more recent predecessors, viewership for Rock's show is also often constrained owing to HBO's cost, since it is a premium cable channel and is not part of most standard cable packages. Hip-hop occasionally surfaces on other television shows, with artists appearing on *Late Night with Conan O'Brien* or in the mid-afternoon time slots such as *The Jenny Jones Show,* which featured an appearance by the Cash Money crew during their spring 2000 tour.

In the mid- to late 1990s, the Internet was also established as an essential force in the delineation and mapping of the virtual hip-hop nation. The relatively new medium was taken up by rap fans and by independent and major corporate labels alike as a new means of communication. Reporting on the emergence of hip-hop on the Internet, *Billboard* (Coleman 1996, 34) noted that both noncommercial fan-based and commercial corporate-sponsored Web sites and chat rooms were slowly proliferating, although they remained underaccessed in comparison to many other music and entertainment fan-oriented Web sites. This was due, in part, to the newness of the medium and to general disparities in home computer ownership and online access among minority youths. The report observed that the industry's Internet presence was less well developed for rap artists than for artists in some other genres, although fan-built Web sites were growing in number and frequently displayed superior graphic quality and a broader range of information than those of established independent labels.

In May 1997 *Billboard*'s rap columnist, Havelock Nelson, reported on the growing influence of a burgeoning hip-hop Internet underground and its capacity to generate new international alliances, expanding and intensifying the bonds of the hip-hop nation (1997b, 23). Developments in Web site programming and rising computer sophistication among teens were in greater evidence by 1998–99, when hip-hop was represented on the Internet with more fully operational informational and commercial Web sites that linked online users to both industry and fan-built pages. The growth of this technological sector facilitated the formation of multiple virtual communities focused on audience tastes and affective fan identification derived from hip-hop, producing a context for fan chat and other interactive activities. Reporting in *Billboard*, the columnist Elena Oumano also cited the introduction of 88HipHop.com, a live "international, online, and interactive video show" that grew out of an online radio show created by Randy Nkonoki Ward and Mark Kotlinski (Oumano 1998, 36). A *Billboard* article on October 31, 1998, noted that despite the rapid exploitation of Internet possibilities by rap and hip-hop, R & B artists and labels were less likely to be represented on the Internet, since both major and independent labels were considerably slower to utilize the available electronic online technologies for R & B promotions and marketing (Shawnee Smith 1998b, 23).

With the advent of various software sound packages and the rise of Internet radio, Napster music file exchange systems, and MP3 music downloading systems, rap is now a central feature on the Internet. Some hip-hop artists are at the forefront of the online music distribution movement. Chuck D and Ice-T, each of whom has a long track record as a social agitator and has struggled against restrictions on his artistic expression, signed with the Atomic Pop recording and Internet company, employing the online technology to promote, market, and distribute their material without either the meddling of corporate executives or the restrictions of traditional bricks-and-mortar retail outlets. Hip-hop labels, including Def Jam, which in June 2000 introduced its online service, 360hiphop.com (dedicated to hip-hop "music, culture, lifestyle, and politics," and, significantly, commercial retailing, with a section titled "buy shit"), are well ahead of many of the industry's major corporations on the technology curve. In many cases, however, these sites are attempting a more comprehensive content-based approach to the medium, moving rapidly away from basic e-commerce concepts of pitching commodities and embarking on more holistic approaches that emphasize hip-hop lifestyles and cultural knowledge, of which material goods are only a segment.

Black Music Divisions and the Shifting Music Industry

Throughout the 1990s the music industry experienced important transformations as corporate concentration intensified and the major entertainment conglomerates jockeyed to maximize their market positions. Within the corporate structures, however, black music divisions remained destabilized throughout the decade, with changes in personnel, market focus, and corporate commitment fluctuating considerably. Many of the transitions among black music divisions were spurred by hip-hop's ongoing growth and penetration of the national cultural consciousness and its global market expansion, although the chasm dividing black consumers continued across generational lines. It was not uncommon for rap to top the pop singles and album charts, and industry executives pondered the question of whether rap might actually overwhelm R & B, as it even more frequently topped the R & B charts.

Consumer patterns among white and minority youth were also under transition, with alternative or modern rock evolving as an important genre among white teens and Latin music (including salsa, club-oriented techno-merengue, and merengue–hip-hop hybrids) spurring new interest among many Latino teens. Still, the sales figures for rap and hip-hop music reflected a consumer appeal that extended far beyond the narrow boundaries of black youth, just as they had a decade earlier when the Beastie Boys, Run-D.M.C., and LL Cool J dominated the charts. Although rap's powerful market presence in nonurban regions had slipped briefly in the early and mid-1990s, white teens continued to consume rap in high volumes. Yet even with more sophisticated and geographically precise data (encompassing suburban malls and music retail chain sales and urban sales at independent retail outlets) generated through the SoundScan sales monitoring system, detailed and accurate racial breakdowns remained elusive. At the Bobby Poe Pop Music Survey convention in June 1993, Billy Brill, Interscope's promotion executive, created havoc with his racist innuendo when he refuted the misplaced belief among radio programming directors that white teenagers did not buy rap, challenging them to "go to a mall. It's the white kids who are buying rap while the brothers are shoplifting." Despite unresearched opinions such as that of one vice president of sales at Tommy Boy Records, who stated that "Dr. Dre is the voice of suburbia," the numbers reflected that, in fact, modern rock acts, including Offspring and Green Day, were strong competitors among the white suburban teen consumer demographic.

Glen Sansone, of the influential *College Music Journal,* identified the relentless quest for authenticity and a commitment to an ideology of "the real" in hardcore rap as likely sources of the shifting tastes across racial lines, citing crucial geographic disjunctures as an accompanying force in rap's reduced sales: "Rap is moving more toward keeping it real and appealing to a certain core market of 15-to-25-year-old black urban fans. White [college DJs] in the middle of the country do make the effort and want to understand it, but they're understanding it less and less" (Boehlert 1995, 19). As the racial and spatial divide widened, some radio stations revived the moribund practice of articulating a firm "no rap " commitment. WHTZ (Z-100) in New York even aired a promo snippet of Green Day to indicate what they would play and a snippet of the Notorious B.I.G. to indicate what lay beyond the aesthetic scope of their playlist.

In mid-1995 *Billboard*'s Havelock Nelson voiced the industry perspective that rap had again entered a phase of "aesthetic fatigue," suggesting that creativity was slumping and many marginal rap music consumers were overlooking hardcore rap to a greater extent by purchasing various hip-hop hybrids (Jamaican dancehall reggae, acid jazz, etc.) or purchasing rap with a strong R & B orientation (1995b, 1). Notwithstanding strong sales by many individual acts, rap's overall market share had decreased between 1993 and 1995, falling from 9.2 percent in 1993 to 7.9 percent by the end of 1994. Rap singles tended to outpace sales of full-length CDs (due in part to the rise of radio hit programming and the influence of single-oriented video play), reflecting that, in the rap industry, artist development still lagged behind that in the pop, rock, and country genres. Furthermore, the rap albums that performed best in the market often featured more melodic hooks and choruses, embracing R & B and crossing over on the charts. Industry executives and some artists complained of an overall sameness, blaming producers for the formulaic reproduction of stylistic forms with little innovation, cleaving toward the norms established within either New York or Los Angeles hip-hop production circles.

The Fugees' 1996 release *The Score* (Ruffhouse) provided what critics agreed was a much-needed aesthetic boost, signaling the rise of a new hip-hop sound that was not easily associated with either the hardcore Northeast production styles or the West Coast's G-funk sound. Industry marketing executives and critics attempted to define the emergent aesthetic as "alternative" rap ("Alternative R & B Tour Should Put Sizzle in Summer Season" 1996, 1), a term that had earlier been assigned to such acts as Arrested Development and Disposable Heroes of Hiphoprisy, each of which stumbled commercially after demonstrating initial promise. Among the key distinctions in the Fugees' sound were the emphasis on live instrumentation and the use of a DJ on the turntables, a respectful yet fresh reinterpretation of classic soul (especially the cover of Roberta Flack's 1973 hit "Killing Me Softly with His Song"), pronounced influences of the Caribbean cultural diaspora (particularly the music of Haiti and Jamaica), and critically acclaimed live concert performances. Several of these features were also observable among other artists in the period, most notably the Roots, whose live performances continue to earn high praise among fellow rap artists.

Industry analysts also continued to speculate that the interventions of major labels in the rap market unleashed a greater number of artists, oversaturating an already crowded market and, in the view of many critics, diluting rap's overall quality. The impressive sales of Dr. Dre's *The Chronic* and Snoop Doggy Dogg's *Doggy Style* (which was the first debut album in the SoundScan era to enter *Billboard*'s Top 200 Chart at number one) and the lucrative financial relationship between Interscope and Death Row Records gained the close attention of top industry executives, yet the major labels' approach to the rap market was frequently formulaic, seeking to capitalize on innovations that in most cases had emerged earlier from acts signed to independent labels. The renewed efforts among the major music corporations to engage with the hip-hop consumer and increase their percentage of sales in the rap market was consequently met with mixed emotions among longtime black music executives.

A rash of appointments within black music and R & B divisions throughout the industry, especially from 1993 to 1997, was initially cause for optimism among blacks in the industry, yet it was also observed that many of the older and more established black music executives were not being promoted or moved to other internal divisions within their companies, in contrast to the standard career patterns among their veteran white executive peers. Rather, they were often demoted or simply replaced by younger, less experienced industry professionals—or, increasingly toward the end of the decade, by musicians and producers with a certain hip-hop market savvy but, in many cases, virtually no executive experience. In 1996 the Harvard Consultation Project, a team of graduate students at the Harvard Law School, conducted a research study on the urban music environment. As they reported in their findings,

No major record labels have a formal training program, and the majority of assignments are "Baptism by Fire." The latest wave of appointments in Urban Music departments and record companies have [*sic*] placed entertainment attorneys, artist managers, and former A&R executives in decision-making positions. The apparent assumption of the majors is that Black "insiders" with close artist connections will result in greater success. (Harvard Consultation Project 1996, n.p.)

While these hiring trends offered the image that major labels were reinforcing their black music divisions and strengthening their commitments to their top black executives, they also had the effect of reducing the inside clout of black executives by thinning the number of those with career longevity, a wealth of industry contacts, and deep experience. As the report further observes, the parameters of responsibility granted to black music executives are often narrowly defined, isolating them to their corporate divisions in a case of de facto ghettoization. They are often not privy to important decisions about their corporations' overall objectives and strategic planning, nor are they positioned within the structures to gain a professional global vantage that would prepare them for greater responsibilities.

Anthony Giddens writes that "locales are typically internally *regionalized*, and the regions within them are of critical importance in constituting contexts of interaction." While his statement is oriented more toward the broader social spectrum of lived experience, it is equally pertinent at the reduced scale of the corporate environment and its internal geographies. The spatially organized "routinized social practices" have a great deal of relevance and import for the deeds and activities—the actual "work"—of those who inhabit these corporate regions and other rational institutional spaces (Giddens 1984, 118). Because the traditions of the industry over time reproduce a mindset that inscribes the black music division as a separate region, top black executives come to envision their role as that of overseers of their division, of black music, and of a segment (albeit a highly influential segment) of the black cultural experience. What they do not attain as easily, owing to the internal spatial structuration of the institution rather than their own shortsightedness, is an overarching perspective of the globally networked corporation and the diversified entertainment conglomerate.

Peter Jackson and Jan Penrose write that notions of race and nation "are articulated by different groups of people at different times and at different spatial scales, from the global to the local. In each case, the idea of 'race' or nation is part of a broader set of ideologies and social practices" (1993, 13). This is to say, as it was in previous chapters, that racial difference in America is almost always linked at some level to spatial difference. In the major music corporations, black executive knowledge was mainly privileged and welcomed at the local and national scales, and their assignments to new posts reflected this.

Black music, including R & B and rap, was not conceived by the major labels as being particularly mobile. It was thought of primarily as a commodity for African-American consumers and hence did not travel well in the global commercial media systems. Black executives were, therefore, hired not for their global perspectives, but for their local, regional, or national contacts and knowledge, a situation that restricted their professional growth. The Harvard Project is critical of the failure among major music labels to groom and prepare black executives for more prominent roles with more widely defined responsibilities instead of isolating them in the racialized enclaves of black music divisions. The report quotes Clarence Avant, the chairman of Motown Records and a board member of Polygram Holdings: "Black executives should not limit themselves to Black Music Departments. They should seek to realize their potential as total executives" (Harvard Consultation Project 1996, n.p.). Their agency to do so, however, is restricted from within the corporations even as they are granted "promotions," since, as the Harvard Project determines, these very promotions can effectively preclude "Black executives from 'crossing over' at the major labels, and they are constantly relegated to positions with grand titles, but duties that amount to little more than being a talent scout" (Harvard Consultation Project 1996, n.p.).

Also imposed on black executives was an emphasis on immediacy and the capacity to generate quick hits while consistently locating new, marketable artists. In either instance, the hiring patterns often indicated another dimension of the marginalization of blacks in the industry, especially since, unlike the case for many of their white counterparts, the mechanisms for grooming artists for longer careers were restricted. Indeed, the space that people are capable of appropriating as a part of their identity is inextricably linked to various resources and options that lie within their range and sphere of control, and in a direct sense, such enabling or debilitating resources include race. The confinement of black executives to black music divisions and the shifts engendered as they leave and enter their executive posts in the fluctuating search for greater authority and responsibility subsequently make it more difficult to halt or reverse the trends of racial marginalization. As this suggests, race, and not professional abilities or corporate loyalty, can be identified as the defining characteristic of black music executives in the corporate institution, and it functions as the central hindrance on their ability to move beyond the confining terrains within the internal corporate geography.

The generational divisions that were evident in the consumer market were also increasingly evident in the corporate structure (relating to both experience in the industry and taste patterns), especially as rap encroached on R & B as the top-selling black music genre. This produced tension for black executives in the industry, who were confronted by two camps: their corporate superiors expected them to perform according to the expediencies of the company, whereas the artists and producers of contemporary black music were asking them to open the gates and grant them greater access to the mediascape. Since the early 1980s, young black rap artists and black-owned management agencies had lamented the incapacity of or deliberate refusals by longtime black executives with ties to major labels to provide support and help establish an early foundation for rap and hip-hop music. They sought either changes in the corporate attitude or the outright removal of veteran black executives who seemed, in their view, destined to stall rap's development. In this regard, it is not insignificant to note that whites in the industry have proven to be highly effective advocates for rap and remain instrumental to its commercial expansion. As the 1996 Harvard Report suggests, however, risk taking—which was already minimally practiced within the industry at large—was even less likely among black executives, who had only limited authority and control within their corporate settings.

Through the 1990s and toward the end of the decade, many black executives and division heads were refused the opportunities for growth and upward movement within their companies and were criticized by artists, on the one hand, for losing contact with "the streets" and by their corporate superiors, on the other hand, for failing to stay abreast of the aesthetics of the street and to dominate the shifting markets. At Elektra, Sylvia Rhone, who had over twenty years of experience in the industry and an advanced business degree from the Wharton School, was promoted to CEO, but hers was—and remains—a relatively rare appointment among women and blacks alike in the corporate music sector. As a result of corporate inequities and the professional restrictions veteran black executives encountered, some left the major-label fold to start their own independent labels, while others established themselves as consultants to younger executives or to young entrepreneurs with independent labels who sought to solidify their position in the business.

While independent labels became more adept at marketing their artists and positioning them in the increasingly crowded rap field (notable was Sean Combs's independent startup, Bad Boy Entertainment, which in 1994 leveraged its first full-length releases by Craig Mack and Notorious B.I.G. into the top of the charts), the major labels also demonstrated a new, more street-savvy approach to marketing, reducing one of the competitive edges from which independent rap labels had traditionally benefited. By the mid-1990s, along with their refocused and redesigned black music divisions, the major labels were reinforcing their status as formidable competitors in the volatile and unpredictable rap market. They did so through more diligent talent recruiting as well as by aggressively pursuing joint ventures and lucrative pressing and distribution deals with smaller independent labels.

The reinforcement of RCA's roster of black artists (including SWV, Martha Wash, and Me Phi Me) was cited under the headline "RCA Broadens Vision for R & B, Rap via New Deals" (McAdams 1993), as were its initiatives in establishing new distribution deals with several labels, most notably Steve Rifkind's Loud Records, after dismal sales among RCA's black music roster and the end of its distribution contract with Jive Records. In pointing to RCA's renewed emphasis on black music, the label's president, Skip Miller, stated, "We're back in the tradition of a full-service company," with the notion of "full service" referring to the inclusion of and commitment to black music. Mercury Records, too, reinforced its commitments to hip-hop in this period, launching a fifteen-city promotional college rap "posse tour" in March 1993 that featured several artists on the roster. Several months later the Atlantic Group also mobilized its black music resources for a push into the rap market with the development and implementation of "It's On!," a coordinated effort involving Atlantic, Interscope Records, EastWest Records, and Delicious Vinyl. The campaign involved the release of compilation recordings featuring artists from the various affiliated labels, extensive street sniper postering, and calculated marketing targeted toward urban-format radio stations.

After severing ties with Ice-T, the Warner Music Group was regarded by many artists as the prime example of major-label deceit, owing to its failure to fulfill its commitments to the rap acts it distributed. Still, in late 1993 and early 1994, the label attempted to recover from Ice-T's departure (and the loss of street ties through his Rhyme Syndicate label), the end of its distribution deal with Cold Chillin' Records, and weak sales of new releases by the Jungle Brothers and Monie Love. Warner executives defensively suggested that it was the creative limitations and shifting market demands that produced poor results from their artists, whereas the artists claimed that the sheer size of the Warner corporate structure led to a slowed production and release process that negatively affected releases of supporting singles and video clips. As part of their renewal strategy, Warner hired a "street promotions team" in an attempt to develop a more regionally sensitive approach to rap marketing.

Revealing Warner's struggle to harmonize its operations according to hip-hop's unique geographic and cultural idiosyncrasies, one Warner product manager explained that "every city is its own little world, and certain techniques only work in certain markets." His statement reflects just how out of touch Warner was at the time, since hip-hop had, from its inception, been structured along local and regional lines with pronounced cultural distinctions. In the year following the announcement of its new black music agenda, Warner's acts remained seriously underrepresented on the rap and R & B charts. The label's black music division relied heavily on the achievements of the Interscope, Qwest, and Giant labels, which Warner distributed. In 1995 Warner again reorganized its black music division, introducing a new executive team following the departure of the influential industry executive and vice president of A & R at Warner, Benny Medina, after the label refused to renew his contract.

Virgin Records announced the appointment of the former Priority Records executive Eric Brooks as chief at its Noo Trybe label in late 1993 as part of an attempt to strengthen its black music division by adding rap and R & B artists to its roster. Among its first projects was the solo release *Diary* by Scarface of the Geto Boys, which accompanied a distribution deal between Noo Trybe and the Geto Boys' Houston-based label, Rap-A-Lot Records. In the same period Scotti Brothers Records, a subsidiary of the television syndication company All American Communications, announced its plan to launch Street Life Records, diversifying its corporate focus by expanding into the growing urban music sector.

In late spring 1995 MCA embarked on a restructuring project, hiring Public Enemy's former producer, Hank Shocklee, and the former vice president of business affairs at Def Jam, David Harleston, as senior vice presidents of the label's black music division (replacing Ernie Singleton, who resigned and moved to Ruthless Records following the death of Eazy-E). The new executives in turn hired the former Def Jam executive Jeff Trotter and the former Stetsasonic frontman Daddy-O. In little more than a year, however, Harleston left the label, and Shocklee was demoted to a senior A & R position when the more experienced executive insider, Ken Wilson, was appointed the new president of the division.

The Sony mega-corporation was also reassigning its resources in order to strengthen its position in the black music sector. In January 1994 the Sony subsidiary Epic Records formed its Epic Street division, acquiring Cold Chillin' Records from Warner Records and establishing distribution ties with Flavor Unit, Immortal, and New Deal as a base for their push into urban music markets. Mobilizing the standard strategy of marketing and promoting their acts through street-level campaigns that target independent retail outlets and clubs, Epic also outlined its intention to conduct research toward developing a more comprehensive profile of the preadolescent demographic. This age group was not generally considered a strong rap market segment, but it was thought that over time it would evolve into a huge hip-hop-influenced consumer group (Reynolds 1994, 13). Sony also reaffirmed its commitment to R & B in the summer of 1995 with a new executive lineup, installing R & B divisions at both its Columbia Records and Epic labels. In 1996 Relativity, a subsidiary wholly owned by Sony that had for years been associated with a range of musical genres, announced its transition to an all-urban roster, concentrating on the label's market strengths and reinforcing Sony's involvement in rap and hip-hop markets on several fronts. Distribution rights for the late Eazy-E's Ruthless Records label were subsequently purchased by Epic in 1997, enabling Ruthless to expand its catalog distribution into overseas markets with greater efficiency and penetration. Beginning in 1993, Clive Davis's "mini-major" label Arista Records, which was already a considerable presence in the R & B market, enjoyed a lucrative arrangement with Bad Boy Entertainment that served both companies well toward the end of the decade. Davis maneuvered to buy Profile Records by 1998 as part of Arista's strategy to expand its rap roster while obtaining Profile's lucrative rap catalog.

The flurry of activity among the major corporate labels was not without its losses. For example, in a move that was at odds with the reinforcement of many black music divisions among the major labels from 1993 to 1996, Motown (itself a division of MCA) laid off twenty-one of its mid-level staff in order to facilitate the move of its corporate headquarters from Los Angeles to New York under the questionable (and ultimately short-lived) leadership of the former Uptown Records chief Andre Harrell, who was appointed in 1995. Similarly, Capitol Records undertook what some industry analysts described as a "systematic extermination of black music" (Reynolds 1996b, 18) as the company folded its R & B operations into EMI Records, laying off eighteen staff members from the label's urban-music division. By mid-decade EMI-Capitol's distribution company, Cema, claimed the fewest charting R & B acts among all of the major companies. Capitol's rationale for the change was that it sought to focus resources on its existing stars, including the rock artists Bonnie Raitt, Bob Seger, and Richard Marx, as well as developing newer rock acts such as the Foo Fighters, Everclear, and Radiohead. Despite indications at the time, Capitol executives claimed that EMI was not being restructured solely as an urban-oriented label. In the fall of 1996, EMI-Capitol sought to reinforce its position in the urban market with the purchase of a 50 percent stake in Priority Records, with which EMI already had a distribution contract. The deal, which displaced fifteen people at Priority, was undertaken to capitalize on the smaller label's strength and recognition in the rap market, especially through its contracts with West Coast artists. The deal also provided Priority with a cash infusion that reinforced its position and allowed it to afford the increasing costs of rap videos and general promotions and marketing.

In the promotions sector, the issue of discrimination against black promoters, which had been a sore point for over thirty years and had been festering with particular intensity since the mid-1980s, surfaced.[1] In late 1998 a coalition of five promotions companies affiliated with the Black Promoters Association of America (BPA) filed a lawsuit alleging "antitrust and civil rights claims, charging a long-standing conspiracy that has kept black promoters from promoting shows by white headliners and top-selling black acts" ("Black Promoters' Suit Underscores Discontent" 1998, 1). With industry trends toward concentration of ownership evolving in the promotions, touring, and venue sector of the entertainment industry (notable in the nationwide expansion of SFX, which consumed many midsize local theaters and outdoor "summer shed" performance centers and booked large summer tours), black promotion agencies became even more alienated from the more lucrative tours and performance sites. Furthermore, with the enhanced presence and profile of major labels in the rap sector, black promoters observed the tendency for the majors to favor white-owned promotions agencies with which they had preexisting business relations. While rap is still more commonly promoted among black-owned agencies, its artists either tour less frequently and/or less widely or play to fewer patrons in much smaller venues than do many of their rock or pop counterparts, making the tours far less profitable by comparison.

The major labels enhanced hip-hop's cultural momentum in mainstream America in the late 1990s and provided many of the mechanisms for rap's consistent distribution throughout North American and global markets, but they did not dominate its character or control its evolution. Indeed, the hip-hop underground has continued to develop according to its own unwieldy agendas, which are often foreign, confusing, and even frightening to major-label executives. In this, the independent labels deserve to be acknowledged since crucial innovations and aethetic shifts have predominantly emerged from independent-label rosters and artists whose contracts are with smaller companies. Toward the end of the decade, as hip-hop continued to extend its influence, individual artists and labels alike experienced the wrath and condemnation of cultural critics and various watchdog organizations that opposed the content and imagery spouted by rappers. Major labels were ill prepared for the levels of tension and drama that could accompany hip-hop, and as they drew closer to hip-hop by signing artists directly to their rosters or establishing co-ownership and distribution deals with independent rap labels, they also increasingly found themselves exposed to attacks by consumers, stockholders, and other activist organizations.

Hip-Hop and Moral Panic: The Controversies Continue

If, during the 1980s, rap was demonized for the outbreaks of audience violence associated with concert performances or, after 1988, for the viciousness of its thematic content, in the 1990s rap artists themselves emerged as the central players in the dramas of street violence, murder, and mayhem. Many critics representing a range of ideological and racial viewpoints were horrified at the seeming tendency of rap artists and their young fans to straddle a line between representational violence or the image of the gangster lifestyle and actual violence and thuggery. In its November 13, 1993, issue, *Billboard* featured an article on page 1 that posed the question: "Music & Violence: Does Crime Pay? Gangsta Gunplay Sparks Industry Debate" (Nelson 1993a, 1). The article cites criminal charges against Snoop Doggy Dogg (who was on trial as an accomplice to murder) and Tupac Shakur (for a litany of offenses, including the shooting of two off-duty Atlanta policemen and aggravated sexual assault) and an incident involving Public Enemy's Flavor Flav (who allegedly fired an unlicensed gun at a neighbor in a fit of jealousy). The next month, an unprecedented front-page editorial in the December 25 issue made plain the bewilderment and simmering outrage:

The headline on the lead story for the Nov. 13 issue of *Billboard* was "Music & Violence: Does Crime Pay?" Although the long-term outlook is uncertain, the initial public and industry responses to a deluge of new or impending releases by various rock, gangsta rap, and reggae/dancehall acts that have associated themselves with mass murderers or have been charged with violent crimes indicates that the answer to our story's woeful question would seem to be yes.

Major-label executives were unprepared for the blurring of actual and fictional gun violence among artists on their rap rosters as the criminal cases involving rap artists accumulated (with variations in their severity or implications). Still, in a perverse twist, the incidents benefited the labels by further fueling the associations between rap's themes of unrepentant gangsta-ism, actual violence, and social chaos, lending the cachet of authenticity to the acts as they simultaneously navigated the mediascape inhabited by their musical personae, the localized places of the 'hood, and the landscapes of the nation's court system. The various charges against rappers reinforced a hardened image that in some cases had been carefully cultivated within the discourse and image of "keeping it real," informing their profiles as outlaws who stray from the status quo and openly defy mainstream values. As the criminal charges against rap artists steadily inched upward, the music journalist Kim Green observed that "these sort of incidents won't affect the sales of anyone's rap records, but they would have an effect at labels tired of paying bail bondsmen, fighting off journalists, etc. Every time a VP gets a call that so-and-so is in jail, it's a problem" (Nelson 1993a, 108).

Of relevance is the fact that many of the cases involving rap as the alleged cause or catalyst of violence were tried in the South, often in county courtrooms, where the nation's strongholds of local and regional conservatism are found. For instance, under the headline, "Jury Weighs Rap as an Accomplice to Murder of a Trooper," *Billboard* described the case of Ronald Ray Howard, who was convicted of killing a Texas state trooper in April 1992 while driving a stolen truck (Beets 1993, 12). The prosecution alleged that Howard was listening to inflammatory gangsta rap, and the officer's wife also filed a civil suit against Tupac Shakur after a tape of *2Pacalypse Now* (1991, Interscope), with several references advocating the murder of police officers, was found in the stolen vehicle. In another incident, on June 14, 1993, a teen in Florida confessed to murdering an elderly woman who objected to the content of the lyrics he was rapping while he listened to Dr. Dre's "Stranded on Death Row" (1992, Death Row) ("Slay Charge vs. Rapping Teen: Victim Complained about Lyrics" 1993, 83). In this case, however, it was the defendant's own lawyers who attempted to exploit rap's purported negative influences, stating that it was a combination of insanity, prescribed medication, and rap's power of suggestion that contributed to his violent actions.

In the midst of the controversies involving rap and its role in criminal activities, the fallout from Ice-T's 1992 "Cop Killer" conflict with Time Warner continued to resonate among rap artists and their labels, sending a chill through the record industry and altering the relationship between major or intermediary companies and rap-oriented independent labels. In early 1993 Ice-T released *Home Invasion* through Priority Records after Warner-controlled Sire Records refused to renew his contract in the wake of the "Cop Killer" debacle. The complications of Ice-T's earlier battle with Time Warner led the corporation to intensely scrutinize *Home Invasion,* and although the lyrics were under review, it was widely believed that the album's cover art, with its graphic depiction of black-on-white violence, was ultimately what forced the severance of the contract (Morris 1993b, 10). Within a month after Ice-T left Sire, Time Warner's cable television network, HBO, also squelched a planned cable series, *Ice-TV,* being developed by the artist, citing reasons unrelated to Ice-T's earlier controversies for their decision not to proceed with the series (Morris 1993a, 94).

During the same period, Time Warner encountered a further incident involving hip-hop when angry teenagers without tickets for a show at the Six Flags theme park in Valencia, California, which featured the headliners TLC (an R & B act) and Paperboy, fought security, looted park stores, and damaged property. Nine hundred police officers responded to the incident at the park, which is part of the extensive Time Warner entertainment empire. Park officials cited the family-oriented nature of the chain and safety concerns as justification for the number of officers summoned to the park, indicating that rap acts would no longer be permitted at the Six Flags Valencia venue (Borzillo 1993, 11). Later that summer, however, the Los Angeles radio station KACE hosted a "Jam for Peace" concert featuring over twenty acts that included such hardcore artists as the Geto Boys, Ice-T, and Bloods and Crips, from the *Bangin' on Wax* project. Performed before an audience of fifteen thousand people, the concert was free of violence.

The controversies surrounding rap content continued, and since gangsta rap was entrenched as a facet of the media terrain and was more easily accessed on radio and music television programs, various organizations displayed an important strategic shift in their protests. In this period rap came under review in rather predictable ways, but the significance lies in the new venues—the new spaces and places—where the attacks on rap were fought. Critics and anti-rap activists more consistently expressed their grievances to media executives, the entertainment industry's annual corporate shareholders meetings, retail sales outlets, and the government, seeking from within the halls of power stronger and more restrictive regulations against the music and its producers. The president of the National Political Congress of Black Women, C. Delores Tucker, rose as a persistent combatant against hardcore gangsta rap and in New York, Reverend Calvin Butts, a pastor at the Abyssinian Baptist Church in Manhattan, attracted media attention with a series of public relations stunts.

In the spring of 1993 Butts embarked on a campaign against rap, explicitly targeting it for what he regarded as its misogynistic, sexist, violent, and racially self-hating character. After making several incendiary public statements in the media and at the pulpit, Butts planned a spectacle in which he intended to run over a stack of rap records, CDs, and cassettes with a steamroller. Writing in the editorial commentary section of *Billboard* on June 19, 1993 (following his public-relations event), Butts emphasized that he was not condemning all rap, only those examples that were negative or whose lyrics he personally found repugnant. He explained that he had demurred when it came to destroying the recorded material with heavy equipment, in order to avoid a direct confrontation between his supporters and counterdemonstrators, but he had "dump[ed] those tapes and CDs in front of Sony's midtown headquarters because that recording company is a major contributor to the production of offensive music" (Butts 1993, 9). On the same issue, urban and Top 40 radio stations, including New York's WBLS and KACE Los Angeles, in 1993 declared their opposition to music with derogatory or sexually explicit lyrics and violent themes, creating a restrictive policy that affected rap just as it was gaining new ground in commercial urban radio. BET, MTV, and Video Music Box followed suit, enacting similar no-violence and no-gun policies.

By this point, the controversies surrounding rap, whether related to its content or to the activities of its main artistic producers, had attracted the attention of a prominent black political elite, with the authority of public office, and the clergy, each turning its critical sights on the industry's rap music sector. Clearly, these developments displayed many of the same tendencies and adopted many similar moral arguments to those that had been applied throughout the years to rock music (Martin and Segrave 1993), suggesting that rap was a corrosive cultural force, that it propagated negative values, or that it was a causal factor in incidents of real aggression, illegal activities, and expressions of moral depravity. Among the main historical differences between the earlier anti-rock protests and the 1990s anti-rap movement was race, since many leaders and spokespeople at the forefront of the later anti-rap cause were black. The opposition to rap's obscenities and representational violence in the 1980s had frequently been dominated by a white conservative elite, and the articulations of distaste were commonly framed in racial and spatial terms as the themes of an unruly ghetto underclass. By the early and mid-1990s, not only were black leaders better represented in official capacities, but they were, as they claimed, also defending the integrity of black culture by challenging the expressive forces of rap and decrying what they perceived as rap's potential for psychological damage and the erosion of civility within the teen and preteen minority demographic.

While views on rap were mixed, it is interesting to retrospectively identify the sources of support and encouragement of rap, especially during a period of intense public condemnation of the genre. For instance, in November 1995 the mayor of Compton, Omar Bradley, announced the formation of the Rap the Vote Foundation, aimed at raising the number of registered voters among the black eighteen-to-thirty-five age demographic. Bradley had earlier confronted Eazy-E and N.W.A. for failing to secure civic permits to shoot their videos in Compton's streets, criticizing the artists for disseminating a skewed and inaccurate image of Compton throughout the world. In his announcement Bradley observed that the highest rate of voter nonparticipation tended to be closely aligned with the demographic associated with the highest concentration of rap music consumption. In a guest column in *Billboard* (Bradley 1995, 9), Bradley explained that rap had amply demonstrated its capacity to circulate progressive political messages and to engage its audiences in sophisticated issues. Concurrent initiatives such as MTV's "Rock the Vote" campaign (later titled "Use It or Lose It") provided another context in which rap artists were called upon as spokespeople for a generation of youth who had become disenfranchised in the nation's political structures. Bradley's aim was to generate renewed interest in the democratic process among minority youth by adding their names to the voter registration rosters at the point of entry to a series of rap concerts.

For many white critics, the resistance to rap among the older black middle class was vindication of a sort, but it also presented a context in which white moral defenders and conservative activists could step back from the controversy, absolving themselves of responsibility by letting their black counterparts take up the battle on their behalf. For their part, many of the more ardent white cultural critics returned their attentions to rock music, later focusing their ire on the shock rocker Marilyn Manson. The racialization of the struggle against rap had resulted in the separation of the conservative white and black cultural watchdog movements as each camp developed its own strategies and discourses, which were then applied to the ostensible protection of their children or their cultural identities.

Representative Cardiss Collins (D-Illinois) called for an official House committee hearing on "controversial sound recording lyrics in the last ten years" (Holland 1994, 1). It was not officially intended as a hearing on rap, although his later comments isolated rap as a major focal point. Collins, who chaired the Subcommittee on Commerce, Consumer Protection, and Competitiveness, stated, "You have to have concerns when you find young people listening to these lyrics. Most of them understand it's just a lyric to a song. I'm of the belief that they're more concerned about the beat, the cadence of the rap than the violence, but I want someone to tell me at a Congressional hearing so that I can have a record of it for the U.S. government, whether or not this is the case" (Holland 1994, 103). Along with C. Delores Tucker, the pop singer Dionne Warwick was a prominent presence at the hearings for the anti-rap activists. Congresswoman Maxine Waters of California voiced her support for rap, stating before the committee, "these are my children. . . . I do not intend to marginalize them or demean them. Rather, I take the responsibility for trying to understand what they are saying" (Dawsey 1994, 60). In the spring and summer of 1995, the PMRC also lurched to life again, stimulating further conflict over music lyrics and CD labeling and refocusing political and critical attention on rap content.

Among the main concerns raised by Butts, Tucker, and Warwick was the prevalence of sexist and misogynist discourses in rap. These themes were also often taken up among women in rap, albeit within less conservative and restrictive terms. MC Lyte, Queen Latifah, Salt 'n' Pepa, and Yo Yo, who were regarded as the highest-profile female rap artists at the time, each proclaimed support for the politics of women's empowerment and solidarity against objectification and subjugation by men, albeit inconsistently. Their contributions were almost uniformly ignored by the establishment's older cultural critics, although Yo-Yo spoke in Washington in defense of rap at the committee hearings. Sister Souljah's more astute (and incendiary) political engagement had previously won her the ire of Bill Clinton in June 1992. By the late 1990s rappers including Da Brat, Eve, Foxy Brown, Lauryn Hill, L'il Kim, Missy Elliot, and Rah Digga were redefining gender relations and expressing themes of female confidence and desire (often within highly sexualized contexts that conservative critics and feminists alike found discomforting), while R & B acts such as Destiny's Child and TLC were also generating attention and sales with tracks such as TLC's "Unpretty" and "No Scrubs" (1999, La Face), which advocated female autonomy and independence.

With the imminent release of the Dogg Pound's *Dogg Food* (Death Row/ Interscope) in 1995, Time Warner, which held a 50 percent interest in the group's distributing company, Interscope (which was, in turn, essential in the formation of Suge Knight and Dr. Dre's Death Row Records), sought to delay the album because of fears that its content would alienate stockholders and create a firestorm of controversy reminiscent of the corporation's earlier publicity dilemma involving Body Count's *Cop Killer*. Tucker purchased stock in Time Warner, enabling her to gain access to the company's annual shareholders meeting. There she took the floor and roundly harangued top executives for maintaining ties with artists and independent labels—especially Death Row—that trafficked in the imagery of aggression and sex.

The moral controversies surrounding Death Row Records were undoubtedly the most intense at the time, often taking absurd turns. For example, in August 1995 it was reported that following her high-profile public-relations campaign against gangsta rap and Time Warner's involvement, Tucker had intended to start her own distribution company, attempting a behind-the-scenes takeover of Death Row that sought to sever the label's relationship with Interscope. Both Interscope and Death Row initiated their own lawsuits targeting Tucker for her actions, although the Death Row countersuit revealed more deeply strained relations with Time Warner by naming its CEO, Gerald Levin, and Michael Fuchs, head of the Warner Music Group, as coconspirators. The conflict eventually led Interscope into negotiations to either repurchase Time Warner's stake in its operations or seek a new corporate partner. In 1995 Time Warner surrendered its co-ownership position with Interscope, though it maintained its distribution arrangement with the label and, under Warner-Chappel, the publishing rights to Death Row material (Cashmore 1997, 168). While early 1995 saw an abundance of gangsta rap releases, by the end of the year there was an observable decrease in the prevalence of explicit gangster themes. Within the industry it was widely speculated that the attacks by various conservative forces, including the Republican senator and 1996 presidential candidate Bob Dole, had continued to exert a chilling effect, especially among the larger corporate distributors, and in some cases contributed to self-censorship among artists who were eager to have their material released to the general market without controversy or restrictions.

In early 1996 Time Warner's 50 percent stake in Interscope was purchased by the Seagram-owned MCA Music Entertainment Group (part of the Universal Music Group, which has since been absorbed by the Vivendi Corporation of Spain), with options to purchase the remaining stake at a later date. MCA-Universal's CEO, Doug Morris, who had been fired from his position as CEO at Warner Music the previous year, stressed that Interscope's real value had been overshadowed by its politicized struggles with high-profile representatives of the conservative Right and that the critical emphasis on Interscope's rap roster and its distribution arrangements with Death Row records had obscured the full range of artists and genres carried by the label. By the end of 1996, Universal Music Group was also embroiled in disputes with Tucker, the conservative critic William Bennett, and Democratic Senator Joseph Lieberman, who continued their attacks on the lyrical content of the works of artists (including Marilyn Manson, Tupac Shakur, Snoop Dogg, and Crucial Conflict) released through Interscope or Universal. In a further chapter in the complicated situation, C. Delores Tucker initiated legal proceedings to sue the estate of the late Tupac Shakur on the grounds that he had slandered her on his multi-platinum Death Row release *All Eyez on Me*. Her suit named both corporate entities, including Death Row, Interscope, Time Warner, Seagram, and Tower Records, and various individuals. Among Tucker's allegations of "defamation of character and reputation" was the assertion that the duress of Shakur's invective had caused her husband to suffer "a loss of advice, companionship, and consortium" ("C. Delores Tucker Sues Tupac's Estate" 1997, 18).

Deliberately timing their attack to coincide with the profitable Christmas sales season, William Bennett and his colleagues castigated the CEO of Seagram, Edgar Bronfman, for allegedly breaking a vow to withhold the release of recordings featuring what they perceived as controversial or offensive content. In a similar motion to weaken the resolve of corporate executives, in April 1997 the chairman of the Texas finance committee, Bill Ratliff, proposed a bill that would forbid the state from investing public funds in media companies that released recordings deemed offensive (within rather narrow parameters of taste and judgment). This followed a similar bill that had earlier been defeated in Maryland. Ratliff had also previously persuaded the Texas state school fund to divest itself of $3.5 million in Seagram stocks after the Seagram-owned Universal Music Group obtained its 50 percent stake in Interscope records. With the established precedence of successful and potentially costly protests, boycotts, and legal challenges, corporate executives, who were responsible for ensuring stability in their companies and consistent returns to shareholders, indicated their intentions to more closely assess their commitments to rap.

Touring toward 2000

The 1996 Harvard Consultation Report on Urban Music explicitly links concert performances and touring with the development of artists' long-term careers and describes the value of live performances in building a loyal fan base. As the report states, the conditions of inequality within the concert industry and numerous shortcomings on the part of promoters and artists themselves contribute to a weakened urban concert infrastructure. While the constraining influences of violent or aggressive incidents at rap concerts had debilitating effects on rap's concert status through much of the 1990s and created further barriers to the genre's tour schedules, rap tours were not altogether stifled.

The headliners of the 1996 Smokin' Grooves tour, sponsored by the House of Blues, included the Fugees, Cypress Hill, Busta Rhymes, A Tribe Called Quest, Spearhead, and the reggae artists Ziggy Marley and the Melody Makers. Billed as a "black Lollapalooza," the tour drew teen audiences from across the racial spectrum and was commercially successful, sending a message to the industry that hip-hop could still be delivered in live concert settings without threat of violence or other disruptions. Furthermore, the tour's consistent organization and professionalism was reproduced at each venue, diminishing some of the negative images ascribed to rap artists and promoters. Some analysts conceded, however, that the inclusion of the tour's closing act, the Marley clan, was a necessary capitulation designed to assuage fears among nervous venue managers and local promoters who were more comfortable with the "laid-back" attitudes and demeanor of the popular reggae act. Even after the successful execution of a second Smokin' Grooves Tour the following year, many rap promoters continued to struggle against the pervasive restrictions instated at many venues and faced insurance rates up to 75 percent higher rates than those charged for rock or pop concerts.

In July 1996 *Billboard* touted the revival of consumer interest in funk, largely because of rap producers' sampling of vintage funk from a substantial archive. On the strength of market indicators such as CD catalog reissues and sales of "greatest hits" compilations, several old-school funk and R & B package tours were mounted that had cross-generational and pronounced cross-cultural appeal, tapping into a strong vein of nostalgia for a more mature audience segment while benefiting from surging support among teen hip-hop audiences. The rekindled interest and commercial potential also enabled increased activity in studios as several classic funk acts recorded new albums, including Cameo, George Clinton and P-Funk, Con Funk Shun, the Gap Band, the Isley Brothers, and the Ohio Players. Further reflecting the links between hip-hop artists and their funk predecessors, Charlie Wilson of the Gap Band signed a contract with Snoop Dogg's Doggystyle Records, was featured prominently throughout his 1996 release *Tha Doggfather* (Death Row), and appeared with him in live performances.

The year 1998 proved to be an active one for hip-hop concerts, with several major tours, including the Elements of Hip-Hop tour (featuring the headliners Common and Rahzel of the Roots and the DJ crew the X-Ecutioners), the annual House of Blues Smokin' Grooves Tour (starring Public Enemy, Gang Starr, Wyclef Jean's Refugee All-Stars, Canibus, and Black Eyed Peas), and the Survival of the Illest tour (with DMX, Onyx, and the Def Squad, among others). The year's top-grossing traveling rap show, Puff Daddy and the Family's No Way Out tour featuring Mase, L'il Kim, the Lox, Jay-Z, Busta Rhymes, Foxy Brown, and the R & B acts Dru Hill, 112, and Usher, stands as a turning point for the touring and promotions sectors, indicating in no uncertain terms that rap presented a viable commercial option in large venue concerts and that it could compete with other major tours on the circuit. In 1999 the Hard Knock Life Tour, headed by Jay-Z, DMX, Method Man, and Red Man, further affirmed the positive commercial message communicated by No Way Out. It was the highest-grossing rap tour ever and generated acclaim as much for its orderliness and violence-free atmosphere as for its celebrity performances and box-office clout.

For agents, promoters, and tour organizers, however, the rapid turn-over of stars and the continuing dilemma of a relative paucity of durable career rap artists also complicated rap's development in the concert realm. As Carl Freed, promoter of the largest regular rap concert production, Summer Jams, noted in *Billboard*, rap tours suffered from lapses in professionalism, experience, and showmanship, all of which require education and skill development:

There's not much longevity in the field. From the record label standpoint, they're not into lengthy careers. They put it out there to sell as many records as they can and move on from there. . . . The artists need to know how shows should work: requests for backstage passes are out of control, time factors are ignored. . . . I think there is an audience out there for straight rap tours, but it is a matter of controlling the artists. (Samuels 1998, 45)

Freed's concerns were realized with the much heralded Ruff Ryders–Cash Money Tour in the spring of 2000.

Seeking to draw on the artists' current market appeal and to bridge the aesthetic and regional differences encompassed by the Ruff Ryders and Cash Money labels' rosters, DMX, Eve, the Lox, and Drag-On represented Ruff Ryders, and the Cash Money Millionaires were represented by the Big Tymers and the Hot Boys, featuring Juvenile, L'il Wayne, B.G., and Turk. Promoters boasted of the tour's unprecedented scale: it had the highest overhead and production costs ever for a rap tour (estimated at $100,000 to $150,000 weekly). Indeed, in the first third of the forty-one-date tour, box-office figures for the consistently sold out arena dates outpaced the per-show figures from the previous year's Hard Knock Life tour by almost two to one (grossing approximately $500,000 per city, according to concert trade insiders). The tour was designed and staged to conform to the performative logic of high-end rock concerts, employing pyrotechnics and large stage props, yet even with its ample budget, the concert staging was assailed in several postconcert reviews for its uneven pacing and an overall lack of substance.

When the tour arrived in Boston for a two-night engagement, with an added appearance by Boston's top rap act, Made Men (featuring former members of Almighty RSO), the *Boston Globe* ran a lengthy feature article touting the unique character of a two-label tour and its theme of mutual support. The discourse of unity across geographic and cultural differences was mobilized by the tour's promoters and by spokespeople for Ruff Ryders and Cash Money Records as they proclaimed that the event had the potential to overcome the common production posse rivalries and regional animosities that frequently cause deep rifts in the hip-hop nation. The CEO and president of Ruff Ryders, Joaquin Dean, stated, "We come from similar backgrounds. . . . We know what family is. Hip Hop is gonna benefit from the touring piece of this, because they're seeing the unity, as far as us collaborating and not fighting" (Anderman 2000a). While the first show, before a sold-out house at the city's Fleet Center arena, unfolded without incident, the following night's concert, on April 3, was marred by a backstage fight between various members of the performing acts and their posses, resulting in the stabbing of five people and the cancellation of the show in mid-concert.

Front-page commentary in the local press the following day was reminiscent of the coverage of Run-D.M.C.'s 1986 Raising Hell tour, with the *Boston Herald* running the headline "Stabbing Melee Erupts at Concert" (Sweet 2000) and the *Boston Globe* announcing "Several Stabbed as Rap Groups Brawl at Show in Fleet Center" (Yaekel and Latour 2000). Nowhere in the media's coverage was it stated that despite the concert's disruption, the 5,500 members of the teen-dominated audience in the front of the house remained calm during the backstage events, of which the audience was not even aware. Few of the media reported that there was no trouble or cause for police intervention among the mixed-race crowd of Boston youth; it was only in the following days that reports more directly emphasized that the incident had remained isolated in the backstage area. Articles over the next two days attempted to establish the cause of the violence, but media and police alike were met with resistance and suspicion by those involved, reinforcing an image of uncooperativeness in the eyes of mainstream authorities and venue management. Several days later, Made Men hosted a brief press conference at which they assailed the Boston police force and the media for unfairly vilifying them, the tour, and rap music.

After the incident, tour promoters acknowledged that intensified scrutiny of the tour by the media, venue managers, insurance brokers, and local law enforcement agencies would surely ensue, leading to the voluntary cancellation of several subsequent engagements and allowing the promoters to refocus the artists and reorganize security (Anderman 2000b; Graham 2000). They were also cognizant of the possibility that the backstage violence could further inflict damage on rap itself, communicating to the public that the genre remained a facet of a volatile cultural domain and that the barrier between representational violence and actual, realized violence was, under certain conditions, quite permeable. As the summer 2000 concert tours were announced, the most eagerly anticipated hip-hop package heading toward arena-size venues was the Up In Smoke tour. The show, featuring Dr. Dre, Ice Cube, Exhibit, Snoop Dogg, Warren G, and Dr. Dre's protégé, Eminem, was an unqualified success, and it was deemed, apart from minor incidents, violence-free. The tour was also a boon to Eminem's CD sales: following a late spring 2000 release, *The Marshall Mathers LP* (Aftermath) sold over 1.5 million copies in its first week, reaching sales of over 7 million units by January 2001. Dr. Dre's *Dr. Dre 2001* (Aftermath) was itself an unmitigated success, surpassing the sales of his earlier release, *The Chronic,* and selling over five times platinum by the end of the year. Still, rap's reputation for violence was again reinforced in August 2000, when, during *The Source* magazine's prestigious Hip-Hop Music Awards, the program was disrupted by a fight that started in the audience and spilled over onto the stage. The cable network UPN, which was filming the program, excised the footage of the brawl and aired the "clean version" the following week without going into the details of the incident.

The New Hip-Hop "Moguls": Suge Knight, P. Diddy, and Master P

For over twenty-five years Berry Gordy's Motown Records stood as the ultimate measure of black entrepreneurial success in the music industry. Rap entrepreneurs had embraced and emulated the Motown model; for example, referring to Eazy-E's industry aspirations as CEO of Ruthless Records, the label executive Jerry Heller suggested that "Eazy was interested in being Berry Gordy" (Powell 1996, 48). An article in the May 1995 issue of *The Source* on Death Row's Suge Knight featured the headline "At Age 28, Suge Knight Has Helped Dr. Dre Establish What Many Are Calling the New Motown." Similarly, Sean Combs explains of his early forays into the music industry, "I was an entrepreneur and a businessman. . . . I knew I wanted to get to a point of Berry Gordy and Quincy Jones" (Gilmore 1997, 54).[2] Interviews among rap producers and label owners commonly cite the Motown label's cultural influence and the historical precedence of Gordy's corporate authority and autonomy, idolizing his methods of grooming and training his acts and his ability to cross-market acts under the Motown logo, idealizing the wealth that he amassed, and admiring the Motown legacy. Older industry veterans also seized on Motown's influence, cautioning this new, younger rap contingent against overlooking or ignoring the staying power of R & B in view of the comparatively short-lived successes of most contemporary rap acts. They pointed out that Motown's vast R & B and soul catalog had sustained the label as it sought more current urban acts, and, they believed even contemporary R & B had a more lasting or timeless potential than rap. The extensive archival catalog was also essential to sustaining the label's brand identity after it was sold (with the master recordings and artist contracts) to Boston Ventures and MCA in 1988. The catalog was also a crucial element of the label's continued relevance through the transitional process as the industry shifted from vinyl and cassettes to CD technologies.

From a business and marketing perspective, Motown's highest achievement could be isolated in the successful branding of the company and its "products"—the music and musicians whose recordings were released under the Motown logo. Motown was easily and instantly recognizable for the consistency of its product and for its meticulous production standards, which aimed firmly at the status quo of the pop charts and at the white consumer market. With Motown, Gordy capitalized on the standardized sound and quality ensured by a stable of excellent (and regularly underpaid) studio musicians and a roster of carefully trained artists with polished performance skills, establishing a powerful brand identity that made the label stand out from others in the industry.

As Nelson George writes, "All of a sudden, in the early months of 1965, the record industry began wondering what was happening in Detroit. . . . In 1964, something else had happened. Motown had a sound" (1985b, 102). While the attention to racial issues and black empowerment granted by scholars and historians in discussions of Motown's influence is not misplaced, the notion of market branding and product positioning is rarely defined or explicitly engaged (though the intertwined issues of "selling soul" and the commercialization of black expression are). Motown products competed in the market against the white-sourced pop music of the period, but it was also necessary for Gordy to locate his label's music in a competitive market alongside black independent labels such as Stax and Philadelphia International Records. Gordy understood, perhaps better than his competition, that corporate and product branding were essential to developing Motown's commercial image, and the label's contemporary legacy is related, to a considerable extent, to brand recognition among audiences and consumers across the racial spectrum (especially those of an older, postwar baby-boom demographic).

It is also significant to note that Motown drew its name from its sited base of operations: Detroit, Motor City. Motown, like its independently owned competitors Stax and PRI, was geographically external to the tight and incestuous industry centers of New York and Los Angeles, a factor that was repeated in hip-hop throughout the mid- to late 1990s, when influential and innovative new rap labels emerged with force from Atlanta or New Orleans. Motown also spoke to the production-line sensibilities of the city's industrial sector, churning out a relatively standardized product with efficiency and precision and distributing it nationwide for mass consumption. In this regard, Berry Gordy was not only in touch with the wider music industry and popular youth tastes, but also displayed an interesting affiliation with Detroit's distinct localized character. As Nelson George (1985b) and Gerald Early (1995) observe, the start of Motown's erosion coincided with the executive decision to uproot the label from its Detroit home between 1970 and 1972, transplanting its base of operations to Los Angeles, where Gordy hoped to more fully exploit the entertainment industry's resources in an attempt to diversify his corporate interests.

Despite its status as a powerful signifier of black autonomy and creativity in the music business (and, to a far lesser extent, film and television production), Motown's status had continued to decline since the 1970s, especially as the label failed to secure a solid footing in hip-hop. Def Jam subsequently emerged among junior rap entrepreneurs as the new model to emulate, and its longevity was rewarded in the form of "money, power, and respect" (The Lox, 1998, Bad Boy) within the general industry. The headline over Bill Adler's liner notes accompanying the Def Jam Tenth Year Anniversary four-CD set (1995)—"Once Again Like It or Not: The Sound of Young America"—simultaneously acknowledges Motown's long shadow over black music entrepreneurship and a changing of the guard in black musical leadership.

Russell Simmons was lionized for his ability to establish a hip-hop legacy and to build a label that proved capable of surviving the vagaries of the rap market. His strategy, like Gordy's before him, was to create a strong brand identity for the Def Jam label and its various spin-off enterprises. But, as Ellis Cashmore (1997) suggests, Simmons was not ultimately enthralled with Gordy's Motown model of success, which depended on white consumer interest; he envisioned a more powerful and broader entertainment base than Gordy ever attained, allowing for extensive synergy and cross-marketing that more accurately reflected the practices of mega-corporations such as Time Warner. As Simmons explained in *The Source*, "There's all this synergistic opportunity in terms of marketing and positioning. Each company is stronger because of another link. . . . They understand the concept of Def Jam: if it's not for the logo, it's no good" ("Hip-Hop Trinity" 1999, 174).

According to the former CEO of Uptown Records and Motown, Andre Harrell, "Russell was the first to really understand that hip-hop was a culture and as such could be translated into a number of different venues" (Muhammad 1999, 88). Def Jam's brand equity, carefully nurtured and protected as the hip-hop culture grew and evolved, enabled Simmons to develop a broader range of entertainment and fashion ventures, branching out of the music business with companies in the fashion, film, television, advertising, promotions, and publishing sectors, as well as initiating several philanthropic ventures designated to benefit disenfranchised urban youth. In the Tenth Anniversary set, Simmons reinforces the importance of the brand, stating, "The consumer picks our logo out of ten thousand pieces of product and makes a connection. . . . I'm selling the Def Jam way of life."

The transition from a model of success based on Gordy's Motown to one based on Simmons's Def Jam is thus important from a generational perspective, with the successful rap upstarts Suge Knight, P. Diddy, and Master P, among others, ascending as independent label owners over the course of the decade. Dubbed the new hip-hop moguls by the media, they established distinctive production and promotional standards by alternately introducing innovative aesthetics (constructed around the stylistic trademarks of their respective in-house production teams, which, within typical corporate branding strategies, ensure consistent product standards); a system for inexpensively producing and distributing films, videos, and accompanying sound tracks featuring their label artists; and importantly, developing strategies for the merchandising of ancillary name-brand commodities (especially clothing and fashion accessories) that conform to or influence teen consumer patterns.

The distinction between many earlier black independent label executives and today's hip-hop entrepreneurs is precisely that they comprehend the wider cultural influences and market opportunities for their companies rather than envisioning them specifically as music labels. As Sean Combs states, "I think that this music is not just a music, it's a lifestyle. I think that people are intrigued by the lifestyle" ("Hip-Hop Trinity" 1999, 173). With greater frequency, new hip-hop entrepreneurs, including artists with their own labels, are strategizing for expansion into other cultural and consumer sectors where hip-hop's styles, forms, and expressions—the elements of the hip-hop lifestyle cited by Combs—can be cultivated on a regional, national, and global scale.

With rap firmly established in the music and entertainment sectors, initiatives to enhance and reinforce artist and entrepreneurial stability and knowledge of the industry acquired crucial relevance. Tales of young, eager, and naive black youth signing contracts that, for example, had them exchanging their lucrative publishing rights for jewelry or a single fixed payment were rife in the industry, although it is essential to acknowledge that independent black label owners were not absolved of responsibility in these practices. Seminars such as Howard University's Cultural Initiative Conference (which began in 1990 and ran through a good part of the decade) and other similar conventions or workshops sponsored by the industry press or record labels attempted to educate those entering the music business and to illuminate the complicated industry topography.[3] For example, the seventh annual How Can I Be Down conference, advertised as "the most powerful platform in the history of Hip-Hop and urban culture," was held in London, England on May 11–14, 2000. (The first six had been held in the United States.) The event featured a global roster of artists and industry executives and enjoyed the corporate sponsorship of Motown Records, Island Def Jam Music Group, Loud Records, and *The Source*. In 1992, responding to the plight of young hip-hop artists and entrepreneurs, Wendy Day founded the Rap Coalition, a nonprofit organization dedicated to addressing "the way urban artists are unfairly exploited in the music industry . . . to support, educate, protect, and unify hip-hop artists and producers—in other words, to keep artists from getting jerked" (see its Web page at www.rapcoalition.org). Since then, Day has been involved in renegotiating artist contracts and major-indie label arrangements, including the $30 million deal in 1998 between Universal and Cash Money Records. The 1996 Harvard Consultation Project also identified the need for training at all levels of the industry, acknowledging that while informal training and mentoring have positive effects, the rap and hip-hop sectors were in drastic need of more formal systems. The report quotes Andre Harrell, who states, "In the music business you have to come ready to be trained. It only took Puffy six months to get a label deal because he was properly trained" (Harvard Consultation Project, 1996, n.p.).

As a model for the young crop of independent label owners, Simmons himself concedes that the new generation of hip-hop entrepreneurs harbor considerable industry savvy: "These young guys have way more power, control and access than I ever had" (Muhammad 1999, 88). Access emerged as a crucial element in the growth of rap and hip-hop in the late 1990s, with aggressive young independent-label owners showing sharper business skills and demonstrating in greater numbers that they could navigate the comparatively unpolished terrains of the 'hood as well as the chic ones of corporate meeting rooms, conducting negotiations with major-label executives. The multi-platinum selling artist and co-owner of Roc-A-Fella Records, Jay-Z, explains, "The worst thing to do is put out work that you've been working on for months or years, put it in someone else's hands and see them drop the ball. . . . At least I know that if it turns out right, it's on me, and if it doesn't turn out right, it's on me" (Shawnee Smith 1998a, 36).

By 1999 the industry had experienced another rush of artists establishing their own recording companies, with L'il Kim's Queen Bee Records, Mase's All Out Records, Missy Elliott's Gold Mine, Mos Def and Talib Kweli's Good Tree Records, and Kurupt's Antra Records. The trend usually involved either mid-size independent labels or major labels, which assisted with promotion, marketing, and distribution. In some cases, as with Cash Money Records, the major labels extended the distribution reach of the smaller labels, while the independent label might also be effective in a consultant capacity, helping position major-label releases and other artists in their rosters. This was a more reciprocal arrangement than had been the case previously.

The entertainment attorney Londell McMillan reinforces the sense of an enhanced knowledge of the industry on the part of young entrepreneurs in hip-hop, noting that "it's become part of the hip-hop culture now to become a business mogul. Rappers are talking about everything from recoupment status to publishing percentages and ownership of their music" (Muhammad 1999, 79). Ellis Cashmore offers a cautionary reading of these trends, however, explaining that the proliferation of independent labels with major-label support "signaled a willingness on behalf of the big corporations to invest money in smaller labels in the expectation of medium-term rewards. The corporations risked money; the labels risked autonomy" (1997, 175). He observes that the market pressures and the tithe to major corporate underwriters do not, in the majority of cases, result in independence but present the conditions under which a small-label owner might "become a titular CEO but an effective employee of a major corporation. So it is with the new heads of the black culture industry: media moguls by name, millionaires by bank balance, but paid staff nevertheless" (1997, 176). By the mid-1990s major-label executives and investors recognized the market potential of rap and finally saw the expanded opportunity of selling this popular lifestyle through an integrated marketing approach encompassing several media simultaneously. Through the example set by Def Jam and its early contracts with CBS/Sony, they were made aware that they risked missing out on the swelling retail growth and consumer interest in hip-hop unless they opened their doors to the new generation. This also meant signing contracts with untested entrepreneurs seeking joint venture deals and investor funding to capitalize on their familiarity and connections with the cultural locus of the 'hood. Some of these were committed to "long money" and an industry career, while others were hoping for "flash cash" and a rapid payoff.

Suge Knight and the "Untouchable" Death Row Records

The Los Angeles–based Death Row label established a corporate brand that was steeped in the image of the 'hood. It dominated the hardcore spectrum of the rap genre by amplifying the discourses of 'hood life and the gangster ethos. Its cofounder and CEO, Marion "Suge" Knight, rapidly earned a reputation in the industry for merging 'hood-oriented survival skills with a corporate leadership style that many viewed as a case study of domination through intimidation and coercion. When Knight started Death Row in 1992 with cofounder Dr. Dre and the investment security of Jimmy Iovine's Interscope Records, he inherited the mantel (once held by Eazy-E and Ruthless Records) of head of the industry's top gangsta rap label, rising above Ruthless, Rap-A-Lot, and other independent labels specializing in the gangsta subgenre. At the label's inception, industry analysts acknowledged that Death Row's major coup from a business perspective was its relatively unorthodox deal with Interscope permitting Knight to retain ownership of Death Row's master recording tapes. This provided the label with an essential asset that eluded many start-up labels, especially those with major financial investments by larger corporate entities. According to Knight, "The first thing to do was to establish an organization, not just no record company. I knew the difference between having a record company and having a production company and a logo. First goal was to own our masters. Without your master tapes you ain't got shit, period" (Powell 1996, 46). The goal of maintaining ownership of master tapes has since become a primary objective among hip-hop entrepreneurs and independent-label owners and constitutes a central facet of negotiations between start-up labels and the larger corporate entities that underwrite their operations.

Profiled in the media, Knight's personal history was commonly delineated in spatial terms, and his connections and loyalties to his neighborhood and the streets from which he came were regarded as key elements to understanding his business persona. For example, *The Source* wrote of Knight: "Originally from the gang-infested streets of Compton (where he continues to maintain a presence to this day), Suge managed to escape some of the drama of the 'hood and enrolled in college" ("The G-Funk Family" 1995, 57). A former varsity football player who went on to play professionally in the National Football League, Knight applied his physical size to his later role as a bodyguard for several artists in the music and entertainment industry, where he is said to have gained his early connections and knowledge of the mechanics of artist contracts and the business. Knight's propensity for surrounding himself with a formidable posse, many with unambiguous gang ties and local turf affiliations, and the legal wrangling surrounding his two top marquee artists, Tupac Shakur and Snoop Dogg, reinforced his image as a threatening force and an industry anomaly.

In *Vibe* magazine, Knight's interviewer, Kevin Powell, self-reflexively observes how the Death Row CEO's street sensibilities pervaded his corporate practices: "I can't help but notice how utterly simple and *ghetto*—in the sense that the underclass has always done what it takes to survive—his logic is" (Powell 1996, 46). Knight himself reflects this point, exclaiming, "Ghetto politics teaches you how to win and really be hungry" (47). The street and the industry boardrooms both represent harsh environments, potentially hostile loci in which negotiations can be highly aggressive, though not explicitly violent. Violent intimidation, strong-arm tactics, and physical threat, however, were considered to be well within Knight's repertory of negotiation "skills" as he methodically assembled his artist roster (Ro 1998). For his part, Knight defended his management style and industry reputation as a matter of "keeping it real," reproducing the ethos of the street and the 'hood that was crucial in his formative stages and that also formed a common thread among his top recording acts. Death Row's brand identity was, as a result, closely linked with the corporate character of the label and its executive leadership, not solely with the content and discourses of gangsterism and 'hood life that provoked most of the attention and controversy in the mainstream media and among cultural watchdogs.

The demise of Death Row came about following a series of grave misfortunes, including the conflicts between its artists (especially between Dr. Dre and Tupac Shakur), various contract disputes between artists and Knight, the ongoing battles with major-label distributors who were leery of carrying Death Row's product, and the unhealthy environment at the label's office and studio complex owing to tensions among posse members with competing gang allegiances (Ro 1998; Marriott 1999). Critics and rap industry observers sensed that the strange and precarious balance between professional ethical standards and the 'hood ethos had tipped drastically toward the latter, throwing the label into a state of perpetual crisis. In 1996 Death Row's co-owner and production ace, Dr. Dre, hastily departed from the label, citing the corporate uncertainty of the previous year, the distractions of the pervasive posse contingent in the studios, and an increasingly tense and dangerous atmosphere on the national front as the label intensified its battle with rappers from New York, specifically those connected with Combs's Bad Boy Entertainment. Later the same year Dre started his own label, Aftermath Records, in a joint venture with Jimmy Iovine's Interscope Records. His first release in 1996, *Dr. Dre Presents . . . the Aftermath,* met with mediocre sales by Dre's standards, but with the release of Eminem's triple-platinum CD, *The Slim Shady LP,* and a solo effort, *Dr. Dre—2001,* in 1999, both his production talents and his business acumen were applauded within the industry.

In September 1996 Death Row's 'hood ethos was further embraced, and the label began its rapid slide from the pinnacle of the rap industry. Following a fight between the Death Row entourage, including Knight and Shakur, and a patron at the MGM Grand Hotel in Las Vegas (who was allegedly affiliated with a Los Angeles branch of the enemy Crip gang), Shakur and Knight were fired on in the streets. Shakur was mortally wounded and died six days later. Knight's involvement in the earlier fracas had been captured on the hotel's video surveillance monitors, and he was later sentenced to prison for parole violation, effectively ending his capacity to function as Death Row's CEO on a daily basis and severely debilitating the label. In 1997, with Knight already incarcerated, the rapidly unraveling Death Row came under federal grand jury investigation for alleged business improprieties and other criminal activities, including laundering of capital assets derived from drug deals. Though the investigation did not target Interscope Records, artists, producers, and several other smaller business associates were presented with subpoenas.

New Orleans–based No Limit Records later obtained Snoop Dogg's contract from Death Row, and the label's roster of lesser-known artists gradually drifted away to seek new contracts elsewhere. At the time of Death Row's demise, Knight was in negotiations with Eric B (of the once-influential act Eric B and Rakim) to establish an East Coast presence with a Death Row branch office in New York. Even though a handful of CDs were released between 1997 and 1999 under the Death Row logo, including commercially successful recordings by Tupac, sound tracks, and greatest-hits packages such as the compilation CD *Chronic 2000* (1999), the label has since been assailed by lawsuits launched on behalf of several former employees, artists, and Shakur's estate, all seeking remuneration for their work or recordings. Upon Knight's well-publicized prison release in August 2001, he announced he had changed the label's name to Tha Row and was planning to resume leadership of the dormant operation.

P. Diddy's Bad Boy Entertainment

Sean "P. Diddy" Combs projects a rather different image than Knight, having been variously portrayed in the media as an earnest but eager former party promoter and intern who worked his way to the top of the rap industry; as a focused entrepreneur with a vision of corporate success; as an arrogant artist, opportunist, and eager social climber; and as a top hip-hop producer with a proven ability to showcase the talent of others while maintaining a keen sense of popular audience tastes. Combs launched his Bad Boy Entertainment label in 1993 and developed it into an influential market presence in only three years. He had graduated through the independent-label ranks via Andre Harrell's Uptown Records (where he started as a college intern and rose to top executive status) before breaking with Harrell and founding Bad Boy with major financial investment from Clive Davis's Arista Records.[4]

Reflecting on his ambitions, Combs cited his predecessors Berry Gordy, Russell Simmons, and Suge Knight for their ability to effectively carry their artists into the mainstream and to influence the popular culture environment: "Bad Boy was kind of modeled on Death Row because Death Row had become a movement. We wanted to model ourselves behind the record companies that were movements, like Motown, Def Jam, Death Row. These were record companies that were the sound of the culture, and we wanted to become another sound of the culture" (Gilmore 1997, 54). Combs explicitly sought status in the industry: "I strive to be known as a mogul entrepreneur" (Gilmore 1997, 72).

The industry initially took notice when Bad Boy was "two for two" after Craig Mack's *Project: Funk the World* went gold and Notorious B.I.G.'s *Ready to Die* went platinum in 1994. Bad Boy's contract with Arista Records gave Combs executive control over marketing and A & R, working within what Combs defined as a nexus where street-savvy production sensibilities, corporate management skills, and his own self-image as a representative of the ideal consuming subject within his target demographic were merged (Reynolds 1995, 18). Bad Boy initially hired a relatively inexperienced staff—most, like Combs himself at the time, were under the age of twenty-five—and the company tended to offer positions to people who, like Simmons and Combs, frequented clubs and were familiar with the street-based impressions among their peer groups. In late 1994, "after catchin' a major ass-whippin' from the West Coast," as Combs described it, New York labels had reasserted their potential for innovation and were displaying a new aesthetic character that borrowed heavily from the melodic character of the West Coast–associated G-funk sound, introducing such compelling rappers as Notorious B.I.G., Jeru the Damaja, and Nas, winning back audiences, and selling more recordings in the process. The general trend toward melodic and R & B–laced rap also assisted Bad Boy's status on radio, facilitating crossover among Combs's artists.

By 1998, with a string of hit singles and albums by Craig Mack, Notorious B.I.G., Mase, the Lox, Faith Evans, and 112, numerous production credits throughout the rap and R & B sector, and his own top-charting compositions, Combs saw Bad Boy Entertainment's total value climb to an estimated $250 million, while he reported personal wealth of over $50 million (LaFranco 1999). When he appeared on the cover of *Forbes* magazine with the entertainment industry's top earner, the comedian Jerry Seinfeld, it was evident that Combs had achieved much of what he had promised: he had an established reputation as one of hip-hop's most skilled label executives, and he was a top studio producer and a number-one-charting rap artist.

The *Forbes* feature states that "in the celebrity-driven, hip-hop world of 1990s music, no one manages an image, exploits it, and protects it better than the young man known as Puff Daddy and as Puffy" (LaFranco 1999, 180). Combs's carefully crafted media image is designed to communicate the signs of wealth and achievement, adhering to a formula that includes wearing fur coats or other luxury clothing apparel and baseball caps in a sartorial blending of styles that semiotically positions him between the 'hood and the fashion runway. Creating what eventually evolved into a visual cliché throughout the hip-hop video genre, Combs in his videos is often seen literally throwing money to the wind in a metaphor for the excesses of successful young entrepreneurial capitalists in the late 1990s. Moving through disparate geographic and cultural landscapes, including the contemporary mediascape, Combs has emerged as a mainstream celebrity with considerable brand equity.

After purchasing a mansion in the exclusive Long Island enclave of the Hamptons, Combs was commonly pictured in the company of other top-flight entrepreneurs and a media-friendly social elite that included Martha Stewart and Donald Trump, and in the hip-hop press he was pictured alongside his R & B protégés or, more often, Bad Boy's extended rap posse. Critics (and so-called envious player haters) took issue with Combs, from his regularly cited hubris (as he himself acknowledged to one interviewer, "Sometimes people say I'm cocky and arrogant, but that comes with it") to his formulaic production style, which, in a manner reminiscent of Hammer's earlier successes, featured long, unexpurgated samples of classic cuts by artists including Led Zeppelin, the Police, and Diana Ross. Accusations were rife that his mainstream corporate interests and tireless business drive led him farther and farther from the streets and ghetto sensibilities that remain crucial to the establishment of hip-hop legitimacy. It seemed to many hip-hop industry observers that despite producing a string of charting hits and, in the case of Notorious B.I.G., recording lasting rap classics, Combs was eroding the hardcore essence of hip-hop with his sustained bid for mainstream crossover success.

On March 9, 1997, following a *Vibe* magazine party in Los Angeles, the Bad Boy marquee star Christopher "Notorious B.I.G." Wallace was gunned down as he left the party accompanied by Combs and the Bad Boy entourage. Coming less than a year after Tupac Shakur's murder, B.I.G.'s death further alarmed the music industry, indicating once again that the gangster imagery and violent themes that formed the foundation of much of the hardcore content was not confined to the lyrics alone but in fact had deadly results in the streets. It was not lost on major label executives that rap, more than any other musical genre and industry sector, was beset with issues relating to violent grudges and deep social schisms that were prone to regular, if not necessarily frequent, eruptions. This was not a concern with rap's paucity of professionalism and training that the Harvard Consultation Project cited; it was a matter of an entirely different and critical kind.

Bad Boy lost its most prominent artist just as his sophomore album, *Life after Death,* was released, and spurred both by genuine consumer anticipation and the additional sensationalism and media attention accompanying his death, the Notorious B.I.G.'s album surged to the top of the *Billboard* charts on April 12, 1997, reaching the number one position in its second week. On April 26, the single "Hypnotize" debuted on the *Billboard* Hot Rap Singles and Hot R & B Singles charts at number one and simultaneously appeared on the Hot 100 Singles chart in the number two position, behind Puff Daddy and Mase's "Can't Nobody Hold Me Down" (Bad Boy, 1997). *Life after Death* received substantial critical acclaim (garnering hip-hop's prestigious prize of a five-microphone review in *The Source*) and went on to sell over four million copies in the North American market, making it one of the most successful rap releases of 1997.

By 1998, still reeling from the loss of Notorious B.I.G., Sean Combs and Bad Boy Entertainment encountered a series of setbacks that some insiders speculated could stall the expansion of Combs's various enterprises and restrict his autonomy owing to the pressures of meeting payments on the Arista advances. Although "Missing You" (1997), a tribute single dedicated to B.I.G. featuring Puff Daddy, Faith Evans, and 112 (sampling the 1983 Police hit "Every Breath You Take"), and Puff Daddy and the Family's debut album *No Way Out* (1997, Bad Boy) each reached multi-platinum status, Bad Boy's R & B releases by Faith Evans, 112, and Total in 1998 sold slowly and received lukewarm reviews. In 1999 the multi-platinum-selling artist Mase announced his retirement and left the label, ostensibly to pursue a more spiritual lifestyle following the release of his lackluster sophomore recording. The Lox underwent a much-scrutinized departure from the Bad Boy label in 1999, publicly declaring a desire to sever their ties with Combs to the extent of wearing "Free the Lox" t-shirts in concert and public appearances, in a gesture that recalled Prince's inscription of "slave" on his face during his battle to leave the Warner label years earlier. Following their departure from Bad Boy, the group signed with the competing Ruff Ryders label and appeared on the spring 2000 Ruff Ryders–Cash Money tour.

Generating the most attention, however, were two incidents that seemed to illuminate Combs's own questionable judgment and cast doubts on his executive leadership. In 1998 he faced charges for assaulting the hip-hop producer and Trackmasters Entertainment executive Steve Stoute in Stoute's office, allegedly beating him with a champagne bottle in a disagreement over Combs's guest appearance in a Nas video. In late 1999 and early 2000 he was again before the courts following a nightclub shooting in New York that involved several members of his entourage, including the alleged gunman, the Bad Boy artist Jamal "Shyne" Barrow. Arrested and charged with possession of an unregistered handgun in the ensuing legal proceedings, Combs and his girlfriend, the singer and actress Jennifer Lopez, received prominent media coverage at the local and national levels. Once again rap was on the front pages of the mainstream press and was the lead story on nationally syndicated television news and entertainment programs. The press interpreted Combs's personal indiscretions as an expression of rap's shortcomings, reaffirming the view that the music and the hip-hop lifestyle were the source of violent and antisocial behaviors.

Much of the coverage of Combs's later crises drew links between rap and its historical associations with violence, reproducing the negative images that hip-hop culture has struggled against throughout its existence and introducing a further destabilizing effect that mitigated its widespread popular acceptance. Among critics of rap, and of Combs in particular, there was a pervasive (and distasteful) discourse that suggested that while young black men might leave the geocultural confines of the 'hood, the 'hood could never be purged from their inner selves. In Combs's case, this was framed as a further example of the inherent racial differences that affect society: in a purported case of manifest destiny, Combs's origins had finally caught up with him.

Comparatively unspectacular sales of several Bad Boy recordings, including Combs's own *Forever,* which was released for the Christmas 1999 sales period, contributed to further speculation throughout the industry that Combs and his Bad Boy empire were in a creative and commercial slump. Quoted in *Black Enterprise,* Combs stated, "None of my companies are based on the success of the record company" (Muhammad 1999, 85). In a similar vein, *Forbes* wrote that "he's trying to build an image for a business enterprise, of which his own rap music act is just a part" (LaFranco 1999, 180). The strategically crafted corporate brand image that Combs established was, over the course of a year, tainted; mediocre product sales in Bad Boy's primary business sector, continued diversification into new, unrelated media and leisure ventures, and accompanying bad press weakened the public's and some industry insiders' confidence in Combs's business projections.

In late 1999 Bad Boy released the single "Whoa" and the full-length CD *Life Story* by Black Rob in a bid to reclaim chart position and to introduce a product that would meet the more discerning taste criteria of hardcore rap fans in "the streets." "Whoa" found its intended audience and was heralded as the season's first official street anthem, appearing on mix tapes and receiving considerable airplay on rap radio as well as introducing a new expression into the mainstream lexicon. Much of the CD had been recorded over a year earlier, however, as indicated by the inclusion of the former Bad Boy act the Lox on one track in which they proclaim their support for the Bad Boy label. Though the album was critically praised and performed reasonably well in the market, the slow release schedule suggested that, as with the major labels, Combs's executive control was hampered by the demands of concurrent projects and an overambitious corporate agenda that was affecting his enterprise's music division. His court case ended in a verdict of not guilty, and 2001 continued to show positive signs for Combs's personal and corporate activities with the release of two films in which he had roles (*Monster's Ball,* directed by Mark Forster, and Jon Favreau's *Made*) and his third LP, *P. Diddy and the Bad Boy Family: The Saga Continues* (Bad Boy), which peaked at number two on the Top R & B Albums chart and the Billboard 200 sales chart. By late August, the lead single, "Let's Get It," featuring G. Dep, Black Rob, and P. Diddy, had reached number five on the Hot Rap Singles Chart.

East-West Conflict and Hip-Hop's "Civil War"

Writing in *Billboard* in 1993, Havelock Nelson articulated a growing complaint within the dispersed hip-hop community:

These days, when one group gets involved in an artistic battle with another, what results is a physical confrontation. In some cases, peace summits even have to be called: New York hip hop is taking itself far too seriously. It's this new breed of musicians leading toward a new frontier. Rap may have started in New York, but it has kept on the move elsewhere. The Apple corps had better check itself.

(Nelson 1993b, 31)

Six years later Robert Marriott recalled the shifting poles of dominance in rap in 1993–94, noting that "this aesthetic quarrel between coastal conglomerates turned into a major media event" (1999, 321). In both cases the emphasis is primarily on an aesthetic transition and the different expressive forms that were associated with various artists and labels representing the East and West Coasts where they were based. With the combatants first venting their antagonisms on wax, many regarded the east-west jousting as another example of hip-hop's propensity for competition—tough talk in a public forum where it was left to hip-hop audiences to evaluate the efforts and determine the winner.

The critical theorist David Harvey explains that the spatial aspects of territorial struggle are deeply implicated in struggles of power and that "the denigration of others' places provides a way to assert the viability and incipient power of one's own place" (1993, 23). Moreover, Harvey claims that "defining the other in an exclusionary and stereotypical way is the first step towards self-definition" (27). It appears obvious that the source of hip-hop's internal unrest throughout most of the 1990s radically exceeds agitation based on mere aesthetic differences, as Nelson and Marriott suggest. Rather, the issues were steeped in a deeper sense of place-based identity and were related to power and authority that crossed and merged the physical space of neighborhoods and geographic regions, the spaces of the commercial market, and the representational spaces of the international mediascape.

An example of the competitive bickering of the early 1990s could be witnessed when Luther "Luke" Campbell, of Luke Records, purchased a full-page advertisement in the summer of 1993 claiming that his single, "Cowards in Compton" (1993, Luke Records), was the "diss of the year," a public response to having been slandered on Dr. Dre's "Nuthin' But a G Thang." The tension and intensity of the ad hominem invectives and interlabel animosities shifted, however, as the forums for attack increasingly included contexts for physical encounters. At the Jack the Rapper Family Affair, an industry conference for black music industry representatives held in Atlanta concurrently with the release of "Cowards in Compton," members of Campbell's and Dr. Dre's posses squared off violently, signaling a trend that was to become more common and more deadly. Numerous columns in *Billboard* in the mid-1990s referred to the concerns among industry executives that rap and hip-hop conventions were turning into opportunities for competing artists, labels, and posses to aggressively settle accounts with each other.

The roots of the battle for national supremacy within the hip-hop nation lie in the history of rap itself. The contestatory traditions that once characterized the local MC and DJ battles in the boroughs of New York have, like rap, grown and expanded. That it has taken such a vicious and violent turn is less easily accounted for, yet this also unfortunately remains consistent with the patterns of youth crime and black-on-black gun violence that daily affect the lives of urban teens. In the aftermath of the April 1999 Columbine High School massacre in Littleton, Colorado, and a handful of similarly conceived attacks, the suburbs also constitute potential sites of gun violence and unannounced eruptions of deadly anger.

Following several aggressive physical encounters between opposing label posses, *Rap Sheet* (with a host of cosponsors representing national retailers, independent record labels, and local media outlets) hosted a caucus in October 1994 dedicated to the mission of "Working towards a Unified Hip-Hop Nation." The event illustrated the early efforts among black industry representatives to respond to the regional and place-based tensions that were affecting hip-hop and to establish dialogue to bridge the rifts. The difficulties this endeavor entailed can be related to Paul Gilroy's observation that "though blacks identify themselves as an exploited group, there are marked and important differences between the political cultures and identities of the various black communities which together make up the social movement" (1987, 230–31).

Hip-hop's diverse factions were directly confronting these differences, and in the process they were confronting their own limits of power and authority, reflecting Gilroy's further insight that "when people find themselves unable to control the world, they simply shrink the world to the size of their community" (1987, 232). While the various rap contingents were not necessarily acting in the interests of their wider communities, they were defensively reinforcing the relevance of their 'hoods, their record labels, and/or their regions as a means of exerting control at some spatial level. In their attempt to derail the violence, artists and label executives discussed possible means of ensuring that the increasingly frequent skirmishes between those affiliated with the East and West Coasts remained conceptual, fought through lyrics and recordings rather than spilling into actual violence as the conflicts, which were based in fierce competition, continued to develop.

During the second annual Source Music Awards, held in New York in August 1995, the tensions continued. Los Angeles–based Suge Knight delivered a thinly veiled challenge to New York's Sean Combs, stating "to all the artists out there—don't go with producers who want to dance up in your videos and be stars. Come to Death Row" (Nelson 1995c, 25). The comments, interpreted as a slight not only against Bad Boy (which had experienced an exceptional year of sales and challenged Death Row in the market) but also against the entire New York rap contingent, sparked an immediate response from the East Coast artists and intensified the antagonisms that had been simmering between the Death Row and Bad Boy camps in particular. At this stage, each label emerged as the symbolic representative of the various nonunified coastal forces that were in conflict.

The hip-hop press also helped to frame the rising tensions in spatial and territorial terms, fueling the conflict with speculations about a brewing "civil war." The May 1996 issue of *The Source* features the Los Angeles artist Ice Cube on its cover flashing the West Coast hand sign and sporting a diamond-studded pendant featuring the same image. The accompanying headline reads, "East vs. West: Inside Hip Hop's Civil War." Ice Cube was an appropriate spokesman for the perspective from the west: he had been a founding member of N.W.A., which catalyzed the market onslaught of gangsta rap. At the time of publication of the issue, Ice Cube was involved in a side project with the group Westside Connection (consisting of Ice Cube, Mack-10, and W.C.), which had recorded the single "Bow Down" (1996, Priority) as an aggressive declaration of West Coast supremacy. The following September Suge Knight was featured on *The Source*'s cover under the headline "It Ain't No East Coast/West Coast Thang." Knight disclaims any east-west antagonisms, choosing instead to situate the issue in relation to spatial identities and the pervasive authenticity debate within hip-hop:

It's about ghetto niggas and phony niggas. You got both on both coasts. I'm down with the ghetto niggas on the East coast and around the world 'cause I'm a ghetto nigga from Compton. . . . Now Puffy, that's a phony nigga. He's frontin', tryin' to be somethin' he ain't.   (Ivory 1996, 176)

The September 1996 issue of *Vibe* pictured Notorious B.I.G. and Puffy Combs on its cover. In the article, which ran under the headline "East vs. West: Biggie and Puffy Break Their Silence," the Bad Boy duo proclaims ignorance of the reasons behind Death Row's vicious sentiments toward them. It seemed that the gangster ethic and street posturing that had permeated the rap genre for the previous eight years had blown up and out of the narrow enclaves where it began, first capturing the attention of the hip-hop media and gradually encroaching on the corporate and institutional fiber of the rap scene in ways that seemed much more attuned to the "street" than to "the executive suite" (to borrow Keith Negus's dichotomous distinction).

The east-west conflict and its accompanying outbreaks of vitriol and violence related to bicoastal and interlabel animosities sent a shiver through the mainstream industry and were often cited as a major reason why many corporate labels felt compelled to deal more cautiously with rap. *Rap Sheet's* second conference on unity in the hip-hop nation, held in the fall of 1995, rededicated its focus to the divisiveness that was eroding hip-hop in this period, although cases of east-west aggression in both representational and physical forms of expression continued. In 1995, for example, the Death Row artists Tha Dogg Pound, with guest Snoop Doggy Dogg, flew to New York to shoot a video in support of their track "New York, New York." Rather than being a tribute to the earlier classic by Bronx artists Grandmaster Flash and the Furious Five, the video featured the visually enhanced Death Row artists crashing through New York, laying waste to the East Coast rap mecca. During the filming of the video, they were the intended targets of gunfire from an unsuccessful drive-by assailant.

The rising concerns were not solely confined to the music industry; at a conference convened in Philadelphia in 1996, the top leadership of the National Association for the Advancement of Colored People intervened to assist in settling disputes between Bad Boy and Death Row as the aggression intensified. Later, Louis Farrakhan, of the Nation of Islam, also offered his services to help broker a resolution in the disputes. Members of the old school—hip-hop's rap, graffiti, and break-dancing pioneers—also expressed their sadness and intention to mend differences, noting that while stylistic and discursive distinctions between artists, producers, and their labels were indeed evident and influential, hip-hop had always accommodated differences of this nature.

One underlying reason for hip-hop's civil war was the belief among artists, producers, and label owners associated with each bicoastal region that neither was receiving sufficient respect from their counterparts.[5] Early California rappers had been explicit in their appreciation and respect for New York artists and the cultural heritage they engendered, although as the market shifted and hip-hop emanating from New York fared less well in the market, regionally dispersed artists sought and failed to receive what they deemed due credit from their eastern rap peers. Ice Cube explains, "It's about what we got to do to get some respect here. We sold platinum and we can rhyme with the best of them and we are not getting our due. . . . New York does not set the standard for hip hop. People need to know that and understand that hip hop is coming out of everywhere" (Hinds 1996, 52–53). According to this rationale, the East Coast biases of the culture industries and the more deeply entrenched connections between various media organs (including magazine publishers and television networks based in New York City) and rap artists produced an environment in which hip-hop producers from the West Coast and other regions were often regarded as unfamiliar and foreign.

Todd Boyd offers an important insight that contributes to an understanding of the expressions of aggression by isolating the yearning for respect in the face of long-term denial of power in one's class background,

which seems to ultimately result in the abuse of power once that person has gained a significant financial and cultural position. . . . It is the mentality of the truly disadvantaged that was formulated in these individuals' childhood and the continued embrace of this mentality long after the circumstances have faded from their lives problematizes their existence. And when these tensions are articulated in public, they tend to be expressed in the same way.   (Boyd 1997, 36)

This perspective does not limit the potential of individuals or social classes to rise above their background, but it does present a viable explanation that does not reside in racial stereotyping or other biased and bigoted interpretations. The codes of the street, which place maximum emphasis on respect and the acknowledgment of achievement, are paramount in this issue, as is the defensive practice of "representing" for one's home turf or territory, especially in the face of perceived disrespect. As Boyd's hypothesis might imply, in the face of chronic, long-standing disrespect individuals will turn the power at hand, no matter how minimal, to their own defense. The failure of artists and hip-hop fans from each coastal region to demonstrate reciprocal respect therefore sowed the first seeds of mutual contempt. The spatial character of the conflict—the emerging civil war across the nation—can, in at least one sense, consequently be traced to the importance of this particular 'hood-oriented sensibility as it was taken up as a cultural factor among young black men from the urban centers of the United States.

A second factor was the ongoing disputes related to market dominance and sales percentages. This had emerged earlier (as I have earlier suggested, harking back to the introduction of N.W.A. in 1988 and Death Row Records in 1992), yet the antagonisms were not expressed in explicit physical violence and murder. The financial rewards accompanying market domination had never been higher, but the rap field was saturated, and the percentage margin for turning a profit was dwindling as more and more recorded product was released and distributed widely. Complicating the matter were two accompanying aspects: the entire music industry was in flux during the late 1990s, and the dominant corporate forces were also experiencing considerable tension and conflict as they sought to gain commercial advantage and global market domination. There was, therefore, a considerable impact on independent labels in all music sectors as these wider industry struggles unfolded. Also, in seeking to secure their positions in discrete markets, the major labels moved quickly and aggressively into each new sector in a highly competitve attempt to dominate. The majors had, by the mid-1990s, awakened to the fuller potentials of rap and were encroaching on hip-hop's cultural terrains, further reducing the market share available to smaller independent companies. Under the effects of corporate investments and other contractual arrangements, the contours of the industry were heavily revised, correspondingly affecting independent urban labels: "like crabs in a barrel trying to escape, black entrepreneurs were prepared to crawl over each other as the major corporations dangled money before them" (Cashmore 1997, 176). One outcome of the situation can be seen with the release of Nas's *It Was Written* on the Columbia Records label (1996); it signaled the first time that a rap recording by an East Coast artist had ever debuted at the number one spot on the *Billboard* Top 200 charts, though the West Coast artists Ice Cube, Snoop Doggy Dogg, and Tupac Shakur, all on independent labels, had done so already.

The logic of the market and the obvious remuneration for success proved to be powerful forces that overwhelmed and displaced the idealistic yet flawed notion of a unified hip-hop nation. As Arjun Appadurai states,

What is new is that this is a world in which both points of departure and points of arrival are in cultural flux, and thus the search for steady points of reference, as critical life choices are made, can be very difficult. It is in this atmosphere that the invention of tradition (and of ethnicity, kinship, or other identity markers) can become slippery, as the search for certainties is regularly frustrated by the fluidities of transnational communication. (Appadurai 1996, 44)

Not only was the use of hip-hop as a "steady point of reference" becoming untenable, but race and place, too, were increasingly regarded as points of irreconcilable difference. Neither the 'hood nor the market were domains of lasting cooperation or unity among black entrepreneurs.

Strong independent labels were also becoming more numerous, and the stakes in asserting a label's identity and attracting consumer interest were high. Failure to effectively brand a record label, to tap into current consumer tastes, and to demonstrate commercial viability with two or three respectable releases (or to demonstrate some other form of commercial promise) generally meant the difference between acquiring major-label financing and distribution for entry into the market on a global scale and continued marginalization on a regional scale. The hip-hop journalist Harry Allen defined the bicoastal conflict in relation to the business environment within which it was structured: "I feel it's highly overrated as a phenomenon. . . . If Suge Knight and Puffy Combs were white people, their story would be called *Hit Men* or *Stiffed*. In any other language, this would merely be called capitalism" (Hinds 1996, 53). Sean Combs concurs with the attitude, explaining in *Rolling Stone,* "To white people, I'm that guy who's in the East-West thing. I'm *not* that motherfucking guy! I'm the guy that every record I produced went platinum. . . . And I'm the guy that wants to make history for my race and wants to be a leader of my race" (Gilmore 1997, 72).

A third contributing factor in hip-hop's internal turmoil involves the growth and success of the genre itself and the enhanced mobility of artists as they toured and traveled the nation. Whereas at an earlier stage in rap and hip-hop's development minimal regional mobility was the accepted norm, by the mid-1990s rap was more lucrative and well established on a broader geographic scale. Owing to higher revenues being taken in by rap labels, better-paid artists, and closer ties to standard music industry practices, those working in the rap sector were more deeply integrated into the circuits and flow of the mainstream culture industries, which also required more frequent travel. With the ascension of hip-hop as a cultural force, there was a corresponding increase in public events associated with hip-hop, creating a context that precipitated greater contact and interaction among artists, producers, and label owners from the nation's urban centers. Contexts in which label posses arrived in full force at parties, music industry conventions, awards ceremonies, and other public events arose more frequently. Under the best circumstances, this contributed to a stronger sense of engagement with other individuals working in the genre. The incidence of violence, however, was also strikingly common as posse members representing the dispersed regional scenes confronted one another with hostility on each other's turf or on foreign turf that neither might claim as "home." The relative distance enabled by battling on recordings was erased, and individuals and their posses converged physically in shared spaces.

When a Death Row colleague was murdered at an Atlanta party for the owner and producer of So So Def, Jermaine Dupri, in September 1995, Suge Knight blamed the death on members of Bad Boy's posse who were also in attendance as invitees. A later public display of aggression between representatives of Death Row and Bad Boy was widely cited following the March 29, 1996, Soul Train Music Awards in Los Angeles, where the Death Row posse, led by Tupac Shakur, allegedly challenged the Bad Boy entourage while a Death Row affiliate wielded a gun in the venue's parking lot. The antagonism between the two labels and their artists was by this point common knowledge, and industry events throughout the country at which both were scheduled to attend acquired an additional layer of tension. Within months, Death Row released Tupac's vicious track "Hit 'Em Up" (the B-side to the single "How Do You Want It"), which explicitly attacked East Coast rappers and the Bad Boy contingent in particular. While the "battle on wax" was within the parameters of acceptable rap practices, the track's vitriol and expressed bitterness left little doubt of Tupac's seething anger and volatility as a soldier defending Death Row's reputation and integrity.

For several years prior to his murder in September 1996, Shakur had been a lightning rod of celebrity controversy, living the "thug life" and adopting the postures of a self-professed "outlaw immortal."[6] He became the newest and most vocal soldier in the Death Row Records posse in 1996, and his hit single "California Love" (recorded with Dr. Dre) clearly stated his regional allegiances. Despite his climbing chart status, he maintained an ongoing bicoastal beef with New York–based Bad Boy Records, its CEO, Sean "Puffy" Combs, and the label's most bankable rap artist, the Notorious B.I.G.

By the time of his death, rumors of the feud between the Bad Boy and Death Row posses were circulating widely, though ongoing police investigations in Las Vegas and Los Angeles indicated that the shooting was almost certainly related to a settling of accounts among Los Angeles Crip and Blood gang sets and was not a conflict between competing record labels. In the aftermath of his death, the sales of *All Eyez on Me* (replete with a cover image of Tupac flashing the West Coast hand sign) accelerated, as did the sales of his earlier releases. Death Row further capitalized on Shakur's passing with rushed distribution of the video for "Life Goes On" (1996, Death Row), which captures the artist's introspective fascination with his own demise. It portrays an angelic Tupac surrounded in heaven by deceased musical luminaries such as Marvin Gaye and Miles Davis.

Following Shakur's death, *Billboard* questioned the legacy of his life and his chosen lifestyle, which was littered with hit releases and criminal charges, in an unprecedented meditation on the tragedy's broader implications. The column, which was far from a eulogy from the industry, interrogated the expression of the "thug life" that Shakur embraced, implicating the industry itself in the promotion and circulation of the images of violence that were central to his oeuvre. However, *Billboard*'s rap columnist, Havelock Nelson, responded to Shakur's demonization in the press as a case of standard procedure when young black men are engaged in violence and murder. Nelson's point is well taken, since the mainstream media tended strongly toward reproducing the litany of wrongs that he had done, yet the hip-hop media identified the balance—and the incredible contradictions—encompassed in his life and art, providing a more fully rounded sense of the man. Still, Nelson also addressed the involvement of the industry:

Since the music industry holds maximum sway with adolescents, it must bear much of the blame for the state of young black culture. It's the industry with a hole in the middle that created the format called "gangsta rap." It has sold artists' Gotti dreams as reality without regard for how the aesthetic gets absorbed into the community. With fewer and fewer veterans working in black music, interacting with fledgling acts, the information needed for growth isn't being exchanged.

(Nelson 1996, 26)

Nelson cites the increasing likelihood that when young rap artists are signed to a label the executives assigned to them will be of roughly the same age; there is seldom any system in place for the training or professional development of artists, let alone the honing of appropriate prosocial skills and attitudes.

Following Tupac's murder in 1996, Dr. Dre left Death Row and commenced recording on the unity track "East Coast Killa/West Coast Killa" (1996, Aftermath) in an attempt to proclaim his neutrality on the issue and to reduce tensions by closing the divide between hip-hop's East and West coasts and between the Bad Boy and Death Row camps. Featuring artists from each coastal region, the accompanying video was also shot on location in New York and Los Angeles. Dre took no chances with the production process lest he be perceived as privileging his West Coast allegiances and further alienate those from the east whose support he sought and needed from a business perspective as he embarked on his new enterprise, Aftermath Entertainment.

Six months after Shakur's death, the Notorious B.I.G. was killed in a similar fashion, gunned down on March 9, 1997, in Los Angeles in what detectives termed a "surgical" drive-by shooting. Once again speculations of an East-West beef circulated within the mainstream and alternative media (and among fans on the Internet), and once again authorities (with little evidence to back their claim) blamed the incident on a gang-related conflict. The media lamented the loss of another rap artist in his prime and made the obvious ties between this incident and the Tupac shooting. The pause within the rap music sector was immediately felt, and artists and executives alike called forcefully for a cease to the conflict and a serious reevaluation of the deadly conditions that were leaving top artists dead at the peak of their careers. In his *Billboard* R & B column, J. R. Reynolds (1997, 18) observed that the immediate outcome of the Notorious B.I.G.'s murder was a chilling effect throughout the hip-hop nation as artists and fans alike reanalyzed the roots of the expression and the attendant ideology of "keeping it real," in the process scrutinizing the east-west rivalry and the absurd extent to which it had apparently evolved.

Appearing on Notorious B.I.G.'s posthumous multi-platinum album release, *Life after Death* (1997, Bad Boy), the track "Going Back to Cali" stands out for the manner in which it slides within the interstices between East and West Coast sensibilities, adapting the title of an earlier LL Cool J track and appropriating several basic sonic characteristics associated with the West Coast sound (most clearly reminiscent of Tupac and Dr. Dre's "California Love"). It is doubtful that this is an homage to the Los Angeles production styles, but neither does it suggest satire or a clear provocation of West Coast artists or those on the Death Row label. Even as Biggie Smalls/Notorious B.I.G. "represents" the East Coast and proclaims his status as the New York rap "don," he still offers respect to his West Coast counterparts, claiming, "If I've got to choose a coast, I've got to choose the East. . . . But that don't mean that a nigga can't rest in the West . . . Givin' L.A. props."

Although the east-west rivalry settled down noticeably following the murders of Shakur and the Notorious B.I.G., defenses of regional authority and domination persisted. The producer and sound engineer David Lotwin explained that from his perspective, "New York is the true essence of hip-hop. . . . This is where it came from. This is where it's real" (Nelson 1997a, 10). Lotwin and others based their perceptions of New York's authenticity on the overall character of the hip-hop scene, with clubs, radio stations, cable access television stations, record labels, and mix-tape producers all functioning in tandem to provide a solid base for the development of new artists and innovative styles.

Many rappers and industry observers were consequently relieved when, in 1997–98, the freestyle phenomenon Canibus and the old-school veteran LL Cool J, both from New York's boroughs, fought a bitter battle "on wax." The lyrical salvos were delivered on LL Cool J's "4,3,2,1" (1997, Def Jam) and "The Ripper Strikes Back" (1998, Def Jam) and Canibus's "Second Round K.O." (1998, Universal). With their return to old-style microphone warfare, the artists demonstrated that disagreements and disputes could still be negotiated in the absence of actual violence or aggression while remaining commercially lucrative. In the years during which the hip-hop's unofficial civil war had intensified, however, labels from several of the nation's regions were quietly emerging as powerful forces in their home market sectors. The earlier assumption that the strongest labels and most innovative artists would necessarily emerge from either New York or Los Angeles was about to be challenged.

Funk and Grits: The Rise of "the Dirty South"

As the antagonisms between the Bad Boy and Death Row camps evolved and regionally affiliated artists representing New York and Los Angeles continued to express their mutual disdain through their recordings, interviews, and personal appearances, hip-hop from the nation's southern geographic and cultural tier was gaining popularity, slowly establishing a firm market and audience base from which to launch new labels and artists. As Tony Green observes, "You could say that, without fear of much contradiction, that southern aesthetics—and by southern, I'm talking about the unreconstructed 'urban/rural' flavor of the Deep South—were central to

'90s hip hop" (1999a, 266). The notion of a "southern" sound requires definitional qualification, however, which, Negus stresses, relates to the ways
in which "particular sounds [are] connected to and come to signify place
identities through quite specific historical circumstances rather than through
any essential connections to a people or piece of land" (1996, 188).

The varied rhythmic and vocal styles emanating from Miami, Atlanta,
Memphis, Houston, and New Orleans through the 1990s and early 2000
generally sounded like nothing else on the charts, creating a crucial alternative to the market's dominant sounds from the two coasts while expressing nuanced distinctions in the manner in which hip-hop culture was lived
and experienced across the South. According to the Harvard Consultation
Project,

there was a time in the music business when being near major metropolitan areas
was important. . . . Many of the reasons to locate near music clusters are no longer
true. In fact, being away from traditional music centers has been an asset for many
Urban Music companies. Clusters create institutional "inbreeding." Thus, bad
ideas and executives are shuttled between different companies in the cluster. . . .
One need not go to rural areas to receive the benefit. In many cases it could be as
simple as moving to an urban area that is growing. . . . In sum, picking a location
could create a distinct culture in the minds of a company's employees and could
make it unique within the industry.   (Harvard Consultation Project, 1996)

In developing artists and promoting them, label strategies had changed little since the earliest stages of rap's development. Independent labels in the
South also started with local and regional promotions and then gradually
worked their product in other regions, commencing with those markets
that indicate potentially receptive audiences.

In September 1994 *Billboard* featured a special report on "bass music"
from the southern states, most notably from Florida and Georgia, observing that it was slowly outgrowing its regionalism and meeting success on
radio and at retail throughout the United States as independent labels such
as Bellmark, Luke, and Pandisc were joined in marketing hip-hop's bass
subgenre by such major labels as Columbia, Island, and Epic. Through the
mid-1990s bass continued to expand regionally; the prominent Florida DJ
Magic Mike appeared in a nationwide Coca-Cola commercial and performed on the Trunk Funk Tour, featuring the 69 Boys, 95 South, and Dis
'n' Dat, which kicked off in Orlando in April 1995. Frequently distinguished
by their graphic representation of scantily clad women, often draped over
elaborately customized or "tricked-out" cars, bass CDs presented an alternative image within hip-hop, turning the discourse away from the street-
tinged themes of gangsta rap through engaging call-and-response chants
that had none of the characteristics for which New York acts were renowned.
Producers and artists also avoided the popular, comparatively lazy G-funk

rhythms in favor of hyper, quickened rhythm tracks, constituting an entirely unique regional aesthetic that was gaining sales momentum across the nation. In distributing bass recordings, the standard efforts geared toward independently owned retail outlets and major retail chains alike were complemented by a distribution structure that included car audio sales outlets and automobile stereo customizing centers. Bass promoters observed that because of the specific contexts of listening to the music in cars (or at home with sophisticated equipment), its main consumers were often skewed toward middle-class and slightly older demographics.

Houston-based Rap-A-Lot Records, founded by CEO James Smith in 1987, is regarded as a groundbreaking label (along with Luther Campbell's Luke Records) in opening the southern rap market. By the mid-1990s Rap-A-Lot was an established mainstay of the rap music industry, having built a regional empire around the chart successes of the Geto Boys and solo releases by the group's most prominent member, Scarface, among others. Smith had formed the label with no prior experience in the recording industry, but after consulting with Lyor Cohen, then a top executive with Def Jam, in New York, he developed a strategy to position Rap-A-Lot as a central entity in the southern rap scene. As Smith's small roster of artists slowly tapped into the southern audiences' musical tastes, displaying aesthetic and thematic content that resonated with local and regional consumers, the label gradually overcame regional radio's resistance to rap unaffiliated with either New York or Los Angeles and earned a favorable reputation in the wider industry. An example of Smith's status in the industry was his role as host for *The Source*'s Gangsta Rap Summit (June 1994), which was attended by rappers from the Northeast, the South, and the West Coast. As Rap-A-Lot's profile rose, it became a beacon for many southern rap artists who were geographically and culturally distant from the bicoastal poles of New York and Los Angeles.

Tony Draper's Houston-based Suave House label, formed in 1988, emerged within the same regional terrain as its main competitor, Rap-A-Lot, whose dominance of the Texas market was largely unchallenged. Initially lacking a top act to anchor the label, Draper signed Eightball and MJG, a Memphis rap duo, and released their debut album, *Coming out Hard*, in 1993. On the strength of sales by these two artists, who released albums in 1993, 1994, and 1995, Draper was able to sign several more southern acts, which solidified his reputation and status in the southern regional rap market while attracting new audiences on a national scale. In 1998 Suave House released Eightball's solo project, an unprecedented triple CD effort titled *Lost,* which was critically well received.

Atlanta's Ichiban Records began as an independent label that boasted a roster including the 1960s R & B stalwarts Curtis Mayfield, Clarence Carter, and William Bell, but serendipity led Ichiban's president, John Abbey, into rap after he secured initial distribution rights to Vanilla Ice's surprising multi-platinum release, *To the Extreme*. The label was instrumental in creating "an explosion for the record in the Southeast and Midwest." Abbey then capitalized on his new market connections in rap, distributing MC Breed's *Ain't No Future in Yo Frontin'* (1991, SDEG) before forming WRAP records, Ichiban's rap imprint (Nathan 1993). Bellmark Records, headed by the former Stax Records executive Al Bell, had nationwide hits with Tag Team's "Whoomp (There It Is)" and Duice's "Dazzey Duks" in July 1993, each of which displayed pronounced bass-style flourishes. Criticizing the hegemony of New York and Los Angeles corporations, which regarded southern aesthetics as parochial or regionally restricted, Bell recalled his days with Stax, noting, "I was told that you couldn't get Miami bass played or sold in large urban centers. But they told me that I couldn't do it with Otis Redding, Sam & Dave, and Isaac Hayes, so I didn't accept that with Duice" (Rosen and Borzillo 1993, 13). Atlanta was emerging as an important hub in the evolving southern market and as a key production zone from which a new hip-hop aesthetic was audible.

In a special feature on Atlanta's rising independent music scene, *Billboard* dubbed it "the New Motown" (D. Smith 1993, A-3), a city where R & B and hip-hop had transformed the local music industry to an extent that is on par with the alternative grunge influences in Seattle. By the late 1990s, Atlanta labels, including John Abbey's Ichiban Records, Dallas Austin's Rowdy Records, Kenneth "Babyface" Edmonds and Antonio "LA" Reid's La Face Records, and Too Short's $hort Records, were each generating substantial sales of rap, hip-hop, and R & B product on a nationwide scale. In early 1996 Public Enemy's former front man, Chuck D, also announced that his new company, Slam Jamz Recordings (formed with financial backing from Columbia Records), would base its operations in Atlanta, signaling a growing dissatisfaction with the New York music establishment.

Jermaine Dupri's Atlanta-based label So So Def Recording is considered within the industry to be an innovative label with a consistent reputation for hit-making and artist discovery. Despite his tender age (which was the subject of a Dr. Pepper® print advertisement in early 2000), Dupri demonstrated ample market savvy by distributing bass-oriented material (by the So So Def Bass All Stars) geared mainly toward southern regional tastes as well as by generating hit material for hip-hop's wider general market. Recognized primarily for his production skills, Dupri was responsible for launching the careers of the multi-platinum artists Kriss Kross, TLC, Da Brat, and Usher, having signed a distribution contract with Columbia

Records in 1992 when he was only nineteen years old. With the release of his debut solo effort, *Life in 1472* (1998, So So Def), Dupri entered the artist realm as a producer-rapper in a mold similar to that of Dr. Dre and P. Diddy before him.

When interviewed in *The Source,* Dupri contemplated the notion that his southern geographic location constrained his industry profile, rendering him marginal in relation to his East and West Coast competitors. He questioned the extent to which executives in New York and Los Angeles comprehend the different references and southern cultural sensibilities that infuse his work and that of his Atlanta-based peers. His concerns are not without foundation; major-label executives also express regional tastes and sign acts accordingly, as indicated by the vice president of A & R at Elektra, Dante Ross, who in 1993 admitted that he had not signed any West Coast artists to Elektra, "mainly because I live in the east. I'm naturally drawn to sounds from here" (Nelson 1993d, 31). Five years later, Dupri's father, Michael Maudlin—president of the Black Records division at So So Def's parent company, Columbia Records—explained that "because he's in Atlanta, people assume that he's not really a part of the game. That attitude is changing as more people are making [power] moves in the South" (Hopkins 1998, 118).

Atlanta's independent record labels have benefited from several key factors, including the influence of black civic leadership. Mayors, city officials, and business leaders have proved their mettle as able supporters of black enterprise, fostering a working environment in which black and white entrepreneurs might flourish in tandem and often in cooperation. The city's traditionally black educational institutions, Morehouse, Spelman and Clark Colleges, also positively influence the area's cultural character, since they are inhabited by thousands of hip-hop aficionados and cultural taste-makers, some of whom capitalize on their proximity to the burgeoning music production scene in their midst by undertaking internships and work-study positions as a means of entering the industry.

As record labels continued to concentrate in the city, executives noted transitions over a six-year period (roughly from 1992 to 1998) that included the emergence of necessary ancillary services, including a rising number of photographers, artists, designers, and printing and record-pressing companies that served the music industry as it evolved. Despite the growing number of record labels and artists, however, Atlanta's music industry leaders lament that the local concert scene often lags behind that of other urban areas, and that many acts test their skills and their performances on the road rather than in their hometown. The steady influx of musicians and producers from other regions and urban centers has also thwarted the emergence of a consistent identifiable aesthetic—an "Atlanta sound"—or a pronounced production style with which individual studios or labels might be strongly associated. Finally, the apparent reluctance among major labels to establish black music division headquarters or satellite offices in Atlanta is an issue, as *Billboard* reported (Reynolds 1996a, 19), and the ancillary music industry services, while growing, still remain far fewer than those in other major music centers such as New York, Los Angeles, and Nashville.

New Orleans Rising:
Cash Money Millionaires and the No Limit Army

The domination of the southern hip-hop landscape by artists, producers, and industry executives from either Atlanta, Houston, or Miami was irrefutable in the early 1990s, but urban centers from across the South were also creating their own unique hip-hop aesthetics and nonderivative subgeneric styles. *Billboard*'s first detailed examination of the burgeoning New Orleans hip-hop scene (Aiges 1994) focused on the local bounce style —a name ostensibly derived from the track "Bounce (for the Juvenile)," by Juvenile. Citing a plethora of local artists who, since 1991, had released homemade cassettes and vinyl singles, *Billboard* explains that New Orleans teen audiences and several key radio stations had quickly warmed to the homegrown bounce genre and that, with a rhythmic foundation bearing some resemblance to regional southern bass styles (especially the uptempo genre emanating from Florida and Georgia), the style had also developed an audience across the southern tier, fanning out into Alabama, Florida, Georgia, and Mississippi. Among bounce's defining characteristics is a chorus structured around simple vocal chants reminiscent of the famous New Orleans Mardi Gras Indian ensembles, which coexist within a network of strong neighborhood affiliations (and which are also featured in several contemporary videos by New Orleans hip-hop artists). As *Billboard* states, the tradition of the black Indian troupes "remains vital in the poor neighborhoods where many bounce artists were raised. That, plus an emphasis on local references, may have stunted bounce's ability to gain an audience outside of New Orleans. But it helps sales locally" (Aiges 1994, 26). Like their older predecessors as well as their contemporaries in the hip-hop culture, the emergent New Orleans artists regularly cited local spaces and places, delineating associations with neighborhoods and housing projects in the New Orleans urban context.

As bounce's popular appeal grew in New Orleans, Baton Rouge, and the surrounding areas, it momentarily overpowered local rap, displacing it from clubs and radio while generating regional sales that regularly out-paced those of top national rap acts, despite the latter's access to better promotions and distribution. A New Orleans independent retailer con-firmed in *Billboard* that "locally produced bounce cassettes routinely sell 200 to 300 units a week—roughly ten times the sales of national rap al-bums" (ibid.). Several rap producers, including DJ Mannie Fresh of the then-upstart Cash Money Records, proclaimed their disdain for the repeti-tive, "silly," and "stupid" bounce style; yet they, too, produced and distrib-uted it, acknowledging its local importance and impressive commercial re-turns. As bounce evolved between 1992 and 1996, hip-hop producers slowly adapted several of its formal elements, merging it more closely with rap's vocal and production styles in an attempt to embrace the locally unique elements of the genre and relocate them within hip-hop's broader regional and national aesthetic forms, streamlining the genre with current tastes on a wider scale. New Orleans bounce was thus influential in establishing a localized musical style that drew from the city's deeper musical traditions, the southern hip-hop styles that flourished throughout the region, and more recent aesthetic developments in North American hip-hop more generally.

Although they recognized the hegemony of New York and Los Ange-les's corporate structures, rising entrepreneurs in New Orleans frequently credited James Smith and his Rap-A-Lot label for introducing southern hardcore hip-hop to the nation and building a credible model to emulate. Because of bounce's narrow appeal, many producers entered the music business with limited or no experience; having a model such as Rap-A-Lot assisted them in orienting their product for the market and establishing local and regional marketing strategies and sales objectives. They also drew from their contacts in the local scene, often recording unseasoned artists in the hope of a hit and that their product might coincide with consumer trends. The independent production networks and links between artists, studio producers, nightclubs, radio programmers, and an eager audience constituency rapidly helped establish a powerful new sector in the New Orleans music scene. As one bounce producer states, "If you do a bounce song locally, independent, you'll make more money than if you do a rap song on a national record label." Another producer cites the potential for a label to net roughly $40,000 on sales of fifteen thousand cassette singles (Aiges 1994, 26). By 1996 the original bounce sound was changing, and the scene within which it had formed began its decline, leading several local producers to consciously reframe the musical and rhythmic structures of their sound in order to bind rap and bounce more closely together than before.

Listed as a local market leader in early 1994, Cash Money Records—with its roster of bounce artists, including local favorites UNLV and Juvenile—maintained a consistent output of bounce product. As the bounce scene flourished, Cash Money, headed by the sibling CEOs Ron and Brian Williams and the label's production ace, Mannie Fresh, rose as a New Orleans production posse. They formed alliances, first within the "home" places of the uptown New Orleans neighborhoods from which the production team hailed—mainly in New Orleans's Third Ward district—and then throughout the city, establishing bonds and professional relationships with artists from other neighborhoods who had strong allegiances to the public housing developments within their own home boundaries. As Ron Williams notes, the label's originary locale provided a dynamic cultural influence, but the tensions of 'hood life were also a continual threat to his business and the capacity to expand and grow: "We come from the New Orleans underground . . . that's the hardest place to establish a business. All the trial and tribulations you go through. [It's] murder. And then after you go through all of it, the reward is niggas trying to take you out" (Green 1999b, 67).

Cash Money was estimated to have sold roughly 100,000 cassettes and CDs annually from 1994 to 1996, building a foundation for their later successes as they entered into the national market more aggressively. By 1997–98, when the label released the Hot Boyz's *Get It How You Live!!* (1997) and the Big Tymers' *How U Luv That* (1998), Cash Money demonstrated its ability to consistently sell units with virtually no video support or major promotional campaign; as evidence, *Get It How You Live!!* sold close to 400,000 copies, reaching the midrange of the *Billboard* Top R & B Albums chart in 1997 and reentering the charts again in 1998 after a brief hiatus. The Williams brothers attracted the attention of the major labels and eventually, in 1998, signed a three-year, $30 million pressing and distribution contract with Universal Records, which provided upfront financing for the label and, importantly, guaranteed that Cash Money would retains 100 percent ownership of its master recordings. The first full-length release under the new arrangement, Juvenile's *400 Degreez,* which featured the hit single "HA," sold an estimated three million copies in 1998 alone, and subsequent releases by the Hot Boyz, L'il Wayne, and the Big Tymers have all benefited from concentrated exposure in the hip-hop press, major video support, and the acts' appearances on the 2000 Ruff Ryders–Cash Money tour. When the tour ended, Big Tymers released *I Got That Work,* which debuted in the number one slot on *Billboard*'s Top R & B/Hip-Hop Albums chart and the number three position on the *Billboard* 200 chart during the sales week ending June 3, 2000, reaffirming the 1996 Harvard Consultation Project's observations on the momentum that results from wider national concert exposure.

The entrepreneurial character of the mid-1990s bounce and hip-hop scene in New Orleans and the formation of local infrastructures contributed to the national and global breakout of rap from the Crescent City and its surrounding area. Leading New Orleans hip-hop into the public eye and the national record charts was Master P, whose origins in the city's Third Ward and the Calliope housing development are, like those of Eazy-E or Suge Knight before him, commonly cited as a reliable indicator of his ghetto authenticity and 'hood survival skills:

> I went from surviving in the jungle the way we survive to moving into corporate America. It's hard not to do what Suge and them did: taking your ghetto actions and forcefully making people feel you. When you in the 'hood, that's the only way people understand you. In corporate America, you dealing with people got lawyers. You can't just do what you used to do: shoot up everybody. Next thing you know, you on the front page of the newspaper. (Marriott 1998, 72)

His first corporate entity, No Limit Records, began during a sojourn in Richmond, California, where he opened a small, independently owned record retail outlet that primarily sold rap and hip-hop recordings. Drawing from his experience in music marketing and retail and studying the operations of Bay area independent rap entrepreneurs (including Too Short and E-40), Master P positioned himself for entry into the production business on an independent footing while improving his skills as a rapper. Following his debut solo LP, *The Ghetto's Tryin' to Kill Me,* in 1993, Master P gradually established something of a reputation in his hometown of New Orleans and in northern California, absorbing the aesthetics and regional taste preferences of each region and merging them as he honed and defined the No Limit brand.

Having observed consistent sales of Priority's artists at the No Limit record outlet and noting that Master P had successfully shipped his own independent releases to small retailers throughout the southern and western regional markets, Priority Records' CEO, Bryan Turner, attempted to either purchase No Limit or establish a fifty-fifty joint venture with the label, but he was rebuffed. Master P later signed a manufacturing and distribution contract with Turner, granting Priority an estimated 15–20 percent share in No Limit while Master P retained the remaining majority percentage. With Suge Knight's Death Row as his model, Master P remained adamant that No Limit would maintain 100 percent ownership of its master recordings as well as retaining autonomy over the label's daily operations and its release schedule.

Master P's microphone skills have often been assailed by critics who deemed them uneven and derivative, leading him to claim, "I'm not a rapper . . . I'm a company executive" (Braxton 1998, 144). Indeed, early recordings reveal a vocal style that often owes much to the phrasing and flow of his fellow southerner, the Rap-A-Lot artist Scarface, whereas later material can frequently be traced to the stylistic influences of Tupac Shakur, whose rap career began in Oakland. These influences are, I believe, significant, for they merge Master P's two dominant geocultural reference points; simply put, he expressed his hip-hop sensibilities within the main aesthetic structures that he had accessed and interpreted during his time in each urban locale. Nonetheless, in all his solo material and that of his protégés, a thick New Orleans drawl is always evident, introducing a distinct quality to the No Limit sound. Recordings are laced with localized references (including references to ritualistic voodoo practices that prevail among several New Orleans religious sects) and regional slang and terminology that, like the expression "bout it, bout it" (from a track of the same name), were more widely adopted and eventually became standard throughout the United States. Master P's trademark moan—his unmistakable signature sound, which is also fundamental to the 1998 No Limit posse track "Make Them Say Uhh,"—can be identified as an entirely unique vocal statement, as easily recognizable in hip-hop as James Brown's soulful exhortations are in 1960s and 1970s funk.

With his second solo LP, *99 Ways to Die;* the No Limit compilation release *Bouncin' and Swingin',* by an amalgamation of artists appearing under the moniker the Down South Hustlers; and the compilation album *West Coast Bad Boyz, Volume 1: Anotha Level of tha Game*, all released in 1994, No Limit displayed a commitment to presenting regional talent from the southern United States and the West Coast in a compelling musical context that also corresponded with wider national tastes. The compilation projects linked artists across an aesthetic range with 'hood-oriented themes of street survival, hustling, and gangster lifestyles, which comprised the main connective thread between the various contributions. Furthermore, releasing three projects in the same year proved to young rappers who were eagerly seeking record contracts and executives at other competing labels that despite its minor, independent status, No Limit was emerging as a formidable force in the southern hip-hop scene.

No Limit's business approach was committed to keeping costs and operating overhead low in order to maximize the profit ratio on sales of recordings and all other merchandise. The label assembled an impressive roster of artists, including Master P's relatives, friends, and acquaintances from New Orleans, and recorded at his self-owned Ice Cream Shop studios in Baton Rouge. The label's ambitious recording and release schedule ensured a steady flow of new commodities for the market and helped to define the label through the late 1990s. The tightly controlled process figured prominently in the label's rise in status to become the top independent rap label in 1998. According to *Forbes,* No Limit was valued at $230 million in 1998, with Master P's personal wealth estimated at $56.5 million, placing him tenth on the *Forbes* list of top entertainment earners, ahead of the next rap representative, Sean Combs, who appeared at number fifteen on the list (LaFranco 1999).

In the case of many independent labels, such as Bad Boy, Cash Money, Death Row, No Limit, and So So Def, the pattern of recording in the labels' own studio complexes under the guidance of one main producer or regular production team emerged as a standard practice. It was solidified with the rise and market dominance of Suge Knight and his Death Row "family," but as P. Diddy and Master P attained market dominance in 1997 and 1998, the emphasis on production posses and rap cliques was further intensified; it was, as some insiders claimed, the year of the clique. Monica Lynch, president of Tommy Boy Records, expressed frustration with the trend: "It's very unhealthy for the business when, in order to get success, you have to have those associations or people don't check for you because you aren't down with the right person" (Nelson 1997c, 35). With in-house production teams, such as Bad Boy's former aces, "The Hit Men," or No Limit's now defunct "Beats by the Pound," the labels developed signature rhythms and sounds that are merged with each rapper's individual vocal style. The approach has its drawbacks, however, as indicated by criticism from many fans and critics that the No Limit production team was ill suited to the label's star acquisition, Snoop Dogg, whose greatest achievements were under the production lead of Dr. Dre at Death Row Records (a relationship that was rekindled in 2000).

Master P engaged in several innovative marketing strategies that helped to build the No Limit brand and reinforce his other, nonmusical ventures. For example, the image of the No Limit tank was successfully established as an unmistakable icon in the hip-hop community, one that is immediately associated with No Limit among fans and consumers. The tank logo is featured prominently on all the label's CDs and is displayed in most publicity photographs of Master P and his top acts, who commonly sport gold or platinum tank medallions encrusted with diamonds. Members of the No Limit posse—known as the "army"—often wheeled a mock tank onstage during their performances throughout 1997–98, and many of their recordings referred explicitly to "the tank" as a synonym for the label itself. Print advertisements announcing upcoming releases in 1998 and 1999 featured the tank logo accompanied by bold copy reading, "No Limit Records. We can't be stopped."

Master P's *99 Ways To Die* included advertisements for a 1-900 No Limit phone sex service, inviting consumers to call and talk with the "No Limit bitches" pictured on the CD sleeve. Through aggressive cross-marketing, Master P advertised future releases by various acts on the No Limit roster inside every new CD, including their release dates and a full-panel image of the CD covers. Gradually the CDs began to advertise a wide range of clothing accessories as Master P introduced his No Limit fashion line, selling via mail order branded clothing merchandise explicitly associated with the label or identified by the tank logo. By the end of 1998, No Limit clothing was also regularly available in independently owned retail outlets and several department store chains.

With the expansion into film production, CDs also increasingly featured images and information about videos and films produced by the No Limit Films division. Utilizing marketing savvy developed in his early forays into the industry, Master P bypassed larger video outlets, stocking his first video film, *I'm Bout It,* in many of the same independent record retail outlets that already handled No Limit product, selling over 220,000 copies in its first week of release (Braxton 1997, 102). Sound tracks for the direct-to-video films proved to be lucrative on the market; *I'm Bout It* (1997) debuted at number one on the Top R & B Albums chart and attained gold record status; Master P's *Da Last Don* (1998) sold four million copies in less than two months, while Snoop Dogg's *Da Game Is to Be Sold, Not to Be Told* (1998) peaked at number one on the Top 200 *Billboard* Albums charts; and the sound track to the feature film *I Got the Hook Up* (1998) reached the upper echelons of the Top R & B Albums chart. *I Got the Hook Up,* produced by Master P and distributed by Miramax, was produced for approximately $3.5 million and generated over $10 million in domestic box-office revenues, garnering even greater revenue in video retail and rentals. In 1999 Master P signed a five-film deal with Artisan Pictures, ensuring that No Limit Enterprises will continue to flourish even as several other sectors of the corporate structure struggled in 1999–2000.

Expanding into real estate (MP Realty) and sports management (No Limit Sports Management), Master P has built No Limit into an influential financial empire in New Orleans and Baton Rouge, where its corporate headquarters are based, reflecting the corporate attitude that "this ain't no ghetto business. . . . I'm trying to extend the No Limit brand in as many areas as possible" (Muhammad 1999, 82). On June 1, 2000, Master P extended his mini-empire, announcing the establishment of No Limit Communications, "a joint venture between himself and New Orleans-based Alliance Network. . . . [The partnership] will provide prepaid telecom products, ranging from local home phone service to long distance calling cards and E-commerce" (Mitchell 2000, 33), with an initial launch in eight urban markets across the United States.

In the Harvard Consultation Project report, a highly experienced black industry leader, Clarence Avant, describes the plight among contemporary black entertainment entrepreneurs:

> We have always been entertainers, but we have never really owned anything. Based on the number of black artists who are successful, we should have more ownership. . . . It's nice to see Oprah Winfrey making money and Quincy Jones producing the Academy Awards, but when you visit the various "Harlems" there has to be ownership of theaters and record stores.   (Harvard Consultation Project, 1996)

Referring to his contractual arrangement with Priority and the importance of his own label ownership, Master P cites freedom and speed as two key facets of his formula at No Limit. They allow the label to respond to shifts in the market and to capitalize on consumer trends while they are still relevant:

> When you're independent you can put out product whenever you want to. You can control your own masters, your own destiny. You don't have to go through the middle man. That's what takes records so long to come out. You got to get so many approvals from so many departments that by the time a record comes out, it's an old record.   (Braxton 1997, 95)

No Limit's peak year of production was 1998, when Master P oversaw the release of approximately twenty full-length recordings. Most achieved gold or platinum sales status. The *Billboard* charts, for instance, reflect No Limit's presence and impact: on January 17, 1998, albums by Mystikal (who has since jumped to the powerful Jive label, home to 'N Sync, the Backstreet Boys, Britney Spears, R. Kelly, Joe, and KRS-One) and Master P were in the top twenty on the Top R & B Albums chart. By April 4, C-Murder's *Life or Death* occupied the number one spot; Silkk the Shocker, Master P, Mystikal, and Young Bleed all placed releases in the top twenty, and three other No Limit releases appeared in the top one hundred. Three weeks later, the sound track album *I Got the Hookup* debuted at number three on the Top 200 Albums chart and reached the number one Top R & B Album position in its second week; on May 23, Fiend's *There's One in Every Family* reached number one on the Top R & B Album chart in its second week, making a total of eleven No Limit releases in the top one hundred. By June 20 Master P's double solo CD, *MP da Last Don*, reached number one on both the Top 200 Albums chart and the Top R & B Albums chart in its second week, with No Limit placing three albums in the top twenty and nine on the Top R & B chart; and on August 15 Snoop Dogg's No Limit debut album entered the chart at number seventy-eight, reaching the number one slot on both the Top 200 and Top R & B Albums charts the following week. This brought the number of No Limit releases located in the August 22 top twenty R & B Albums to four; a total of twelve releases were represented in the top one hundred for the week ending August 22.

In 1999, however, there was a notable decrease in the number of No Limit releases and in the label's overall sales, although Master P's solo album *Only God Can Judge Me* debuted at number two on the *Billboard* 200 in November 1999. As Master P developed and launched new ventures, some industry observers questioned whether No Limit was overextended. Still others speculated that the label's slump was due in part to a reduced release schedule, precipitated by a declining interest in the No Limit sound among consumers as overall competition increased and several other southern labels, such as Cash Money, asserted themselves in the market. The spring 2000 release of the single "Wobble Wobble" and the subsequent full-length release *Goodfellas* introduced the 504 Boyz (featuring Master P, Silkk, Mystikal, C-Murder, and Krazy) as No Limit's latest act. The album debuted on May 11 at number one on the Top R & B/Hip-Hop Albums chart and number two on the *Billboard* 200, behind 'N Sync's record-breaking release *No Strings Attached*. As a collective consisting of several of the top artists on the No Limit roster, the 504 Boyz are based conspicuously on the successful model of Cash Money's Hot Boyz and were portrayed in press photos and in their video wearing the 504 logo (the New Orleans telephone area code) alongside their No Limit brand sportswear. A late example of hip-hop's dynamic rise, the 504 Boyz create a powerful link between the local and the transnational or global spheres of media, technology, and commerce, representing for their hometown as well as their record label posse, marketing geography and industry in equal prominence.

Epilogue

❋

In the year 2000, hip-hop looked and sounded considerably different than it did when it was still primarily located in the streets and parks of the Bronx and Harlem. Moreover, it came to *mean* differently, acquiring great depth and sophistication as it evolved as a standard facet of everyday and everynight life for an entire generation of youths and consumers. As the genre has grown and matured, its cultural reach has also expanded, and the ghetto or 'hood, while remaining a powerful spatial foundation for much of the ideological thought that pours into hip-hop's cultural practices, is no longer its sole or even dominant geocultural reference. Benefiting from myriad globalizing forces, including the Internet and worldwide media distribution systems, hip-hop is more than ever situated within the global-local nexus and what might be defined as the contemporary hip-hop industrial complex. As this indicates, hip-hop's spatial expansions and its thematic, discursive, and rhythmic content are inextricably bound to the corporate exigency of global commerce; tremors in one realm can have major repercussions in the other.

There are so many examples of spatiality and emphases on geocultural themes and issues in rap and hip-hop that any attempt to comprehensively embrace them is fruitless. Paul Gilroy accurately assesses the research dilemma:

One of the things I find troubling in debates about rap is that I don't think anyone knows what the totality of its hypercreativity looks like. . . . I can't keep up with the volume of hip-hop product anymore. I don't know if anyone can. There is simply too much of it to be assimilated, and the kinds of judgments we make have to take that volume into account. It's a flood—it's not a flow, it's a flood actually—and bobbing up and down in the water is not enough. (1992, 309)

Hip-hop 's ubiquity, rate and volume of output, and incontestable commercial appeal have produced sometimes subtle indicators of its wider social impact. For example, as the term "the 'hood" has seeped up from the "underground," having been popularized through rap and the hip-hop media, it has entered into the standard vocabulary of the social mainstream. Today it is not uncommon to hear individuals who are quite distant from hip-hop as either fans or consuming audience members erroneously referring to their upscale or gentrified enclaves as "the 'hood," dipping into hip-hop's linguistic forms as a sly display of urban chic. This phenomenon and the curious cultural effects that can and do emerge through hip-hop's cross-cultural appeal also inform Marc Levin's 1999 feature film *White Boys* and the James Toback film *Black and White,* which was released in the spring of 2000.

As this book has illustrated, however, the 'hood is not just *any* place; the term cannot simply be used to define *any* neighborhood. As I have endeavored to explain, the 'hood is the product of a unique spatial sensibility that permeates the hip-hop culture. It is a spatial construct that can be traced through a series of transformative moments, having usurped other, earlier spatial constructs that have been historically defined within black cultural practices, including music, literature, and cinema.

As with most subcultural groups, those who subscribe to the hip-hop lifestyle and live within its range of attitudes and practices have developed their own internally coherent styles, codes, and elaborate systems of meaning. Over the years, teenagers have implemented these codes and signs to communicate the importance of spatiality, and in the past ten years there has been a strong turn toward place-based value statements that inform individual and collective identity affiliations. Rap has become an essential element in the formation of spatial politics and the politics of place upon which different "players" and posses base their identities in an arena that is characteristically obsessed with identity and public profile. To express the emergent spatial practices upon which these identity affiliations are founded, youths have devised an entirely new lexicon and medium through which to describe the spaces and places of the contemporary urban land-scape. This is one of rap's most important social functions, and it is absolutely essential we acknowledge it if we are to understand the music's role in the lives of its young fans and consumers.

The examples of hip-hop's late-1990s spatial articulations are, however, interesting in their diversity and their clear sense of hip-hop's global status: Mase's *Harlem World* (1997, Bad Boy) incorporates the name of a once-crucial uptown New York nightclub while simultaneously evoking a local-global dynamic that speaks to the artist's position within both his home locus and the international music industry. The cover images of the Wu-Tang Clan's second release, *Wu Tang Forever* (1997, Loud), and Wu-Tang alumnus Gza/Genius's *Beneath the Surface* (1999, MCA) also reflect global perspectives, the former via a simply conceived Wu-Tang corporate logo with the group's distinctive "W" overlaying an image of the globe, and the latter through a whimsical image of Gza's logo impressed deeply into the face of the earth as if from a falling comet. The global scale also figures prominently in the Def Squad (comprised of Redman, Erick Sermon, and Keith Murray) release titled *El Niño* (1998, Def Jam/Jive), which metaphorically refers to the global disruption of standard patterns that the artists seek to achieve through their storm and fury. *Global Warning*, by the Rascalz (1999), explicitly articulates hip-hop's global impact in its title while employing the images of household-product labels warning the consumer about the product's combustibility, toxicity, or explosiveness. Concerns with temporality and the significance of the global transition into a new millennium also emerged, most notably on Busta Rhymes's *Extinction Level Event* (1999, Elektra) and *Anarchy* (2000, Elektra), with their cover art and lyrical themes depicting vast urban devastation, or Method Man's *Tical 2000: Judgment Day* (1998, Def Jam), which depicts the artist as a techno-cyborg entity. Each example reveals the creeping millennial ("Y2K") stress and paranoia that were experienced on a global scale, implying through their postapocalyptic scenarios that the world as we know it has ended.

Within hip-hop, rap constitutes a primary vehicle for the expression of spatial sensibilities from a youth perspective, and in its many subgeneric forms it has risen as one of the more distinct sites for social debate on the contemporary convergences of youth, race, space, and place. Rap's expansive development has contributed to a widened sense of connection among the artists, producers, record labels, and audiences throughout the world, producing further cases that reflect the global character of the culture. In a 1998 feature article titled "Global Rap Pulse," *Billboard* observed that rap continued to solidify its base in foreign markets as local artists in European and Asian urban locales adapted the genre to their own regional linguistic dialects and turned the themes toward culturally relevant issues. As in the North American market, global rap frequently remains reliant on the output of independent labels, while small-scale entrepreneurs capitalize on the opportunities offered by an art form that is in most cases only marginally associated with mainstream corporate labels. In corresponding fashion, a network of underground nightclubs and radio outlets have emerged as crucial forces in nurturing the burgeoning rap scenes in various internationally dispersed urban contexts, reproducing many of the trends that had been essential in rap's formative stages in the United States.

Through the early 1990s, Canadian artists struggled to define their hip-hop identities, often being accused of being derivative of what were deemed more "authentic" U.S. styles and stances, or of being copyists who attempted to replicate the sounds of successful U.S. artists. Canadian media outlets were deemed unresponsive to rap, even as the U.S. media accommodated it more fully in the late 1990s. The Canadian artist Maestro (formally Maestro Fresh Wes) released his third full-length album, *Naaah, Dis Kid Can't Be from Canada?!!* (LMR Street), in 1994 after having moved to New York two years earlier in the attempt to sustain his career in a more receptive environment.

By 1998 Canadian rap acts had experienced a surge of creativity and public interest, with Toronto's Choclair, Ghetto Concept, Kardinal Offishal, Mathematik, Solitair, and Saukrates; Montreal's Dubmatique; and Vancouver's Rascalz acquiring national market profiles and, in Choclair's case, U.S. attention (F. Williams 2000). With its anthemic announcement that Canadian rap was not to be underestimated, the Rascalz joined forces with fellow artists Thrust, Checkmate, Kardinal Offishall, and Choclaire on the national unity track "Northern Touch" (1998, BMG), bridging "the T-dot" (Toronto) and "Van City" (Vancouver) and representing for Canada. Toronto's Beat Factory label played a crucial role in popularizing many of the Canadian rap and hip-hop artists domestically through its biannual *Rap Essentials* compilation CD in the mid-1990s, although distribution for Canadian artists was generally thin. The debut in 2000 of the television program *Drop the Beat* on Canada's CBC network provided a new avenue for exposure for many of the nation's top rap acts. Based on the fictional activities of a campus radio station's hip-hop program, *Drop the Beat* presents a unique perspective on Canada's urban music scene.[1] The concurrent release of a sound track CD (*Drop the Beat* [2000, Universal]) featured several of the Canadian artists listed above, accompanied by high-profile U.S. artists such as Canibus, Common, Ja Rule, Rahzel, and Erykah Badu.

In France, rap artists gained a larger share of market sales between 1993 and 1996. The government's instatement of a domestic radio broadcast regulation in 1995 mandating 40 percent domestic content provided a boost for French rappers as stations scrambled to fill their airtime with viable music. In 1998 *Billboard* featured the Czech group Chaozz, which was developing a loyal national following despite a general public unfamiliarity with hip-hop and its cultural foundations in U.S. urban contexts (Legge 1998, 13). Later that year a detailed report on Cuban hip-hop was published that described both the country's economic constraints and the limiting effects of the U.S. trade embargo and offered insights into the strategic innovations displayed by rap artists who have developed their skills under these difficult conditions (Shawnee Smith 1998c, 46).[2] Indeed, in the latter half of the 1990s, there was consistent coverage of non-U.S. rap and hip-hop in the industry press and in ancillary, fan-oriented media, providing an elaborated sense of consumer interest and artist and industry production around the world.

Amidst these trends, with the genre's twentieth anniversary looming, rap advertising in the music press also shifted noticeably, enunciating hip-hop's temporality and longevity rather than emphasizing the spatiality of "the street" as the dominant locus of legitimacy. For example, in *Billboard's* end-of-year special feature on rap (Dec. 5, 1998), an advertisement for Sony displayed a photograph of a box of vinyl records in milk crates—representing both a DJ's professional tools and the hip-hop archive—under the slogan "We're just getting started." Tommy Boy Records adapted the aesthetics and tone of advertisements for Altoid® mints with the copy, "Supporting Hip-Hop since 1981: Curiously Strong Music." Jive comes closest to a street-oriented advertising image, featuring a neighborhood butcher shop recast as a "beat market" and copy reading "Still Doin' It in '99." Standing out among the labels with its unambiguous emphasis on place and the locational mapping of the urban environment, a Columbia Records advertisement depicts a map based on the layout of the New York subway system, with artist's names, including the Fugees, Cypress Hill, Nas, Will Smith, and Sporty Thievz, corresponding to subway stations and accompanying ad copy reading "This is how we ride."

Hip-hop loudly displays and articulates the fluctuating scales of meaning and experience that have been seen since its inception in mid-1970s New York. Urban youths have continued to employ rap and the powerful visual and symbolic forms of hip-hop in their project of remapping the urban terrain. The term "mapping," for all of its academic potency, is appropriate here since it captures the sense of an active engagement with the social, political, and economic realms that underlie the contemporary cultural landscape. Hip-hop's processes of cultural mapping have produced a valuable body of work that defines the spatial relations between the 'hood, the region, and the nation, and that, more broadly, describes minority teen existence within the global-local contexts of an interactive, wired world. This is cartography on the move, and over the past twenty years rappers have, like the "super rapper" Muhammad Ali before them, feinted, jabbed, and rapped against the system, challenging and opposing the dominant sociospatial configurations. In so doing, they have introduced a series of alternatives that express the needs, concerns, and desires of urban minority youth at the end of the twentieth century and into the new millennium.

As I have argued, the material conditions and social dynamics connecting a range of variables have not remained constant since rap first emerged as a facet of the hip-hop culture. Rather, they have been in continual flux and have undergone transformations that profoundly influence the lives of teens across the racial and class spectrum for whom rap is a central cultural practice and commodity. At the dawn of rap's third decade, minority teens, and a sizable segment of white teens as well, have given voice to serious sociospatial concerns that are asserted with intensity. In some, but still far too few, cases this voice constitutes an assault on the barriers that divide the spatial realms of difference, of "the other." Still, the color line that Du Bois long ago identified as America's primary constraint continues to divide the races in America. Small children and teenagers are growing up in a society where de facto segregation of neighborhoods and schools is common.

One need not look far to see that the stakes are indeed high for many minority youths in America; receding urban crime statistics and the diminishing influences of the crack scourge notwithstanding, many black and Latino teenagers remain at risk, confronting the fears of neighborhood violence, the negative outcomes of inadequately allocated educational funding, unequal economic opportunities, limited employment options, and the persistence of higher rates of teen pregnancy, sexually transmitted diseases, and HIV infection. With occasional exceptions, relations between the sexes are also generally conflicted, and the unequal distribution of spatial power between young men and young women remains a serious problem within hip-hop circles.

In reporting the tragic and senseless (and at this writing, still unsolved) deaths of twenty-five-year-old Tupac Shakur and twenty-four-year-old Notorious B.I.G., the hip-hop media reminded readers that while the incidents resulted in an immeasurable loss to the rap community, the crisis of urban gun violence is an American problem that disproportionately affects young black men. By contrast, the mainstream media often seemed unable to focus on anything beyond the celebrity angle, placing the emphasis on the individuals and framing the murders as a logical outcome of the gangsta-ism that is perceived as thematically endemic to rap: live by the sword, die by the sword. Slowly, artists from the two coasts and across the hip-hop nation are attempting to settle differences through carefully scripted public statements, high-profile joint public appearances, and guest spots on each other's recordings. The spatial dimensions of authority, power, and pride and the geocultural roots of a particular desire for respect may not fully disappear, but, for the time being players in the rap game seem willing to accept that regional and local differences are not enough to go to war over. Already there is evidence, as rap artists age and mature and have children of their own, of a new conciliatory attitude that may in fact be a healthy result of rap's longevity.

There is much room for optimism, and rap's ability to provide a communicative medium within hip-hop endures as the joys and fears of youth are expressed and the contexts of existence, both positive and negative, are defined. We are only now witnessing the processes through which rap also communicates the voices of older men and women, as the members of hip-hop's first pioneering generation articulate concerns and values that do not fixate on the lifestyles of youth alone. Rap, therefore, provides a powerful cultural means through which changing identities, often forged under duress, are written onto the social map. The diverse range of narratives and discourses, along with regionally dispersed rhythms and flows, continue to shape the territories and loosely circumscribed boundaries of the hip-hop nation.

Notes

❉

Notes to Introduction

1. Ronald Formisano points out that the term "homie" was first used among native and middle-class northern blacks in reference to "the mostly poor, rough-edged newcomers" from the South who poured into northern cities after 1945 (1991, 35).

2. While "the 'hood" remains the most prominent and frequently used term and constitutes the main referential structure within which discourses of place cohere, it is by no means the only one. Other expressions such as "around the way" are also used to describe the neighborhood environment in various contexts.

Notes to Chapter 1

1. As an indication of the distinctions between "rap" and the broader term "hip-hop," the rap artist KRS-One explains that "rap is something you do, hip-hop is something you live" (Howell 1995, 40). Rap is the music of hip-hop and provides the culture's central form of articulation and expression.

2. In this instance, I am thinking of subcultural theories of youth and resistance (i.e., Chambers 1986; Hebdige 1988), but the emphasis on signification and "semiotic guerilla warfare" that characterizes much of the British research does not translate quite so easily in contemporary American contexts pertaining to hip-hop culture.

3. For a collection of analytical essays on the black public sphere, see *Public Culture* 7, no. 1 (fall 1994), special issue.

4. One example of this is the 1995 Mario Van Peebles film *Panther* (1995), which spawned two hip-hop albums: in addition to the recorded sound track, *Pump Ya Fist: Hip Hop Inspired by the Black Panthers* (1995, PolyGram) was issued to coincide with the film's release.

5. Describing "a response to the forces of globalization," Robins describes a phenomenon whereby "purified identities are constructed through the purification of space, through the maintenance of territorial boundaries and frontiers" (1991, 42). This argument is also central to Gilroy 1987 as it pertains to British nationalism(s), "the English," and U.K. blacks. See also Formisano 1991 for an example of the notion of purified identities, defensive postures, and localized resistance to externally imposed authority.

Notes to Chapter 2

1. See, e.g., Jones 1963, esp. chap. 8.
2. This point is evident in Holman 1984, which describes the ethnic and racial composition of early break-dance crews while also offering an interesting introduction to the commercial development of break-dancing.
3. For a detailed overview of the graffiti underground in the late 1970s and early 1980s, see Castleman 1982 and the 1982 film *Wild Style,* directed by Charlie Ahearn and starring many prominent New York spray artists from this period. Many contemporary hip-hop magazines, including *The Source,* continue to feature public graffiti work from around the world.
4. Joel Garreau identifies a phenomenon called the "Edge City," which he determines is the third stage of a trajectory from suburban housing areas, to malls and retail and consumption spaces, to fully functional cities that have sprouted at the frontier of older, traditional city boundaries (Garreau 1988).
5. This claim has serious implications and is based on a questionable reading of contemporary crime trends throughout the early 1990s in which blacks were more vigorously policed and more likely to be found guilty of crimes than other minorities and whites. For an overview of the subject, see Donziger 1996.
6. See the cover story, "Silicon Alley 10003," in the Mar. 6, 2000, issue of *New York.*
7. See also N. Smith 1996.
8. This was reflected in the mid-1990s in the Boston area, where civic officials, police departments, and other affiliated adults miscomprehended teen leisure practices and the dynamics of "the mosh pit." See the *Boston Globe* articles "Violence Halts Green Day Concert: 70,000 Angry Fans Spark Mosh Melee," Sept. 10, 1994, and "10 Arraigned in Plymouth Concert Uproar: Police Say Punk-Rock Show Halted To Avert Dancing," Jan. 16, 1995.
9. Marketing to Generation X emerged as a growth industry in the 1990s, as numerous magazines dedicated issues to the topic. See *Newseek,* summer/fall 1990 ("The New Teens: What Makes Them Different"); *Time,* July 16, 1990 ("Twentysomething"); *Business Week,* Aug. 19, 1991 ("Young Americans: The Under-30 Generation"); and *Atlantic,* June 1990 ("Growing Up Scared") and Dec. 1992 ("The New Generation Gap: Twentysomethings and Fortysomethings"). *Swing,* which made its debut in November 1994, explicitly targets "men and women in their 20s." In the latter half of the decade, youth marketing has intensified across commercial and entertainment sectors.
10. See, e.g., the emphasis on race and society comprising the feature stories of *Newsweek:* "The New Politics of Race," May 6, 1991; "Tackling a Taboo: Spike Lee's Take on Interracial Romance," June 10, 1991; "Beyond Black and White," May 18, 1992; and "The Hidden Rage of Successful Blacks," Nov. 15, 1993. See also *Time,* "The Two Americas: E Pluribus Unum?" May 18, 1992.
11. For a detailed ethnographic study of this phenomenon, see Jones 1988.
12. I use the terms "hip-hop culture" and "hip-hop nation" as common expressions within the subcultures that I am describing. For example, the Feb. 8, 1999, issue of Time featured the headline "Hip Hop Nation: After 20 Years—How It's Changed America," overlaid upon a photo of Lauryn Hill. The expressions are also relevant in relation to Nelson George's (1989) term "R & B world," employed to explain musical and extramusical cultural phenomena in the late 1980s.

Notes to Chapter 3

1. The history of *Billboard*'s chart designations is itself an interesting study. The first black music chart, running from 1942 to 1945, was called the Harlem Hit Pa-

rade. From 1945 to 1949 the widely criticized title Race Records was in effect; it was replaced in 1949 by Rhythm and Blues, in a shift away from a racial identification to a musically based designation. After a hiatus from November 1963 to January 1965, all black music was assigned to the pop category. The Rhythm and Blues title was maintained until August 1969, when it was replaced by the Soul charts, in keeping with the sociopolitical tenor of the times (Garofalo 1994, 278). In 1982 the Hot Soul Singles and LP charts were renamed Hot Black Singles and Top Black Albums in order to reflect "the diverse nature of music that field now encompasses" (June 26, 1982, 3). In October 1990 the debate over race music resurfaced, precipitating a reinstatement of R & B chart designations. On June 6, 1992, a Hot Rap Singles chart was added that greatly overlapped the existing R & B singles listings. In December 1999 the charts again shifted with the introduction of the Hot R & B/Hip-Hop Singles and Tracks (with accompanying sales *and* airplay charts) and the Top R & B/Hip-Hop Albums alongside the Hot Rap Singles chart.

2. I thank Keir Keightley for drawing this technical point to my attention.

3. For an interesting critical assessment of this period, see Michael C. Dawson's "A Black Counterpublic?: Economic Earthquakes, Racial Agenda(s), and Black Politics," in *Public Culture* 7, no. 1 (fall 1994): 195–223.

4. For an interesting discussion of the evolution of generational differences and contemporary hip-hop sensibilities, see Boyd 1997.

5. For a compelling and detailed overview of the filming in the Bronx and resultant community protest against the film's production and release, see Perez. 1985.

6. It is important not to lose sight of the fact that rap did not emerge solely from within the constrained economic conditions of the American ghetto landscape. Within these urban sites, it also evolved alongside the developing narco-economy that was being fueled by the growing trade in crack cocaine.

Notes to Chapter 4

1. Noting the ways, for example, that disco became identified with and fell under the purview of the predominantly white jet-set crowds associated with clubs like New York's Studio 54, or the manner in which the Motown songbook was repositioned as the sound track to depictions of white nostalgia in the 1983 Lawrence Kasdan film *The Big Chill*.

2. For a description of this proprietary logic in practice, see the chapter in George 1992 titled "Rappin' with Russell: Eddie Murphying the Flak-Catchers."

3. One article addressing this phenomenon is Samuels 1991. He attempts to account for the broader implications of white youth's consumption of rap, however, by basing most of his analysis on only the most hypermasculine, racist, and aggressive examples within the genre.

4. See George 1993, 44–50, in which the author discusses rap's formative years with hip-hop's "founding fathers," Afrika Bambaataa, Grandmaster Flash, and Kool DJ Herc.

5. In the spring of 2001, Combs emerged victorious from his court case involving illegal gun possession charges, and at a press conference he announced he would change his "nom de rue" to P. Diddy.

6. Among other prominent artists in the era were UTFO, the Real Roxanne, Melle Mel, and the former Treacherous Three member Kool Moe Dee.

7. The phenomenon of "reverse crossover" caused considerable consternation among many blacks in the business. For a discussion of the issue at the time, see George 1984.

8. In a special section of *Billboard* titled "The World of Black Music," Harry Weinger reported on crossover trends on stations featuring rap: "There is a noted

increase in the white audience's acceptance of contemporary rap and funk as the grassroots efforts of Tommy Boy and Profile Records pounded their way into the mainstream. . . . The suburban spread of rap and the new found life of the war horse ballad form bode well for artists and programmers alike" (Weinger 1984b).

9. Sales of CD players and disks were in a rapid upswing in this period as standards and quality were being established across the industry. *Billboard* reported that in 1982 when they first became available at retail, 25,000 CD players were sold. In March 1986, reports on small and medium-size record retailers and on CBS reflected the industrywide growth of CDs and the impact on annual sales revenues (Lichtman 1986; Sippel 1986; Goodman 1986). Later that month the RIAA released figures that indicated the drop in sales for LPs between 1984 and 1986 was 18 percent and that the rise in CD sales for the same period was 291 percent. Although prerecorded cassettes were the dominant configuration for 1985, it was reported that market saturation and a hard-to-measure rate of home taping was resulting in declining sales of cassettes and audiocassette components (Horowitz 1986).

10. By most accounts, Motown's golden period as "the voice of young America" ended in 1972 when the label's founder, Berry Gordy, moved the operation from Detroit to Los Angeles.

11. Known in the early 1980s as Dr. Jeckyll, Harrel formed half of the rap duo Dr. Jeckyll and Mr. Hyde, which had several charting releases. Later he was an executive with Def Jam before starting his own successful label, Uptown Records.

12. *Billboard* reported that in 1984 rap shows had sold out the 9,000-seat Greensboro Coliseum and the 14,000-seat Atlanta Omni performance center.

13. For a detailed analysis of the issues and impact the PMRC and other conservative watchdog groups had on popular music and the industry, see Garofalo 1997, 423–39.

Notes to Chapter 5

1. For further illustration of the divergences between old and new school rap as well as for testimonial evidence of the old school influence on subsequent generations of rap artists, see the 1995 rap documentary *The Show*.

2. In the his announcement of rap's Grammy Award category, Greene also said that Grammy categories would be assigned to hard rock, bluegrass, and fusion.

Notes to Chapter 6

1. Hip-hop's timeline can be roughly divided into three general eras: old school refers to the period from 1978 to 1986; middle school covers the period between 1987 and 1992; and new school extends from 1993 to the end of the decade. The expression "now school" is occasionally employed in reference to hip-hop's present state.

2. Luther Campbell's Skyywalker label caught the attention of the creator of *Star Wars*, George Lucas, who controlled proprietary rights to the name. A legal battle ensued, and the court ruled in favor of Lucas, leading Campbell to change the name of his label to Luke Records in 1990.

3. See Garofalo 1997, 257–64; Ward 1998.

4. The Flavor Unit posse at the time included such rap notables as Queen Latifah, Monie Love, Apache, Lakim Shabazz, and Naughty by Nature (the latter, perhaps more than the rest, explicitly refer to their origins as New Jersey rappers hailing from 118th Street, "Illtown," in East Orange). After internal restructuring, the posse's most bankable star, Queen Latifah, occupied a more prominent leadership role in Flavor Unit Management.

5. Known as the Dogg Pound, the posse at the time included Snoop Doggy

Dogg, Nate Dogg, Dat Nigga Daz, and Kurupt, among others who represent the Los Angeles, Compton, and Long Beach areas.

6. For a detailed examination of the Florida bass phenomenon, see the special March 1994 issue of *The Source*.

7. For more detailed examinations of the political and religious foundations of message rap, see Eure and Spady 1991; James 1992; and Allen 1996.

8. Addressing the relatively minor industry consideration for Seattle's black artists, Sir Mix-A-Lot's Rhyme Cartel Records released the conspicuously titled *Seattle: The Dark Side* in 1993. The cover prominently proclaims that the release "flips the script. No Grunge . . . just Rap and R&B . . . SeaTown style."

Notes to Chapter 7

1. In March 1989 *Billboard* reported that Norby Walters, who throughout the 1980s was "the largest booking agency in the black music field" and had been instrumental in mounting the first New York Fresh Fest Tours and numerous R & B and rap package tours, faced trial in Chicago on racketeering charges stemming from his alleged mob ties. The agency's troubles contributed to the void in major concert tours by black artists.

2. While alterations to *Billboard*'s sales research methods and chart evaluation system were partially responsible for the meteoric ascent on the charts of *Efil4zaggin*, the album also reached the public without major advance media hype. Released on Eazy-E's Ruthless Records label and distributed by the independent Priority Records, it soared to number one in advance of a single release and without the benefit of an accompanying video; these were sales based on N.W.A.'s established reputation for solid production, compelling street-tough lyrics, and a "buzz" within the hip-hop scene itself.

3. For an overview of the internationalization of hip-hop and a partial discography, see Schwartz 1999.

4. For a more detailed examination of why artists do or do not maintain relations with the 'hood, see C. Jones 1995, 43–46.

5. Bill Clinton's appearance on MTV had a similar effect among young voters as he manipulated the generational differences between himself and President George Bush to his advantage, altering the way modern political campaigns approach young voters.

Notes to Chapter 8

1. As an example of the conflation of youth, race, and danger, see the cover of the Canadian news magazine *Maclean's* (May 18, 1992), which, in the aftermath of urban riots ostensibly spurred by the acquittal of California police officers in the beating of Rodney King, pictured a black male teenager wearing a hooded sweater under the headline "Young, Black and Angry."

2. For a compelling analysis of this dynamic with careful attention to two specific episodes of *The Fresh Prince of Bel Air*, see Zook 1999.

3. In the case of *Straight Out of Brooklyn,* this is the specific locale of the Red Hooks housing development, home to director Matty Rich. The low-income housing depicted in *Juice* remains anonymous, although the city is clearly New York and the locale is representative of Harlem, Brooklyn, or the Bronx.

Notes to Chapter 9

1. George 1988, 88–89, cites Berry Gordy's decision to work with the William Morris Agency in the early and mid-1960s in booking his top Motown acts. He by-

passed Queen Booking, the black-owned agency with which he had worked previously, once his artists gained momentum and achieved wider success on the pop charts.

2. Hip-hop magazines such as *The Source* and *Rap Sheet* emerged as influential forces by sponsoring various conferences and educational seminars that addressed hip-hop's direction and elements of the professional music business. In many cases these gatherings provided the context for probing analysis of internal issues, including the discourses of sexism and misogyny, representational violence, and the ongoing issue of East Coast–West Coast antagonism. With special issues focusing on crucial issues to youth and members of the hip-hop nation, these magazines were woven into the culture as important communicative organs, shaping the discourses and illuminating the key issues that influenced the evolution of hip-hop.

3. Arista's interest in Bad Boy Entertainment is estimated to have involved an initial $15 million cash investment and, following renewals, a substantial credit line estimated at $50 million and other cash and credit incentives (Gilmore 1997, 54). *Forbes* confirmed the figure of $50–55 million for Arista's advance against future earnings, explaining that Arista owned 50 percent of Bad Boy. Combs's contract gives him the option to buy back his master recordings and Arista's stake in the company by 2003 (LaFranco 1999, 185).

4. For an insightful interrogation of the concepts and actions relating to respect, deference, and defensiveness among black and Latino teens in urban America, see Anderson 1994.

5. Among Tupac's transgressions were the shooting of two off-duty police officers in Atlanta in 1993, a sexual assault in 1993 that led to his conviction and imprisonment the following year, and an assault on the film director Allen Hughes in 1994. While on trial for sexual assault, Shakur was also robbed at gunpoint and shot five times in New York, setting in motion a series of accusations implicating Sean Combs and the Notorious B.I.G. of Bad Boy Entertainment in the ambush.

Notes to Epilogue

1. The CBC's *Drop the Beat* features Michie Mee, who had a minor Canadian hit with her single "Jamaican Funk" (1990, First Priority/Atlantic).

2. For a detailed ethnographic account of the enabling and constraining factors in Cuban hip-hop, see Pacini Hernandez and Garofalo 1999–2000.

Bibliography

✳

Acland, Charles. 1995. *Youth, Murder, Spectacle: The Cultural Politics of "Youth in Crisis."* Boulder, Colo.: Westview Press.

Adams, John. 1994. "Setting as Chorus: an Iconology of Dallas." *Critical Survey* 6, no. 2: 180–87.

"A Day in the Hood: Rolling With Cypress Hill." 1992. *Rap Sheet,* July, 18–21.

"A Day In the Hood: The Bloody." 1992. *Rap Sheet,* October.

Adler, Jerry. 1990. "The Rap Attitude." *Newsweek,* March 19, 56–59.

Adorno, Theodore. 1989. *Introduction to the Sociology of Music.* New York: Continuum.

Agnew, John. 1993. "Representing Space: Space, Scale and Culture in Social Science." In *Place/Culture/Representation,* edited by James Duncan and David Ley. London: Routledge.

Aiges, Scott. 1994. "Home Grown Bounce Music Rules Big Easy's Rap Roost." *Billboard,* March 19.

"Album Deals, Video Promote Longer Careers: Rappers Gain More Staying Power." 1989. *Billboard,* August 19.

Allen, Ernest, Jr. 1996. "Making the Strong Survive: The Contours and Contradictions of Message Rap." In *Droppin' Science: Critical Essays on Rap Music and Hip Hop Culture,* edited by William Eric Perkins. Philadelphia: Temple University Press.

"Alternative R & B Tour Should Put Sizzle in Summer Season." 1996. *Billboard,* April 13.

Althusser, Louis. 1971. *Lenin and Philosophy, and Other Essays.* London: New Left Books.

Anderman, Joan. 2000a. "Hip-Hop's Family Value." *Boston Globe,* April 2.

———. 2000b. "Promoters Say Mayhem Might Hurt Future Tours." *Boston Globe,* April 5.

Anderson, Elijah. 1994. "The Code of the Streets." *Atlantic Monthly,* May, 80–94.

Appadurai, Arjun. 1996. *Modernity at Large: Cultural Dimensions of Globalization.* Minneapolis: University of Minnesota Press.

"Artists on Image: Rappers Answer Critics, Pinpoint Resistance to Youth Wave." 1988. *Billboard,* December 24 [special section on rap].

Baker, Houston A., Jr. 1993. *Black Studies, Rap, and the Academy.* Chicago: University of Chicago Press.

Baker, Soren. 1999a. "Magazine Leads Hip-Hop into Mainstream." *Los Angeles Times,* December 22.

———. 1999b. "The Ten Count." *Rap Pages,* October, 114–120.

Beets, Greg. 1993. "Jury Weighing Rap as an Accomplice to Murder of a Trooper." *Billboard,* July 3.

Berland, Jody. 1988. "Locating Listening: Technological Space, Popular Music, Canadian Mediations." *Cultural Studies* 2, no. 3: 343–58.

Berry, Venise. 1994. "Redeeming the Rap Music Experience." In *Adolescents and Their Music: If It's Too Loud, You're Too Old,* edited by Jonathon Epstein. New York: Garland.

Bhabha, Homi. 1990. "The Third Space." In *Identity: Community, Culture, Difference,* edited by Jonathan Rutherford. London: Lawrence and Wishart.

Billboard. 1984. Special issue, *Spotlight: The World of Black Music,* June 16.

"Black Promoters' Suit Underscores Discontent." 1998. *Billboard,* December 5.

Blair, M. Elizabeth. 1993. "Commercialization of the Rap Youth Subculture." *Journal of Popular Culture* 27, no. 3 (winter): 21–33.

Blanton, Kimberly. 2000. "Survey Shows Stock Surge Boosted Many." *Boston Globe,* January 19.

Blatt, Wendy. 1990. "Innovatin' Indies: Creative Strategies Chase Word-of-Mouth Warriors onto National Stage." *Billboard,* November 24 ["Spotlight: Rap"].

Boehlert, Eric. 1995. "Hip-Hop, R & B Culture at the Crossroads: Rap's Grip on Suburbs Loosens as Teens Turn to Modern Rock." *Billboard,* June 3.

Borzillo, Carrie. 1993. "Rap Shows Banned at Six Flags after Brawl." *Billboard,* May 1, 11.

Boyd, Todd. 1994. "Check Yo Self, before You Wreck Yo Self: Variations on a Political Theme in Rap Music and Popular Culture." *Public Culture* 7, no. 1 (fall): 289–312.

———. 1997. *Am I Black Enough for You? Popular Culture from the 'Hood and Beyond.* Bloomington: Indiana University Press.

Braxton, Charlie. 1997. "Master P's Theater." *XXL* 1, no. 1.

———. 1998. "General P's Last Stand." *The Source,* July, 137–44.

Bradley, Omar. 1995. "Hip-Hop Generation: American as Apple Pie." *Billboard,* November 18, 9.

Butts, Reverend Calvin O. 1993. "Rolling Out an Agenda for Rap." *Billboard,* June 19, 9.

Carr, Tim. 1983. "Talk That Talk, Walk That Walk." *Rolling Stone,* May 26, 18–25.

Cashmore, Ellis. 1997. *The Black Culture Industry.* New York: Routledge.

Castells, Manuel. 1985. "High Technology, Economic Restructuring, and the Urban-Regional Process in the United States." In *High Technology, Space, and Society,* edited by Manuel Castells. Beverly Hills: Sage.

———. 1989. *The Informational City: Information Technology, Economic Restructuring, and the Urban-Regional Process.* New York: Basil Blackwell.

Castleman, Craig. 1982. *Getting Up: Subway Graffiti in New York.* Cambridge, Mass.: MIT Press.

"C. Delores Tucker Sues Tupac's Estate: Rap Critic Charges That His Lyrics Slander Her." 1997. *Billboard,* August 16, 18.

Certeau, Michel de. 1984. *The Practice of Everyday Life.* Berkeley: University of California Press.

Chambers, Iain. 1985. *Urban Rhythms: Pop Music and Popular Culture.* London: MacMillan.

———. 1986. *Popular Culture: The Metropolitan Experience.* London: Methuen.

———. 1990. *Border Dialogues: Journeys in Postmodernity.* New York: Routledge.

———. 1993. "Cities without Maps." In *Mapping the Futures: Local Cultures, Global Change,* edited by Jon Bird, Barry Curtis, Tim Putnam, George Robertson, and Lisa Tickner. New York: Routledge.

———. 1994. *Migrancy, Culture, Identity.* New York: Routledge.

Chin, Brian. 1985. "Warner, Tommy Boy Link: Some Distribs Blast Move." *Billboard*, December 28, 1.

———. 1987a. "Rap Taps Into Mainstream Market." *Billboard*, June 6, 26.

———. 1987b. "Small Labels Maintain Street Sense: DJ Mixers Value Indie Ties." *Billboard*, May 9, 33.

Cohen, Lyor. 1987. "Run-D.M.C., Beasties Together: On Tour: A Dispatch from the Front Lines." *Billboard*, September 12, 9.

Cohen, Stanley. 1972. *Folk Devils and Moral Panics: The Creation of the Mods and Rockers*. New York: Basil Blackwell.

Coleman, Lauren. 1996. "The Community @ Cyberspace." *Billboard*, November 26 ["Spotlight Rap"].

Cox, Meg. 1984. "If a Big Beat Zaps You Out of a Nap, the Music Is Rap." *Wall Street Journal*, December 4.

Cross, Brian. 1993. *It's Not About a Salary: Rap, Race, and Resistance in Los Angeles*. London: Verso.

"Culture, Violence, and the Cult of the Unrepentant Rogue." 1993. *Billboard*, December 25.

Dannen, Fredric. 1990. *Hit Men: Power Brokers and Fast Money Inside the Music Business*. New York: Vintage.

Darden, Joe. 1987. "Choosing Neighbors and Neighborhoods: The Role of Race in Housing Preference." In *Changing Patterns of Racial Segregation*, edited by Gary Tobin. Newbury Park, Calif.: Sage.

Davies, Wayne, and David Herbert. 1993. "The Social Construction of Communities: Creating and Identifying Senses of Place." In *Communities Within Cities: An Urban Social Geography*. London: Belhaven Press.

Davis, Angela. 1981. *Women, Race, and Class*. New York: Random House.

———. 1989. *Women, Culture, and Politics*. New York: Random House.

Davis, Mike. 1989. "Homeowners and Homeboys: Urban Restructuring in LA." *Enclitic* 11, no. 3.

———. 1992. *City of Quartz: Excavating the Future in Los Angeles*. New York: Vantage Books.

Dawsey, Kierna Mayo. 1994. "Caught Up in the (Gangsta) Rapture: Dr. C. Delores Tucker's Crusade against 'Gangsta Rap'." *The Source*, June, 58–62.

Dawson, Michael C. 1994. "A Black Counterpublic? Economic Earthquakes, Racial Agenda(s), and Black Politics." *Public Culture* 7, no. 1 (fall): 195–223.

Decker, Jeffrey Louis. 1993. "The State of Rap: Time and Place in Hip Hop Nationalism." *Social Text* 11, no. 1: 53–84.

"Def Jam: A Label in Tune with What's Popular on the Street." 1985. *Billboard*, April 20 [special section on Rush Artist Management].

Dennis, Reginald. 1997. "Welcome to *XXL*." *XXL* 1, no. 1.

Dery, Mark. 1990. "Public Enemy: Confrontation." *Keyboard* (September): 81–96.

Diawara, Manthia. 1993. "Black American Cinema: The New Realism." In *Black American Cinema*, edited by Manthia Diawara. New York: Routledge.

DiMartino, Dave. 1991. "Back Catalogs Moving Into Front Seat: Labels Get Ready For Surge of Reissues." *Billboard*, March 23, 11.

Donloe, Darlene. 1990. "Mintin' Majors: Big Guns Train Sights on Explosive Street Market." *Billboard*, November 24 ["Spotlight: Rap"].

Donziger, Steven R., ed. 1996. *The Real War on Crime: The Report of the National Criminal Justice Commission*. New York: Harper Perennial.

Du Bois, W. E. B. 1967 [1899]. *The Philadelphia Negro: A Social Study*. New York: Benjamin Blom.

———. 1994 [1903]. *The Souls of Black Folk*. New York: Dover.

Duncan, James, and David Ley. 1993. "Introduction: Representing the Place of the

Future." In *Place/Culture/Representation,* edited by James Duncan and David Ley. London: Routledge.

Duncan, Simon, and Mike Savage. 1989. "Space, Scale and Locality." *Antipode* 21, no. 3: 179–206.

Dyer, Richard. 1979. *Stars.* London: British Film Institute.

Dyson, Michael Eric. 1993. *Reflecting Black: African-American Cultural Criticism.* Minneapolis: University of Minnesota Press.

Early, Gerald. 1995. *One Nation Under a Groove: Motown and American Culture.* Hopewell, N.J.: Ecco Press.

Entman, Robert. 1994. "African-Americans According to TV News." *Media Studies Journal* 8, no. 3 (summer): 29–38.

Entrikin, J. Nicholas. 1991. *The Betweenness of Place: Towards a Geography of Modernity.* Baltimore: Johns Hopkins University Press.

Eure, Joseph, and James Spady, eds. 1991. *Nation Conscious Rap.* New York: PC International Press.

Farr, Jory. 1994. *Moguls and Madmen: The Pursuit of Power in Popular Music.* New York: Simon and Schuster.

Fernando, S. H., Jr. 1994. *The New Beats: Exploring the Music, Culture, and Attitudes of Hip-Hop.* New York: Anchor Books/Doubleday.

Flores, Juan. 1994. "Puerto Rican and Proud, Boyee! Rap, Roots, and Amnesia." In *Microphone Fiends: Youth Music and Youth Culture,* edited by Andrew Ross and Tricia Rose. New York: Routledge.

Flynn, Sean. 1990. "2 Live Crew's New England Tour Provokes controversy." *Billboard,* July 28, 3.

Ford, Robert, Jr. 1978. "B-Beats Bombarding Bronx." *Billboard,* July 1, 65.

———. 1979. "Jive Talking N.Y. DJs Rapping Away in Black Discos." *Billboard,* May 5, 3.

Formisano, Ronald. 1991. *Boston Against Busing: Race, Class, and Ethnicity in the 1960s and 1970s.* Chapel Hill: University of North Carolina Press.

Foucault, Michel. 1980. *Power/Knowledge: Selected Interviews and Other Writings, 1972–1977.* New York: Pantheon.

Freeman, Kim. 1985. "Indies Stake in Street and Third World Music May Prove a Goldmine." *Billboard,* June 15.

Fraser, Nancy. 1992. "Rethinking the Public Sphere: A Contribution to the Critique of Actually Existing Democracy." In *Habermas and the Public Sphere,* edited by Craig Calhoun. Cambridge, Mass.: MIT Press.

Frith, Simon. 1983. *Sound Effects: Youth, Leisure, and the Politics of Rock 'n' Roll.* London: Constable.

———. 1988. *Music for Pleasure.* New York: Routledge.

———. 1996. *Performing Rites: On the Value of Popular Music.* Cambridge, Mass.: Harvard University Press.

Gaines, Donna. 1991. *Teenage Wasteland: Suburbia's Dead End Kids.* New York: Harper Collins.

Garofalo, Reebee. 1990. "Crossing Over: 1939–1989." In *Split Image: African Americans in the Mass Media,* edited by Jannette Dates and William Barlow. Washington, D.C.: Howard University Press.

———. 1992. "Popular Music and the Civil Rights Movement." In *Rockin' the Boat: Mass Music and Mass Culture,* edited by Reebee Garofalo. Boston: South End Press.

———. 1994. "Culture versus Commerce: The Marketing of Black Popular Music." *Public Culture* 7, no. 1 (fall): 275–87.

———. 1997. *Rockin' Out: Popular Music in the USA.* Boston: Allyn and Bacon.

Garreau, Joel. 1988. *Edge City: Life on the New Frontier.* New York: Anchor Books/ Doubleday.

Gates, Henry Louis, Jr. 1988. *The Signifying Monkey: A Theory of African-American Literary Criticism*. New York: Oxford University Press.

George, Nelson. 1982. "Rap Disks Open Doors for New Breed of Producers." *Billboard*, June 5.

——. 1984. "The World of Black Music." *Billboard*, June 16.

——. 1985a. "The Rhythm and the Blues." *Billboard*, March 30, 57.

——. 1985b. *Where Did Our Love Go? The Rise and Fall of the Motown Sound*. New York: St. Martin's Press.

——. 1986a. "The Rhythm and the Blues." *Billboard*, May 31, 23.

——. 1986b. "The Rhythm and the Blues." *Billboard*, July 26, 23.

——. 1987. "The Rhythm and the Blues." *Billboard*, July 11, 20.

——. 1988a. "Indie Sound Blossoms via Multifaceted Deals: Rap Breaks Through to Majors." *Billboard*, February 20, 1.

——. 1988b. "The Rhythm and the Blues." *Billboard*, March 12, 25.

——. 1989a. *The Death of Rhythm and Blues*. New York: E. P. Dutton.

——. 1989b. "The Rhythm and the Blues." *Billboard*, April 8, 20.

——. 1992. *Buppies, B-Boys, Baps, and Bohos: Notes on Post-Soul Black Culture*. New York: Harper Collins.

——. 1993. "Hip-Hop's Founding Fathers Speak the Truth." *The Source*, November, 44–50.

——. 1998. *Hip Hop America*. New York: Viking.

George, Nelson, Sally Banes, Susan Flinker, and Patty Romanowski. 1985. *Fresh: Hip Hop Don't Stop*. New York: Random House.

"The G-Funk Family." 1995. *The Source*, May, 50–57.

Giddens, Anthony. 1984. *The Constitution of Society: Outline of the Theory of Structuration*. Berkeley: University of Berkeley Press.

Gilmore, Mikal. 1997. "Puff Daddy." *Rolling Stone*, August 7.

Gilroy, Paul. 1987. *There Ain't No Black in the Union Jack: The Cultural Politics of Race and Nation*. Chicago: University of Chicago Press.

——. 1992. "It's a Family Affair." In *Black Popular Culture*, edited by Gina Dent. Seattle: Bay Press.

——. 1993a. *The Black Atlantic: Modernity and Double Consciousness*. Cambridge, Mass.: Harvard University Press.

——. 1993b. *Small Acts: Thoughts on the Politics of Black Cultures*. London: Serpent's Tail.

——. 1994. "'After the Love Has Gone': Bio-Politics and Etho-Poetics in the Black Public Sphere." *Public Culture* 7, no. 1 (fall): 49–76.

Gilroy, Paul, and the Centre for Contemporary Cultural Studies Race and Politics Group. 1982. *The Empire Strikes Back: Race and Racism in 70s Britain*. London: Hutchison.

Giroux, Henry. 1994. *Disturbing Pleasures: Learning Popular Culture*. New York: Routledge.

——. 1996. *Fugitive Cultures: Race, Violence, and Youth*. New York: Routledge.

"Global Rap Pulse." 1998. *Billboard*, December 5 ["Spotlight Rap and Hip-Hop"].

Goldberg, David Theo. 1993. *Racist Culture: Philosophy and the Politics of Meaning*. Cambridge, Mass.: Blackwell.

Goodman, Fred. 1984a. "Indies Express Concern: 12-Inchers: Majors Move In." *Billboard*, July 28, 1.

——. 1984b. "New Product Mix Broadens Base of Retail Renewal." *Billboard*, June 16.

——. 1986. "CBS Predicts Modest '86 Industry Upturn." *Billboard*, March 15, 3.

Graham, Renee. 2000. "Hip-Hop Doesn't Deserve the Rap for Violence." *Boston Globe*, April 5.

Gracyk, Theodore. 1996. *Rhythm and Noise: An Aesthetics of Rock*. Durham, N.C.: Duke University Press.

Gramsci, Antonio. 1971. *Selections from the Prison Notebooks*. New York: International.

Green, Tony. 1999a. "The Dirty South." In *The Vibe History of Hip Hop*, edited by Alan Light. New York: Three Rivers Press.

——. 1999b. "Money Changes Everything." *XXL*, April, 64–70.

Greenberg, Steve. 1999. "Sugar Hill Records." In *The Vibe History of Hip Hop*, edited by Alan Light. New York: Three Rivers Press.

Grossberg, Lawrence. 1987. "Rock and Roll in Search of an Audience." In *Popular Music and Communication*, edited by James Lull. Newbury Park, Calif.: Sage.

——. 1991. "Rock, Territorialization, and Power." *Cultural Studies* 5, no. 3: 358–67.

——. 1992. *We Gotta Get Out of this Place: Popular Conservatism and Postmodern Culture*. New York: Routledge.

——. 1994. "The Political Status of Youth and Youth Culture." In *Adolescents and Their Music: If It's Too Loud, You're Too Old*, edited by Jonathon Epstein. New York: Garland.

Grosz, Elizabeth. 1992. "Bodies-Cities." In *Sexuality and Space*, edited by Beatriz Colomina. New York: Princeton Architectural Press.

Guerrero, Ed. 1993. *Framing Blackness: The African American Image in Film*. Philadelphia: Temple University Press.

Gunst, Laurie. 1995. *Born Fi Dead: A Journey through the Jamaican Posse Underworld*. New York: Henry Holt.

Gupta, Akhil, and James Ferguson. 1992. "Beyond 'Culture': Space, Identity, and the Politics of Difference." *Cultural Anthropology* 7, no. 1: 6–23.

Hager, Steve. 1984. *Hip Hop: The Illustrated History of Break Dancing, Rap Music, and Graffiti*. New York: St. Martin's Press.

Hall, Stuart. 1977. "Culture, the Media, and the 'Ideological Effect.'" In *Mass Communication and Society*, edited by James Curran, Michael Gurevitch, and Janet Woollacott. Beverly Hills: Sage.

——. 1992. "What Is This 'Black' in Black Popular Culture?" In *Black Popular Culture*, edited by Gina Dent. Seattle: Bay Press.

Hall, Stuart, Chas Critcher, Tony Jefferson, John Clarke, and Brian Roberts, eds. 1978. *Policing the Crisis: Mugging, the State, and Law and Order*. New York: Holmes and Meier.

Haring, Bruce. 1989. "Many Doors Still Closed to Rap Tours." *Billboard*, December 16, 1.

Harper, Phillip Brian. 1989. "Synesthesia, 'Crossover,' and Blacks in Popular Music." *Social Text* 23 (fall–winter): 102–21.

Harris, Leonard. 1993. "Postmodernism and Utopia: An Unholy Alliance." In *Racism, the City, and the State*, edited by Malcolm Cross and Michael Keith. London: Routledge.

Harvard Consultation Project. 1996. *Harvard Report on Urban Music*. Cambridge, Mass.: Harvard Law School.

Harvey, David. 1989. *The Condition of Postmodernity: An Enquiry into the Origins of Cultural Change*. Oxford: Basil Blackwell.

——. 1993. "From Space to Place and Back Again: Reflections on the Condition of Postmodernity." In *Mapping the Futures: Local Cultures, Global Change*, edited by Jon Bird, Barry Curtis, Tim Putnam, George Robertson, and Lisa Tickner. New York: Routledge.

Haymes, Stephen N. 1995. *Race, Culture, and the City: A Pedagogy for Black Urban Struggle*. Albany: State University of New York Press.

"Heavy Metal Bands Are Rocking Top 40 Playlists." 1987. *Billboard*, June 20, 1.

Hebdige, Dick. 1987. *Cut 'n' Mix: Culture, Identity, and Caribbean Music*. New York: Methuen.

———. 1988. *Hiding in the Light*. New York: Routledge.

Hennessey, Mike. 1988. "Insurer Cancels Coverage for Promoter of Rap Show." *Billboard*, December 24, 6.

Hinds, Selwyn Sefu. 1996. "Don of the Westside." *The Source*, May, 50–58.

Hine, Thomas. 1986. *Populuxe*. New York: Alfred A. Knopf.

"Hip-Hop Trinity." 1999. *The Source*, February, 168–76.

Hirsch, Paul. 1990. "Processing Fads and Fashions: An Organization-Set Analysis of Cultural Industry Systems." In *On Record: Rock, Pop, and the Written Word*, edited by Simon Frith and Andrew Goodwin. New York: Pantheon.

Hirschberg, Lynn. 1996. "Does a Sugar Bear Bite? Suge Knight and His Posse." *New York Times Magazine*, January 14.

Hoban, Phoebe. 1998. *Basquiat: A Quick Killing in Art*. New York: Penguin.

Holland, Bill. 1994. "House Panel to Examine Rap." *Billboard*, February 19.

Holman, Michael. 1984. *Breaking and the New York City Breakers*. New York: Freundlich.

hooks, bell. 1988. *Talking Back: Thinking Feminist, Thinking Black*. Toronto: Between the Lines.

———. 1990. *Yearning: Race, Gender, and Cultural Politics*. Boston: South End Press.

———. 1992. *Black Looks: Race and Representation*. Boston: South End Press.

Hopkins, Tracy. 1998. "The Accidental Mogul." *The Source*, August, 114–18.

Horowitz, Is. 1986. "CDs Hold the Fort: RIAA: '85 Shipments Flat." *Billboard*, March 29.

Howell, Ricardo. 1995. "Evolution of a Revolution." *The Source*, June, 40–43.

"Indies Keep Rap Product Popping: Despite Sales Slowdown, Genre Maintains Steady Profile." 1982. *Billboard*, July 17, 6.

Ivory, Steven. 1996. "Family Matters." *The Source*, September.

Jackson, Peter, and Jan Penrose. 1993. *Constructions of Race, Place, and Nation*. Minneapolis: University of Minnesota Press.

James, Darryl. 1992. "Rakim: The Five Percent Science." *Rap Sheet*, October.

Jameson, Fredric. 1984. "Postmodernism, or the Cultural Logic of Late Capitalism." *New Left Review* 146 (July–August): 53–92.

Jargowsky, Paul, and Mary Jo Bane. 1990. "Ghetto Poverty: Basic Questions." In *Inner City Poverty in the United States*. Washington, D.C.: National Academy Press.

Jeffries, John. 1992. "Toward a Redefinition of the Urban: The Collision of Culture." In *Black Popular Culture*, edited by Gina Dent. Seattle: Bay Press.

Joe, Radcliffe, and Nelson George. 1979. "Rapping DJs Set a Trend." *Billboard*, November 3, 4.

Jones, Charisse. 1995. "Still Hangin' in the 'Hood: Rappers Who Stay Say Their Strength Is from the Streets." *New York Times*, September 24.

Jones, LeRoi. 1963. *Blues People: The Negro Experience in White America and the Music That Developed from It*. New York: William Morrow.

Jones, Simon. 1988. *Black Culture, White Youth: The Reggae Tradition from JA to UK*. London: Macmillan.

Judy, R. A. T. 1994. "On the Question of Nigga Authenticity." *boundary 2* 21, no. 3: 210–22.

Katz, Cindi, and Neil Smith. 1992. "L.A. Intifada: Interview with Mike Davis." *Social Text* 10, no. 4: 19–33.

Keith, Michael, and Steve Pile, eds. 1993. *Place and the Politics of Identity*. New York: Routledge.

Kelley, Robin D. G. 1996. "Kickin' Reality, Kickin' Ballistics: Gangsta Rap and Postindustrial Los Angeles." In *Droppin' Science: Critical Essays on Rap Music and Hip Hop Culture*, edited by William Eric Perkins. Philadelphia: Temple University Press.

———. 1997. *Yo' Mama's Disfunktional: Fighting the Culture Wars in Urban America.* Boston: Beacon Press.

LaFranco, Robert. 1999. "I Ain't Foolin' Around—I'm Building Assets." *Forbes,* March 22, 180–86.

"Learning Lessons of Prince Success: Majors Look to Youth Movement Gains, Challenge Platinum." 1985. *Billboard,* June 15 ["Spotlight: World of Black Music"].

Lebon, Manuel. 1999. "Codigos musicales para la cultura urbana." *El Universal de Venezuela,* January 7.

Lee, Spike, and Lisa Jones. 1989. *Do the Right Thing.* New York: Fireside.

Lefebvre, Henri. 1991. *The Production of Space.* Oxford: Basil Blackwell.

Legge, Michele. 1998. "Czechs Check Out Hip-Hop: Polygram's Chaozz Is Leading Act." *Billboard,* February 28.

Lewine, Edward. 1995. "The South Bronx? It's a State of Mind." *Bronx Beat,* March 13.

Ley, David. 1989. "Modernism, Post-Modernism, and the Struggle for Place." In *The Power of Place: Bringing Together Geographical and Sociological Imaginations,* edited by John Agnew and James Duncan. Boston: Unwin-Hyman.

Lichtman, Irv. 1986. "CD Sales Fueling Conn. Operation." *Billboard,* March 15, 27.

Light, Alan. 1992. "About a Salary or Reality? Rap's Recurrent Conflict." In *Present Tense: Rock and Roll and Culture,* edited by Anthony DeCurtis. Durham, N.C.: Duke University Press.

Lipsitz, George. 1990. *Time Passages: Collective Memory and American Popular Culture.* Minneapolis: University of Minnesota Press.

———. 1994a. *Dangerous Crossroads: Popular Music, Postmodernism, and the Poetics of Place.* New York: Verso.

———. 1994b. "We Know What Time It Is: Race, Class, and Youth Culture in the Nineties." In *Microphone Fiends: Youth Music and Youth Culture,* edited by Andrew Ross and Tricia Rose. New York: Routledge.

Lopiano-Misdom, Janine, and Joanne De Luca. 1997. *Street Trends: How Today's Alternative Youth Cultures Are Creating Tomorrow's Mainstream Markets.* New York: Harper Collins.

Lusane, Clarence. 1993. "Rap, Race, and Politics." *Race and Class* 35, no. 1: 41–56.

"Mainstream vs. Mean Streets." 1991. *Billboard,* November 23 ["Spotlight: State of Rap"].

"Major Label Rap Hit: Boogie Boys 'Fly' on Capital." 1985. *Billboard,* September 28, 63.

Marriott, Rob. 1998. "American Gothic." *Vibe,* May, 68–76.

———. 1999. "Gangsta, Gangsta: The Sad, Violent Parable of Death Row Records." In *The Vibe History of Hip Hop,* edited by Alan Light. New York: Three Rivers Press.

Martin, Linda, and Kerry Segrave. 1993. *Anti-Rock: The Opposition to Rock 'n' Roll.* New York: Da Capo Press.

Massey, Doreen. 1992. "A Place Called Home." *New Formations* 17 (summer): 3–15.

———. 1994. *Space, Place, and Gender.* Minneapolis: University of Minnesota Press.

Massood, Paula. 1996. "Mapping the Hood: The Genealogy of City Space in *Boyz N the Hood* and *Menace II Society.*" *Cinema Journal* 35, no. 2 (winter): 85–97.

McAdams, Janine. 1990. "Wrapping Up the Year Rap Went to the Top." *Billboard,* December 22.

———. 1991a. "Credibility and Commerciality." *Billboard,* November 23 ["Spotlight: State of Rap"].

———. 1991b. "N.Y.'s 'Da Joint' Puts Acts on da Road to Overseas Venues." *Billboard,* December 14.

———. 1991c. "The Rhythm and the Blues." *Billboard,* January 12, 23.

———. 1991d. "The Rhythm and the Blues." *Billboard*, January 19, 31.

———. 1991e. "The Rhythm and the Blues." *Billboard*, October 12, 24.

———. 1993. "RCA Broadens Vision for R & B, Rap via New Deals." *Billboard*, February 13.

McChesney, Robert W. 1999. "The New Global Media: It's a Small World of Big Conglomerates." *Nation*, November 29, 11–15.

MC Eiht. 1995. "Once Upon a Time in Compton." *The Source*, February, 52–57.

McLaughlin, Milbrey W. 1993. "Embedded Identities: Enabling Balance in Urban Contexts." In *Identity and Inner-City Youth: Beyond Ethnicity and Gender*, edited by Shirley B. Heath and Milbrey W. McLaughlin. New York: Teachers College Press.

Meyrowitz, Joshua. 1985. *No Sense of Place: The Impact of Electronic Media on Social Behavior*. New York: Oxford University Press.

Michner, Charles. 1972. "Black Movies." *Newsweek*, October 23, 74–81.

Miller, Ivor. 1994. "Creolizing for Survival in the City." *Cultural Critique* (spring): 153–88.

Mills, David. 1990. "The Gangsta Rapper: Violent Hero or Negative Role Model?" *The Source*, December, 30–40.

Minh-ha, Trinh. 1987. *Of Other Peoples: Beyond the Salvage Paradigm*. Discussions in Contemporary Culture 1. Seattle: Bay Press.

Mitchell, Gail. 2000. "The Rhythm and the Blues." *Billboard*, June 10, 33.

Moleski, Linda. 1987. "Rap Tour Wrap Up." *Billboard*, October 17, 34.

Morris, Chris. 1986. "Venue Reads Riot Act Following Melee: Run-D.M.C. Gig Spurs Arena Policy Changes." *Billboard*, August 30, 7.

———. 1993a. "HBO Scraps Plans to Run Program Featuring Ice-T." *Billboard*, March 6, 94.

———. 1993b. "Priority New 'Home' for Ice-T: Questions Remain over Warner Bros. Split." *Billboard*, February 13.

Muhammad, Tariq. 1999. "Hip-Hop Moguls: Beyond the Hype." *Black Enterprise*, December 1999, 78–90.

Nathan, David. 1989. "Rap Video: Underground Giant Begins to Stir Sales in Untapped, Unmapped Home Vid Jungle." *Billboard*, December 16 ["Spotlight: Rap"].

———. 1993. "Ichiban Records Taking the Rap: Has Foot in Past while Exploring New Music." *Billboard*, February 13.

Neal, Mark Anthony. 1999. *What the Music Said: Black Popular Music and Black Public Culture*. New York: Routledge.

Negus, Keith. 1996. *Popular Music in Theory: An Introduction*. Hanover, N.H.: Wesleyan University Press.

———. 1999. "The Music Business and Rap: Between the Street and the Executive Suite." *Cultural Studies* 13, no. 3: 488–508.

Nelson, Havelock. 1991. "Mergers, Money, and Marketing." *Billboard*, November 23 ["Spotlight: State of Rap"].

———. 1993a. "Music and Violence: Does Crime Pay?" *Billboard*, November 13.

———. 1993b. "Radio Acceptance Eases for Hard Rap: Top 40, R & B Embrace Acts One Shunned." *Billboard*, August 28.

———. 1993c. "The Rap Column." *Billboard*, August 28, 31.

———. 1993d. "The Rap Column." *Billboard*, October 19, 30–31.

———. 1993e. "Rapping Up '93: After Chronic Growing Pains, Hardcore Gains Easy Acceptance, Hip-Hop Takes a Flying Leap Into the Mainstream." *Billboard*, November 2 ["Spotlight: Rap"].

———. 1995a. "Compton Mayor Forms Rap the Vote: New Group to Produce Voter-Registration Concerts." *Billboard*, November 10, 18.

———. 1995b. "Hip-Hop, R & B Culture at the Crossroads: Hip-Hop, Rap Wrestle with Predictability as Demand Dips." *Billboard*, June 3.

———. 1995c. "The Rap Column." *Billboard*, August 26, 25.

———. 1996. "The Rap Column." *Billboard*, October 5, 26.

———. 1997a. "Hip-Hop's Home Remains on the Cutting Edge." *Billboard*, October 25.

———. 1997b. "The Rap Column." *Billboard*, May 31.

———. 1997c. "Rap, What's Up: The State of the Nation." *Billboard*, Nov. 22, 31–50 ["Spotlight: Rap"].

Nelson, Havelock, and Michael Gonzales. 1991. *Bring the Noise: A Guide to Rap Music and Hip Hop Culture*. New York: Harmony Books.

Olalquiaga, Celeste. 1992. *Megalopolis: Contemporary Cultural Sensibilities*. Minneapolis: University of Minnesota Press.

Olson, Yvonne. 1988. "As Rap Goes Pop, Some Say Black Radio Is Missing Out." *Billboard*, June 18, 1.

Oumano, Elena. 1998. "Words & Deeds." *Billboard*, October 17, 36.

Pacini Hernandez, Deborah, and Reebee Garofalo. 1999–2000. "Hip Hop in Havana: Rap, Race, and National Identity in Contemporary Cuba." *Journal of Popular Music Studies* 11–12: 18–47.

Pasternak, Clay. 1987. "Alive and Well: Independents Enjoy a Major Turnaround." *Billboard*, May 2, 9.

Perez, Richie. 1985. "Committee against Fort Apache." In *Cultures in Contention*, edited by D. Kahn and D. Neumaier. Seattle: Real Comet Press.

Pike, Jeff. 1990. "At Long Last, Seattle Is Suddenly Hot: Nastymix, Sub Pop Put It on Musical Map." *Billboard*, August 18.

Plasketes, George. 1992. "Romancing the Record: The Vinyl De-Evolution and Subcultural Evolution." *Journal of Popular Culture* 26, no. 1 (summer): 109–22.

Powell, Kevin. 1996. "Live From Death Row." *Vibe*, February, 44–50.

Quart, Leonard, and Albert Auster. 1996. "A Novelist and Screenwriter Eyeballs the Inner City: An Interview with Richard Price." *Cinéaste* 22, no. 1: 12–17.

"The Rap Attitude." 1990. *Newsweek*, March 19, 56–63.

"Rap Records: Are They Fad or Permanent?" 1980. *Billboard*, February 16, 57–59.

"Rap Rocks: Two Managers Are Aiming for Broader New Wave Crossover." 1983. *Billboard*, May 28, 50.

"Rap Visionary Russell Simmons: 'It's More than Making Records, It's Building Careers.'" 1985. *Billboard*, April 20 [special section on Rush Artist Management].

"Reality Check." 1994. *The Source*, June, 64–75.

Relph, Edward. 1976. *Place and Placelessness*. London: Pion.

Reynolds, J. R. 1994. "New Urban/Hip-Hop Label Takes Epic to the Street." *Billboard*, January 22.

———. 1995. "Combs' Bad Boy Label Makes Good: Record Co. Is Intimate, Youthful Workplace." *Billboard*, May 20.

———. 1996a. "The Rhythm and the Blues." *Billboard*, March 2, 19.

———. 1996b. "The Rhythm and the Blues." *Billboard*, March 9, 18.

———. 1997. "The Rhythm and the Blues." *Billboard*, May 16, 18.

Robins, Kevin. 1991. "Tradition and Translation: National Culture in its Global Context." In *Enterprise and Heritage: Crosscurrents of National Culture*, edited by John Corner and Sylvia Harvey. New York: Routledge.

Ro, Ronin. 1998. *Have Gun Will Travel: The Spectacular Rise and Violent Fall of Death Row Records*. New York: Doubleday.

Rose, Tricia. 1989. "Orality and Technology: Rap Music and Afro-American Cultural Resistance." *Popular Music and Society* 12, no. 4: 35–44.

———. 1990. "Never Trust a Big Butt and a Smile." *Camera Obscura* 23: 108–31.

———. 1994a. *Black Noise: Rap Music and Black Culture in Contemporary America*. Hanover: Wesleyan University Press.

———. 1994b. "A Style Nobody Can Deal With: Politics, Style, and the Postindustrial City in Hip Hop." In *Microphone Fiends: Youth Music and Youth Culture*, edited by Andrew Ross and Tricia Rose. New York: Routledge.

———. 1997. "Cultural Survivalisms and Marketplace Subversions: Black Popular Culture and Politics into the Twenty-first Century." In *Language, Rhythm, and Sound: Black Popular Cultures into the Twenty-First Century*, edited by J. Adjaye and A. Andrews. Pittsburgh: University of Pittsburgh Press.

Rosen, Craig. 1993. "TV Eyes Rap for Ratings." *Billboard*, April 17.

Rosen, Craig, and Carrie Borzillo. 1993. "Labels Love the Single Life: Indies Invade Hot 100." *Billboard*, July 17.

Russell, Deborah. 1993. "Beyond The Box and MTV: Alternative R & B Busts Moves on Local Vidshows." *Billboard*, June 12 ["Spotlight: R & B"].

Ryden, Kent. 1993. *Mapping the Invisible Landscape: Folklore, Writing, and the Sense of Place*. Iowa City: University of Iowa Press.

Sack, Robert D. 1992. *Place, Modernity, and the Consumer's World: A Relational Framework for Geographical Analysis*. Baltimore: Johns Hopkins University Press.

Sacks, Leo. 1989. "The Majors: Marketing the Revolution down the Street, around the Corner, and around the World." *Billboard*, December 16 ["Spotlight: Rap"].

Samuels, Anita. 1998. "The Trials of the Touring Trail." *Billboard*, December 5 ["Spotlight: Rap and Hip-Hop"].

Samuels, David. 1991. "The Rap on Rap: The 'Black Music' That Isn't Either." *New Republic*, November 11, 24–29.

Schwartz, Mark. 1999. "Planet Rock: Hip Hop Supa National." In *The Vibe History of Hip Hop*, edited by Alan Light. New York: Three Rivers Press.

Scruggs, Charles. 1993. *Sweet Home: Invisible Cities in the Afro-American Novel*. Baltimore: Johns Hopkins University Press.

Sengupta, Somini. 1996. "In Their Own Image: The Source Led the Way." *New York Times*, April 28.

Shields, Rob. 1991. *Places on the Margin: Alternative Geographies of Modernity*. New York: Routledge.

———. 1996. "A Guide to Urban Representation and What to Do about It: Alternative Traditions of Urban Theory." In *Representing the City: Ethnicity, Capital, and Culture in the Twenty-First-Century Metropolis*. New York: New York University Press.

Shocked, Michelle, and Bart Bull. 1992. "L.A. Riots: Cartoons vs. Reality." *Billboard*, June 20, 6.

Shuker, Roy. 1994. *Understanding Popular Music*. New York: Routledge.

Shusterman, Richard. 1991. "The Fine Art of Rap." *New Literary History* 22: 613–32.

Simone, Timothy Maliqalim. 1989. *About Face: Race in Postmodern America*. New York: Autonomedia.

Sinclair, Upton. 1906. *The Jungle*. New York: Signet.

Sippel, John. 1986. "ALMAS Hi-Fi Says CDs Will Account for Half 86 Gross." *Billboard*, March 15, 28.

"Slay Charge vs. Rapping Teen: Victim Complained about Lyrics." *Billboard*, July 3, 83.

Smith, Danyel. 1993. "The New Motown: 'The Big Peach' Is Home to Some of the Best and the Brightest of R & B." *Billboard*, August 21.

Smith, Neil. 1996. *The New Urban Frontier: Gentrification and the Revanchist City*. New York: Routledge.

Smith, Neil, and Cindi Katz. 1993. "Grounding Metaphor: Towards a Spatialized Politics." In *Place and the Politics of Identity*, edited by Michael Keith and Steve Pile. New York: Routledge.

Smith, Sam. 1991. "Rap Looks for Acceptance Abroad: Hammer, Ice Break into Euro Market." *Billboard*, March 30.

———. 1994. "Saving Our Cities from the Experts." *Utne Reader*, September–October, 59–75.

Smith, Shawnee. 1998a. "Artists Take Control with Their Own Labels." *Billboard*, December 5 ["Spotlight: Rap and Hip-Hop"].

———. 1998b. "Record Companies Fine-Tune R & B Presence on Internet." *Billboard*, October 31, 23.

———. 1998c. "Words & Deeds." *Billboard*, September 19, 46.

Soja, Edward. 1989. *Postmodern Geographies*. London: Verso.

Soja, Edward, and Barbara Hooper. 1993. "The Space That Difference Makes: Some Notes on the Geographical Margins of the New Cultural Politics." In *Place and the Politics of Identity*, edited by Michael Keith and Steve Pile. New York: Routledge.

Sorkin, Michael, ed. 1992. *Variations on a Theme Park: The New American City and the End of Public Space*. New York: Noonday Press.

Stolzoff, Norman C. 2000. *Wake the Town and Tell the People: Dancehall Culture in Jamaica*. Durham, N.C.: Duke University Press.

Strauss, Stephen. 1995. "Teen Murders Soar, Study Says." *Globe and Mail* [Canada], February 18.

"'Street Music' Label: Tuff City Rapping via Epic Tie." 1984. *Billboard*, February 11, 35.

Sudjic, Deyan. 1992. *The Hundred Mile City*. San Diego: Harcourt Brace.

Sweet, Laurel. 2000. "Stabbing Melee Erupts at Concert." *Boston Herald*, April 4.

Tate, Greg. 1992. "Posses in Effect: Ice-T." In *Flyboy in the Buttermilk: Essays on Contemporary America*. New York: Fireside.

Terrell, Tom. 1999. "The Second Wave." In *The Vibe History of Hip Hop*, edited by Alan Light. New York: Three Rivers Press.

Terry, Ken. 1988. "Grammys Get New Categories." *Billboard*, June 4.

Toop, David. 1984. *The Rap Attack: African Jive to New York Hip Hop*. Boston: South End Press.

———. 1991. *Rap Attack 2: African Rap to Global Hip-Hop*. New York: Serpent's Tail.

Tuan, Yi-Fu. 1974. *Topophilia: A Study of Environmental Perception, Attitudes, and Values*. Englewood Cliffs, N.J.: Prentice-Hall.

———. 1977. *Space and Place: The Perspective of Experience*. Minneapolis: University of Minnesota Press.

———. 1979. *Landscapes of Fear*. New York: Pantheon.

Turner, Graeme. 1990. *British Cultural Studies: An Introduction*. Boston: Unwin-Hyman.

"TV's 'Arsenio Hall' Having an Impact on Urban Radio." 1989. *Billboard*, August 19.

"Value of 12-Inch Single from LP Questioned." 1980. *Billboard*, February 16, 51.

Vincent, Rickey. 1996. *Funk: The Music, the People, and the Rhythm of the One*. New York: St. Martin's Griffin.

Wagner-Pacifici, Robin. 1994. *Discourse and Destruction: The City of Philadelphia versus Move*. Chicago: University of Chicago Press.

Wallace, Michele. 1996. "Doin' the Right Thing." *Village Voice*, May 21, 10–14.

Wallis, Roger, and Krister Malm. 1990. "Patterns of Change." In *On Record: Rock, Pop, and the Written Word*, edited by Simon Frith and Andrew Goodwin. New York: Pantheon.

Ward, Brian. 1998. *Just My Soul Responding: Rhythm and Blues, Black Consciousness, and Race Relations*. Berkeley: University of California Press.

Warren, Donald. 1975. *Black Neighborhoods: An Assessment of Community Power*. Ann Arbor: University of Michigan Press.

Watkins, S. Craig. 1998. *Representing: Hip Hop Culture and the Production of Black Cinema.* Chicago: University of Chicago Press.

Weinger, Harry. 1984a. "'New York City Fresh Fest': Hip-Hop Heading for Huge Halls." *Billboard,* September 29, 40.

———. 1984b. "Widening World of Crossover Sparks Black Radio Resurgence." *Billboard,* June 16.

West, Cornel. 1989. "Black Culture and Postmodernism." In *Remaking History: Discussions in Contemporary Culture,* edited by Barbara Kruger and Phil Mariani. Seattle: Bay Press.

———. 1993. *Race Matters.* Boston: Beacon Press.

Whitmire, David. 1995. "Experts Fear Crime Wave as Our Children Grow Up." *Boston Herald,* January 11.

Williams, Frank. 2000. "Sexual Chocolate." *The Source,* May, 142–45.

Williams, Raymond. 1977. *Marxism and Literature.* New York: Oxford University Press.

Wilson, William Julius. 1996. *When Work Disappears: The World of the New Urban Poor.* New York: Vintage.

Winner, Langdon. 1986. *The Whale and the Reactor: A Search for Limits in an Age of High Technology.* Chicago: University of Chicago Press.

Wolfe, Tom. 1987. *Bonfire of the Vanities.* New York: Farrar Straus and Giroux.

Wood, Joe. 1999. "Native Tongues: A Family Affair." In *The Vibe History of Hip Hop,* edited by Alan Light. New York: Three Rivers Press.

"The World According to Ice-T." 1991. *Rap Pages,* October.

X, Malcolm. 1966. *The Autobiography of Malcolm X.* New York: Grove Press.

Yaekel, Tara, and Francie Latour. 2000. "Several Stabbed as Rap Groups Brawl at Show in Fleet Center." *Boston Globe,* April 4.

Zen, DJ. 1994. "Makin' the Hood Go 'Round: After Years of Putting in Work, Compton's Most Wanted Ain't Surrendering." *Rap Pages,* June, 36–43.

Zook, Kristal Brent. 1992. "Reconstructions of Nationalist Thought in Black Music and Culture." In *Rockin' the Boat: Mass Music and Mass Culture,* edited by Reebee Garofalo. Boston: South End Press.

———. 1999. *Color by Fox: The Fox Network and the Revolution in Black Television.* New York: Oxford University Press.

Index

✳

Library of Congress Cataloging-in-Publication Data
Forman, Murray, 1959–
The 'hood comes first : race, space, and place in rap and hip-hop / Murray Forman.
p. cm. — (Music/culture)
Includes bibliographical references and index.
ISBN 0-8195-6396-x (cloth : alk. paper) — ISBN 0-8195-6397-8 (pbk. : alk. paper)
1. Rap (Music)—Social aspects. 2. Hip-hop. 3. African American youth—Social life and customs. I. Title: Race, space, and place in rap and hip-hop. II. Title. III. Series.
ML3918.R37 M67 2002
782.421649—dc21 2001055920